The Bank of Israel

The Bank of Israel

Volume 1

A Monetary History

Haim Barkai
Nissan Liviatan

2007

03-1012029

OXFORD
UNIVERSITY PRESS

Oxford University Press, Inc., publishes works that further
Oxford University's objective of excellence
in research, scholarship, and education.

Oxford   New York
Auckland   Cape Town   Dar es Salaam   Hong Kong   Karachi
Kuala Lumpur   Madrid   Melbourne   Mexico City   Nairobi
New Delhi   Shanghai   Taipei   Toronto

With offices in
Argentina   Austria   Brazil   Chile   Czech Republic   France   Greece
Guatemala   Hungary   Italy   Japan   Poland   Portugal   Singapore
South Korea   Switzerland   Thailand   Turkey   Ukraine   Vietnam

Published by Oxford University Press, Inc.
198 Madison Avenue, New York, New York 10016

www.oup.com

Oxford is a registered trademark of Oxford University Press

Library of Congress Cataloging-in-Publication Data
Barkai, Haim [date]
  The Bank of Israel.
     p. cm.
  Includes bibliographical references and index.
  Contents: v. 1. The monetary history of Israel / Haim Barkai
     and Nissan Liviatan—v. 2. Selected topics in Israel's monetary
     policy / edited by Nissan Liviatan and Haim Barkai.
  ISBN-13 978-0-19-530072-7; ISBN 0-19-530072-6 (v. 1)
  ISBN-13 978-0-19-530073-4; ISBN 0-19-530073-4 (v. 2)
  1. Bank Yisra'el.   2. Banks and banking—Israel.
  3. Money—Israel—History.   4. Monetary policy—Israel.
  I. Liviatan, Nissan.   II. Title.
  HG3260.A7B40 2007
  332.4'95694—dc22 2006024501

9 8 7 6 5 4 3 2 1
Printed in the United States of America
on acid-free paper

To Nurit and Carmela

Preface

Several years ago, when David Klein had just started his term as governor of the Bank of Israel, he asked me to edit a book to commemorate the golden anniversary of Israel's central bank, which had been established in December 1954. My first reaction was hesitant, but later I was convinced that it would be possible to embark on a serious research project to commemorate the event. This is especially the case in Israel, which during those fifty years had completed a cycle in macroeconomic development: loss of control of inflation and the reestablishment of price stability within the framework of a different monetary system. I saw in the explanation of this cycle a professional challenge that deserved a research project.

Thus, I returned to the governor with a practical proposition based on the following principles: (a) The authors shall be given full academic freedom to express their views, even though the Bank of Israel is financing the project. (b) To safeguard the objectivity of the research, the editors shall choose the authors from the ranks of academia, excluding economists and officials of the bank, and the bank shall pay them at prevailing world rates. (c) To benefit from the views and experience of the top Bank of Israel officials who implemented the bank's policies in the past, the authors shall interview these officials and summarize their views about the policies undertaken during and after their terms in office. The Governor accepted these principles willingly and even made some suggestions about the practical implementation of the project.

I then asked Professor Haim Barkai to join me as coeditor. He is an expert on the historical background of the establishment of the Bank of Israel and the conduct of monetary policy over time. He has written extensively on monetary policy in Israel and has chaired the advisory council of the bank. Together we wrote volume 1, which deals with the monetary history of Israel during these fifty years and beyond. This volume divides the fifty-year interval into three main periods: from the establishment of the State of Israel in 1948 to the outbreak of the Yom Kippur War in 1973 (by Haim Barkai), the great inflation era 1973–85 (jointly by Haim Barkai and Nissan Liviatan), and developments from the 1985 stabilization to the present day (by Nissan Liviatan). This volume includes also an overview which was written jointly by the two authors.

We devoted volume 2 to the investigation of several important issues that deserve additional clarification. Nathan Sussman performs an econometric evaluation of the bank's reaction function, Michael Michaely analyzes the process of liberalizing Israel's foreign-exchange market, Jacob Paroush surveys the history of banking supervision in Israel, and Oved Yosha (who, to our deep regret, died during the course of the project) outlined the research on competition and concentration in the banking sector. The actual research on this subject was carried out by his colleagues, Sharon Blei and Yishay Yafeh. Nachum Gross reports on a series of interviews that he conducted with top officials of the Bank of Israel, including governors, directors of the Research Department, and other people in key positions (excluding incumbents). We take this opportunity to thank them all for their cooperation.

In this research project, we benefited from the insights and experience of many people. Let us mention just a few: David Kochav, Eliezer Sheffer, Ephraim Kleiman, Karnit Flug, Yossi Djivre, Ami Barnea, Yaacov Lavi, Gideon Shur, Meir Sokoler, Zvi Eckstein, and Zvi Herkowitz. We also wish to thank the discussants of an early version of the book at a conference that we held in December 2003—Assaf Razin, Michel Strawczynski, Alise Brezis, David Elkayam, Efraim Sadka, Yoav Friedman, Dani Tsiddon, Rafi Melnick, Nadav Halevi, and Avi Tiomkin—and the organizer of the conference, Sigi Tsur.

The Bank of Israel offered us all the assistance that we needed: free access to its database and all technical help in research and processing of the data. We thank our research assistants, Yevgenia Dechter and Asaf Nagar, who did an excellent job.

The book was originally written in English (except for the chapter by Paroush) and then was translated into Hebrew for the Hebrew edition of the book, which was published by the Bank of Israel in November 2004. This required a tremendous effort on the part of the Publications Unit of the bank, under the remarkable leadership of Moshe (Bari) Bar-Natan. In the preparation of the present revised edition, we benefited greatly from the excellent editing of Naftali Greenwood, who not only helped us with English language usage but also helped in improving the clarity of the presentation in the text.

It goes without saying that all the views expressed in this book are those of the authors; the Bank of Israel bears no responsibility for anything written in this book. We wish to thank David Klein, Governor of the Bank of Israel as this book was being prepared for publication, for granting us complete academic freedom.

It is with deep sorrow that I report the death of Professor Haim Barkai, my coeditor and close friend, in May 2006.

Nissan Liviatan
Jerusalem

Contents

Tables and Figures

TABLES

FIGURES

The Bank of Israel

Overview

Israel's monetary history, originating in the first post–World War II decade, was geared to and influenced by that era, which was characterized by moderate inflation in leading industrial countries and high rates of inflation in Latin America. As the last decade of the twentieth century saw the demise of chronic inflation in Latin America and, in fact, inflation worldwide appeared to phase out, Israel joined the trend.

Thus, in the fifty years since the establishment of the Bank of Israel in December 1954, Israel has come full circle on inflation. Initially, from the mid-1950s through 1960, inflation ran at low single-digit rates. Such rates were regained only in the closing phase of the 1990s, and effective price-level stability did not follow until the succeeding decade, that is, the first years of the twenty-first century. In between, inflation soared to a threshold of double digits in the first half of the 1960s, made a brief three-year retreat to low single digits, and took off again in the early 1970s, promptly crossing the double-digit barrier. Inflation crossed into triple-digit territory at the end of that decade and accelerated to almost hyperinflation by the first two quarters of 1985. The stabilization policy of 1985 pulled the system back from the brink and a decade at low double-digit rates furthered the transition to price stability at the turn of the millennium.

This study surveys the macroeconomic developments linked to this inflation cycle and provides an analytic framework for their analysis. From this perspective, the story—the full circle of inflation—begins in the mid-1950s, when Israel's economy was run on the basis of monetary dominance pegged to the Bretton Woods system of fixed exchange rates, which gave the country a nominal anchor.[1] In the 1970s, the economy switched effectively to a regime of

3

fiscal dominance and shed the nominal anchor. Finally, in the wake of the 1985 stabilization program, the exchange rate was again given a nominal anchor— initially the U.S. dollar and, later, a basket of currencies. In the succeeding decade, the 1990s, the exchange-rate anchor was replaced with inflation target- ing and a more flexible exchange-rate regime. At that time, the economy grad- ually returned to a monetary dominance regime in which the credibility of the price-stability goal had to be reestablished.

Notably, the recent return to price stability in Israel came about not under some version of the erstwhile Bretton Woods regime of partially fixed exchange rates but rather under a regime of monetary and fiscal rules.[2] In this respect, Israel followed a global trend, in which price stability was secured not by the classical gold standard, as in the pre–World War I era, but by a regime of rules (e.g., the Maastricht guidelines) that ensure monetary dominance.

When we speak of monetary dominance, we mean a regime in which fiscal policy internalizes the goals of monetary policy on the basis of a strong mone- tary anchor. Fiscal dominance, in contrast, denotes a regime that sets fiscal targets—say, public expenditure and deficits—but lacks a nominal target. Such a regime imposes on the monetary authorities the task of ensuring (temporary) macroeconomic equilibrium.

THE 1950s AND 1960s: THE ESTABLISHMENT OF THE BANK OF ISRAEL (BOI) AND THE "RUNNING IN" PERIOD

Monetary policy in Israel has usually followed the international pattern. In the 1950s and 1960s, it was implemented within the framework of the Bretton Woods regime run by the International Monetary Fund, which Israel joined in 1954. This regime provided a nominal anchor for, and imposed monetary dis- cipline on, all IMF member countries. In modern macroeconomic termi- nology, the regime adopted by Israel in the mid-1950s was one of monetary dominance, in which fiscal policy internalized the monetary goals of price stability that the Bretton Woods regime dictated. Accordingly, fiscal policy based itself on two parameters that were essential for the maintenance of the exchange-rate regime: low deficits and a low public debt/GDP ratio (table I.1). During this period, there was little need for a monetary policy per se that an independent central bank would administer; after all, the Bretton Woods regime provided the requisite relatively credible nominal anchor. The extreme example of such a regime is the gold standard, in which full credibility of the ER anchor ruled out the very possibility of the adoption of an independent monetary policy by a central bank, especially in small economies. This may explain the secondary role of the BOI in Israel's economic scene during this period. The BOI charter furnished the newly established central bank with the standard arsenal of monetary instruments common to all industrial econo- mies. Thus, the Bank of Israel Law, 5714-1954,[3] empowered the BOI to operate a discount window and engage in open-market operations in domestic and foreign exchange. The law allowed, but did not require, the bank to accommo- date the government directly up to a specified ceiling in terms of the size of the

Table I.1. Economic Indicators 1960–73*

		1960–66	1967–69	1970–73
(1)	Operational deficit of general government	−4.01	4.78	11.38
(2)	Annual change in monetary base	1.84	1.69	3.22
(3)	Inflation Tax[1]	1.51	1.00	2.88
(4) = (1) − (2)	Total general-government deficit less seigniorage	−5.84	3.09	8.16
(5) = (1) − (3)	Total deficit minus inflation tax	−5.52	3.78	8.50
(6)	Net real interest payments	1.33	1.76	3.55
(7) = (1) − (6)	Primary deficit of general government	−5.34	3.02	7.83
(8) = (7) − (2)	Primary deficit of general government less seigniorage	−7.18	1.33	4.61
(9) = (7) − (3)	Primary deficit minus inflation tax	−6.85	2.02	4.95
(10)	Net public debt[2]	66.81	60.40	79.28
(11)	MB/GDP (m)	12.12	13.20	12.74
(12)	Inflation (% annual), (π)	7.15	1.99	16.07
(13)	MB—growth (% annual)	17.11	14.23	29.89
(14)	Real interest rate (r)			
A	On government bonds[3]	5.07	5.48	5.50
B	On bank loans[4]	8.04	13.13[6]	3.2[6]
C	Actual interest payment[5]	1.99	2.91	4.48
(15)	GDP growth (n)	8.54	10.13	9.01
(16)	Unemployment rate	4.26	7.00	3.15

*Rows 1–10: % of GDP.
[1]im = $((1 + r)(1 + \pi) - 1)$*m, r from (14)a; i = nominal interest rate.
[2]Methodology: Dahan and Strawczynski (1999).
[3]Real yield to redemption of CPI-indexed bonds.
[4]1960–72 real interest rate on unrestricted bank credit (*Source*: 1968–72 Manzli Series).
[5]Actual interest payments, average of annual ratios (6)/(10).
[6]From Table 4.9.
Source: BOI.

regular government budget. The BOI was also allowed to set reserve ratios for the commercial banks. Theoretically, then, it could determine the money supply by manipulating the two determinants of supply, the monetary base (MB) and the money multiplier.

However, the law did not allow the BOI management to exercise these two prerogatives at its unrestricted volition, even with the support of its advisory bodies. Such actions required the approval of the government. In practice, the Ministerial Economics Committee, representing the government at large, invoked its right to encroach on the BOI's management of monetary policy by, among other things, maintaining the financial repression regime that it had inherited from the wartime arrangement that the British Mandatory Government had created. Furthermore, the provision of the Bank of Israel Law that required formal government approval of changes in minimum reserve ratios effectively, although not formally, barred the central bank from using its control of the size of the monetary multiplier. Furthermore, the required approval of the issue of central-bank debentures precluded the BOI from implementing the open-market instrument, thereby reducing its clout in the financial markets. Consequently, an ad hoc arrangement adopted to finance the extraordinary costs of Operation Kadesh (the "Sinai Campaign" of 1956)—central-bank accommodation of the leap in the fiscal deficit by means of creative accounting—evolved into standard operating procedure from the late 1960s on. Specifically, short-term loans taken from the BOI, which were limited by law, were converted into long-term debts at the end of each year.

Despite the shortcomings of the monetary regime, Israel's economy performed remarkably at first. The problematic aspects of the monetary regime became visible only in the 1970s, when some of the underpinnings of the regime collapsed. Israel's growth rate during the initial period, about 10% annually, was part and parcel of the rapid global economic expansion that followed World War II. Moreover, Israel's growth rate outpaced the global average. Although this was partly due to the low point of departure, Helpman (1999) shows that in the 1960s Israel grew faster than countries with a similar per-capita GDP. (This advantage was lost in later years.) One reason was the outward orientation of the Israeli economy and its high degree of openness to foreign trade; indeed, the volume of its exports plus imports has long been a significant share of GDP (Razin and Sadka, 1993).

Although the scope of general government expanded rapidly, the fiscal primary and operating balances were in surplus in the decade from the mid-1950s to 1966, indicating that the increase in tax revenues originated in growth. The revenue flow was supported by rising unilateral receipts in foreign aid and reparation accounts, a steady flow of donations from Jewish communities abroad, and a still-small level of transfer payments by the government. The large influx of immigrants in the 1950s and through the mid-1960s strained the absorption capacity of the labor market through 1965, resulting in relatively high unemployment rates, especially among recent immigrants. Effectively, however, the economy attained full employment in 1960 and, despite a brief interruption during the 1966–67 slowdown, maintained it through the 1970s and the early 1980s. Inflation stayed within single digits through 1969 (see table I.1). The management of monetary policy in this period faced various constraints. The Bretton Woods regime potentially allowed for the conduct of an independent monetary policy by permitting controls on capital flows. Indeed, the Israeli government applied comprehensive and tight foreign-currency controls within the framework of the financial-repression system that had been inherited from the Mandate period. Until 1970, however, monetary policy was constrained by a legacy of the Ottoman period, a de jure ceiling on the interest rate. Although this constraint was irrelevant during the Mandate years due to very low interest rates, which reflected the crisis and deflation in the world economies, the somewhat more lenient Israeli version, legislated in 1957, became strongly relevant as inflation rose in the early 1960s. Furthermore, the direct intervention of the Ministry of Finance in the allocation of commercial bank credit, a practice adopted from the very beginning, had a significant effect. In the 1960s, the ministry institutionalized this conduct by establishing "directed credit" as a major component of total commercial-bank credit, allocated on the basis of government criteria and at substantially lower interest rates than the tranche of "free" (unrestricted) bank credit. This inevitably made an effectively restrictive monetary policy, if and when required, less feasible.

This method of administering the monetary dimension of the economy accorded with the Keynesian doctrine that prevailed as the deflationary years of the late 1920s and the 1930s still loomed in the background. According to this doctrine, monetary policy should surrender priority in macroeconomic management to fiscal policy and its instruments, which are subject to the direct control of the political community, and should keep interest rates low in order to create strong incentives for investment.

This regime proved consistent with the comparative price stability imposed by the Bretton Woods system as long as the fiscal management internalized its nominal constraints. In fact, Israel behaved as if it were a member of a "currency bloc" formed by the Bretton Woods system and abided by its rules. The expectations of low inflation were deeply rooted as long as the Bretton Woods exchange-rate regime existed. It should be borne in mind that the phenomenon of long-term ("chronic") inflation, as distinct from hyper-inflationary eruptions, is a recent feature in economic history and was not part of the world's collective memory at the time, although its stirrings had long been evident in Latin America (Pazos, 1972).

The role of government in the Keynesian concept of economic management referred to the *macroeconomic* regime and not to the pervasive micro-level intervention that characterized Israel and many developing countries. The financial repression associated with this regime was apparently part of the notion that only government can stimulate and steer economic growth—the very opposite of the turn-of-the-century view, which gave primacy to the private sector. Moreover, it was widely (and perhaps correctly) believed that the infrastructure for a young economy could be most efficiently created under the strict guidance of government. Within this conceptual framework, the government assumed primacy in allocating investment and facilitated the implementation of this principle by imposing a regime of regulation and intervention in the capital market. Only much later was it argued, with the backing of evidence, that such a regime in a more mature economy stifles economic growth. Indeed, Yosha et al. show in Volume II of this study that while it is preferable to have a more concentrated and less competitive financial sector in a small economy, the opposite is true in a developed economy, which provides better opportunities for risk diversification.

The aforementioned economic philosophy regarding the role of monetary and fiscal policies represented attitudes in Western Europe. It was also the traditional political message of the Israeli Labor Party. The Labor Party, oriented to rapid development and linked to the social democratic tradition of Western Europe, ran Israel's affairs of state for almost three decades, through 1977, and faced weak parliamentary opposition during the first two of these decades. It was this political hegemony that enabled the Ben-Gurion government in 1952 to initiate and successfully implement a New Economic Policy (NEP) that involved a major devaluation, a 10% tax on money balances, and a merciless slashing of government deficits. Although the NEP imposed severe temporary hardships on the employment and living standards of the population, it managed within two years to lead the economy to the threshold of a decade of rapid growth.

Another manifestation of the political strength of the Labor-led governments came to light in the mid-1960s. To redress a major current-account deficit after a devaluation in 1962 failed to move the system toward that target, the Labor Government under Levi Eshkol, just returned to power with a larger majority than before in the wake of a highly divisive election campaign, felt that it could afford politically to orchestrate a restrictive fiscal policy that would lead to a major economic slowdown in 1965–67. The country's reward for this demonstration of political resolve was the extermination of the price inflation that had erupted at the beginning of that decade, thereby creating leeway for the resumption of 10% annual growth in the noninflationary environment of the interval after the Six-Day War, 1967–69.

The main challenge to monetary policy from the late 1950s on was the need to sterilize the large and rising inflows of unilateral payments received by households from German restitution and immigrant transfers. These, coupled with unilateral transfers to general government, widened the variance of the expanding monetary base. Furthermore, the two exchange-rate realignments of 1962 and 1967, which increased proportionally the domestic-currency value of the current inflows, presented the BOI with the challenge of having to stanch significant inflation of the money supply. These factors were augmented by difficulty in keeping the rate of increase of money on an even keel, that is, roughly commensurate with the rate of economic growth. As it happened, the BOI did manage to hold the expansion rate of M_1 to 14%–15% on annual average during its first fifteen years, that is, through 1969. It achieved this in part by setting up special accounts for recipients of transfers from abroad. Since the monetary expansion in this period was not totally out of line with the 10% annual average rate of economic growth, inflation was held to moderate rates of 5%–6% on annual average, with only two outlying years in the 9%–10% range.

This monetary performance, which kept inflation (almost) at bay, was supported among other factors by fiscal surpluses in most years during this time interval (see table I.1), clearly reflecting the discipline imposed by the Bretton Woods rules. The Bretton Woods regime did allow staggered realignment of official exchange rates with crawling "effective rates" that reflected export subsidies and import imposts, given with the IMF's overt consent following usually covert advice.

The infrastructure of relative monetary stability during the aforementioned period was composed of several conflated factors: (a) the growing global economy and Israel's emphatic participation in it; (b) domestic political stability;

(c) a sound fiscal stance; (d) the absence of major exogenous shocks; and (e) the monetary anchor provided by the Bretton Woods regime. These elements, contributing jointly to economic stability during the first fifteen years of the BOI's operations, disappeared one-by-one in the successive fifteen years (1970–85)—the chronic high-inflation era.

THE "LOST DECADE"

The Israeli economy, like the economies of many other countries, operated at over-full employment in the late 1960s, after the 1967 war had caused a long-term increase in the fiscal deficit (table I.2). The combined effect of these two

Table I.2. Economic Indicators 1974–84*

		1974–77	1978–80	1981–83	1984
(1)	Operational deficit of general government	15.98	13.55	12.25	14.53
(2)	Annual change in monetary base	1.97	1.44	2.04	3.00
(3)	Inflation tax[1]	3.36	3.71	3.59	9.95
(4) = (1) − (2)	Total general-government deficit less seigniorage	14.00	12.11	10.21	11.53
(5) = (1) − (3)	Total deficit minus inflation tax	12.62	9.84	8.66	4.57
(6)	Net real interest payments	5.25	8.47	9.35	11.53
(7) = (1) − (6)	Primary deficit of general government	10.73	5.07	2.90	3.00
(8) = (7) − (2)	Primary deficit of general government less seigniorage	8.75	3.63	0.87	0.00
(9) = (7) − (3)	Primary deficit minus inflation tax	7.37	1.36	−0.68	−6.95
(10)	Net public debt[2]	113.41	140.26	157.38	170.94
(11)	MB/GDP (m)	8.36	4.74	2.62	2.18
(12)	Inflation (% annual), (π)	40.07	97.49	141.23	444.88
(13)	MB—growth (% annual)	30.54	47.83	127.74	438.17
(14)	Real interest rate (r)				
A	On government bonds[3]	2.45	0.13	1.63	4.30
B	On bank loans[4]	−4.39	2.05	12.46	62.05
C	Actual interest payment[5]	4.63	6.04	5.94	6.74
(15)	GDP growth (n)	3.24	4.13	2.91	2.21
(16)	Unemployment rate	3.40	3.77	4.87	5.90

*Rows 1–10: percent of GDP.
[1]im = $((1 + r)(1 + \pi) − 1)*m$, r from (14)a; i = nominal interest rate.
[2]Methodology: Dahan and Strawczynski (1960–82), BOI (1983–02).
[3]Real yield to redemption of CPI-indexed bonds.
[4]Real interest rate on revolving-credit facilities.
[5]Actual interest payments, average of annual ratios (6)/(10).
Source: BOI.

factors caused inflation to accelerate. Additionally, the Bretton Woods regime collapsed in the early 1970s, and the global economy reeled under the cost effects of the twin energy crises of 1973 and 1979. Concurrently, in the industrialized countries Keynesian economic philosophy gave way to the "monetarist revolution" led by Milton Friedman. In the late 1970s and early 1980s, then, these countries applied highly restrictive monetary policies to control inflation. In some developing countries, however (especially in Latin America), the loss of the nominal anchor provided by the Bretton Woods system instigated a "chronic-inflation regime" pegged to nearly universal indexation arrangements. Such arrangements were thought capable of overcoming the need to face the Phillips Curve tradeoff between inflation and unemployment.

Domestic political and economic instability in the 1970s prompted Israel to join the club of "chronic-inflation economies," the members of which were mainly Latin American countries, which were much lower than Israel on the scale of economic development. The main contributory factor here was the shattering of political stability as Labor Party hegemony was terminated in the elections of 1977 and power was transferred to a Likud-led coalition that commanded a shaky parliamentary majority. To cope with the political turbulence, both leading parties adopted populist fiscal policies before and after these elections and in subsequent election campaigns. The result, in 1973–84, was a "lost decade" characterized by low growth, high inflation, and financial crises amid policy seesawing.

The collapse of Labor's lengthy political hegemony began with the political firestorm generated by the Yom Kippur War of October 1973. Although Labor survived the post-armistice election campaign, the new government lacked the parliamentary and public strength to risk its political fortunes by slashing civilian consumption expenditure and transfers in order to make room for the tremendous expansion of defense expenditure. In fact, transfer payments grew even in the crisis year of 1974. This, however, did not improve the political fortunes of the last Labor-led government that would hold office in the inflationary era; it was replaced by its rival, a Likud-led coalition government, in 1977.

The next two Likud governments that ran the country through October 1984 were even weaker in parliament than the last Labor government, as underscored by the midterm change of finance ministers in each. Both governments were reluctant to put their budgetary house in order. Accordingly, domestic and total deficits at annual average rates of some 15% of GNP[4] were the rule of the realm for almost the entire fifteen-year period ending in 1984 (table I.2). In terms of the prevailing classification of the comparative roles of the components of the economic system, this period should be labeled as a "fiscal-dominance" era. Indeed, the switch from monetary dominance to fiscal dominance was the main characteristic of the difference in macroeconomic regime that distinguished the "lost decade" from its predecessor. There was no monetary target to defend; the only function left to monetary policy was to react to external and internal shocks in order to maintain a semblance of short-term equilibrium. Inflation during the lost decade was characterized by a series that exhibited the properties of a random walk with a positive drift, so that any shock (usually associated with a balance-of-payment crisis) resulted in a stepwise increase.

Political instability was reflected not only in huge fiscal deficits. For domestic reasons, ruling governments could not afford the emergence of comparatively high unemployment rates. Thus, they headed off any increase in interest rates, however temporary, that might trigger a recession. The combination of swollen deficits and the constraint of continuous full employment robbed the BOI of any possibility of implementing tight monetary policies.

The momentum of real 10% annual growth amid full (and, from 1971, *over-full*) employment did endure briefly after the outbreak of the October 1973 war. From 1974 through 1985, however, annual growth rates slumped to 3.3% annually and 1.1% per capita, as against 1.9% per capita growth in industrial countries such as the United States and Germany.

Inflation took its first stepwise increase in 1970, climbing to low double-digit rates. By the first three quarters of 1973, preceding the war, it had escalated to an annual rate of 22%. All relevant indicators suggest that this was "demand-pull inflation," that is, it was fueled by surging domestic demand. As inflation continued to accelerate from 1974 on, however, "cost-push" factors associated with the energy crisis, which afflicted the whole group of oil-importing countries, became dominant. Demand elements associated with war-related defense expenditure and cost shocks related to the prices of energy and basic commodities, supported by monetary accommodation, conflated to propel the domestic price level to a new and much higher step. Annual inflation climbed to 40% by mid-decade and smashed through the triple-digit threshold by decade's end, underlining the fact that monetary control was in tatters and had become irrelevant as an instrument of economic control.

As noted, the domestic political instability that surfaced in the wake of the Yom Kippur War was a significant factor in the dynamics that generated the large fiscal deficits of the "lost decade." The trend began, however, after the 1967 Six-Day War with the disappearance of the crucial fiscal discipline that the monetary-dominance regime had imposed. The operating budget veered from surpluses through 1966 to deficits in subsequent years. The average deficit from the Yom Kippur War to 1984 was routinely in double digits of GDP and the average level by 1968–77 was already 9%. Such deficit levels make inflation virtually impossible to control.

CONSTRAINTS ON MONETARY POLICY DURING THE "LOST DECADE"

Excluding attempts at suasion, the BOI had no say in matters of fiscal policy during that period. Thus, even if it had had complete freedom to pursue a restrictive monetary policy by applying the twin instruments that the law placed at its disposal—open-market sales, controlling the size of the monetary base, and bank reserve requirements, which control the value of the money multiplier—it could not have done much to alleviate the monetary avalanche generated by the huge fiscal deficits of the 1970s and the first half of the 1980s.

The deficits, in turn, led to the ballooning of current national domestic and foreign debt in the 1970s and early 1980s, exacerbating the risk of general-government insolvency and reducing the credibility of its sustainability (tables I.1 and I.2).

Since under a fiscal-dominance regime it is the task of monetary policy to react to external and internal shocks, the BOI favored maxi-devaluations and matching increases in controlled prices in order to facilitate a "surprise inflation" strategy. Such a strategy exploits the long-term nature of wage accords, meaning that any increase in the price level creates surprise inflation effects. The idea was to erode real wages and create a short-term real devaluation, thereby temporarily reducing the government's real deficits and improving the balance-of-payments current account. Such "discretionary policies" evidently fueled medium-term inflation expectations and, in turn, raised the long-term inflation rate. The discretionary-policy regime was a counterpart of the fiscal-dominance model, which excludes a nominal anchor and orders monetary policy to achieve some sort of short-term equilibrium in any way possible.

In view of the mission imposed on the BOI—to maintain high employment and to support a highly expansionary fiscal policy—an active restrictive monetary policy was obviously out of the question. Any attempt to march a significant distance down the restrictive road would not only have been inconsistent with the task of maintaining low rates of return on government paper but would also have dampened (temporarily) macroeconomic activity, leading to higher unemployment rates. Thus, although growth rates during the "lost decade" were sluggish to begin with, any increase of unemployment in the post–1973 war period, however brief, was anathema to the political community in view of the political instability that was characteristic of the three governments that held office during this time. By implication, the BOI reflected the Zeitgeist by accepting the dominance of the Ministry of Finance.

Thus, for better or worse, the BOI did not attempt to contain the spiraling expansion of the money supply. What it attempted to do, with general success, was to reduce the *variance* of the rate of monetary expansion rather than the long-term expansion rate itself. One manifestation of this policy was the stabilization of the variance of inflation rather than its trend. This at least helped to mitigate uncertainty, reducing the real cost of running the economy and offering the system an obvious benefit.

By the late 1970s, it was realized by the government that the inflationary regime was counterproductive despite widespread indexation. This led to some early stabilization attempts, which failed for reasons including, principally, the lack of the political power required to initiate a credible budget cut and stanch the expansion of the public debt. Eventually, the public took matters into its own hands. In 1984, it refused to buy more government bonds, forcing the BOI to finance the fiscal deficits by selling foreign reserves and increasing reliance on seignorage. This signaled the final reckoning with reality, forcing the era of large fiscal deficits to an end.

From an economic point of view, this suggests that the attempt to adhere to a monetary regime that had been consistent with stable and rapid economic growth in the Bretton Woods environment failed during the "lost decade." Amid the vicissitudes of the flexible exchange-rate system and the unsettled political environment of that time, it could not function properly. This became increasingly clear as the years went by. The actual change of regime, however, had to wait. It took a stalemated election in July 1984 to create the political environment that made the system ripe for change.

THE 1985 STABILIZATION AND ITS AFTERMATH

The 1985 stabilization program was the definitive watershed in the formulation and implementation of macroeconomic policy in Israel. In more than one sense, it established over time the advent of monetary policy as an inherent and indispensable component of the economy's control and guidance system.

The main reason the previous stabilization attempts failed was the parliamentary weakness of the governments in power. The 1985 program, in contrast, was carried out by a National Unity Government composed of the two dominant parliamentary powers, Labor and Likud, which had roughly equal parliamentary representation. Thus, the coalition government that set the program in motion, buttressed by the religious parties, was supported by more than 75% of the House. The plan also enjoyed exogenous backing in the form of successful action by the industrialized countries to reduce their (much lower) inflation rates in the first half of the 1980s, signaling the onset of the "non-inflationary era" in the global economy. This change in attitude toward inflation spread even to chronic-inflation countries in Latin America. Thus, Argentina and Brazil joined the trend by launching stabilization programs, at approximately the same time as Israel was planning to launch its program.

The new government in Israel, established in October 1984, had two main missions to accomplish: to withdraw military forces from Lebanon and to stamp out inflation. The missions seemed closely linked because the military redeployment made room for a substantial budget cut that supported the disinflation policy. The use of wage and price controls in the 1985 stabilization in the context of a social pact was criticized in some academic circles. The critics pointed out the failure of stabilization programs in Latin America, which froze the exchange rate and implemented price controls, but failed as a result of lack of fiscal support. However, the Israeli stabilization program centered on cutting the fiscal deficit. The controls were intended only to facilitate a "soft landing" from the extreme inflation. As it happened, the controls imposed were excess baggage from the economic standpoint because the drastic classical policy measures—highly restrictive fiscal and monetary policies—created a state of excess supply. Be this as it may, the controls were invoked as a temporary measure only and were dismantled by the end of 1986. The more fundamental principles of the program, however, have been upheld ever since.

The stabilization program enunciated several fundamental principles of macroeconomic policy that were maintained down the road, allowing disinflation

to become a permanent feature of the economic landscape. The main principles of the program included a de jure injunction against the financing of fiscal
deficits by the BOI (the April 1985 "non-printing law"), the adoption of a policy of low fiscal deficits to stanch an increase in the national debt, and an inherent reliance on a nominal anchor, ruling out the use of surprise inflation tactics
as an instrument for the attainment of nonfinancial objectives such as a cut in
real wages, a real devaluation, and a cut in the fiscal deficit. This regime sired a
relatively conservative set of macroeconomic features: a declining debt/GDP
ratio, stable and moderate budget deficits, and a low inflation tax. This more
market-oriented environment allowed Israel to elevate its growth performance
to rates exceeding those of the European Community (on the continent) and
matching those of the United States (table I.3).

The nominal anchor assumed different forms: First, it was based on a fixed
exchange rate against the U.S. dollar. Then it was pegged to a five-currency basket. In the third stage, the anchor was defined in terms of a fixed (horizontal)
exchange-rate band. Finally, it was redefined as a nominal inflation target
supported by a sliding exchange-rate band that widened over time. The main
message in all phases was that the exchange rate should no longer be used to
create a price shock, as had often been the case during the period of high and
accelerating inflation. Thus, surprise-inflation tactics would no longer be
invoked in the implementation of monetary policy.

The credibility of the exchange-rate anchor in the first crucial quarters of
the stabilization policy was supported by a $1.5 billion aid package from the
United States. The long-term credibility of fiscal discipline was enhanced by the
"non-printing law," an amendment to the Bank of Israel Law that repealed
Section 45a of the original 1954 statute that had allowed the government to
borrow from the central bank to finance its fiscal deficit—an option that
governments used frequently and massively in the 1970s and early 1980s. In the
long run, the amendment had a major effect on the BOI's degrees of freedom
in the running of monetary policy.

The interim target was attained. In a feat of political stamina and perseverance, the annual inflation rate plunged from 400%–500% to 15%–20% by early
1986, three to four quarters after the process began. On the whole, fiscal policy
supported the disinflation strategy in the spirit of monetary dominance. The
budget was pruned drastically as subsidies were cut by a major 5% of GDP and
defense expenditure by 3%. The latter cutback was abetted by the pullback of
forces in Lebanon and the eight-year-long Iran-Iraq war, which mitigated the
threat to Israel's eastern front. The rapid disinflation, obvious to all and sundry
by the third and fourth quarters of the program, generated a "reverse Tanzi
effect" by significantly reducing the negative inflation effect that had been eroding real tax revenues in the last phase of the inflationary era. This, of course,
supported the effort to cut the deficit.

The BOI's technique in running the process was effected by a much slower
reduction of the rate of interest on its funds—and consequently the commercial banks' overdraft rate—than the pace of disinflation. The instrument used
for this purpose, that is, for the implementation of the monetary restriction

Table I.3. Economic Indicators 1986–2002*

		1986–89	1990–94	1995–99	2002–02
(1)	Operational deficit of general government	0.96	4.51	4.55	3.47
(2)	Annual change in monetary base	0.83	0.67	0.59	0.43
(3)	Inflation tax[1]	1.13	0.56	0.41	0.31
(4) = (1) − (2)	Total general-government deficit less seigniorage	0.13	3.84	3.96	3.04
(5) = (1) − (3)	Total deficit minus inflation tax	−0.17	3.95	4.14	3.16
(6)	Net real interest payments	9.66	6.93	5.66	5.20
(7) = (1) − (6)	Primary deficit of general government	−8.70	−2.42	−1.11	−1.73
(8) = (7) − (2)	Primary deficit of general government less seigniorage	−9.53	−3.09	−1.70	−2.16
(9) = (7) − (3)	Primary deficit minus inflation tax	−9.83	−2.98	−1.51	−2.04
(10)	Net public debt[2]	135.78	102.61	85.73	83.60
(11)	MB/GDP (m)	5.33	3.62	3.93	4.92
(12)	Inflation (% annual), (π)	18.22	14.14	7.13	2.64
(13)	MB—growth (% annual)	18.57	20.60	17.70	9.34
(14)	Real interest rate (r)				
a	On government bonds[3]	2.46	1.14	3.20	3.36
b	On bank loans[4]	29.10	8.66	12.83	13.45
c	Actual interest payment[5]	7.11	6.75	6.60	6.22
(15)	GDP growth (n)	3.67	6.13	4.05	1.85
(16)	Unemployment rate	7.13	9.84	7.16	9.00

*Rows 1–10: percent of GDP.
[1]im = $((1 + r)(1 + \pi)-1)$*m, r from(14)a; i = nominal interest rate.
[2]Methodology: Dahan and Strawczynski (1999).
[3]Real yield to redemption of CPI-indexed bonds.
[4]Real interest rate on revolving-credit facilities.
[5]Actual interest payments, average of annual ratios (6)/(10).
Source: BOI.

specified in the stabilization policy document, was clumsy yet immediately effective: quantity control of bank credit. This conservative strategy generated high positive real interest rates throughout the stabilization interval. Simultaneously, the BOI initiated a major move on what may be identified as its home turf—the "directed-credit" component of commercial bank credit. Hitherto, the central bank had very little if any say about the volume and the price of this major fraction of the commercial banks' total outstanding credit accommodation and of its own indirect contribution to that tranche. Therefore, this important component of bank credit—30%–40% of total commercial bank credit from the 1970s to the mid-1980s—and its contribution to the money supply had been off-limits to monetary policy. Now, however, in a process stretching over several years through 1990, the directed component of bank credit, a highly significant privilege for its beneficiaries in the agriculture, manufacturing, and construction industries, was phased out. This had far-reaching consequences for several major manufacturing and construction firms that were household names in Israel. Some of them collapsed. Without the termination of directed credit, however, monetary policy never could have been liberated from its thirty-year confinement. The mirror image of the process was the loss of clout at the Finance Ministry and several other government ministries and agencies, which forfeited part of their turf. Yet by the late 1980s, as the success of the stabilization policy and what it represented was conceptually absorbed, the political community and the electorate finally acknowledged that there was no alternative to the process. This signaled the acceptance in Israel of the OECD economic model.

A basic issue in macroeconomic management is whether a monetary regime can impose fiscal discipline on the government. In 1983, a plan to "dollarize" the economy (to adopt the U.S. dollar as the Israeli currency) as an instrument of fiscal discipline had failed because—among other reasons—the need to stabilize the economy was not considered critical at the time. The situation changed dramatically in the 1990s, when Israel realized that it had no alternative but to join the bandwagon of the industrialized countries, which were granting their central banks greater freedom by means of new legislation (in the cases of the Bank of England and the European Central Bank) or by established praxis (the Federal Reserve Bank). This gave "teeth" to monetary-policy objectives and created the necessary political conditions for the fiscal authorities to support the monetary strategy of disinflation in the spirit of monetary dominance.

THE EMERGENCE OF AN INDEPENDENT MONETARY POLICY

Israel's monetary policy in the 1990s pursued a disinflation strategy similar to that adopted by many industrialized and developing countries. The cornerstone of the disinflation policy was the entrusting of its implementation to an independent central bank that enjoys the support of the government. The most conspicuous feature of the disinflation strategy in the mid-nineties was an increase in the real interest rate on central-bank funds (usually involving a shift from negative to positive real rates). The OECD countries invoked this strategy in the early 1980s; the developing countries of Latin America and Israel did so in the 1990s. The theoretical foundation of the need to raise the real interest rate in *money-based* disinflation processes may be linked directly to the monetary crunch that usually accompanies disinflation processes. This became the characteristic feature of the Israeli economy in the second half of the 1990s.

The raising of real interest rates in the medium term is explainable by reference to the assumption of sticky domestic prices and Rogoff's "conservative central banker." When the inflation target is reduced drastically, a conservative central banker will not expand the stock of money immediately in order to reduce the nominal interest rate in tandem in order to align it with the new target. This behavior is prescribed by the fear that such a move may be interpreted as inflationary finance. Instead, the banker will adjust the money supply to the target gradually. This equilibration of the money market, however, initially entails a high real interest rate and, in turn, an increase in unemployment.

This argument may be generalized for an open economy by means of a modified version of the Dornbusch model of "overshooting" (Dornbusch, 1976, 1980, chap. 12; Liviatan, 1980). In a nutshell, if the slowdown of monetary growth leads to a larger reduction in the exchange rate than in domestic prices (real appreciation), rational expectations entail an increase in the expected real devaluation and, with it, the real interest rate. This sequence of events seems to correspond to the Israeli experience.

There are alternative ways of explaining the real interest increase in the disinflation processes of the OECD countries and Israel. Clarida, Gali, and Gertler (1999) present a model—a variant of the Taylor equation—in which the key rate depends on the deviation of expected inflation from the inflation target. In this model money is endogenous. However, this model explains reactions to short-term shocks but not an increase in the key interest rate in the medium term. To explain the latter within the framework of the Clarida model, we must assume the presence of a lingering credibility gap or the pursuit by the BOI of a lower target than the declared one, accompanied by a slow learning process by the public (probably due to its lengthy experience with inflation).

While these moves refer to the medium term, the overall strategy requires the active use of the short-term key rate to establish the credibility of the central bank's commitment to price stability. In Israel, this was accomplished within the framework of the regime of government-set inflation targets. Israel's inflation targeting was accommodative when first invoked in the early 1990s but afterwards became increasingly aggressive in forcing rapid disinflation. Since 2002, the annual target has been set permanently at 1%–3%. The BOI's task in this construct is to make sure that the price level attains the target. In principle, the target represents a consensus between the government and the BOI. In practice, however, the government has often been critical of the severity of the measures that BOI has taken to hit the target, especially aggressive rate-hiking in cases of inflation spikes. This conflict between the government and the BOI is the inevitable result of the model in which the government uses the central bank to tie its own hands against the temptation to succumb to inflation pressures.

In the second half of the 1990s, the increase in the interest rate within the constraint of the exchange-rate band created a massive short-term inflow. When the BOI sterilized the inflow, the risk premium of the exchange rate climbed and a fiscal burden (a "quasi-fiscal" deficit) came about due to the interest-rate spread, as the BOI paid higher rates domestically than the global market rate on its foreign-currency assets. Simultaneously, however, the BOI's tactics introduced a conservative macroeconomic strain that was fully consistent with the "OECD model." This reduced the country risk and, correspondingly, made the exchange rate less volatile. On the whole, then, Israel's financial stability improved in the second half of the 1990s, as reflected by the increase in long-term capital inflows, which were largely independent of the short-term interest differential. The fact that Israel avoided a financial crisis in 1998 in response to the Russian and Southeast Asian financial mayhem in the summer of that year is a case in point. The increased financial stability, however, was attained at the cost of a recession that intensified in later years.

The monetary strategy of the BOI could not have worked without the support of the restrictive fiscal policy. The continuous and coterminous process of foreign-exchange liberalization, implemented in the 1990s, was abetted by rising pressure from the international capital market which, for this reason, was inadvertently mobilized to impose the required fiscal discipline on the government. This laid the foundations of a monetary-dominance regime, in which the Ministry of Finance has internalized the constraints of price stability and, in view of BOI policy, contributes to the avoidance of financial crises. The internalization of constraints entailed, first and foremost, adherence to the constraint of a sustainable path of the public debt and a corresponding policy of relatively low fiscal deficits (table I.3). Within the framework of this regime and its basic feature of transparency, there is no room for the surprise-inflation policy that in times of rampant inflation had been an inherent component of the tool set. Nobody today would suspect the BOI of pursuing surprise-inflation tactics in order to increase employment (as proposed by the Barro-Gordon game models) while it is criticized left and right for being more conservative than the Fed.

The move toward monetary control instead of accommodation in formerly inflationary economies actually reflected a more profound change in economic strategy: an ever-increasing shift to a market-oriented economic environment. This change took place against the background of the collapse of Soviet-style centrally planned economies and the failure of the Prebish "chronic-inflation" economic model in Latin America. As the world became less inflationary and as the industrial countries' economic setup emerged as the winning model, disinflation became part of the transition to the new economic regime.

This tendency was reinforced by the growing influence of globalization in world capital markets, which made it risky to be an outlier in the rate of inflation. As noted, the globalization process indirectly supported price stability in Israel (and many other countries) by imposing fiscal discipline on the government. This is because Israeli policymakers today are strongly mindful of their country rating in global capital markets, and the rating services attribute great importance to the state of the budget. The Israeli public, too, seems more willing to accept constraints imposed by the global capital market than constraints imposed by their own government, presumably because it considers the former "objective." At a deeper level, there is a consensus that the Israeli economy should adopt international standards. The BOI contributed to the imposition of this discipline by its continued support of the liberalization of the balance-of-payments capital account, thereby expediting the country's integration into the global capital market.

The strategy described above managed to reduce domestic inflation to internationally accepted levels by the late 1990s, although external and internal shocks that caused occasional spikes blur the picture. The success of the disinflation, however, came at the price of a lengthy recession that subjected the BOI's policies to public criticism.

CRITICISMS OF THE BOI's MONETARY POLICY

It has been argued correctly (e.g., by Ben-David, 2003) that Israel's speedy integration into the global market has had adverse effects on income distribution by tending to raise the wages of skilled workers and lower those of the unskilled. Since this establishes a prima facie case for a more gradual integration into the global economy, it is an indirect critique of the BOI's policy of pushing relentlessly for liberalization of the foreign-exchange market. However, as usually occurs with this kind of criticism, it is rather hard to establish in practice whether the cost of slowing integration outweighs its benefits.

A similar argument can be made about "traditional industries," such as textiles, that found it harder and harder to compete in world markets as disinflation and forex liberalization proceeded. There is a highly reasonable case for allowing these industries to adjust to the globalization process more gradually. In many respects, Israel seems to have been inadequately prepared for integration into the global economy . However, the implications of this argument for the conduct of monetary policy, if any, are debatable. The jury still appears to be out.

Finally, the BOI's high real interest policy after the implementation of the stabilization policy in 1985 and, specifically, in the 1990s, has been strongly criticized. However, in the OECD countries, too, it was common practice to raise real interest rates during the disinflation process due to credibility problems, and the real interest rate of the BOI does not seem to be out of line with that of Southern Europe during the disinflation process. The BOI's critics acknowledged the need to raise interest rates in order to reduce inflation but argued that the BOI had become overly restrictive in comparison with the practice of central banks in major industrialized countries. Indeed, there is indeed evidence that the BOI in recent years has been tougher on inflation than the Fed and totally oblivious to the unemployment aspect of the business cycle. Its tight monetary policy has undoubtedly abetted the recession that has festered since 1997.[5] In response, the BOI has argued that Israel's inflationary history requires a tough monetary policy, especially in the absence of an OECD-type fiscal consolidation underlined by the relevant Maastricht rules. Recent econometric studies suggest that the jury is still out on this topic, too.

It is noteworthy in this context that the very notion of appointing an "independent central banker" reflects the view that the banker's mission entails a tougher stance on inflation than that of the political community. The very purpose of such a banker would be to tie the government's hands against the accommodation of inflation pressures. In view of the so-called Rogoff model, the appointment of a tough central banker who has a strong preference for price stability may be socially beneficial in the long run even though such a banker would pay little attention to the current state of unemployment. It is well known, however, that a central bank may be *too* independent in its pursuit of the target of price stability. What is at issue, then, is whether the BOI's recent disinflation policies have been inconsistent with the social consensus about the trade-off between the speedy transition to price stability and its cost in terms of recession.

We may evaluate this issue from two perspectives. First, the inflation-target regime is supposed to reflect a government-BOI consensus about the agreed course of inflation and, by implication, about its cost. This seems to pose a simple question: did the BOI adhere to such a consensus or did it "play tricks"? The answer, somewhat surprisingly, is not straightforward. In this context, we may also consider the evaluation of the BOI's policies by the democratically elected government and by knowledgeable people in academia.

The first question is hard to answer for two reasons, conceptual and statistical. The conceptual problem is that the BOI may implement its policies (or "play its tricks," as some may prefer) in a way that influences the government in setting the inflation target. By pursuing a tighter monetary policy than the one agreed upon, for example, the BOI may create a monetary environment that is conducive to the adoption of a low-inflation target. This, it is claimed, is what happened after the steep but short-lived depreciation of the NIS in October 1998 (occasioned by global financial mayhem at the time). Thus, the consensus itself is potentially subject to foul play. Indeed, Sussman's econometric study (in volume II) suggests that in the second half of the 1990s the BOI conducted its interest policy as if its target were zero inflation instead of the positive and downward-sloping target that had been announced.

The second aspect is more technical: how to identify criteria by which one may determine intentionality. Canzoneri (1985), taking up a similar question in the context of information asymmetry, suggests that in principle this problem may be solved by setting a limit for the path of deviations from the declared policy. In practice, the parameters for such a test are rather subjective. A relevant piece of information is that inflation in Israel was below target for three years in a row, 1999–2001. In 2002, inflation was far above target because in December 2001 the BOI, finally submitting to recurrent heavy pressure from the Prime Minister and the Minister of Finance, slashed the key rate drastically. In response, the annual inflation rate leaped from about 1.4% in the last quarter of 2001 to 7% by the middle of 2002. The BOI reacted swiftly, jerking the key rate from 3.8% to 9.1% within five months. This led to negative inflation in 2003, as against an inflation target of 1%–3%. These facts give many observers the impression that BOI did pursue a monetary policy that was tougher than the one agreed upon.

Sussman's aforementioned econometric study reinforces this conclusion somewhat by noting a change in the relationship between actual inflation and the inflation target during the 1990s. While the BOI tended to err on the upper side of the target in the first half of the decade, actual inflation tended to be below target in the second half. Since the price level was quite volatile during that period, it is difficult to determine whether the results are statistically significant. Nevertheless, the study reinforces the impression that the BOI conducted a tougher monetary policy than the consensus would have favored.

Another approach to the problem is to consider the attitude of the government toward the BOI's policies. Did the government behave as if the BOI had "cheated" it? Maybe. In December 2001, the prime minister, Mr. Sharon, successfully prevailed on Governor Klein to slash the key rate, clearly suggesting that the government's reading of monetary policy considered it excessively restrictive. However, the financial turmoil that followed this step convinced the government that it is preferable to let BOI control the monetary system, which it did by reversing the December 2001 move rapidly and drastically. By inference, although the government was dissatisfied with the pace of rate cutting, its own process of learning-by-doing convinced it that pressuring the governor can be counterproductive. Finally, we may also note that the community of economists in academia has treated the BOI's monetary strategies not with raucous criticism but with acquiescence.

These facts, as we construe them, support the view that although the BOI's tough monetary policy may have fallen outside the social consensus, the deviation was not large enough to justify a confrontation between the BOI and the government. However, the "brinkmanship" policy of the central bank may eventually backfire because the government has the option, in due course, of replacing the governor with a successor who will reverse his or her policies. This seems unlikely with the appointment of Professor Stanley Fischer as governor.

While there is criticism of the BOI's monetary policy there does not seem to be an obvious alternative to it. An alternative strategy would presumably reduce the pace of disinflation in the hope that it will stimulate growth. But these results are uncertain; a slower pace of disinflation might signal a weaker commitment to price stability and endanger the integration of Israel in the world capital market. Thus there is a wide gray area within which the BOI can conduct its policies. The criticism focuses essentially on the dosage of the treatment and not the treatment itself. The right dosage, however, is of course very difficult to determine empirically.

Admittedly, central banks inherently prefer high interest rates when in doubt. This may be due to the fact that the harm caused by excessively high interest rates is harder to detect than the ravages of excessively low rates. Overly high rates neither deplete the foreign reserves nor generate any visible crisis. Their effect is more insidious, manifested in a substantial lag in the slowdown of economic activity, which once it occurs may be blamed on other factors. Excessively low interest rates, in turn, may result in an immediate financial crisis. An obvious case in point was the drastic rate cut in December 2001 and its consequences in terms of the impact on the exchange rate, which was translated rapidly and vehemently into price inflation.

Those who argue that the BOI succumbed too easily to the interest-rate syndrome inherent in the modus operandi of central banks do have a case. On the whole, however, central banks have been very successful in delivering price stability to the world's economies since the mid-1980s or so. The Bank of Israel shares in this success. Indeed, it succeeded against much tougher inflationary odds—a much more turbulent and inflationary environment, of much longer persistence—than those confronted by central banks in the OECD countries. Consequently, the BOI has established itself as the anchor of Israel's financial stability.

By the same token, it must be admitted that the central banks have not found a way to cope with the economic recession that spread across the globe after the end of the second millennium. Israel has shared in the slump—in the form of a severe recession—and the BOI shares in the failure to stem it. Moreover, since 2001 or so, the BOI has clearly been out of step with the expansionary countercyclical policies adopted by its "big brothers," the Fed and the European Central Bank.

PART I

THE FORMATION AND DEVELOPMENT OF THE ISRAELI MONETARY SYSTEM, 1948–73

1

Emergence of the Monetary Texture and Macroeconomic Developments, 1948–54

THE MONETARY LEGACY OF THE BRITISH MANDATE

To trace monetary developments during the formative period of the Israeli economy—the "supply and rationing" era of 1948–51—and what may be described as the diametrically opposite policy thrust that followed, the market-oriented New Economic Policy (NEP) of 1952–54, a short reference to "pre-history" may offer illuminating insights on comings and goings during the first chapter of Israel's monetary history.

The Department of Issue, the initial skeleton of the Israeli monetary system that made its debut in August 1948, looked at first glance much like the Currency Board that Israel had inherited from the British Mandate. This Currency Board regime, initially used by the British raj to run the monetary system of India from the last decade of the nineteenth century,[1] was subsequently set up throughout the British Empire. The monetary systems of the post–World War I Mandatory dependencies were fashioned along the same lines.

The Palestine Currency Board came on board in 1927, establishing a Palestinian currency in lieu of the Egyptian currency that, issued by a similar currency board, had been the country's declared legal tender since 1919. The PCB, located in London, was given sole legal power to issue banknotes. Its modus operandi was straightforward and simple: it would sell or purchase one Palestine pound (PSP) for one pound sterling. Assets over and above the (sterling) liquidity required for day-to-day business would be invested in gilt-edged bonds, that is, British government (and Dominion) debentures. Accordingly, the PCB had a 100% reserve ratio.[2]

The strict indexation of the Palestine pound to the pound sterling meant that the country operated on a fixed exchange-rate regime with sterling and the sterling bloc throughout almost the entire Mandate period, and with the dollar and other currencies between 1927 (effectively 1925) and 1931—before the sterling was floated and depreciated. The prewar rules, of course, permitted unrestricted capital movements and what was effectively a free-trade regime. Finally, although accommodation of credit to the government of Palestine was excluded by definition, the British government's restrictive fiscal policy in the interwar period obviated net borrowing from any source. (In fact, the national debt of the United Kingdom declined somewhat during that time.)[3] Thus, the British government did not use the potential credit facility that the basic operating rules of the Empire currency boards made available to the British fiscus.

These constraints were jettisoned when World War II began. Currency controls were imposed, first restricting capital movements and foreign trade (the latter also due to the ever-worsening shortage of shipping space) and later controlling prices in conjunction with rationing. This set of regulations, today described as a "financial repression" regime, changed the effective rules of the monetary game in Palestine even though the operating rules of the Palestine Currency Board remained unchanged until the board stopped issuing Palestine currency in 1948.

The monetary aggregates in table 1.1 and the corresponding figure 1.1 underline the difference in kind between the interwar and the war years. Thus, M_1, for which the series starts in 1931, expanded at an annual rate of around 17% during the last eight prewar years and at twice that rate, 34% per year, during the six war years, 1940–45. It is also quite clear that the monetary base, which in those years was identical with currency in circulation, was the main factor on the monetary scene. The somewhat more rapid expansion of demand deposits in the early 1930s through 1935 was clearly linked to the major structural

Table 1.1. Monetary Aggregates in the Mandate Period, 1927–47[1]

	Average Annual Rates of Change (percent)		
	Currency in Circulation (1)	Demand Deposits[2] (2)	M_1 (1) + (2) = (3)
1927–31	12.0	—	—
1932–35	30.0	34.3	32.7
1932–39	17.8	15.6	16.9
1940–45	31.2	34.7	33.6
1940–46	26.2	29.4	27.7

[1]End-of-year balances.
[2]Based on Szereszewski series for deposits with Jewish banks only (Szereszewski, 1968, Table 10, p. 66). Deposits with Jewish banks and cooperative credit societies accounted for 79 percent of the total in 1946 (Heth, 1994, Table A-9, p. 26).
Sources: Columns (1)–(3): Halperin, 1954; Tables VII and X: according to *Statistical Abstract of Palestine 1944–45*, pp. 86–90, and *General Monthly Bulletin of Current Statistics*, January–February 1948, p. 31. Estimates of demand deposits for 1931–35 are Halperin's own estimates.

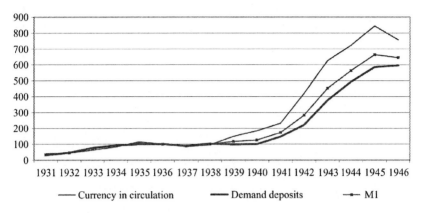

Figure 1.1. Monetary Aggregates in the Mandate Period, 1931–46 (1936 = 100)

change that Palestine's economy underwent during these years—the strong upturn in Jewish immigration and the corresponding rise in capital imports. The rates of inflow were quite volatile during the 1930s, from 34% annual expansion in 1932–35 to zero growth in 1936–39. Obviously this reflected the depressed business conditions that affected the real dimension of the economy in view of global political tension. Indeed, the 1935–36 Abyssinia crisis, the 1938 confrontation in Europe (the "Munich" episode), and the prewar jitters in 1939 generated runs on banks. Although there were several minor failures among the plethora of small private institutions that surfaced in Palestine between 1933 and 1936 (Heth, 1994, pp. 15–21), the banking system survived due to its strong liquidity position and sound solvency. The 1936–39 Arab uprising and the British government's political reaction to it—the reduction of Jewish immigration and the inevitable effect of this measure on capital imports—had a similar dampening effect on the expansion of demand deposits during this period and, thus, on the pattern of the money supply.

The concurrence of rapid expansion of monetary aggregates and rapid GNP growth—at an annual average of 8.4% in the 1930s and almost 11% during the war era and in the postwar years through 1947, generating a corresponding demand for money—affected the price level in opposite directions. M_1 expanded at nearly a 17% annual rate in 1931–39, about twice the 8.4% annual rate of NDP growth.[4] However, the price level hardly budged; both consumer and wholesale prices were about 10% higher at the end of 1939 than at the end of 1931 and, thus, at about the 1930 level in effective terms (figure 1.2). By implication, something other than growth of product and, correspondingly, of national income affected the demand for money during that period. Thus, it is quite reasonable to impute the acceleration of demand for money to the far-reaching modernization process, which of course involved the process of "monetization," that the two national components of the population were undergoing. This boosted demand for money over and above the level suggested by a unitary income elasticity of demand.

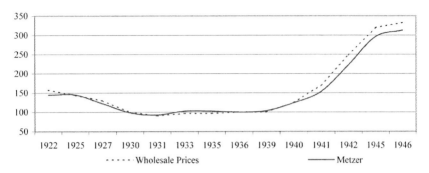

Figure 1.2. Price Patterns 1922–47 (1936 = 100)

The supply of base money, effectively Palestine pound banknotes, was dependent solely on the foreign balance. However, since the current account was always in deficit, the monetary base could be increased only in the event of a capital inflow that surpassed the current-account deficit. A fraction of this inflow was allocated to the public at its choice to accommodate its growing demand for cash. Thus, the expansion of the monetary base was clearly demand driven, suggesting an infinitely elastic supply curve of Palestinian pounds at the current interest rate, which in those days was set in London and other world markets at a low and stable level. Although the money supply—M_1 including demand deposits—was somewhat more flexible, since the banking system maintained fractional reserves and had discretion in setting reserve ratios, the data for the 1930s clearly show that M_1 and the monetary base grew at similar rates. This means that the volume of M_1, too, was similarly determined by demand.

Accordingly, the nominal demand for money (M_1) grew at a rate determined by the growth rate of real product, multiplied by the stable price level, plus the significant—highly significant for the Arab population in particular—monetization process. By implication, the price level in Palestine, where free trade was effectively the norm, was "supply determined," that is, set by prices in the global market. The stable wholesale prices and the rather stable cost of living in the 1930s (table 1.2 and figure 1.2), then, reflect the stable pattern of world market prices after they toppled at the turn of the decade into the trough of the post-1929 global economic crisis.

The advent of war abruptly changed the monetary rules of the game. The financial-repression apparatus that the United Kingdom installed at home when the war began was immediately and inevitably imposed on the dependencies, including Palestine. Free capital movements (with non-sterling-bloc countries) were abolished and transport connections with locations outside the Middle East became increasingly tenuous. The restrictions mounted over time as the expanding theaters of the war effectively destroyed the free-trade facility. Finally, Britain's fiscal rectitude in the interwar years was jettisoned. The expansionary fiscal policy, coupled with military expenditures in Palestine and the Middle East—which were formally conceived as exports of Palestine—inevitably entailed the monetization of these expenditures by means of the printing press,

Table 1.2. Price Patterns, 1922–71[1]

	Cost of Living				Wholesale Prices
			Office of Statistics		
	Metzer (1)	Szereszewski (2)	Jewish (3)	Total (4)	(5)
Indices: 1936 = 100					
1922	144.2	138.2	—	156.6	157.4
1930	98.4	104.2	—	106.0	99.4
1931	92.7	95.5	—	95.6	90.7
1935	102.6	110.6	—	94.7	96.5
1936	100.0	100.0	100.0	100.0	100.0
1939	103.3	102.9	104.3	101.3	100.3
1940	124.1	123.6	118.8	118.4	124.4
1941	153.2	152.7	153.5	160.2	169.9
1945	295.8	294.7	254.6	244.9	319.4
1947	316.7	315.4	—	—	—
Annual average rates of change (percent)					
1928–31	−7.2	−7.2	—	−9.6	−12.2
1936–39	0.2	1.0	1.4	0.4	0.0
1940–45	19.2	19.2	16.0	15.9	21.3
1940–47	15.0	15.0	—	—	—
1946	5.7	5.7	3.6	3.9	4.0
1947	1.3	1.8	—	—	—

[1]Columns (1)–(3) refer to alternative estimates of prices in Jewish markets. The Szereszewski and Metzer estimates are adjustments of the basic Government Office of Statistics cost of living index (Column 3), which is available through 1946 only. Columns (4) and (5) are Government Office of Statistics estimates. No alternative wholesale price index is available.
Sources: Column (1): Metzer 1998, Table A-21, p. 241; columns (2): Szereszewski, 1968, Table 13, p. 73; columns (3)–(5): *Statistical Abstract of Palestine,* 1944–45, and *General Monthly Bulletin of Current Statistics,* February 1948.

by the PCB, among others. Since the option of a corresponding increase in imports from the United Kingdom and from other sterling-bloc countries was hardly practical, these "increased export revenues" inflated Palestine's monetary base and its money supply. The significance of these expenditures and, in turn, their impact on the monetary aggregates, is underlined by their very size. Military expenditures in Palestine were seven times greater in 1940 than in the last prewar year, 1938. At their peak in 1941, they were almost 14 times greater than in 1938. That year, these military procurements absorbed almost 38% of Palestine's Net Domestic Product. By 1946, the proportions had reverted to a factor of eight and almost 16% of NDP (Gross and Metzer, 1999, pp. 306–8, tables 2 and 3).

Thus, although the economy of Palestine prospered enormously during the war years, growing at annual average rates of about 10% in the six years through 1945 and nearly 11% in the last eight years of the British Mandate (through 1947), it could not cope with the avalanche of money that ensued. The annual average expansion rates of M_1—34% and 28% in 1940–45 and 1940–46, respectively (table 1.1)—supported by the war restrictions on imports, generated severe demand-pull inflation. The price level climbed by a factor of three, by 19% on annual average during the six war years or by about 17% annually if the significantly lower inflation of consumer and wholesale prices in 1946 is included. By 1948, this lengthy stretch of inflation had inevitably dashed expectations that a decade of stable or falling prices in the 1930s had generated. A conceptual environment of inflation expectations took over.

A solid monetary system, based on a currency board that operated separately from the political administration and maintained complete transparency in its assets and liabilities, was one of the most significant legacies of the Mandate era for the economic and political institutions of Israel. The inheritance also included an experienced, solid, solvent, and highly liquid commercial banking sector that strictly followed the modalities of banking in developed countries, with their prescription of rather conservative guidelines for the proper conduct of business. The system had demonstrated its ability to survive serious financial pressure by having withstood three politically generated runs on banks in the second half of the 1930s despite the lack of a lender of last resort and the Mandatory authorities' adamant refusal to offer even token assistance.[5]

On the negative side of the balance sheet of the Mandatory legacy, the lengthy period of inflation (1940–47) invested households and firms, the Histadrut (the all-powerful General Federation of Jewish Labor in Palestine), and the political community with entrenched inflation expectations. Furthermore, the new and inexperienced Israeli government inherited a comprehensive legal and administrative framework of financial repression that included tough currency controls; a legal ceiling for the nominal interest rate (inherited from the Ottoman period) that was much lower than the wartime inflation rates; price controls and rationing; and a system, operating since 1943, of wage and price indexation, coupled with a highly favorable conceptual attitude toward government control and micromanagement of the economy.

The favorable attitude toward comprehensive government involvement in running the economy was of course not specific to the nascent State of Israel. In the first postwar decade, it was dominant in a Western European public opinion that had internalized the memory of the economic downturn and crisis that began in the 1930s and lasted until World War II. This view also prevailed in the North American political community at the time, as manifested in the U.S. Employment Act of 1946. Both political spheres, the Western European and the American, had of course been subjected to the influence of the frame of mind articulated by Keynes in his 1936 *General Theory of Employment, Interest and Money*.

THE DEBUT OF THE ISRAELI CURRENCY

Although Palestine was legally excluded from the sterling bloc in February 1948 by resolution of the British Government, the Government of Israel did not rush to take action on the monetary front. The United Nations resolution of November 29, 1947, to partition Palestine into two states within an economic and monetary union, precluded any official moves by the Jewish side in this area during the politically sensitive pre–Declaration of Independence interval between November 29, 1947, and May 15, 1948. The highly delicate diplomatic situation continued to prescribe caution on these issues even in the first months of independence. Foreign-policy considerations still inhibited moves that could be made on this front. In the summer of 1948, the country's ongoing war for survival prompted its stewards to identify other priorities as more urgent.

The issue was forced in the middle of August 1948, leading to the expansion of the newly acquired political sovereignty to the monetary realm. The precipitating event was the complete stoppage of the issue of currency by the PCB on June 1, 1948, strangling the national cash flow.[6] The rapid and highly successful transition to an Israeli currency was implemented within a month after the Government of Israel and Anglo-Palestine Bank (APB) concluded a covenant on August 16, 1948, establishing a Department of Issue at the bank.

The covenant and the enabling legal framework, incorporated into the Bank Note Ordinance and the Currency Ordinance (both enacted on the same day), established the new currency as legal tender. Neither the covenant nor the new legal framework was the product of sorcery. That the documents could be placed on the table was due to a lengthy process of secret deliberations and subsequent negotiations that the APB Board of Directors initiated in October 1947. The initiative of Eliezer Siegfried Hoofien, Chairman of the APB Board, and his protracted efforts for this cause, starting immediately after the U.N. resolution of November 1947, were inevitable in more than one sense. As the banking institution established by the Zionist Organization in the first decade of the twentieth century, the owner of its voting shares, and the country's dominant bank—holding more than 50% of total deposits with the Palestine commercial banking system in 1946 (Heth, 1994, p. 26, table A-9)—APB was the obvious instrument of choice. Its size, its financial expertise, and, particularly, its lengthy reputation for solidity were obvious assets for the successful launching of a new currency, which in ordinary times and a fortiori in wartime was crucially dependent on credibility and trust.

Eliezer Kaplan, the treasurer of the Jewish Agency in the two quarters preceding the Declaration of Independence and the first minister of finance in the Provisional Government of Israel that served from May 15, 1948, nevertheless sought outside expert opinion. Two (Jewish) monetary experts of world stature, among others, were consulted: Sir Jeremy Reiseman, then Vice-Chairman of the Board of Lloyds Bank in England, and Harry D. White, the American Executive Director at the IMF who, in his earlier function as Assistant Secretary of the Treasury of the United States, had negotiated the Bretton Woods agreement with Keynes.

The main issues involved were: (1) the significance of awarding a monopoly on issuing currency, the quintessential public good, to a private firm; (2) the degree and means of control of the state over this agency; (3) the time limit of the monopoly; (4) the composition of the portfolio of assets that the issuing agency would acquire as a quid pro quo for the outstanding currency balance; and (5) the exchange rate to be set for the new currency in terms of the old one, that is, the Palestine pound, and effectively in terms of sterling.

Apart from the restricted time dimension of the right of issue—set at three years with six months' notice of repeal by either side—the terms of the covenant between APB and the government closely resembled those of the renowned English Bank Act of 1844. Accordingly, APB was to set up a separate, legally distinct Department of Issue, the profits or losses of which would be credited or debited to the government budget. The Government would appoint two members of the department's management committee as its representatives. Finally, on "major policy issues"—the volume of credit to be granted to the government and the rate of discount to be set from time to time by the Department of Issue—the management of the department would take the government's point of view "into consideration."[7]

In regard to the first of these crucial issues, the size of government credit, the covenant imposed a limit by stipulating a reserve ratio of at least 50% of total currency in circulation. The reserves of the Department of Issue were defined as gold, foreign exchange, and Palestine pounds that the department would acquire in exchange for its own notes. The department was also to offer a rediscount facility for Treasury bills and commercial paper (Ottensooser, 1955, p. 111). To assure transparency and, thereby, to acquire and maintain credibility, the department undertook to publish its balance sheet at the end of every month. Implicitly, the publication of this document would constrain the government's reliance on the printing press.

To make outstanding Palestine pound notes and the assets and liabilities of the banking system convertible into the new Israeli currency, a rate of exchange had to be established. The rate chosen, 1 : 1, was made the law of the land in the Currency Notes Ordinance, legislated on the same day (August 16, 1948) that the Bank Note Ordinance had enshrined the covenant as law. In retrospect, the huge difference between the British and Palestine inflation rates in 1940–48—about 80% and significantly beyond 200%, respectively (in terms of official consumer price indices)—makes the 1 : 1 choice seem quite out of line. Yet this factor, which indeed became highly relevant in the longer run, was not mentioned at all, to the best of our knowledge, in the deliberations on that issue. Just the same, in view of the extreme uncertainty that the war conditions and the corresponding diplomatic struggle imposed on this novice among states, the public-relations dimension of the move to an Israeli currency—the matter of credibility and its corollary, acceptance—was undoubtedly high on the agenda. The public at large, which of course was unaware of the linkage between exchange rates and relative changes in price levels and completely ignorant about the difference between the rates of inflation in Palestine and the United Kingdom, considered the 1 : 1 rate self-evident. Accordingly, it was the policymakers' inevitable choice.

Furthermore, since the only alternative to the 1 : 1 rate would have been a higher rate for the Palestine pound, the rate chosen offered an additional benefit: avoidance of the immediate monetary inflation that a higher exchange rate for the Israeli version of the Palestine pound would have caused. Whether the policymakers considered this aspect is anyone's guess. This is said in particular of the APB executives, whose background in finance and banking left them poorly versed in the finesse of relative prices and the linkage between the exchange rate and the current account of the balance of payments in the longer term.

These matters of substance were negotiated until the very last minute before the covenant was signed. The implementation of the pact, scheduled for the next day (August 17, 1948), meant that stocks of new currency notes had to be available at every bank branch countrywide. It could never have taken place had not Mr. Hoofien, acting on behalf of APB, placed an order for banknotes inscribed with the name of Anglo-Palestine Bank over his signature and that of Mr. A. Bart, the general manager of the bank, back in April of that year. Hoofien, who thus deserves the title of father of the Israeli currency, took this action in the absence of any agreement, even in draft form, that would empower the bank to issue currency. The bank's established reputation with the public did, of course, impart credibility and confidence that contributed to the success of the conversion and the rapid acceptance of the new currency even though uncertainty about political future of the state, even in the short term, was still high.[8]

The Department of Issue, during its tenure of slightly more than six years— twice as long as originally envisaged—followed in the footsteps of the Palestine Currency Board in more than one sense. It never rediscounted commercial paper, even though its constitution allowed it to do so. The only meaningful difference was in the nature of its collateral: whereas the PCB portfolio had been dominated by Treasury bills and investments in gilt-edged UK bonds,[9] that of the APB Department of Issue was dominated by Israeli government paper—Treasury bills and, from June 1949, also "Land Bonds." The Bank Notes Law, passed at that time, amended the 1948 Bank Notes Ordinance and the covenant with APB to allow Land Bonds to count, along with gold and foreign exchange, as reserve assets of the Department of Issue.[10]

Thus, technically speaking, there was hardly a difference between the portfolio of the Department of Issue and that of the Palestine Currency Board in terms of the source and formal quality of the collateral for outstanding base money. The inscription on the securities in these portfolios was different, of course: those of the department were signed by the Government of Israel and those of its predecessor by that of Great Britain. The difference that mattered, of course, was the fact that from August 1948 it was the budget deficit of Israel, instead that of the United Kingdom, that could be (partly) financed by the creation of base money. Until World War II, the British government had not resorted to deficit financing and, therefore, did not tap the financing potential of the Palestine Currency Board or any other board of its kind in the Empire. The war inevitably changed all this; the cash flow needed for the war was (partly) financed by the legally available money-creation facility of these currency boards. In the case of Palestine, this is obvious from the fact that the PCB had boosted the annual average rate of base money expansion from less than 2% in 1936–39 to almost 39% between June 1939 and June 1945 (Szereszewski, 1968, p. 69, table 11; figure 1.1).[11]

This underscores the relevance of fiscal policy for the rate of base money creation even in a monetary regime based on a currency board, in which the issue of currency depended conceptually on an inflow of foreign exchange while its outflow was strictly controlled. This factor—the potential impact of fiscal policy on the time pattern of the money supply—was obvious to those involved in the creation of the Department of Issue. The prescribed 50% reserve ratio, established in response to the pressure from the APB management, was obviously designed to serve as a bulwark against budget-driven inflation of the monetary base.

However, as the Department of Issue opened for business, it advised the commercial banks that it would be ready to rediscount at its discount rate any volume of Treasury bills that they might offer. This made the bills fully liquid—tantamount to a component of the bank reserves and, thus, of what may be termed the "effective" monetary base (table 1.5). This move, which furnished the monetary system with an expansionary potential that reflected the government's cash-flow requirements, was presumably approved, or at least not opposed, by the APB management. The bank's directors must have regarded this facility as an inherent component of the services of a department such as this.

The inflationary potential of the monetary base gained further momentum as the 50% reserve ratio, meant as a protective screen against overexpansion of the monetary base, was undermined by the June 1949 Bank Note Law that replaced the 1948 Bank Note Ordinance. The new statute added Land Bonds—a new long-term government debenture—to the list of reserve assets in the portfolio of the Department of Issue. The Ministry of Finance justified this change in the permitted composition of the department's reserve assets by citing a technical requirement. Under a May 1949 agreement with the British government, an initial portion of Israel's blocked sterling balances would be released in order to finance essential imports. Since the release process continued for more than two years, maintaining the 50% reserve rule would ultimately cause a corresponding reduction of currency in circulation. To avoid this effective contraction of the monetary base, an inconceivable prospect under the economic and fiscal circumstances of the time, the Land Bonds were created as a surrogate asset for the rapidly dwindling sterling balances. It goes without saying that the directors of APB, who did not object to and presumably approved the department's commitment to discount Treasury bills at the rates proposed, were quite unhappy with the June 1949 Bank Note Law. The statute created a loophole for the circumvention of the 50% reserve constraint on the expansion of currency in circulation, and the directors knew it.

The loophole became a fact of life by the end of 1949, even though the department's gold and foreign-exchange balances at the end of that year were still more than 50% of the highly inflated (during that year) outstanding balance of currency in circulation (table 1.3). This means that the technical case for the sale of Land Bonds to the department did not warrant this operation in 1949. Be this as it may, Land Bonds were the main source for evening out the Treasury's cash flow from the very beginning, reflecting a fiscal deficit

Table 1.3. Main Items on Department of Issue Balance Sheet, 1948–54[1]

	Gold and Foreign Exch[2] (1)	PCB Notes[3] (2)	Land Bonds (3)	Treasury Bills (4)	Currency in Circulation (5)
(Thousand IL)					
1948: September	—	26,500	—	—	26,500
1948: December	6,832	18,823	—	5,000	30,655
1949	28,362	317	16,680	4,740	50,099
1950	10,887	—	49,920	13,070	73,877
1951	2,762	—	77,136	20,410	100,308
1952	12	—	77,136	20,410	119,888
1953	4,526	—	77,276	56,480	138,012
1954 Nov.	53,930	—	77,266	30,110	157,187
Average annual rates of change (percent)					
1948					79.1
1948–51					48.5
1952–54					16.2

[1]End-of-year data, except for the end of September 1948, the first full month of operation of the Department of Issue. The 1954–55 entries refer to the balance sheet of the Bank of Israel, which opened for business on December 1, 1954, and absorbed the accounts of the Department of Issue.
[2]The gold and foreign-exchange assets in 1948–51 were frozen sterling balances. These balances, although not all of them, were counterparts of the PCB notes collected from the public and from Israeli bank portfolios in 1948 as the Palestine pound was converted into the Israel pound.
[3]PCB notes: Palestine Currency Board Banknotes.
Sources: Kleiman (1977), Table III-5, p. 249 and p. 248, on which date the end-of-September 1948 volume of converted Palestine pounds to Israel pounds is reported (see also Ottensooser, 1955, p. 112).

of 30%–40% of GNP in fiscal years 1949/1950 and 1950/1951 (table 1.4). The huge injection of liquidity in 1949, boosting currency in circulation by 63%, was implemented almost fully by means of these sales. The balance of Land Bonds, starting from scratch in 1949, expanded by a factor of 4.6 in the two succeeding years and became the mainstay of the expansion of the monetary base—even though a significant fraction of these bonds did serve during these years as surrogates for the plummeting balance of foreign reserves as the release of frozen sterling balances continued steadily. The main factor behind the expansion of the monetary base by a factor of 3.3 in 1948–51 (three years plus one quarter) was the expansion of the Land Bonds component in the asset portfolio of the Department of Issue. By the end of the period, the bonds accounted for 77% of total assets (table 1.3).

The rate of discount of Treasury bills set by the Department of Issue ranged from 1.70% to 2.30% per annum (Ottensooser, 1955, p. 113), similar to the rates in industrialized countries.[12] Such rates seemed to leave considerable leeway for a restrictive monetary policy, even though the 9% maximum interest rate ordained by the aforementioned Ottoman statute would remain the law

Table 1.4. The Fiscal Balance, 1948/49–1955/56[1] (ratio to GNP and resources, percent)

	Gov. Expendit./Resources[2] (1)	Tax Revenues/Resources (2)	Gov. Expendit./GNP (3)	Tax Revenues/GNP (4)	Unilateral Receipts/GNP[3] (5)	Absorption/GNP (4) + (5) = (6)	Excess Expendit./GNP (3) − (6) = (7)	Foreign Loans/GNP[4] (8)
1949/50	—	—	54.4	11.2	8.9	20.1	34.3	2.0
1950/51	43.9	10.2	55.2	13.1	5.5	18.6	36.6	3.7
1951/52	35.1	11.2	42.4	14.0	5.0	19.7	22.7	4.7
1952/53	29.7	11.5	38.4	15.6	8.2	23.8	14.6	7.5
1953/54	28.8	12.9	36.8	17.7	6.7	24.4	12.4	6.3
1954/55	31.8	13.6	39.8	18.9	13.3	32.2	7.6	7.0
1955/56	28.4	15.4	39.6	21.4	10.7	31.1	8.5	5.4

[1]The expenditure and tax data for the entries in the table refer to fiscal years (April 1–March 31) except for 1948/49, in which the data refer to May 15, 1948–March 31, 1949. The GNP, resources, and government-unilateral-receipts data used to calculate the ratios of fiscal expenditures and receipts refer to calendar years. The time incongruity of the series used to derive the ratios entered in the table has no significant effect for our purpose. The technical device of adjusting the time dimension of the series by means of the conventional technique (nine months and three months of the preceding year) is arbitrary in any case. The quality of the entries for 1948/49 and 1949/50 does not meet the standards of the data from 1950 onward.

[2]Domestic use of resources—GNP plus import surplus.

[3]Government unilateral receipts from abroad. Their value in terms of Israeli pounds (IL) was calculated in terms of the current (relevant) official exchange rate—IL 0.357 per dollar in 1951/52, IL 1 per dollar in 1952/53, and IL 1.8 per dollar from 1953/54 onward.

[4]Long-term funds borrowed abroad, converted into Israeli currency at the same exchange rates as the entries in Column (5). The ratios refer to GNP.

Sources: Columns (1)–(2): Halevi-Klinov (1968): Table 61, Column (7), p. 148, and Table App. 1, pp. 232–233, Columns (3) and (11); columns (3)–(4): Morag (1967), Table App. 1, Table B-13, based on Treasury Dept., First Report of State Revenues, 1956, Table 1, p. 45; column (5): calculated on the basis of Halevi-Klinov (1968), Tables 57 and 58, pp. 128–129; column (8): the foreign loan data are culled from Halevi-Klinov (1968), Table App. 10.

of the land until 1957. Although these interest rates looked quite reasonable to many in what might be described as the "Israeli financial community" and dominant "opinion" in political circles, they were widely off the mark. In an economic environment of 19% annual average inflation during the world war, a falloff to 3.5%–4% in 1946–47, and reacceleration to an annual average rate of almost 27% in 1948, this seems obvious today. Inflation expectations were undoubtedly higher in Israel than in the industrialized countries, most of which had cut their inflation rates to low single-digit rates by then. In particular, it hardly seems possible that inflation expectations in Israel in the last quarter of 1948 and the first quarter of 1949 were lower than the 9% interest ceiling. In any case, the rationale for the maintenance of 2% discount rates in industrialized countries had by 1950 become a matter of dispute between the political community and the managements of central banks.[13] To apply similar rates in a nascent economy that had experienced a decade of inflation at levels verging on 20% and was still embroiled in a war was an altogether different proposition.

Amid these constraints—the government's cash-flow needs, the 2% discount rate on government paper, and the double-digit inflation in 1948, which had generated entrenched inflation expectations—the new management of the Department of Issue, led by its director, Dr. E. Lehman, a senior member of the APB staff, had to start navigating between the Scylla of the requirements of the government budget and the Charybdis of a highly liquid banking system. The maneuvering had to be done in an environment that subjected firms and households to the pull of strong inflation expectations fueled by robust aggregate demand and mounting inflation.

FISCAL DOMINANCE AT CREATION

Above it was suggested that the government's cash-flow constraint in the summer of 1948 finally overcame its reluctance to equip the new state with its own currency, a move that was clearly inconsistent with the chapter and verse of the UN resolution of November 1947. Indeed, cash flow would be the decisive factor in determining the pattern and momentum of monetary developments for the next three years, until 1951.

Thus, a survey and analysis of monetary developments during this genesis period of the Israeli economy must refer first and foremost to the fiscal dimension of the first years of independence. The series on general- and central-government expenditure and taxation in the late 1940s and the early 1950s, presented in table 1.4, underscores the contours of the fiscal impact on the macroeconomy generally and on the monetary sector particularly during the six and a half years preceding the establishment of the central bank.

The ratios of total government expenditure to GNP and to domestic uses (GNP plus the import surplus), presented in Columns (3) and (1) of the table, recount the essentials of Israel's government expenditure "at creation." When a country is mired in a total war of survival, government inevitably absorbs a major share of economic resources. The armistice agreements that Israel concluded in early 1949 made little difference on this account, since the country was already in the throes of its first wave of mass immigration, peaking in 1951, which more than doubled its Jewish population within only 3.5 years. Thus, the very high general-government expenditure ratio, about 55% of GNP in the two first full years of that period, fell to a still-high 42% of national production capacity in fiscal year 1951/1952.[14]

Taxation, the conventional vehicle of government financial absorption from the household and business sectors, was not a practical instrument for this purpose at that stage of affairs. Even a revenue system and administration with a lengthy tradition and technical expertise, relying on comprehensive tax legislation and linkages throughout the economic system, would have struggled to cope with a government expenditure flow at 40%–50% of GNP. Although the Government of Israel had inherited the skeleton of a revenue department from the Mandatory administration, this organ had neither the manpower nor the technical ability to collect taxes on a scale characteristic of modern industrial economies. Neither had it the legal infrastructure to establish a tax base that would allow it to collect taxes at even 20%–25% of GNP.[15] The very rough estimates of the expenditure/GNP and tax revenue/GNP ratios in 1948/1949 and 1949/1950 (table 1.4), showing ratios of 50% for the former and about 11% for the latter in each of the two years, underline the impact of the fiscal gap and, thus, the strain imposed on the economic system. Even the significant improvement in the tax absorption ratio in the following two fiscal years, 1950/1951 and 1951/1952, to about 14% of GNP—reflecting both the rising efficiency of the tax administration and the expansion of the tax base due to new legislation— hardly made a meaningful difference.

Taxation, however, was not the only significant source of general-government absorption. Unilateral receipts from abroad—initially, contributions from the United Jewish Appeal, boosted from 1951 on by U.S. grants and later (from 1953 on) by German reparations payments—also replenished the coffers of general government. Thus, a more reasonable approximation of general-government absorption would add the flow of (the dominant) fraction of these unilateral payments from abroad to the tax revenue flow, as shown in column (6) of table 1.4. According to this definition of general-government absorption, the absorption ratios in the 1949–51 period verged on 20% of GNP annually. Just the same, absorption ratios of this magnitude amid expenditure/GNP ratios of 55% as in 1949 and 1950, and even 42% as in fiscal 1951/1952, hardly mitigated the impact of the requirements of general-government finance on the monetary dimension of the economy. Overspending still ran at about 35% of GNP in the first two years and 23% in fiscal 1951–52, when the government cash flow was improved by an increase in unilateral receipts (U.S. government aid) and a substantial upturn of the inflow on capital account (due to proceeds from sales of Israel Bonds).

Thus, to accommodate the country's cash flow during its first fifteen quarters of existence (May 1948–March 1952), the government of Israel had to resort substantially to the printing press. This, of course, was the very practice that the executive agency in the realm of finance and economics, represented by the APB Board of Directors, had attempted to constrain by enshrining the 50% reserve ratio of the Department of Issue in legislation and by stipulating the original specification of the department's reserve assets. These safeguards, as stated, had already been undermined by the 1949 Bank Notes Law, which added Land Bonds to the set of reserve assets.

THE MOMENTUM OF MONETARY EXPANSION: 1948–51

The series of monetary aggregates (table 1.5) in the entire 75-month period that preceded the establishment of the Bank of Israel (September 1948– November 1954) offers a revealing perspective on the impact of the fiscal strains. It also allows us to identify two subperiods that differ altogether in the momentum of monetary expansion and other inherent features of the inflation process.

The conspicuous difference in the rate of expansion of the money supply between the 1949–51 period, during which the quantity of money expanded at an annual average pace of 34%, and the 1952–54 interval, during which it grew by only 13%, speaks for itself. Even though monetary inflation in the second subperiod also looks significant, the comparison actually understates the gap between the rate at which the monetary balloon was inflated in the first sub-period and deflated in the second because it excludes the annual average growth rate of M_1 between May and December 1948 from the estimate. If we make due provision for the quality of the estimate for May 1948, bringing the period of inquiry to forty-two months—May 1948 through the end of 1951— we find that the average annual rate of monetary inflation was several percent-age points higher than the 34% rate noted above.

The significant difference between the growth rate of the currency compo-nent of M_1 and that of demand deposits in the first subperiod, through the end of 1951—about 50% and 27%, respectively (table 1.5)—points to the factor that powered the process. The rate of expansion of currency in circulation, a liability of the Department of Issue, was about 50% in the first subperiod, fully reflecting the increase of government debt to the department net of a slight contraction of foreign reserves, which scraped the bottom of the barrel that year.[16] It goes without saying that this rate of currency expansion could not have taken place had the Land Bonds not emerged as a reserve asset of the Department of Issue in 1949 and allowed the fiscal cash flow to be sustained. Without the bonds, government expenditure would have been drastically constrained in view of the bulging deficit (table 1.4). The 1949 legislative amendment that added Land Bonds to the components of Department of Issue reserves opened a bottleneck that would have restricted the expansion of government expenditures and the corresponding inflation of the money supply.

The significantly slower rate of expansion of means of payment (M_1)—at an annual average rate 34% slower than that of currency in circulation

Table 1.5. Monetary Aggregates, 1949–54

	M_1			Bank Reserves[2]	Monetary Base[3]	Treasury Bills		Commercial Bank Credit	
	Currency[1] (1)	Demand Deposits (2)	Total (3)	(4)	Effective (1) + (4) = (5)	Bank Portfolio (6)	Total (7)	Public (8)	Total[4] (9)
Annual average rates of change (percent)									
1949–51	49.9	26.8	33.8	26.0	37.0	29.9	37.1	45.0	41.3
1952–54	17.3	10.2	13.0	14.5	16.0	—	—	21.6	14.6

[1]Currency held by the public.

[2]Bank reserves include cash, Treasury bills (and Land Bonds in 1950 and 1951 only), and 3% financial institution loans (Ottensooser, p. 121).

[3]Formal MB: total currency in circulation (banknotes + coins) is equal to currency held by the public plus currency in bank tills. The effective monetary base is the sum of the formal base plus Treasury bills (and Land Bonds in 1950 and 1951 only) plus 3% financial-institution loans (Ottensooser, 1954, pp. 121–122).

[4]Total commercial bank credit is the sum of credit to the public and to the government.

Sources: Columns (1)–(3), 1948 through 1953: Kleiman (1977), p. 250, and sources cited by him; Sanbar-Bronfeld (1973), Tables 2 and 4, for 1954 and 1955; 1949–1955: Central Bureau of Statistics, *Statistical Abstract of Israel,* 1954/55, Table XXIII-3, p. 196, and *Statistical Abstract,* 1956/57, Table XX-III-4, p. 127; and Sanbar-Bronfeld (1973), Tables 2 and 3, pp. 5 and 7 respectively. Column (4): Central Bureau of Statistics, *Statistical Abstract* 1955/56, Table XXII-2, p. 198.

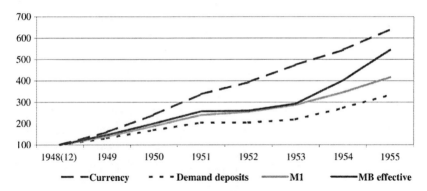

Figure 1.3. Monetary Aggregates, 1948–55 (12/1948 = 100)

(figure 1.3)—reflects among other things a change in the public's behavior. It is clearly illuminated by the implied currency deposit ratios shown in table 1.5, which leaped from 0.36 at the end of 1948 (and even less in May of that year) to 0.44 in 1949 and 0.60 at the end of 1951. The rising trend of the ratio indicates a powerful negative internal drain through 1953, albeit at reduced momentum in the last-mentioned year. The pattern is clearly explicable in terms of the demographics of the time, the first mass-immigration era, which dominated the socioeconomic features of the emerging Israeli economy. The population of recent immigrants, which by late 1951 had already equaled that of the nonimmigrants in size, was of course much less likely to be bank customers. This internal drain did reduce the rate of expansion of the reserves and, in turn, of M_1. At an annual growth rate of 37%, however, the expansion of base money still underwrote a very significant inflation of the means of payment during the 1949–51 subperiod.[17]

Potentially, a countervailing force to this rapid expansion of bank reserves and its implications for bank credit and the corresponding supply of money did exist: an increase in the reserve ratios of the banking system. The reserve-ratio series reported in table 1.5 suggests that, despite slight ups and downs, the banking system maintained a consistent and very high liquidity ratio of 50%–51% between 1948 and 1951. This was indeed higher than the (semi-)legal minimum ratio that the Examiner of Banks had set at 45% in November 1950 and raised to 50% in April 1951 (Heth, 1966, pp. 92, 94)—the ratio that the banks actually maintained at the time. Accordingly, this early attempt to create an instrument that the authorities could use to impose monetary restraint came to naught.

The commercial bank-credit series shown in the table points to strong demand for bank credit by the public, which the banking system could meet without breaching that novel departure—the late-1950 "semi-legal" minimum reserve ratio and its upward adjustment in early 1951. Bank credit expanded by 45% on annual average in 1949–51, far outpacing the M_1 growth rate as the banking system accommodated the robust demand of business and households for credit. With an ample supply of Treasury bills that the Department of Issue stood ready to buy at a rate of discount of 2% and later 2.5%, the rates charged for commercial bank credit averaged 5%–5.5% through 1951. Only 5% of bank loans carried interest in the 7%–9% range. The public's appetite for credit, in the context of the surging inflation expectations, was obvious and had a corresponding effect on the money supply (Heth, 1966, pp. 214–15, tables 84–85).

The combined effect of the public and the banking system, expressed in terms of their choices of currency/deposit ratios, and of the bank liquidity ratios caused the money multiplier to decline slightly in the 1949–51 interval; this eased the monetary avalanche somewhat. The dampening effect, however, reflected an internal drain rather than a restrictive reserve-ratio policy on the banks' part. The slight declining trend of the money multiplier turns our focus to the factor that precipitated the inflation of the money supply, the monetary base. At one remove, this, of course, reflects the fiscal onslaught described above.

SUPPRESSED INFLATION

The Pressure Builds

In view of the huge import surplus during these years—65% and 52% of GNP in 1950 and 1951, respectively (Halevi and Klinov, 1968, p. 234), the obvious real quantity to consider when analyzing the impact of the expansion of money on prices in these years is evidently the domestic-uses series (table 1.6). Reliable data on this real aggregate, available only from 1950 on, suggest a 20% increase in the flow of resources available for private consumption, gross investment, and government domestic demand in 1951.

Table 1.6. GNP, Resources, and Employment, 1949–55

	Gross National Product[1] (1)	Domestic Use of Resources (2)	Employment (3)	Unemployment Rate (percent) (4)
Indicies: 1954 = 100				
1949	(42.8)[2]	—	56.1	9.5
1950	57.6	75.2	75.8	6.9
1951	75.4	90.6	92.4	6.1
1952	81.0	89.2	97.7	7.2
1953	82.0	87.4	96.2	11.3
1954	100.0	100.0	100.0	8.9
1955	112.2	112.7	103.4	7.4
Annual average rates of change (percent)				
1951	31.0	20.5	28.3	—
1948–51	(32.7)	—	—	—
1952–54	9.9	3.3	2.7	—

[1]GNP in 1955 prices.
[2]Gaathon's estimate of nominal national income, deflated by index of nominal wages in manufacturing.
Sources: Columns (1)–(2): Halevi-Kiinov (1968), Table App. 2, p. 234, derived from Central Bureau of Statistics, *Statistical Abstract of Israel* No. 17, 1964–1965, and Lubel (1958); columns (3)–(4): Barkai (1990), Tables 1–2, pp. 99–100; column (6): Sanbar-Bronfeld, Table 3, p. 7; columns (6)–(7) Central Bureau of Statistics, *Statistical Abstract of Israel*, 1954/55, Tables XXIII-2, 4, and 5, pp. 195, 198–199; columns (8)–(9): Heth (1966), Table 49; and Heth (1994), Tables A-10, B-1, and B-2.

This rate of growth may be an overestimate if applied to the entire 1948–51 interval. The pace of imports was maintained at the price of the total depletion of foreign reserves in late 1951, when the British government released the last batch of blocked sterling balances that households, firms, and banks in what had become Israel had amassed during the Mandate period.[18] This means that the 34% annual growth rate of the money supply during the three years ending in December 1951 was accommodated by no more, and presumably even less, than a 20% annual increase in the flow of sources for domestic uses. One would expect this gap to have had a significant impact on prices.[19]

Inspection of the cost-of-living series in table 1.7, however, suggests that the actual effect on prices of the rapid monetary inflation during those three years was moderate. Prices actually declined somewhat in 1949 and, although rising in the following year, were still lower at the end of that year than at the end of 1948. Overall, the measured increase in the cost-of-living index from 1948 through the end of 1951 was 11%. Most of the upturn occurred in the last year of the period, reflecting the global inflation occasioned by the Korean War. The increase in domestic prices that year, as against the 1950 level measured in terms of "official" controlled prices, was about 20%.

The seeming inconsistency between very rapid monetary expansion, far outpacing the growth rate of real sources, and the moderate changes in the price level was a reflection of the price-controlled, tightly rationed markets. The legal and administrative framework that administered the controls had been inherited from the Mandate, which had invoked it during the lengthy world war. However, while Western Europe had already made much progress in decontrol by 1951—Wilson's "bonfire of controls" in Britain in early 1951 is a case in point—Israel engineered a major extension of its price-control and rationing regime in the first quarter of 1951. The government decided to go ahead with this move even though it was about to face municipal elections and general elections later that year.

The inconsistency between the 140% increase in the quantity of money between the end of 1948 and of 1951 and the very small 11% rise in prices, as measured by the official Consumer Price Index, underlines the complete divorce that had come about among the flow of purchasing power, and thus the corresponding expansion of demand for goods in the markets, and the official supply prices during this period.

The forces that pounded on the wall that separated demand from available supply in the price-controlled "official" markets are plainly evident in the alternative price series presented in table 1.7 and the corresponding figure 1.4. The growing divergence between the real-estate price series and consumer prices, and similarly between the black-market dollar exchange rate and the official rate, illuminate the situation. The slight 7% official devaluation of the Israel pound against the dollar, in the wake of the November 1949 devaluation of the pound sterling against the dollar, was severely dwarfed by the almost 600% rise in the black-market price of foreign currency by the end of 1951. The tremendous buildup of pressure generated by money-supply inflation and controlled prices is underscored by the series of noncontrolled real-estate prices, which climbed by a factor of 3 during the three years at issue.[20] This suggests a

Table 1.7. Prices and Exchange Rates, 1949–55

	Prices			Wages[1]			Exchange Rates[3]		
	Implicit GNP (1)	Cost of Living (2)	Real Estate[2] (3)	Nominal (4)	Real (5)	Formal (6)	Effective Imports[4] (7)	Black Market (8)	Real[5] (7)/(1) = (9)
Indices: 1954 = 100									
1948	—	(42.1)	—	29.4	69.8	18.5	—	16.7	—
1949	—	36.8	39	31.3	85.1	19.8	21.5	22.5	—
1950	46.1	39.0	54.9	33.6	86.2	19.8	22.3	34.9	48.4
1951	53.5	46.9	120.9	43.1	91.9	19.8	22.0	115.5	41.1
1952	74.6	78.1	135.2	73.1	93.5	19.8	44.7	92.4	59.9
1953	92.8	93.0	109.3	88.1	94.7	19.8	64.9	103.7	69.9
1954	100.0	100.0	100.0	100.0	100.0	100.0	100.0	100.0	100.0
1955	110.3	104.8	107.7	108.8	103.8	180	122.9	107.8	111.4
Annual average rate of change (percent)									
1951	16.1	20.3	120.2	28.3	6.6	0.0	−1.3	230.9	−15.1
1952	39.4	66.5	11.8	69.6	1.7	0.0	103.2	−20.0	45.7
1954	7.8	7.5	−8.5	13.5	5.6	405.1	54.1	−3.6	43.1
1955	10.3	4.8	7.7	8.8	3.8	80.0	22.9	7.8	11.4
1949–51	—	3.7	—	13.6	9.6	2.3	—	90.5	—
1952–54	23.2	28.7	−6.1	32.4	2.9	71.6	65.7	−4.7	34.5

[1] Nominal wages in manufacturing.
[2] Borochow's index number series for land prices in Jerusalem. Series for several Tel-Aviv locations, culled from the same source, show the same pattern.
[3] US dollar exchange rate.
[4] Effective exchange rate for imports.
[5] The real effective exchange-rate series, which represents the nominal effective exchange rate for imports, standardized in terms of the two relevant price indices, represents the nominal exchange rate plus several components. See Michaely (1968), Table B-2, p. 24.

Sources: Columns (1), (4), and (8): Patinkin (1960/67), Tables 13, 47, and Table App. B, pp. 142–143; column (2): Central Bureau of Statistics, *Statistical Abstract of Israel* No. 29, 1978, Table X-2, p. 267; column (3): Borochov (1965), Table 1, p. 349; columns (6) and (7): Michaely (1968), Tables B-1 and D-4, pp. 23 and 88, respectively.

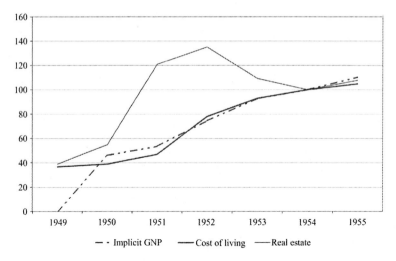

Figure 1.4. Prices, 1949–55 (1954 = 100)

characteristic buildup of inflation pressure that bursts its seams in legally feasible directions such as, in the Israeli case, prices of land or "key money" dwellings. It also applied, of course, to illegal transactions such as those in the foreign-exchange black markets, the series of which is shown in table 1.7.

Patinkin's series of real-money balances, shown in table 1.8 and the corresponding figure 1.5, offer another way of demonstrating the macroeconomic

Table 1.8. Measures of Nominal and Real Quantity of Money[1]

	Money Balances: Nominal M[1]		Prices		Real Balances	
			Consumer		Consumer Prices[2]	
	(1)	(2)	(3)	(4)	(5) = (1)/(3)	(6) = (2)/(4)
Indices: 1948 = 100; 1950 = 100						
1948	100.0	—	100.0	—	100.0	—
1949	138.5	—	103.4	—	133.9	—
1950	182.3	100.0	98.3	100.0	185.5	100.0
1951	240.6	132.0	108.6	110.5	221.5	119.5
1952	265.6	145.7	172.4	175.4	154.1	83.1
1953	311.6	170.9	220.7	224.6	141.2	76.1
1954	392.0	215.0	248.2	252.6	157.9	85.1
1955	472.3	259.0	262.0	266.6	180.3	97.1

[1]The real-quantity-of-money series represents annual averages of M_1, standardized by the corresponding, price indices.
[2]Real balances are the ratio of the index of the nominal quantity of Mi and the corresponding entry for the cost-of-living index, on the basis of 1948 and 1950, respectively.
Sources: Columns (1)–(4) and (6)–(7): Patinkin, 1960, Table 39, p. 110.

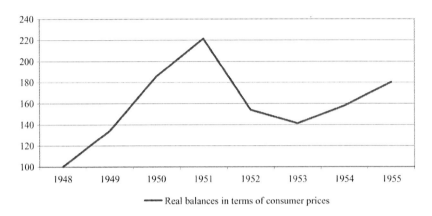

▬▬ Real balances in terms of consumer prices

Figure 1.5. Pattern of the Real Quantity of Money, 1948–55 (1948 = 100)

pressures that the money-supply inflation generated in terms of the Consumer Price Index. These series show an increase by a factor of 2.2 in the real value of the money supply, in terms of controlled prices, between the middle of 1948 and the middle of 1951—a 30% growth rate on annual average.

Yet another indicator of the pressures in the domestic markets is a series describing the trend of real wages. A proxy for this variable may be derived by deflating the manufacturing nominal wage series by the official CPI series (table 1.7).[21] The labor market was of course not free. It was regulated by means of (partial) wage indexation and controlled implicitly by the behavior of the Histadrut, the leadership of which was part and parcel of the political forces that dominated the government. These factors sustained the control and rationing policy that at first—say, until the middle of 1950—was largely supported by public opinion. Under the circumstances—war followed by mass immigration that doubled the Jewish population during the period at issue—the Histadrut accepted the policy of wage restraint in principle even though it opposed formal wage controls, which were not applied in any case. Just the same, real wages (nominal wages deflated by the CPI) rose steadily at a 9.6% annual average rate in 1949–51. By implication, the real income of the nonimmigrant population climbed significantly during a three-year period of strict price controls and rationing. This could not but support the real wealth-effect pressure on the official markets that was being generated by very rapid real monetary inflation, in official cost-of-living terms, during this period.

The Controls Disintegrate

By the summer of 1950, the spread of black markets to all corners of the economy had become a fact of life that brought public opinion and the political community to their feet in alarm. Thus, in response to an appeal by the minister of supply and rationing, Dov Joseph,[22] the prime minister, David Ben-Gurion, put his prestige on the line. In September 1950, before the cost effect of the Korean War leap of world-market prices struck Israel's markets, Ben-Gurion took to the airwaves and decried the black-market phenomenon. His jawboning, however, proved futile. The severe pressure a money supply that more than doubled between May 1948 and September 1950 had brought to bear on the markets, coupled with the significant growth of the real income of the nonimmigrant population, doomed this attempt at moral suasion to failure ab initio.

Nevertheless, the government, cringing under the brutal pressure of absorbing and integrating the masses of immigrants, attempted to stay on course in terms of its expenditure. To facilitate the existing pattern of fiscal policy, it expanded the scope of rationing and tightened price controls during the summer of 1951. What finally doomed the composite policy of supply-and-rationing and comprehensive controls, however, was not only the failure to contain the ever-growing spread and momentum of the black markets, but also the loss of support of public opinion and its concomitant, the political rationale for maintaining controls and rationing. The Korean War price explosion in world markets had by now washed ashore in Israel, prompting the government to raise controlled prices by 20% in 1951 to reflect rising dollar import prices. Had the government wished to sterilize the impact of the price developments in world commodity markets, it would have had to institute a major increase in subsidies. The swollen budget deficit (37% of GNP in fiscal 1950/1951—table 1.4), however, ruled this out. The depletion of foreign reserves due to the tremendous gap between imports and exports (the former exceeding the latter by a factor of 6–7)—induced, although clearly not solely, by an overvalued currency that penalized exports and domestic production in general—ultimately undermined the economic rationale of the attempt to maintain the supply-and-rationing policy.

Furthermore, by 1951, more and more politicians realized that a policy that they could implement only by subsidizing "vital imports" in order to maintain a highly overvalued currency was also an "antiproduction" policy. The agricultural sector, which wielded significant political leverage in these years, also discovered this rather quickly as farmers, although producers in a sellers' market for food, could not capitalize on this situation legally because their supply prices were controlled. The temptation to divert increasing fractions of farm produce from official price-controlled marketing channels to irregular markets that could offer much higher prices proved irresistible.

These developments led to a reevaluation of the conceptual thrust of economic policy. The reassessment was propelled by an unexpected turn of events in the campaign ahead of the Second Knesset elections in July 1951. Although the issue that led to the breakup of the coalition and the dissolution of the Knesset (parliament) before the end of its four-year term belonged to the sensitive domain of relations between secular and Orthodox Jews, the unexpected yet dominant feature of the ensuing campaign was the economy. Under the slogan "Let Us Live in This Country," the small, liberal, market-oriented General Zionist Party trebled its parliamentary strength to twenty members (out of 120) while the left-wing bloc lost almost 10% of its representation.[23] With the election campaign out of its way and the economic crisis boiling over— controlled prices leaping by 10% between January and September 1951 and the foreign reserves swiftly tending to zero—the political leadership understood that a major redirection of economic policy was the only option.

THE NEW ECONOMIC POLICY (NEP), 1952–54

The outcome of these political and economic events was a decision to embark on a major revision of economic policy that would culminate with the formulation of what later surfaced as the NEP—the New Economic Policy. The thrust of this set of policy measures involved a shift from a comprehensively controlled system toward market-oriented rules of the game. The plan was conceived in the second half of 1951, finalized in January 1952, and presented to the Knesset in a speech by Prime Minister Ben-Gurion on February 9, 1952. Preliminary moves for its implementation, focusing on fiscal policy, were already in the making by late 1951.

The Fiscal Lever

It took some time to convince the political community, led by Ben-Gurion—a domineering personality who was poorly versed in even the most basic economic notions—that it was impossible to continue running an economy with an effective fiscal deficit of 23% of GNP, the level attained in fiscal 1951/1952.[24] What finally carried the day was the total depletion of foreign reserves in late 1951, meaning that paying for a tanker load of crude oil—the country's only primary energy source—had become nearly impossible. Changing the fiscal policy was thus absolutely imperative.

Accordingly, the first and most crucial item in the program was the government's resolution in July 1951, after the elections, and its corresponding commitment to put its fiscal house in order. It proposed to accomplish this by balancing its regular budget, entailing first and foremost expenditure constraints and increases in tax revenues. The avoidance of deficit spending in the regular budget proved to be a difficult task indeed. It involved, among other things, a major 20% cut of the defense budget in fiscal 1952/1953, prompting the chief of staff of the Israel Defense Forces to resign. Still, this measure was entirely within the power of the government, which exerted control over its expenditure level and had the power of taxation. The sizable "development budget," in contrast, was to be financed by receipts from abroad: unilateral transfers to the government, long-term credit from foreign governments and international financial institutions, and Jewish sources.[25]

This required long-term prospects of a stable and significant inflow of funds from abroad in both the unilateral-receipts account and the capital account of the balance of payments. With an import surplus of almost $300 million in 1950 and $360 million in 1951, as against the total depletion of the foreign reserves, and the commitment to finance a substantial development budget, mainly by receipts from abroad, the expected inflow of funds on these two accounts had to be $300 million per year at least.[26] By the middle of 1951, it was clear that Jewish philanthropy abroad could be counted on for $90 million–$100 million annually—a far cry from what was considered adequate or absolutely necessary for a development budget that would suffice for the invest-ment in infrastructure and housing, not to mention productive industry, to absorb the immigrants of 1948–51.

Two major efforts to bolster the inflow on the unilateral receipt account were successfully driven through in 1951. The first was the inclusion of Israel in the group of countries receiving U.S. economic aid. Although no long-term com-mitment was made, a flow of aid at $30 million–$40 million annually began in 1952. At first (through 1954), this aid was given mainly in the form of declining grants, but later it was replaced with highly subsidized very long-term credits.

The second and politically highly controversial move was the conclusion of a reparations agreement with West Germany, negotiated in 1951 and approved after a tumultuous debate in the Knesset and riots in Jerusalem in January 1952, just one month before the New Economic Policy was presented to and formally adopted by the house. In the agreement, West Germany undertook to pay a fixed sum in marks amounting to $70 million–$80 million annually, in terms of current dollars, for ten years. These three sources—Jewish fundraising abroad, U.S. aid, and German reparations—were expected to improve Israel's general-government cash flow and its foreign currency inflow by $180 million–$200 million per year during the coming decade.[27]

To close the remaining gap, the government established the Independence Loan ("Israel Bonds") Organization to sell long-term Israel government bonds abroad, initially in the United States. Although the bonds would pay interest at rates somewhat higher than the nominal rate on U.S. government paper, the premium would not, of course, compensate for the high risk of Israeli debt as perceived by capital-market players at the time.[28] This source—which, due to its noncompetitive interest rate, had from the outset the air of a semi-contribution to Israel—was expected to generate $40 million–$50 million annually for the development budget. The residual gap of, say, $40 million–$50 million, could be bridged by long-run compulsory borrowing from the domestic contractual sav-ings industry, that is, pension funds and insurance companies. This debt would be indexed to the CPI or the dollar at significant real rates of interest.

This conceptual design of general-government finance took shape in the last two quarters of 1951, before the formal unveiling of the New Economic Policy in the first quarter of 1952. Its implementation is already visible in the 1951/1952 fiscal balance. The ratio of excess expenditure to GNP fell dramati-cally that fiscal year—to a still-high 23% as against 37% in the previous fiscal year (table 1.4)—mainly due to a significant reduction on the expenditure side. As the NEP program gathered momentum after its formal inauguration in February 1952, the excess expenditure/GNP ratio narrowed again to 15% of GNP in fiscal 1952/1953, chiefly due to a major cut in the defense budget. Spending cuts and rising tax revenues accounted for 5 percentage points of the improvement of nearly 8% of GNP in the fiscal balance in 1952/1953. An increased inflow of unilateral receipts, mostly reflecting a significant increase in U.S. government aid, contributed more than 3 percentage points.

The contribution of the unilateral receipts account to general-government "revenue"—identified as such because, like tax revenue, it did not have a positive

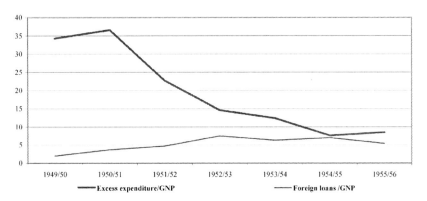

Figure 1.6. Excess Expenditure and Foreign Loans, 1948/49–1955/56 (ratio to GNP: percent)

effect on the national debt—made a major difference in fiscal absorption during the implementation of NEP. The share of unilateral receipts in total absorption leaped from about 20% of general-government absorption in 1951/1952 to 24% in 1952/1953, the year of the first NEP budget, and crossed the 30% line by 1954/1955 due to a substantial improvement in tax revenue and the rising inflow of German reparations payments.

Thus, by the time the Bank of Israel opened for business in December 1954, these developments on the absorption side of the ledger and a small reduction on the expenditure side (from 42% of GNP in fiscal 1951/1952 to 40% in fiscal 1954–55), had reduced the excess expenditure/GNP ratio to 7.6% of GNP— roughly equal to the injection of funds into the general-government cash flow from the balance-of-payments capital account (figure 1.6). Although this inflow caused the long-term foreign debt to increase, it offered the government immediate relief by reducing its reliance on the Department of Issue—the printing press—to even out its cash flow. It is this that identifies the NEP as an all-out departure from the fiscal-dominance policy of 1948–51, in which an accommodating monetary policy marched to the orders of fiscal requirements.

The Design and Implementation of the NEP

The first item on the agenda of the February 1952 New Economic Policy, a necessary condition for the implementation of the rest, was the restrictive fiscal policy described above. As noted, the implementation of this part of the program began in the last two quarters of 1951, after the general elections in July, as is plainly evident in the "excess expenditure" column of table 1.4. The second plank of the program pertained to the monetary sector. In this respect, the government undertook to stop selling Treasury bills and Land Bonds to the Department of Issue and the banking system. The performance of this commitment had become a fait accompli even before the prime minister rose to make his statement (Ottensooser, 1955, p. 133). What Ben-Gurion did not mention on this occasion was another item on the monetary agenda: a decision to impose a 10% tax (formally, a compulsory loan) on means of payment, that is, cash and demand deposits. The proclamation and implementation of this measure were delayed by a technical constraint and went through four months later, in June 1952.[29]

Finally, the Prime Minister unfurled the most dramatic item of the program: an immediate and major devaluation of the Israel pound (IL). A set of three exchange rates would be installed: the existing rate of IL 0.357 to the dollar and two "new" rates—IL 0.714 and IL 1.00 to the dollar, denoting a devaluation of 100% and 180%, respectively. Although this triad of multiple exchange rates was conceived as a temporary measure, no date for its expiration and the restandardization of the exchange rate was set. The principal aim of the devaluation was to reduce the import surplus and, thereby, improve the current account of the balance of payments. This move inevitably sent a cost shock reverberating through the economy.[30]

The purpose of the multiple exchange-rate setup was to mitigate the immediate cost effect of the devaluation on prices, especially those of "essentials." Thus, the lowest rate of exchange was initially applied to crude oil and grain imports only, the second rate to all other foreign-trade transactions, and the third and highest rate to unilateral receipts and capital-account transactions. In view of the quantitative importance of unilateral receipts and capital imports, even though they flowed mainly into government coffers, the highest rate had immediate monetary implications because the conversion of foreign funds on private account and by nongovernment organizations provided them with 2.8 times more Israel pounds per foreign-currency unit than they would have received at the standard rate. Therefore, the devaluation had the inevitable effect of monetary expansion as far as households and the business sector were concerned.

Concurrently, it offered major relief to the cash flow of the government and of the Jewish Agency. The higher exchange rate on foreign funds—whether received unilaterally or on capital account—absolved the government from having to borrow from the Department of Issue. Thus, the impact of general government on the monetary aggregates was neutral. Nevertheless, the higher exchange rate improved the general-government cash flow, thus refurbishing at least the image of fiscal policy.

Though hardly mentioned in the Prime Minister's New Economic Policy statement (February 2, 1951) and in the response of the minister of finance, Mr. Kaplan, in the Knesset debate on the program, an inherent feature of the NEP was the repeal of rationing. This, in turn, involved a major relaxation of price controls and a full pass-through of costs to prices for a significantly narrowed-down basket of "essentials" that would still be price-controlled but no longer rationed. The cost effect of this process was to be softened by the attempt to ease the immediate impact of the devaluation on production costs and prices by means of the aforementioned contrivance of three exchange rates, with the lowest temporarily held at the previous level of IL 0.357 to the dollar.

The post-devaluation leap of the price level in 1952 was in fact largely a reflection of a cost effect—the pass-through of import costs—and the government depicted it as such. However, it was also an expression of improved profit margins. Thus, from a long-term perspective, it was more than the mere pass-through of costs. The determined easing of price controls was indeed designed to give producers—particularly in agriculture—an immediate incentive to increase production and redirect supplies from the black markets back to the newly decontrolled regular channels of distribution. Therefore, it was not only a change in pricing technique but also an expression of a change of mindset and the resetting of priorities. In more than one sense, it represented a "crossing of the Rubicon," in which the warlike, siege-inspired rationing mentality to which the system had been subjected for more than a decade was replaced by a policy that stressed production and producers, that is, a market-oriented policy.

THE MONETARY DIMENSION OF THE NEP

The leap of prices in 1952—nearly 67% in terms of the official Consumer Price Index and about 40% in terms of the more comprehensive and, therefore, more representative index of implicit GNP prices—seemed indicative of an acceleration of inflation but was actually its very opposite. As the London economists would express it in their postwar terminology, it served as an instrument of "disinflation"—deflation in prewar terminology. What it deflated was the monetary balloon that had formed during the 45-month interval between September 1948 and January 1952. The disinflation process could not have succeeded without the effective monetary restraint that was imposed starting in the first quarter of 1952. The minister of finance, Mr. Kaplan, stressed this aspect of the program in his response during the debate in the Knesset (February 18, 1952). At that stage, with the tax on M_1 only in the offing, he underlined the commitment to stop issuing of Treasury bills and Land Bonds, that is, to refrain from increasing their outstanding balance as a way to even out the government's cash flow.

The government honored its undertaking with a vengeance, as the time pattern of the money supply shows. The 37% rate of expansion of the "effective" monetary base in 1949–51 was reduced to only 16% during the three years of the NEP, 1952–54 (table 1.5). The nominal quantity of M_1 grew at an annual average rate of 34% during the three years terminating at the end of 1951 and by only 13% per annum the following three years, those of the NEP. Furthermore, in the crucial kickoff year of the program, 1952, the monetary base expanded by only 1% and M_1 by 6% (figure 1.3). This slashing of the expansion rate of monetary aggregates obviously reflected the 10% tax on outstanding balances, implemented in June 1952, as the new banknotes arrived from the printers in the United States. The impact of the money tax is clearly visible in the demand deposit curve, which remained at the end-1951 level at the end of 1952 (figure 1.3).

The distinguishing feature of commercial banking-system operations as the New Economic Policy came on board in 1952, and during the struggle for the NEP's survival in the next two years or so, was initially inconsistent with the attempt to apply monetary restraint. In response to the strong demand for credit that the 1952 money tax fueled, the banking system stepped on the accelerator at first. Thus, credit to businesses and households (table 1.5) expanded by 20% in

1952, grew at a peak annual rate of 30% in 1953, and increased at a relatively slow 17% pace in 1954, bringing the annual average for the period to 22%. The obverse of this picture was the abrupt decline of bank reserve ratios, from 50% in 1951 to 42% and 38% in 1952 and 1953, respectively, and the corresponding turnabout of the money multiplier from a trough of 1.45 in 1951 to 1.56 in 1953.

This, of course, means that the two determinants of the M_1 expansion rate changed roles as the NEP was being implemented. During the monetary inflation period, 1949–51, the monetary base powered the avalanche and the money multiplier continuously reduced its impact on the expansion of M_1. During the first stage of the implementation of NEP—say, through the first quarter of 1954—the relative impact of these factors was reversed; the money multiplier served as the main vehicle of monetary expansion.

Identifiable economic players lurked in the background of this technical classification. The dominant entity, which determined the pace of the monetary-base expansion through 1951 and was responsible for its major slowdown as the NEP was implemented through 1954, was the government. Two entities set the pace of the money multiplier as the NEP went into effect: households and firms, the decisions of which were expressed in terms of the currency/deposit ratio. The other player on the scene was the commercial banking system, which chose its effective reserve ratios at it saw fit. However, since the negative internal drain continued in 1952 and 1953, as it did from 1948—expressed by the peak currency deposit ratio of 0.73 in 1953 (implied by table 1.5), the banking system alone called the expansionary shots. This was expressed in terms of the major decline of reserve ratios to a trough of only 38% in 1953, far below the (semi-legal) "requested" minimum ratio that the Examiner of Banks had set at 50% in March 1951 and, from then on, at an even higher plateau for increases in outstanding credit balances.[31] In view of the cost effects of the ongoing devaluation process, these expansionary moves by the banking system in 1953 seemed inconsistent, especially in terms of their timing, with the requisite monetary restraint. At an average reserve ratio of 38%, as in 1953, the banks seemed to be committing a flagrant breach not only of the spirit of the policy but also of the letter of the law.

The interesting aspect of this behavior is that the banks' transgressions of the "requested" reserve ratios and, in turn, these transgressions' expansionary impact on bank credit and, correspondingly, on the money supply in 1952 and 1953, were inspired by the Ministry of Finance itself. To relieve the pressure that the money tax and the leap of prices inflicted on the money and real markets in 1952, the pressure in 1953, and the cost effects generated by the elimination of the two lowest exchange rates of the 1952 triad , the Ministry of Finance began to issue banks with "certificates of permission" that allowed banks to expand the credit accommodation for preferred sectors and activities, for example, exports, beyond the reserve limit (Heth, 1966, p. 93). Eventually, however, the authorities became aware of the monetary implications of this haphazard way of providing credit for businesses. Furthermore, the economy was dealt another highly significant cost shock by the (July 1953) decision to raise the top exchange rate again—by 80%, to IL 1.8 to the dollar. The impact of this development and the process of the planned final elimination of the two lowest exchange rates in the triad that had been established in February 1952 and set in motion earlier that year, meant inevitably that monetary restraint became the order of the day.

Since a second squeeze on the monetary base by means of another tax on money balances was out of the question, the instrument of choice for the requisite tight monetary policy was a direct restriction on the expansion of bank credit. Accordingly, the Examiner of Banks imposed early in 1954 a very strict credit volume requirement based on the banking system's outstanding credit balances at the end of November 1953 (Heth, 1966, p. 93). This directive, by hiking the effective bank reserve ratio from 38% to 56% in one stroke, lowered the growth rate of credit to the public from 30% in 1953 to 14% in 1954 and elicited an all-time low money multiplier of 1.34. This additional tightening of monetary policy in 1954, by means of the money-multiplier component, lent the NEP vital support at a crucial time, the last quarter of 1953, when its success or failure dangled on a thread.

The annual average expansion rate of the money supply during the three-year NEP period, 13%, was not significantly out of step with the growth rate of domestic resources (GNP plus the import surplus). Real resources (GNP and the import surplus) grew by more than 10% on annual average during that time. Thus, the annual average gap between the increases in the supply of and demand for liquidity in 1952–54 fell into the 3%–4% range.[32]

This excess and a well-known feature of the disinflation process—an inherent lag in the change in price expectations—were evidently the factors that continued to drive the price level up by 13% on annual average in 1953 and 1954, in a process of an open yet clearly declining inflation rate. The 7.5 inflation rate in 1954, in terms of both the Consumer Price Index and the implicit GNP price index, despite the 80% formal devaluation that inflicted another cost shock in 1953 and 1954, were correctly interpreted at the time as indicators of success. Strong evidence of the resounding success of the NEP in the war on inflation was the dramatic collapse of real-estate prices in 1953 and 1954, supported of course by the significant decline in the black-market dollar exchange rate. The former indicator is retrospective; only the latter was known to the public in real time (table 1.7 and figure 1.4).

The highly significant braking effect of the conflation of strict control of the expansion of nominal monetary aggregates and a soaring price level is revealed by data on the pattern of real money balances, derived by deflating the nominal quantity of money by relevant price-level series. Patinkin's estimate of these series (Patinkin, 1956, p. 78 table 4, and 1960, table 39) is shown in table 1.8 and figure 1.5 in terms of an index of the real value of money (M_1) balances.

The series of columns (6) and (7) in the table reflect the estimate that Patinkin derived by deflating the nominal money series by the Consumer Price Index. The entries in Column (8) were derived by deflating the same nominal money series by the more broadly based implicit GNP price index. The outstanding inflationary effect of the 1948–51 period and the forceful application of the monetary brakes in 1952–54 are illustrated by the series in column (6) or, alternatively, the series in column (7) for the base year that was shifted from 1948 to 1950. As the real monetary base expanded by a factor of 2.3 times between the middle of 1948 and the end of 1951, the real money supply grew by a factor of 2.2: the 40% contraction of the real monetary base in 1952 was followed by an abrupt 30% decline in the real money supply that year alone. In 1954, both real aggregates were still lower, by 27% and 29%, respectively, than at the end of 1951—even though GNP and, correspondingly, domestic uses were 33% and 10% higher, respectively, than in 1951.

Since the pattern of fiscal policy was dominant in determining the expansion rate of the monetary base, the dramatic turnaround in real monetary aggregates during the NEP suggests that fiscal policy was now accommodating monetary policy, as promised by Prime Minister Ben-Gurion in his February 1952 statement about the essentials of the NEP and as emphasized in Minister of Finance Kaplan's response to the debate in the Knesset. Thus, the NEP may be defined as a monetary-dominance policy—the sine qua non for measures designed to implement a comprehensive and major program of reducing and sterilizing inflation.

THE REAL EXCHANGE RATE

The significant tightening of monetary policy in early 1954 was also motivated by considerations related to the attainment of the second target of the NEP: slashing the deficit on the balance-of-payments current account. To meet this target, an improvement in the trade account seemed necessary. Therefore, the success of the whole exercise was pegged to another major effective devaluation requiring a significant immediate increase in the real exchange rate.

However, the price explosion of 1952 that hiked consumer prices by almost 67% in 1952 and eroded real balances by 30%, thereby offering the restrictive monetary policy the support it needed by whittling down the real value of money, had concurrently done the same to the real exchange rate. Even though the nominal effective exchange rate for exports was almost twice as high at the end of 1952 as at the end of 1951, and even though the rate for imports was even higher, prices in terms of consumer and GNP prices were 67% and 40% higher, respectively. The estimated real exchange rates, deflated by the CPI and the implicit GNP price index, indicate that despite the major (average) nominal devaluation in 1952, the real exchange rate did not increase significantly over its level in 1950. Furthermore, the comparison with the real exchange rate in 1949, available only in terms of consumer prices (table 1.7), shows no improvement whatsoever in the real rate. Another indicator of the need for another move on the exchange rate was the trend in real wages available to economic players. Indeed, as column (5) of the aforementioned table shows, real wages rose by almost 7% in 1952–54.

Thus, by early 1953, it was quite clear that a further significant adjustment of the nominal exchange rate had to take place if the balance-of-payments target was to be met. Such a measure, however, would create another cost shock, part of which was already in the works due to the need to move additional components of imports from the two lowest exchange rates to the highest rate, which was 2.8 times higher than the formal rate preceding the February 1952 devaluation.

The visible and obviously necessary erosion of the real exchange rate, in terms of both domestic prices and nominal wages, led in March 1953 to the formation of an Expert Committee on the Balance of Payments and the Exchange Rate. In its report, presented in July of that year, the panel suggested a further devaluation of 80% on the basis of the highest rate (IL 1.00 to the dollar) set in February 1952, when the NEP was adopted as the official policy. The committee also recommended the rapid abolition of the official multiple exchange-rate system that had been implemented on that occasion.[33]

The government adopted the policy recommendation of the majority and initially added a fourth formal exchange rate that was nine times higher than the official rate of January 1952. The two lowest rates were finally abolished by the end of 1953 and the last vestige of the February 1952 triad of rates, IL 1 to the dollar, was eliminated by August 1954. IL 1.80 to the dollar became the sole exchange rate de facto and was finally declared the official rate in July 1955.

Since the *effective* exchange rate on exports and imports was higher by 43% and 89%, respectively, in 1955 than at the end of 1953 (Michaely, 1971) and domestic prices were only 13% higher, the real effective exchange rate on exports was about 27% higher than at the end of 1953. The margin of the effective exchange rate on imports was even wider—more than twice as high as the effective exchange rate at the end of 1951. This provided domestic industries with a high protective shield and created at least the potential of an improvement of the trade balance in the context of rapid growth.

MISSION ACCOMPLISHED

As one would expect, and as policymakers at the time had expected, the highly restrictive fiscal and monetary measures slowed the economy. GDP was flat in 1953 and the unemployment rate climbed swiftly in 1953 and continued to advance in 1954. However, the rate of price inflation fell to 7.5% in 1954 and decreased again in the following year. The declining trend in inflation in 1954, 1955, and the rest of the decade was sustained despite the cost shock inflicted on the system by the final (NEP) move on the exchange rate in 1953–54, which elevated the "effective exchange rate" by more than 50% in 1954 (table 1.7). These two developments—disinflation and a substantial rise in the nominal exchange rate and, correspondingly, the real rate—sent a favorable message to the tradable sector of the economy.

With inflation down to 5% in 1955—a rate not out of line with comparative rates in the United Kingdom and most West European countries—and with a major improvement in the real exchange rate that made it possible to lower the current-account deficit to a manageable level, the mission of the NEP in terms of its twin targets seemed to have been accomplished. The program had placed the economy firmly on the ladder of a decade of rapid sustainable growth based on rising productivity.

The NEP left government finances in much better shape due to the effect of growth on the tax base in addition to the rapidly increasing rate of tax coverage as a result of legislation, which was supported by a major improvement in tax administration. Finally, the haphazard management of the monetary dimension of the economy, navigated hitherto by the Ministry of Finance and leading Bank Leumi executives who had little formal power in any case, was replaced by a full-fledged central bank—the Bank of Israel—which prepared to open its doors for business on December 1, 1954.

2

The Establishment of the Bank of Israel: The Legal and Institutional Framework of Israel's Central Bank

DRAFTING THE BANK OF ISRAEL LAW

The Drafting Process

After the third and final reading of the Bank of Israel Law in the Knesset in August 1954, the final stage of the drawn-out preparations for the establishment of a central bank in Israel was rapidly completed. On December 1, 1954, the Bank of Israel opened for business.

The Department of Issue, established in August 1948 as a distinct legal entity within Bank Leumi le-Israel (see chapter 1), was moved to the central bank in its entirety. Simultaneously, the Department of the Examiner of Banks was moved from the Ministry of Finance to the Bank of Israel. A Research Department also went into action on the inaugural date. Thus the process of setting up the Bank of Israel came to an end.

No one had expected the Department of Issue to endure for more than six years. The length of its tenure had been a major bone of contention in the summer of 1948, when the covenant that established it was being negotiated. The three-year period set forth in that document had been a compromise between the durations proposed by Bank Leumi management and by the government.[1] The denouement envisioned by all sides was the establishment of a central bank. A committee tasked with preparing for the formation of this institution was set up early in 1951. Its chair was Minister of Finance Eliezer Kaplan himself, and two of its other five members were David Horowitz, Director General of the Ministry of Finance, and Eliezer S. Hoofien, Chair of Bank Leumi, who had engineered the introduction of the Israel currency in 1948.

The committee promptly dispatched its secretary, Dr. Lehman, Director of the Department of Issue, to meet with monetary experts in North America and several South American countries, where central banks recently had been established. Little else happened until early in 1953. It was Levi Eshkol, Kaplan's successor as minister of finance, who moved ahead quickly. Almost immediately after taking office in June 1952, Eshkol reshuffled the committee by co-opting, apart from Hoofien and Horowitz, Peretz Naphtali, Minister of Agriculture; Judge A. Witkon; and A. Bart, General Manager of Bank Leumi. Hoofien and Horowitz, now acting as a subcommittee, prepared an outline of a draft of the proposed central-bank legislation in which the mission, management instruments, and role of the institution in controlling and running the country's monetary and financial systems were set forth. In March 1953, the government made the final decision to set up the central bank, designated David Horowitz as its first governor, and instructed Horowitz to make preparations for the establishment of the bank at the earliest feasible date. Within a year, early in the summer of 1954, Lehman drafted the Bank of Israel bill in its final form. After review by the committee, the bill was submitted to the government.

After the government approved the draft, it was sent on to the Knesset for a first reading in which it passed unanimously. The bill was then submitted to the scrutiny of a group of experts in New York. The group included Robert Triffin of Yale University; Luis Rasminsky, then one of the governors of the Bank of Canada; Edward Bernstein, erstwhile head of the IMF Research Department; and Henry Bloch, then the secretary of the Economic Department of the United Nations Organization. After systematically examining the sections of the bill, they proposed various adjustments that were minor with one significant exception: they unanimously recommended deleting the clause that would empower the central bank "to set, from time to time, the rate of exchange." This, they said, was clearly a political decision that should be made by the government.[2]

The International Context

This scrutiny of the bill by a learned group of experts, all of whom were deeply involved in the theory and the practice of the management of monetary or fiscal policy in the industrialized world, could not but reflect the monetary Zeitgeist. Their recommendation on the exclusion of the exchange rate from the central bank's sphere of authority and responsibility mirrored the dominance of the Bretton Woods fixed-exchange-rate system in theory and practice.

The discussion on and legislation of the Bank of Israel Law in 1953–54 were inevitably influenced by the Keynesian conceptual framework that was dominant in the first postwar decade. The Keynesian construct, by focusing on fiscal policy as the instrument of choice in macroeconomic management, presumed intensive government involvement in the macro sphere, with monetary policy in a not highly relevant niche.

By the early 1950s, however, the trend toward greater freedom of central banks to pursue (restrictive) monetary policies was in plain sight. The well-known 1951 "accord" between the administration and the Federal Reserve Bank in the United States initiated the process of releasing monetary policy from its world war shackles. The coterminous change of government from Labour to the Conservatives in the United Kingdom and the market-oriented policies of Ludwig Erhard, Minister of Finance in West Germany, meant that Western Europe was moving in the same direction.

Accordingly, the revival of monetary policy had become a fact of life as the Bank of Israel Law progressed from its first draft in late 1953 to its third and final reading in the Knesset in August 1954. The shift was symbolized by the gradual disappearance of the 1%–2% discount rate in the United States and the effective repeal of Dalton's similar "bank-rate rule" in the financial markets of Western Europe after two decades of dominance. A rapidly growing reliance on monetary instruments as devices of macroeconomic control was clearly visible by 1953 as monetary policy emerged from the doldrums of the 1930s economic crisis and the world war.[3] These developments inevitably affected the vision of those involved in crafting the Bank of Israel bill.

The Domestic Context

The Israeli economy of 1954 was much different in size and performance than the one that had emerged in 1948 from three decades of Mandatory rule. GNP had more than doubled since 1949; the population and the labor force had grown somewhat less. The import flow was 50% higher than in 1949 and that of exports had grown even more vigorously. However, Israel's very dependence on foreign trade and, particularly, on a strong inflow of real resources— that is, a large import surplus—had grown significantly in absolute terms and, therefore, had become a crucial fact of life. Finally, although tight currency controls and import licensing still dominated Israel's international trade scene in the late 1940s and early 1950s, the austerity program and its corresponding rationing of basic commodities were on their way out due to the NEP, signaling a reduction of government involvement in micromanagement of the economy. In this respect, Israel was following the Western European process, although its process lagged behind. In terms of its performance and living standards, Israel in 1955 was still far from the standards of the industrialized world, even though Europe in particular was still recovering from World War II.

It was obvious to all and sundry that Israel's terms of reference were those of the industrialized countries. By implication, its monetary institutions were expected to reflect the rules and the legal framework of that world. This was the mission that the Israeli team in charge of preparing the rules of the game for the central bank, supported by the opinion and scrutiny of the aforementioned group of international experts, attempted to perform. These efforts were reflected in various aspects of the Bank of Israel Law that were meant to establish an infrastructure for the Israeli monetary system.

TARGETS AND INSTRUMENTS

Following a brief chapter on "Interpretation and Definitions," Chapter 2 of the Bank of Israel Law, 5714–1954, spells out the objectives that the central bank is to "promote by [means of] monetary measures": "stabilization of the domestic and foreign value of the currency" and "high levels of employment, national income, and capital investment."[4] This statement of objectives clearly reflects the prevalent attitude in the early 1950s, according to which the target of a central bank is not only to maintain price stability but also to contribute directly to the performance of the real dimension of the economy.

The instruments made available to the BOI included the entire classical set that came into being in the late nineteenth century and had been used since then by central banks in leading industrial countries to guide and affect the nominal dimension of the economy. Thus, Section 42 of the law empowered the BOI to operate a discount window: "[T]he Bank may provide finance to every commercial bank by discounting bills of exchange, promissory notes, or other documents." Section 46 empowered the bank to engage in open-market operations: "(a) The Bank may buy and sell government securities and also other securities denominated in Israeli currency and bearing a fixed interest rate; (b) the Bank may exercise its power under this Section whenever it is necessary, in the opinion of the Governor, to increase or reduce the size of means of payment." To facilitate open-market operations, the bank was even empowered to issue its own securities, *subject to government approval* (Section 47). Section 41 permitted the BOI "to purchase gold, foreign currency, and foreign government bonds," that is, to conduct foreign-currency operations that would affect the money supply much as open-market operations would. In the same section, the government was instructed to consult with the governor of the Bank of Israel before making any decision relating to the exchange rate.

Section 49 empowers the Bank to set legal reserve ratios for commercial banks and to specify the composition of their reserve assets. Section 53 empowers the bank to impose credit ceilings on commercial banks and to set specific and different ceilings for different kinds of credit. The wording of this section, and that of Section 49, referring to reserve ratios, gave the central bank the power of qualitative control over bank credit and, thereby, effectively to discriminate in terms of price and availability among lines of credit "by use."[5]

Thus, the letter of the law allowed the Bank of Israel to implement monetary policy by means of two conventional instruments that central banks possess: control of the monetary base and control of the money multiplier. It is the product of these two variables, of course, that determines the supply function of money. The alternative statement of the supply function of money, in terms of the sum of the monetary base and total commercial bank credit, similarly identifies the central bank's potential ability to affect equilibrium in the money market by applying the same instruments: changing the magnitudes of the monetary base and of (total) commercial bank credit, which depend on the banking system's effective reserve ratios and reserves. The former may be affected by the central bank's open-market policy; the latter may be influenced by its power to set reserve ratios and by the level of the credit ceilings that Section 53 allows the governor to impose.

However, the governing institutions of the BOI were not given carte blanche for the application of these two instruments, that is, an open-market policy to affect the monetary base and the setting of minimum reserve ratios to control the money multiplier. The BOI would need government approval to set reserve ratios (Section 49) and issue its own debentures (Section 47). In view of the specific Israeli circumstances in this regard—initially the absence of a significant outstanding volume and, later, the very small size of the liquid national debt in terms of the relevant economic aggregates—this meant that *restrictive* open-market operations would not be implemented unless the government, meaning the Ministry of Finance, approved them.

Finally, the law provided the governor of the Bank of Israel with a mechanism of explicit moral suasion that would serve the bank as an instrument of monetary restraint. Section 35 required the governor to publish "a report about an increase in means of payment" if this aggregate grew by more than 15% during any twelve-month period.[6] The choice of this specific rate of expansion probably reflects an implied estimate of the feasible growth rate of GNP, correctly perceived as the dominant determinant of the demand for money. Since long-term growth expectations in the early 1950s were presumably no higher than 10% per annum—assuming that the committee of experts that reviewed the draft of the bill had expected even this much growth—the 15% threshold left some leeway for a "low" (endemic) inflation rate, which in the early 1950s was still a fact of life in Western Europe.

Central banks in industrialized countries did not use such an instrument and do not do so today. Its presence in the Israeli statute may be considered an early attempt at transparency—a notion related to central-bank monetary policy that emerged in industrial countries four decades later, in the 1990s. Its inclusion in the law undoubtedly reflected the presumption, representative of the state of mind in the first post–World War II decade, that endemic inflation was an inherent feature and, therefore, a significant problem that the stewards of macroeconomic policy faced. The factual context that inspired the inclusion of this section in the central-bank legislation was the fifteen-year period of inflation that Palestine/Israel had just experienced (see chapter 1). This provision was probably unique in central-bank laws. Even developing countries, many of which were setting up such institutions and preparing the legal framework for their operation during those years, included no such section in their laws.[7]

GOVERNING BODIES OF THE CENTRAL BANK

The inherent confrontational milieu in which central banks and treasuries operate has always been the universal rule of the realm. However, it has been "more inherent" in the Israeli case than elsewhere, since in Israel the central-bank law (Section 45) explicitly entitled the government to a *direct credit facility* from the central bank at a significant magnitude in terms of macroeconomic aggregates. For three decades, through 1985, the political community considered this accommodation, set at "up to 20% of the total budget in a given fiscal year," as a natural supplement that the government could use to even out its cash flow.[8] The wording limits the benchmark for this constraint to the regular budget only. Yet it was precisely through the regular budget that the government did most of its spending.

Thus, if the government requested a short-term advance and the Bank of Israel refused, as it could under the law, the governor of the bank would find himself at loggerheads with the government's representative, the minister of finance. Needless to say, the governor would be at a disadvantage in such a confrontation during Israel's first decade, as would be such an official in any industrialized country in the decade after World War II. In the major countries of South America, this feature remained dominant for most of the second half of the twentieth century. The revolving door for governors in South America through the 1990s is an obvious case in point.[9]

Israel's political environment was quite different; the first governor of the Bank of Israel held the post for seventeen years and all but one of his successors have completed at least one full five-year term. Just the same, the Bank of Israel Law placed the governor in a very weak position to withstand Finance Ministry pressure on monetary matters, which are formally his bailiwick. This was due to the management structure that the BOI Law imposed on the bank. The structure reflected the clearly stated preference of David Horowitz, the first BOI governor and one of the two members of the informal subcommittee who were asked to finalize the draft of the BOI Charter. Under the relevant sections of Chapter 4 of the Law, the Bank of Israel has neither a board of governors nor a statutory committee for monetary policy.[10] Admittedly, in an economy as small as Israel's was at the time, there would have been no justification for a statutory committee if a board of governors were running the show at the top of the pyramid. Accordingly, the decision-making prerogative in monetary affairs, as in almost all other subjects, was vested in the governor personally.[11] A seven-member Advisory Committee and a broader forum—a fifteen-member Advisory Council (including the seven members of the Advisory Committee), none of them an employee of the central bank, were to serve as the supreme deliberative authority. Both entities were chaired by the same person and the governor attended their meetings even though he was not a member. Both were conceived as advisory bodies per se; neither ever took a vote on any issue.

Sections 8, 9, 12, 15, and 17 of the Bank of Israel Law describe the appointment procedure, length of service, and powers of the governor, including his/her function as the "advisor to the government on monetary and other economic subjects" Sections 20–26 describe the appointment procedure, length of service, and functions of the Advisory Committee and the Advisory Council. Section 49 requires "prior consultation with the Advisory Committee as a condition for seeking government approval of the issue of Bank of Israel securities"—an option that has not been exercised to this day.

Section 49 also equipped the Advisory Committee with the only power that proved to be of practical significance during the BOI's first three decades: as a precondition for the government's consideration and approval of any proposed change in the compulsory liquidity ratio of the commercial banking system, the committee was to debate the topic and express its consent.

Thus, without the support of a statutory board of governors or a similar panel specifically in charge of monetary-policy decisions, the Governor went "naked into the negotiating chamber" with the minister of finance whenever the latter, having received the approval of the Knesset Finance Committee, asked for the sort of "temporary accommodation" that the BOI explicitly allowed him to request. The governor's statutory function as the government's economic advisor and, in this capacity, as a nonvoting member of the Ministerial Committee on Economic Affairs imposed a further constraint on his/her management of monetary policy. The governor's membership on this panel, which was subjected to budget pressures occasioned by mass immigration in the 1950s and 1960s and an exploding defense budget from the middle 1960s on, clearly put him in an awkward situation that would not have been muted had he operated as an "outsider."

The sheer magnitude of government in the Israeli economy and the fiscal strain imposed on the system by requisite infrastructure investments and ever-rising defense expenditures suggest that a restrictive monetary policy should have been employed during almost the entire three-decade period that preceded the repeal of the provision allowing the BOI to give the government the aforementioned direct credit accommodation. The implementation of such a policy meant first and foremost the prevention of significant growth in government credit. It would also require, for most of the time, a selling posture in the open market and corresponding moves on the legal minimum level of bank reserves. However, any move in these directions entailed government approval. Thus, the Governor and the other members of the Ministerial Committee on Economic Affairs seemed to be on a perpetual collision course. In this respect, the support of a board of governors might have made a difference in the running engagement between the monetary authority, which everywhere had been setting monetary policy, and the political community that set fiscal policy.

THE "NO-PRINTING LAW" AND THE LEVIN COMMISSION

During the BOI's first three decades, its enabling statute was amended fourteen times. Since the amendments related to technicalities, hardly anyone other than, say, auditors and lawyers, knew about these changes in the legal infrastructure. Amendment 15, however, is an altogether different story in terms of both public awareness and economic and political impact. The amendment was comprised of seven Hebrew words only: "The Bank shall not lend to the Government." Passed in July 1985 and predated to April 1 of that year, it made history.

The amendment, popularly termed the "no-printing law," repealed Section 45 of the original BOI Law, which had allowed the BOI to extend significant credit to the government in terms of major economic aggregates, in order to even out the fiscal cash flow. It was the extensive use of this option by successive governments that had saddled Israel with triple-digit inflation from 1979 on, which surged by the second quarter of 1985 to rates verging on hyperinflation. Thus, the amendment was a sine qua non condition for the success of the stabilization policy that was activated on July 1, 1985, for the purpose of bringing inflation under control for good.

The amendment was a bitter pill for the incumbent Government, and the political community at large, to swallow. It imposed a tough fiscal restriction that entailed a drastic reduction of the budget deficit. It was, however, crucial for the attainability of the target of the policy—an immediate collapse of inflation from annual rates of several hundred percent in the first two quarters of 1985 to the 10%–20% range, where it would reside for the next ten years or so. Later, particularly in the second half of the 1990s, the amendment, which imposed fiscal discipline, was central in the BOI's successful attempt to establish the monetary dominance that allowed it to attain its ultimate target, price stability, at the turn of the twenty-first century.

However, both major issues discussed above—the BOI's management structure and the restatement of its mission, that is, its policy targets—remain unresolved as the central bank celebrates its golden anniversary. The rationale for adjusting the BOI Law, legislated in the middle of the past century, to the realities and modus operandi of global money markets at the beginning of the twenty-first century, is not specific to Israel. The need for such an adjustment is evident in major industrialized countries where central banks have been operating for a century if not more. The 1998 Bank of England Act and the legal framework of the European Central Bank (ECB), which opened the same year as the euro was born, are obvious cases in point.

The significant change in the BOI's stance and the influence of its measures on the domestic financial markets and the economy at large since 1985, coupled with the growing strength of central banks on the world stage, prompted the government in December 1997 to appoint a special commission under Supreme Court Justice Dov Levin. The commission was instructed to review the BOI Law and propose relevant changes for its adaptation to the realities of twenty-first-century domestic and global money and capital markets. In its comprehensive report, submitted in 1998, the panel recommended various changes in the BOI Law, including the appointment of a board of governors and a monetary-policy committee. To this day, the recommendations have not been adopted. The main objection of governments on both sides of the Left–Right divide concerns the committee's proposal to restate the "role of the Bank" in the BOI Law, a turn of phrase that actually refers to the central bank's monetary-policy objectives. Section 3 of the 1954 law expressed the goal of monetary policy in terms of striving for price stability but specified a *high level of employment* as a policy target on equal terms with price stability. According to the Levin Commission proposal, the law should adopt the formula spelled out in the Blair government's Bank of England Act and the ECB Charter (both in 1998),[12] which gives the monetary-policy goal clear priority to price stability. Employment and growth would also figure in the wording of the statute, the committee said, but only as secondary concerns that, although relevant, should not interfere with the main mission of the monetary authority, the assurance of price stability.

The BOI management accepted the Levin Commission's recommendations en bloc, including the proposed major change in the central bank's management structure and the phrasing of monetary-policy goals. The political community, not prepared to cross the Rubicon on this issue, demurred.

THE LEGAL INTEREST-RATE CEILING AND
FOREIGN-EXCHANGE CONTROLS

Variations on the Theme of the Usury Law

The legal context in which monetary policy was implemented comprised more than the Bank of Israel Law, of course. Such a context inevitably reflects the political balance of power, and in this case implementation took place within constraints imposed by two additional acts: the 1939 Mandate Law that imposed universal currency control and the Usury Law, legislated in 1957 as the successor to an Ottoman statute.

Even after the appearance of the BOI on the monetary scene in late 1954, the Usury Law, then in its Ottoman version as carried forward by the Mandate, remained in effect. The interest ceiling that the statute had established, 9%, had no economic significance during the two decades between the world wars, since prices declined through the early 1930s and leveled off through 1939. With the U.K. bank rate holding at 2% since 1931, the market (debitory) interest rates in Palestine, set by commercial banks, were far under the de jure ceiling.

The price pattern during the World War II era was altogether different, of course. The price level in Palestine climbed by 15% on annual average in 1939–47. During that time, then, the Ottoman interest-rate ceiling would have been effective had controls on banks' lending rates been enforced. This, however, was not the case. Commercial banks and other lending institutions used a host of techniques, such as commissions and up-front deduction of total interest, to charge market-level rates that blatantly exceeded the 9% ceiling. Furthermore, the penalty for circumventing the Usury Law probably suggested to them that they would risk little by following this trail.[13] Thus, much commercial bank credit, and a fortiori credit business outside the banking system, was probably transacted at "gray-market" rates that surpassed the legal ceiling.

The same reasoning applied in the 1948–54 period, surveyed in chapter 1, when the monetary environment resembled that under the pre-independence Palestine Currency Board. Now, however, annual average price inflation ran at a 17.0% pace and peaked at 66% in 1952 (table 1.7). Thus, the 9% interest ceiling was a dead letter for most of the period preceding the establishment of the Bank of Israel. At the time the BOI came aboard, the law was being disregarded right and left. Although the BOI Law empowered the governor to set maximum interest rates for commercial bank credit and deposits and to use the credit window to influence market rates (Sections 43, 46, and 56), the central bank preferred not to step into the fray.

This state of affairs persisted through 1957. By then, as the political environment had evolved and bank credit had rapidly become more important in running the economy, the banking system itself began to frown on circumventionist practices. Pressure from the major commercial banks—supported by the BOI, which also looked askance at the semi-legal situation—finally led to the repeal of the Ottoman law and its replacement with an Israeli law based on the principles of traditional usury laws. Yet by empowering the minister of finance to set maximum interest rates and adjust them according to circumstances, the new statute made the system much more flexible. It also explicitly ruled out the treatment of indexation of the debt principal as interest. Thus, lenders who issued indexed credit at lawful interest rates would not have to bear inflation risk. On the other hand, the new law criminalized the receipt of interest payments at nominal rates exceeding the ceiling (Heth, 1966, p. 97).

Although it upheld the principle of capping the interest rate, the new legislation offered the financial sector greater flexibility by adjusting the legal ceiling to 10% for loans to farming and manufacturing and 11% for all other business and household uses. These limits remained in effect until 1970, when the minister of finance, Pinhas Sapir, used the powers granted him by the law to abolish them for good.

The significantly lower inflation rates that followed the success of the New Economic Policy—3%–5% per annum through 1960 (table 1.7)—presumably made the difference in the deliberations preceding the 1957 legislation. The new and higher interest ceilings were part of a deal between participants in the debate representing the commercial banking system, who proposed the outright repeal of the ceiling, and those representing agriculture, who had substantial political clout and were heartily supported in this matter by manufacturing interests. The inflation rates at the time (4.6% and 5.2% in 1956 and 1957, respectively) may have induced the bankers to believe that the higher legal nominal rate would approximate the effective equilibrium rate in the financial markets, even for unindexed credit. Thus, the proposed rates, 10% and 11%, might eliminate or at least significantly reduce the scope of the gray-credit markets.[14]

This reading of the omens proved correct for the 1956–60 interval, as inflation rates declined to less than 4% on annual average. Therefore, the banking sector was under less pressure from the gray-market competition. The effect, however, was temporary. As inflation escalated in 1961–66 to 7.7% on annual average and more than 9% in some years, the commercial banks worked their way back into these credit markets, which soon accounted for a substantial fraction of total bank credit. They did so using a (questionable) legal loophole that allowed them to circumvent the interest ceiling—by creating a large semi-legal money market within the banking system itself, the so-called bill brokerage market. This market, which consisted of a growing fraction of bank credit transactions, complicated the management of monetary policy until the interest ceiling was repealed.

The repeal, however, was bought at a steep cost to the central bank's freedom to implement monetary policy for the next fifteen years. To compensate the farming and manufacturing interests, the subsidized "directed credit" component of commercial bank credit, which had grown haphazardly in the 1960s and gave its beneficiaries a significant subsidy, was finally institutionalized. Its share in outstanding credit of the commercial banking system climbed from 30%–40% in the 1960s—an appreciable level in itself—to the 40%–50% range in the 1970s. Accordingly, the impact of monetary policy was effectively excluded from this fraction of the determinant of the money supply and of its rate of change. The low legal ceiling on interest rates, which had constrained the central bank's maneuvering room in the money and capital markets during its first fifteen years, through 1970, would do so even more emphatically during the next fifteen years, through 1985, although in a different guise. The difference was a matter of technique rather than of substance.

Implications of the Exchange-Rate Regime and Exchange Controls

The economic and financial environment within which Israel's monetary policy would operate was obviously affected by the exchange-rate regime and foreign-exchange controls. The Bretton Woods operating rule, compulsory for all members of IMF, dictated a fixed-exchange rate regime during the 1954–74 period. Although exchange-rate adjustments were allowed, they required IMF approval. Israel's exchange rate adjustments, of course, were few and far between. No adjustment was made during the BOI's first seven years. From then until the adoption of a crawling peg in 1975, four adjustments took place: in 1962, 1967, 1971, and 1974.

Thus, the official exchange rate was an instrument rather than an endogenous macroeconomic variable that continuously reflected real, monetary, and price developments in the economy. Although inflation in 1955–60 had fallen to an annual rate of 4.0% in Consumer Price Index terms, the continuously rising pattern of the price level meant that prices were about 26% higher at the end of 1960 than in 1954. Therefore, the effective exchange rate on all foreign-trade transactions was continuously adjusted upward between the official devaluations in 1954 and February 1962 and further down the road. Duty surcharges and explicit export subsidies were the main devices used to carry out this strategy. These, of course, applied neither to the unilateral transfers (reparation payments) that flowed into government coffers nor to personal restitution receipts and donations, which figured significantly in Israel's foreign-exchange receipts. Obviously, too, the adjustments did not apply to transfers of funds on capital account, which were made at the official exchange rate. This meant that the system had to be run on the basis of a multiple exchange-rate regime that inevitably entailed tight foreign-exchange controls.

Israel had inherited the controls en bloc from the Mandate. From the late 1950s on, they were gradually relaxed for transactions on trade account. Thus, importers no longer had to apply for foreign-currency allocations and exporters could use some of their foreign-currency receipts to pay for imported inputs. Even then, however, the system was not formally dismantled as controls on unilateral transfers and capital-account transactions were strictly maintained. A formal repeal of the former would have thwarted the continuation of the latter.

Accordingly, tight foreign-exchange control was the rule of the realm in the BOI's first two decades. With the exception of the 1977–78 interlude, in which the newly installed government made a dash for partial liberalization (see chapter 7, in this volume) matters continued in roughly this fashion in the central bank's third decade and, in an attenuated fashion, more than a decade beyond 1985. Only afterwards, when a process of decontrol was initiated and systemically pursued, were the last vestiges of this system abolished. By then, a new century had begun.

The most significant practical feature of the exchange-control setup, from the point of view of the management of monetary policy by the central bank, was the administration of the controls by a department of the Ministry of Finance. This endowed the latter with serious clout in monetary affairs. In other words, even though the textbooks describe exchange controls as a device that unhinges domestic money and financial markets from the rest of the world, reality is usually much different. The formally closed door had inevitable and, usually, illegal loopholes. It also had a legal key, kept in the pocket of the minister of finance. Even a partial and temporary opening of that door, reflecting a more liberal attitude toward applications for permits to borrow abroad—something that the Finance Ministry considered justified—had monetary implications with which the central bank had to cope.

EPILOGUE

The most important added value that the BOI generated in its early years was its emergence as a distinct institution in general government and a counterpart of the Ministry of Finance. These two players in governance have maintained the sort of love-hate relationship, manifested in the periodic ebbs and flows of tension that one encounters in all industrialized countries and should expect to encounter in view of their different missions and responsibilities. While the Finance Ministry focuses on the short term and is subjected to constant pressure from the political community, it is the mission of the central bank to take the medium and long run into consideration and to keep the value of the currency—and the price level—in its sights.

This, of course, means that the integration of the BOI into the institutional framework of general government in the closing quarter of 1954 quickly made a significant difference. It added a new player to the institutional team that held overarching responsibility for assuring relative monetary and macroeconomic stability. The BOI's mission, especially when adhered to strictly, inevitably curtailed the degree of freedom of government ministries—particularly that of the Ministry of Finance, which until December 1954 had been running the macroeconomic show by itself.

To work out a modus vivendi between these institutions, the mission of one of which was to constrain the latitude of the other, a delicate and intrinsically unstable equilibrium had to be brought about. Levi Eshkol, who took over as finance minister in 1952 and would serve as such for more than a decade, and David Horowitz, the first governor of the BOI and its only governor during its first seventeen years, had to face that challenge.

3

Groping for and the Emergence of Monetary Policy, 1954–66

GROWTH AND PRICES

The emergence of the Bank of Israel and its consolidation as an important player in governing the country and, in particular, its economy occurred at an opportune time in terms of the major economic aggregates. The success of the 1952 New Economic Policy (NEP) was evident by the end of its first year, even though its last phases of implementation entailed a further stepwise devaluation of the currency through 1954. The 20% leap in the GNP growth rate in 1954 relative to 1953, although partly reflecting a rebound after the stalling of growth in the two previous years, was a clear omen. Double-digit annual growth continued in 1955 and 1956 as well (table 3.1), even though the country experienced severe political strain during these years and followed a military collision course leading to the Sinai Campaign (Operation Kadesh) in November–December 1956. This growth pattern, at annual rates of about 10% in GNP and resources available to the economy (gross product and the import surplus), would remain the order of the day until the middle of 1965.

If a cyclical pattern in the movement of real aggregates could be discerned during this time, it did so only toward the very end, in the last two quarters of 1965, in terms of the rate of GNP and employment growth (figures 3.1 and 3.2). It became a headline phenomenon in 1966 when growth slowed abruptly from the 9%–10% rates experienced for more than a decade to only 1%, meaning a decline in per capita GNP that year. By 1966, however, Israel had an altogether different economy than it had had in 1954. GNP was almost three times higher and per capita product had increased by 60%, even though the population had grown by 50% during the interval.

Table 3.1. Real Economy Indicators, 1954–67

| | Indices, 1954 = 100 | | | | | | | |
	GDP (1)	Resources[1] (2)	GDP Per Capita (3)	Employment (4)	Unemployment Rate (Percent) (5)	Imports ($ million) (6)	Exports ($ million) (7)	Import Surplus ($ million) (8)
1954	100.0	100.0	100.0		9.2	373.4	140.9	232.5
1955	113.9	109.4	110.0	100.0	7.4	432.2	144.3	287.9
1956	124.4	114.3	114.8	98.1	7.8	536.6	178.5	358.1
1957	135.1	118.8	117.9	109.6	6.9	557.8	223.1	334.7
1958	144.7	124.3	122.0	112.4	5.7	561.5	216.5	345.0
1959	163.0	134.0	133.3	115.3	5.5	586.2	266.8	319.4
1960	176.1	143.5	136.7	119.8	4.6	682.0	336.0	346.0
1961	195.3	160.4	141.2	127.5	3.6	843.5	397.9	445.6
1962	214.8	185.3	146.0	134.5	3.7	969.7	503.2	466.5
1963	237.4	200.0	150.7	138.1	3.6	1054.9	606.7	448.2
1964	260.9	227.3	153.3	145.8	3.3	1228.2	655.7	572.5
1965	285.4	241.8	162.2	150.1	3.6	1269.3	748.9	520.4
1966	288.2	241.1	159.7	149.2	7.4	1317.0	872.1	444.9
1967	294.9	238.9	158.2	141.8	10.4	1480.1	949.3	530.8
Annual average rates of change (percent)								
1955–60	9.9	6.2	5.3	3.7	6.3	10.6	15.6	6.9
1961–66	8.6	9.0	2.6	3.7	4.2	11.6	17.2	4.3

[1]Real domestic resources: GNP plus import surplus.

Sources: Column (1), 1954–1960: Central Bureau of Statistics, *Statistical Abstract of Israel* 1978, Table VI-2, p. 163; 1960–1967: BOI database; column (2): Halevi-Klinov (1968), Table App. 2, p. 234, and BOI database; column (3): Halevi-Klinov (1968), Table App. p. 235, and BOI database; columns (4)–(5): Central Bureau of Statistics, *Statistical Abstract of Israel* 1978, Table XII-1, p. 338; column (6)–(8): Halevi-Klinov (1968), Table 50, p. 115; and BOI, *Annual Report* 1964, Table III-1, and similar tables in other reports.

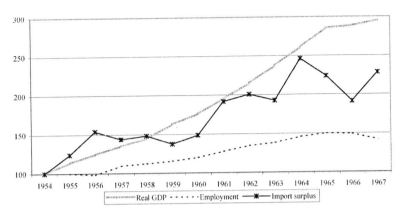

Figure 3.1. Real GDP and Employment, 1954–67 (1954 = 100)

The growth process had its counterpart in the foreign-trade and payments sector. Exports had nearly quintupled (in real dollar terms) during the twelve-year period and imports had grown 3.5 times over. However, since the import surplus had ballooned by 40%, foreign payments were subject to strain, albeit at declining intensity over time. This was evidenced in the rising foreign reserves/import ratio, from about one month of imports in 1955 to somewhat more than three months in 1960 and slightly less than six months in 1966. Just the same, the strain on foreign payments always remained at the top of the macroeconomic and political agenda and led to major moves that culminated in 1962 with a large devaluation.

The pattern of the price level—its rate of change—does clearly display a cyclical feature; its turning point occurred in 1960 (figure 3.2). Despite vigorous growth that pushed the economy into the full-employment range by 1959–60, the annual rate of change of the price level had been declining continuously for six years (1954–59), even though the government had abandoned rationing and steadily reduced its involvement in setting consumer prices. Inflation in the terminal year of the first subperiod, 1959, was exceptionally low: 1.6% and 2.6% in

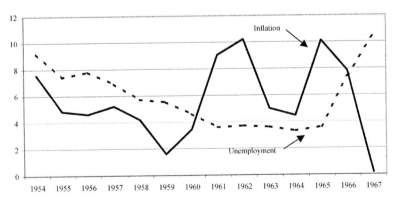

Figure 3.2. Annual Inflation and Unemployment Rates (percent), 1954–67

terms of the Consumer Price Index and the GNP deflator, respectively, even though the unemployment rate declined from 7.4% in 1955 to 5.5% in 1959 and 4.6% 1960 (table 3.2). The declining trend of inflation, placing Israel's rate of price changes in that of the group of industrialized countries, stopped abruptly in late 1960 as the economy moved onto a full-employment level of activity. Price changes leaped to an annual rate of 9% in 1961 and to an even higher rate in 1962, an eventful year in Israel's economic affairs.

This change in the "price climate" may be summarized by comparing the annual average inflation rates in the two subperiods: 4.1% in CPI terms in the five-year interval between 1955 and the end of 1959, during which rates followed a declining pattern, and 7.2% in the seven-year 1961–66 period, in which the general trend was upward. The signals emitted by the pattern of the price level during the declining trend period and in the succeeding interval were evidently more significant than the absolute levels and the gap between the two averages would suggest, due to their effect on the direction of price expectations. The 9% leap in 1961, as the economy crossed the threshold to full employment, followed by a postdevaluation upturn to 10% in 1962 and a sequence of somewhat lower and volatile inflation rates through 1966 (figure 3.2), undoubtedly expressed a change toward an inflationary environment.

Members of the political community, reflecting a typical microeconomic mindset, tended to attribute this significant change in the "price climate" to rising costs. Although this explanation sounded reasonable to the "man in the street," the relevant data indicate that it does not hold water. The obvious candidates to represent cost-shock factors were rising import costs, set by world market dollar prices, and/or a higher (effective) exchange rate, and, finally, higher nominal wages. However, world market dollar prices trended down through 1963. The effective import exchange rate did not rise in 1960–61 by more than it had risen during the declining price-level period of 1956–60. The same statement applies to wages through the third quarter of 1961 (table 3.2). Furthermore, the substantial dampening effect on unit cost of vigorously rising factor productivity during the early 1960s, as in the 1955–60 interval, neutralized the effect of the slowly rising nominal input cost on prices (table 3.3). Even a cautious reading of the data in the table suggests that the substantial dampening effect on unit cost in 1960–61 easily neutralized the impact of the slowly rising nominal input cost on prices. As the price climate took its inflationary turn in 1960–61, cost effects were hardly visible.

A NOTE ON THE TIME PATTERN OF DEMAND FOR MONEY

The 15% annual rate-of-expansion threshold that, according to the BOI Law, was to trigger the publication of a report on the increase in means of payment refers to the supply dimension of money. Its relevance for the management of monetary policy, however, should be perceived and considered with reference to the time pattern of demand for money. Although the BOI Law did not explain the reasoning for the choice of a 15% annual rate as the trigger for "going public"—for publishing a report—the rate was not plucked out of thin air.

Table 3.2. Exchange Rates, Wages, and Prices, 1954-67

| | Exchange Rates | | | Wages | Prices | | | | | | | |
| | Effective | | | | Consumer | | | $[1] | | IL[1] | | |
	Official (1)	Imports (2)	Exports (3)	Nominal (4)	End Year (5)	Ave. (6)	Implicit GNP (7)	Import (8)	Export (9)	Import (10)	Export (11)
Indices, 1954 = 100											
1954	100.0	100.0	100.0	100.0	100.0	100.0	100.0	100.0	100.0	100.0	100.0
1955	100.0	105.9	122.9	110.6	104.8	105.9	110.3	113.7	109.5	137.5	115.6
1957	100.0	128.0	129.7	135.2	115.4	120.0	129.1	101.0	107.4	130.9	114.1
1958	100.0	137.3	130.6	142.4	120.2	124.1	135.2	98.0	93.7	138.2	108.8
1960	100.0	149.2	142.7	156.1	126.3	128.0	142.2	95.1	94.7	138.2	111.6
1961	100.0	153.8	144.7	171.7	137.7	136.6	154.5	93.1	93.7	153.0	108.9
1962	166.7	173.8	142.9	193.0	151.8	149.4	167.1	96.1	97.9	157.8	115.3
1964	166.7	173.8	144.7	237.8	166.4	167.5	191.0	98.0	102.1	164.7	121.0
1965	166.7	177.8	145.7	279.4	178.2	180.4	209.3	100.0	108.4	169.9	136.5
1966	166.7	179.8	154.7	332.7	192.1	194.7	227.5	100.0	106.3	174.2	146.1
1967	194.4	184.3	168.9	334.0	192.5	198.0	231.8				

Annual rates of change (percent)

Year	(1)	(2)	(3)	(4)	(5)	(6)	(7)	(8)	(9)	(10)	(11)
1954	—	—	—	—	7.6	12.2	7.7				
1955	0.0	5.9	0.0	10.6	4.8	5.9	10.3				
1956	0.0	12.2	22.9	13.0	4.6	6.4	10.2	5.9	5.3	18.7	7.6
1958	0.0	7.2	2.3	5.3	4.2	3.4	4.7	-11.2	-1.9	-4.8	-1.3
1959	0.0	5.0	0.7	4.9	1.6	0.8	2.6	-2.9	-9.8	1.9	-3.9
1960	0.0	3.6	6.6	4.5	3.4	2.3	2.8	0.0	-3.3	3.6	-0.8
1961	0.0	3.1	2.5	10.0	9.0	6.7	8.9	-3.0	1.1	0.0	2.6
1962	66.7	13.0	1.4	12.4	10.2	9.4	8.2	-2.1	-1.1	10.7	-2.4
1963	0.0	0.6	-1.3	10.9	5.0	6.6	8.2	1.1	4.5	1.6	5.2
1965	0.0	2.3	0.7	17.5	7.1	7.7	9.6	2.0	4.3	4.4	5.0
1966	0.0	1.1	0.7	19.1	7.8	7.9	8.7	2.0	6.2	3.1	12.7
1967	16.7	2.5	6.2	0.4	0.2	1.7	1.9	0.0	-1.9	2.5	7.1

Annual average rates of change (percent)

Year	(1)	(2)	(3)	(4)	(5)	(6)	(7)	(8)	(9)	(10)	(11)
1955–59	0.0	7.6	6.8	8.4	4.1	4.6	6.6	-0.5	-0.8	5.9	1.9
1960–66	7.6	3.2	1.5	12.1	6.7	6.5	7.4	0.3	1.6	3.5	3.2
1961–66	8.9	3.2	1.4	13.4	7.2	7.2	8.1	0.3	2.5	3.5	3.9

[1] Average import and export prices in dollar and IL terms. Terms refer to the four years 1956–59 only.

Sources: Columns (1), (5), and (6): Central Bureau of Statistics, *Statistical Abstract of Israel*, 1971, Table X-2; columns (2)–(3): Michaely, 1968, Table D-1, p. 88; 1962–67: Amiel (1972), Table 2, p. 27; column (4) *Annual Report* 1960, Table IX, p. 81; Central Bureau of Statistics, *Statistical Abstract of Israel* 1971, Table XI-22, p. 301; column (7), 1954–60: Halevi-Klinov, Table App. 4, p. 236; 1961–67: *Annual Report*, 1999, Table App. II-2, p. 253: column (8)–(9): Central Bureau of Statistics, *Statistical Abstract of Israel* 1978, Table VIII-2, p. 214; columns (10)–(11): Import and export dollar prices from Columns (8) and (9), multiplied by corresponding entries of effective import and export exchange rates in Columns (2) and (3).

Table 3.3. Real Exchange Rates and Real Wages, 1954–67

	Exchange Rates[1]						
	Effective						
	Official	Imports	Exports	Terms of Trade	Wages[2]	Unit Cost[3]	Factor Productivity
	(1)	(2)	(3)	(4)	(5)	(6)	(7)
Indices, 1954 = 100							
1954	100.0	100.0	100.0	100.0	100.0	100.0	100.0
1960	70.3	104.9	100.3	95.7	121.9	98.7	126.1
1961	64.7	99.6	93.7	100.0	125.7	94.9	131.5
1966	76.0	82.0	70.5	108.6	170.8	106.4	158.6
1967	87.0	82.5	75.6	106.5	168.6	90.4	164.3
Annual average rates of change (percent)							
1955–60	−5.7	0.8	0.1	−0.7	3.4	−0.2	3.9
1955–61	−6.0	−0.1	−0.9	0.0	3.3	−0.7	3.8
1961–66	1.1	−3.5	−4.9	1.8	4.9	1.1	2.6

[1]Real exchange rates: nominal rates deflated by GNP prices.
[2]Real wages: nominal rates deflated by consumer prices.
[3]The series represents Gaathon estimates for the ratios of nominal wages and (nominal) product per employee (*Annual Report* 1964, Table B-10, p. 27) as a proxy for the pattern of unit cost. Similar estimates for 1965–67 are based on Central Bureau of Statistics, *Statistical Abstract of Israel.*
Sources: Columns (1)–(3) and (5): Table 3.2; column (4) Central Bureau of Statistics, *Statistical Abstract of Israel* 1978, Table VIII-2, p. 214; column (6): *Annual Report* 1964, Table B-10, p. 27; 1965–67: nominal average product of labor according to GNP, employment and wage series in Central Bureau of Statistics, *Statistical Abstract of Israel* 1971, Table VI-1, pp. 146–147; and Table XI-22, p. 301; column (7), 1954–60: Gaathon (1971), App. 3, Table A-6; 1964–67: *Annual Report* 1966, Table B-7, and *Annual Report* 1968, Table B-5.

For better or for worse, the authors of this section of the law implicitly chose this rate in view of the time pattern of demand for means of payment, associated first and foremost with the trend of real income that a rapid growth process, such as the one expected, would set in motion. Accordingly, the actual growth performance that ensued—9%–10% per annum, more or less, between 1954 and 1973—was not out of line with the implied expectations. Thus, the income-driven rising demand for money paved the way to noninflationary rapid expansion of the money supply, constrained of course by the income elasticity of demand for money.

A set of BOI studies written about this feature suggests that unitary elasticity of demand is, for our purposes, a reasonable approximation of the actual income elasticity of demand for money in Israel during the two decades ending with the Yom Kippur War (Offenbacher, 1985). During that period, the economy was also subjected to the sort of monetization process that is characteristic of developing economies. In the Israeli case, it was driven by the lengthy process of absorbing mass immigration and the growth of the Arab sector of the economy, which was subjected to a major monetization process occasioned by its rapidly rising dependence on trade and markets. Finally, the rather strong deceleration of inflation that commenced in 1953 had a positive effect on demand for money by lowering inflation expectations. The last-mentioned effect, however, changed direction in 1960 as inflation took off again. Overall, this suggests a time pattern of rising demand for real balances—money—at an annual average rate of 11%–13% during the two decades ending in 1973.

THE EMERGENCE OF MONETARY POLICY

A bird's-eye view of the pattern of the major monetary aggregates in the BOI's first decade or so would suggest a clear break in the slope of the curves that describe the evolution of these variables. The slopes of M_1 and the monetary base were significantly steeper in 1960–65 than in the preceding 1957–59 period. Another break occurred in 1965–66, when the rate of increase slowed severely (figure 3.3). The corresponding annual average expansion rates of the monetary base and of M_1 underline the difference in monetary momentum between the two distinct subperiods, 1954–59 and 1960–65. The annual expansion rates of the monetary base and M_1 climbed significantly, from about 13% and nearly 16%, respectively, in the 1955–59 interval to 19% and 18% in the succeeding six years, 1960–65, even though war finance did not play a role at the time (table 3.4).[1] Thus, despite the war-finance effect in 1956, the expansion rate of M_1 at first—in the second half of the 1950s—was not significantly out of line with the 10% growth rate of GNP. However, it definitely strayed beyond the GNP growth rate in the first half of the 1960s. Note also the change of tack in the monetary aggregates. In the first period, the money supply grew much faster than the monetary base; in the second period, its rate of expansion was somewhat slower than that of its counterpart. The watershed marks the emergence of monetary policy.

The abrupt change in the rising trend of these two monetary aggregates in 1960, when both the monetary base and M_1 ballooned by more than 20%, was perceived at the time as an ominous deviation from the norm (Barkai and Michaely, 1963, pp. 30–31). Since the economy had clearly attained full

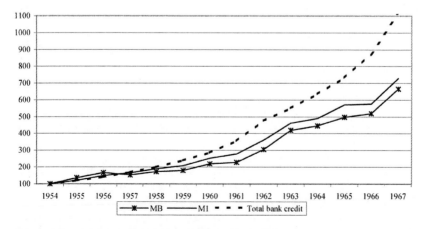

Figure 3.3. Monetary Aggregates, 1954–67 (1954 = 100)

Table 3.4. Monetary Aggregates, 1954–67[1]

	Monetary Base (1)	M$_1$ (2)	M$_2$ (3)	Outstanding Credit Balances	
				Banks[2] (4)	Total[3] (5)
Indices, 1954 = 100					
1954	100.0	100.0	100.0	100.0	100.0
1960	219.4	252.6	248.6	286.3	286.4
1961	228.3	278.1	268.1	355.3	356.5
1966	519.6	576.1	548.1	685.6	877.1
1967	665.9	728.4	777.2	919.3	1115.1
Annual rates of change (percent)					
1955	35.9	20.4	22.7	10.2	19.6
1956	22.6	23.3	20.2	15.6	17.8
1957	−8.1	11.4	11.7	21.0	20.3
1958	12.5	14.5	13.4	18.7	18.0
1959	4.3	10.0	9.5	24.0	20.1
1960	22.2	21.3	21.6	26.3	19.2
1961	4.1	10.1	7.8	24.1	24.5
1962	33.5	29.7	25.5	29.4	33.8
1963	37.5	28.1	25.6	19.5	15.8
1964	6.3	6.1	5.3	−10.4	15.3
1965	11.8	16.5	15.4	12.5	15.3
1966	4.4	0.9	6.7	23.7	19.5
1967	28.2	26.4	41.8	34.1	27.1
Avg.:1955–59	13.4	15.9	15.5	17.9	19.2
S.D.:1955–59	16.9	5.7	5.7	5.3	1.2
Avg.:1960–65	19.2	18.6	16.9	16.9	20.6
S.D.:1960–65	14.2	9.5	8.9	14.6	7.4
Avg.:1960–66	17.1	16.1	15.4	17.9	20.5
S.D.:1960–66	14.1	11.0	8.9	13.6	6.7

[1] End-of-year balances.
[2] Total credit accommodated by the commercial banking system, including the total outstanding balance of directed credit, part of which was BOI's quota—identified as "discounts" on the balance sheet of the central bank.
[3] Total credit available to customers: total credit from the commercial banking system (Column 4) plus government credit intermediated by banks, financed by special "government deposits for loans" with the banks.
Sources: Columns (1)–(3): Sanbar-Bronfeld, Table 3, p. 7, Table 4, p. 9, Table 6, p. 222; p. 9. See also *Annual Report* 1964, Tables XV-2 and XV-6, *Annual Report* 1967, Tables XV-3 and XV-7, and *Annual Report*, 1962, Table XIV-3; columns (4)–(5): *Annual Report*, 1962, Table XIV-13, *Annual Report* 1964, Table XV-9, and *Annual Report* 1967, Table XV-10.

employment in the first quarter of the 1960s, this attitude was fully warranted. After all, the BOI had been formally in charge of the monetary sector for six years and should have overcome its teething pains by then. This reading of the omens intimated by the data on monetary aggregates and prices by the third quarter of 1960 resulted in a call for action.

The quest for monetary policy began at once in what may be described as the BOI's running-in period, that is, the central bank's very first quarter of operation. On March 30, 1955, the Governor of the BOI had no choice but to publish his first *Report on the Increase of the Means of Payment* under Section 35 of the Law, since means of payment had grown by more than 15% (18.6%) in the year ending on January 31, 1955. Since the bank had been up and running in only the last two months of the twelve, the aberrant expansion of liquidity did not really take place on the BOI's watch. However, on November 15, 1955, the bank had to publish another means-of-payment report, its second within its very first year of operation. At issue this time was a six-month interval only, ending on July 31 of that year. During this very brief period, the money supply increased by 17.3%, implying an annual average expansion rate of 37.6% if this rate were to persist for the next six months.[2] The two reports amounted to more than a preamble to monetary policy; such reports—five in number, not counting the first—were effectively the only policy instrument that the central bank wielded through 1960. The decline of inflation rates to low single-digit levels through 1959, within the range of inflation in industrialized countries, offers at least a partial explanation of BOI's six-year delay in the attempt to apply the conventional set of instruments that the law placed at its disposal.

A Call for Action: Monetary Developments in 1960–61

It was the change in the price climate, already evident by October 1960, that called for action. By the third quarter at the latest, the central bank knew that M_1 had been expanding since January at an annual pace that ultimately came to 21%. With unemployment falling below 4% despite a new wave of immigration, these data clearly suggested that the rapidly growing economy was operating either at or not far from full employment. Thus, in the November 1960 *Report of the Governor on the Increase of the Means of Payment*—the seventh in less than seven years since the inauguration of the central bank—the first recommendation refers to "restricting the rate of expansion of bank credit . . . in order to prevent the expansion of means of payment at a rate higher than GNP growth."[3]

In the last section of the recommendations, the BOI for the first time stated its first and second preferences among the instruments of monetary policy: "If the repeal of the law that establishes a maximum interest rate is unacceptable, liquidity ratios should be used as the instrument of an active policy to control the volume of credit" (*Report of the Governor on the Increase of the Means of Payment*, 1960, pp. 21–28). In the August 1957 means-of-payment report, there had already been a reference to liquidity ratios. This, however, referred to the "simplification" and "unification" of the minimum liquidity requirements that had been imposed haphazardly starting in 1951, before the Bank of Israel came into being. This move, implemented in January 1958, set the legal minimum liquidity ratio at 58% of the balance of outstanding deposits. Banking institutions, however, were given special dispensation to lower the ratio by up to 20 percentage points for the accommodation of "directed credit," at interest rates significantly lower than market rates, to "priority" sectors and borrowers that the government specified. Thus, the "net" minimum liquidity ratios were set at 38% of "deposits for which domestic-currency liquidity was required." Concurrently, however, rather stiff penalties for breaching the liquidity rules were imposed.[4]

Inspection of the series of the effective ratios that the banking system maintained in 1955–1960 indicates that this cleaning of the stables had no monetary implications (table 3.5). Thus, "the new liquidity requirements on deposits denominated in Israeli currency did not mean an effective increase in the average liquidity ratios. They meant only a unification of the ratios that were applicable at different banking institutions" (Sanbar and Bronfeld, 1973, p. 218).[5] The two liquidity series in table 3.6—the official effective rate and the corresponding estimate that applied the legally specified liquid assets to current-account balances only—show clearly that liquidity ratios were not used as an instrument of policy between 1958 and 1960. Both series declined through 1959 and recovered in 1960 but to a lower level than in 1958. Accordingly, the supply of money expanded by 12% on annual average in 1958–59, slightly outpacing the increases in GNP and resources available for domestic use. The 21% expansion of M_1 in 1960 was plainly aberrant in terms of the annual rates in the 1957–59 period (table 3.4). These developments prompted the BOI in late 1960 to take the explicit initiative of plunging into the cold waters of active monetary policy.

The moderate expansion of M_1 between 1957 and 1959 reflects an outstandingly low average growth rate of the monetary base and a rising positive multiplier effect. The money multiplier was 1.47 in 1957 and 1.60 by 1960. The entries in table 3.6, however, indicate that this did not reflect a change in BOI policy on liquidity ratios. Most of the expansionary rise of the multiplier traced to the internal injection generated by the public's decision to reduce its currency/deposit ratio significantly, from 0.7 in 1957 to 0.54 in 1960.

The BOI's Response: Money-Multiplier Control

The most interesting feature in this context is that the money multiplier in 1960, when M_1 grew by 21%, was the same as in 1959, when M_1 expanded by only 10%. The slight tightening that the banking system implemented, expressed in a 1.6 percentage point increase in its effective liquidity ratio even though the formal requirement had yet not been changed, merely canceled out the expansionary effect of the internal injection that was manifested in the currency deposit ratio (table 3.6). The stability of the multiplier in 1960 indicates that the large expansion of the money supply that year traced entirely to its second determinant, the monetary base, which expanded by 22%.

These developments underlay the initiative, stated explicitly in the Bank of Israel's means-of-payment report in November 1960, to move into the fray headfirst by taking restrictive monetary action. The statement, reflecting the BOI's groping for an effective instrument to take control of monetary developments, spelled out the alternative available to the central bank: it would be the money multiplier variable that the BOI would attempt to manipulate in its effort to contain the rate of monetary expansion. To bring this about, the

Table 3.5. Banking System Aggregates

| | Free | | Bank Credit | | | | PAZAK + TAMAM Deposits[5] | |
	Bank Resources[1] (1)	Bill Brokerage[2] (2)	Total[3] (3) = (1)+(2)	Directed Credit[4] (4)	Grand Total (5) = (3) + (4)	Demand Deposits (6)	IL - Index (7)	$ (millions) (8)
Indices, 1954 = 100								
1954	100.0	—	100.0	—	100.0	100.0	—	—
1960	197.5	100.0	221.6	244.2	291.9	287.6	10375.0	69.4
1961	230.9	212.5	293.0	280.8	370.0	309.6	16891.7	112.6
1966	428.4	1823.2	1048.2	905.8	1276.3	622.4	84791.2	339.7
Annual rates of change (percent)								
1955–59	7.9	—	7.9	16.0	14.8	15.0	—	—
1955–60	12.0	—	14.2	25.0	19.7	19.3	—	—
1960–66	15.3	62.2	31.1	25.9	25.2	15.2	—	—

[1]The series of "free credit" from bank resources was derived by subtracting the series of directed credit accommodated by commercial banks from the series of total credit balances. The directed-credit series was derived from *Annual Report* 1959 Table XIV-11, *Annual Report* 1960 Table XIV-14, and similar tables in each *Annual Report* during the 1960s.

[2]The entries for bill brokerage were derived from Sanbar-Bronfeld series. The first entry available refers to 1960; therefore, the rate of change refers to 1961–66.

[3]The totals for free credit include also the bill-brokerage balances as derived from the Sanbar series.

[4]The directed-credit series includes the Bank of Israel component and the much larger component of accommodation by commercial banks. The entries for the Bank of Israel component are based on *Annual Report* 1960, Table XIV-13, and similar tables in other *Annual Reports*.

[5]The IL index of PAZAK-TAMAM deposits also reflects change in nominal exchange rates in the aftermath of devaluations. The rates of change in the IL and dollar value of deposits refer to 1956–60.

Sources: Columns (1) and (3): for 1954–60, *Annual Report* 1960, Table XIV-13, Column (4). 1960–66: Columns (1), (2), (4), and (5), Sanbar-Bronfeld (1973), Table 6, p. 222. Column (6): *Annual Report* 1958, Table XIII-1, *Annual Report* 1964 XV-2, *Annual Report* 1967 Table XV-3. Columns (7) and (8): Sanbar-Bronfeld (1973), Tables 4 and 9.

Table 3.6. Liquidity Ratios, Money Multiplier, and Credit Ratios

| | Liquidity Ratios (percent) | | | | Currency Deposit Ratio[3] (percent) | Money Multiplier[4] | Credit Ratios (percent) | | |
| | Legal | | Effective | Calculated[2] | | | Directed[5] Credit | Bill Brokerage[6] Credit | Gov.[7] Credit |
	Formal (1)	Net[1] (2)	(3)	(4)	(5)	(6)	(7)	(8)	(9)
1954	—	—	—	—	74.5	—	—	—	22.4
1955	—	—	39.6	47.0	71.2	1.45	—	—	28.5
1956	—	—	40.9	46.2	76.7	1.44	30.6	—	29.8
1957	—	—	40.9	45.6	69.8	1.47	34.4	—	29.4
1958	58.0	38.0	38.8	43.5	63.1	1.53	32.7	—	29.0
1959	58.0	38.0	36.5	40.4	58.2	1.60	33.2	—	26.6
1960	58.0	38.0	38.1	42.5	53.8	1.60	32.3	9.6	22.1
1961	62.0	40.0	34.2	37.9	53.8	1.68	29.3	16.2	22.0
1962	63.5	41.5	39.4	42.2	50.8	1.62	33.6	25.9	25.1
1963	69.0	47.0	46.6	49.1	49.9	1.51	34.6	31.7	22.8
1964	69.0	47.0	45.4	45.2	53.1	1.56	34.2	36.3	21.0
1965	68.0	44.0	47.3	48.9	62.6	1.46	35.1	38.9	19.9
1966	65.0	40.0	44.5	45.6	60.6	1.51	34.4	40.3	17.3

[1]The difference between the formal and net legal minimum liquidity ratios represents the "recognized" maximum allowance from legal liquidity requirements for the granting of directed credit to customers eligible therefor.

[2]Ratio of actual reserve balances to demand deposits.

[3]The currency deposit ratios were derived from series of currency and means of payment, *Annual Report* 1960, Table XIV-3 and similar tables in previous and subsequent *Annual Reports*.

[4]The money multiplier was calculated from the well-known expression $(1 + cu)/(re + cu)$, where cu and re are currency deposit and liquidity ratio (of Column (4)). The calculated liquidity ratios were used to derive the money-multiplier series.

[5]Ratio of outstanding directed credit balance to grand total outstanding credit balance of the commercial banks (at end of year). The grand total commercial bank credit does not include the bill-brokerage component of commercial bank credit intermediation, which first appeared in 1960.

[6]The ratio of the bill-brokerage balance to the grand total of commercial bank credit.

[7]The ratio of the government development budget credit accommodation intermediated by commercial banks to the grand total of commercial bank credit.

Sources: Columns (1)–(3): Sanbar-Bronfeld (1973), Table 5; column (5): *Annual Report* 1964, Table XV-2, Table XV-3; columns (7) and (9): *Annual Report* 1960, Table XIV-13; and similar tables in subsequent *Annual Reports*; column (8): Sanbar-Bronfeld (1973), Table 6.

central bank would invoke the legal minimum liquidity ratio and back it by imposing stiff penalty charges for violations.

The aforementioned passage in the "Recommendations" section of the report also suggests that the choice of this instrument—or at least the exclusive reliance on it—was not the BOI's first preference. The reference to the "political constraint" that thwarted the repeal of the Usury Law, which capped legal interest rates at 11%, implied that at the current (annualized) inflation rate, which surpassed the ceiling by the fourth quarter of 1960, any attempt by the central bank to control the monetary base was practically off-limits.

The suggested policy move that the bank announced in November 1960 was not implemented until five months later, at the end of the first quarter of 1961. The formal liquidity ratio was hiked by 4 percentage points to 62% but the maximum dispensation for directed credit to privileged sectors was raised by 2 percentage points, to 22%. This yielded a minimum net liquidity ratio of 40%, instead of 38%, for banks that used their own full quota of directed credit. The tightening move in March 1961, which allowed the commercial banking system to comply with the higher required minimum reserve ratios gradually, did not slow the expansion of total credit accommodated to commercial bank customers; this parameter climbed at annual rates of 24.5% in 1961 and 34% in 1962, the fastest rates since 1955 (table 3.4). This led to a second tightening move of the same kind at the end of October 1961. Formal liquidity ratios were raised again by another 1.5 percentage points, to 63.5%, yielding a 41.5% net minimum liquidity ratio for banks that used up the full directed-credit quota.

Inspection of the effective liquidity ratios (table 3.6) shows that those reflecting the behavior of the banking system and determining the value of the money multiplier moved significantly downward in 1961, instead of upward as required by the stated interim target of monetary policy. The relevant series indicates that neither of the measures implemented in 1961 to raise the effective liquidity ratios of the banking system attained its goal by year's end. In fact, whether we refer to the BOI's official estimate—the "effective ratio" representing the entire set of deposits for which banks were legally required to maintain liquid reserves, or to the alternative "calculated" estimate, which attributes total bank reserves to demand deposits only, liquidity ratios declined significantly during that crucial (predevaluation) year. Instead of rising to the required 40% level, they slipped from 38%, the de jure ratio in 1960, to an effective ratio of only 34% at the end of 1961. It took the banking system until the end of 1963 to reach the ratio set in March 1961—a lag of about twenty months. The even higher ratio set in November 1961, 41.5%, was also attained at a two-year lag.

Lags are unavoidable in physical contexts and even more so in economic linkages. The authorities acknowledged this by giving the banks a period of time to adjust their supply of credit to the new, tighter liquidity requirements. They did so by the specifying a "recognized deficit" of required reserves that was set to fall to zero by a stipulated date. Accordingly, penalty rates for missing the liquidity-ratio target were charged only for reserve shortages exceeding the "recognized deficits" in the respective periods of time. However, in the full-employment context of the early 1960s and the corresponding brisk demand for credit, banks—which, on the whole, kept their liquidity ratios within the limit prescribed by the 1958 legal floor until 1960 (Sanbar and Bronfeld, 1973, p. 220)—did not respond rapidly to the attempt to stanch the rate of monetary expansion, preferring instead to accommodate the vigorous demand for bank credit. They manifested this preference, among other things, by doubling the volume of "bill brokerage credit" in 1961 even though this subjected them to penalty charges.[6] Accordingly, "free" (nondirected) commercial bank credit expanded at an annual rate of 32%. This strong demand was clearly affected by inflation expectations that had been generated by the leap of inflation to about 9%, as had been demonstrated by the price data of June 1961 at the latest, and by corresponding expectations of a forthcoming and long-delayed official devaluation (*Annual Report*, 1961, pp. 249–50).[7]

Thus, even though the banks' liquidity ratios surpassed the legal floor in the first quarter of 1961, they plunged below it by the end of the year, only partly due to the restrictive policy measures adopted in March. This apparently reflected the profit consideration, since the banks took this route even though "the reserve shortage of the banking system, for which they had to pay a penalty rate of 10%, climbed to an unprecedented scope" (*Annual Report*, 1961, p. 258). Amid the macroeconomic exuberance of the time, the ballooning of this "nonrecognized" deficit by a factor of almost three in the third quarter of the year was a clear omen that the banking system could not and did not try to disregard.

The attempt at monetary restraint that the central bank had instigated in early 1961, which was tightened by the second twist of the minimum liquidity ratio in October of that year and by the June directive expanding the list of liabilities subject to the liquid-reserves requirements, was not immediately effective. This meant that the monetary environment in the first quarter of 1962 had not been properly prepared for the major macroeconomic policy move that was about to be taken, a major devaluation that inevitably involved a push on the monetary accelerator. The BOI's steps during that crucial year were indeed in line with the predilection that it had expressed in the November 1960 means-of-payment report. However, the resulting reduction of the value of the multiplier, finally attained in 1962, was too little and too late. The expansion rate of M_1 in 1962, almost 30%, proves the point. This was obviously also due to the corresponding and even higher expansion rate of the monetary base in the wake of the major nominal devaluation implemented that year.

STRUCTURAL BACKGROUND OF THE 1962 DEVALUATION

The immediate and main purpose of the major 67% formal devaluation of the Israel pound in early February 1962 was the correction of the balance-of-payments current account. In view of the size and the rapidly rising trend of the import surplus (table 3.1) to 19%–20% of GNP in 1960 and 1961 (Halevi and Klinov, 1968, p. 233), it was perceived as unsustainable in the long run. The vigorous inflow of unilateral transfers from abroad did finance 80%–90% of the import surplus; the rest was covered by the net capital inflow, which had also allowed a fivefold increase in the (dollar-denominated) foreign reserves between 1956 and 1961 (table 3.7). However, a significant portion of the

Table 3.7. Patterns of Selected Bank of Israel Asset and Liability Balances, 1954–67

	Foreign Reserves[1]		Net Government Liabilities (3)	Discounts[2] (4)	Monetary Base[3] (5)	Foreign Reserves (6)	Government Liabilities (7)	Tradeable Government Securities (8)	Discounts (9)	Monetary Base (10)	MAKAM[4] (11)
	IL (1)	Dollar (2)									
Indices, 1954 = 100						*Ratios to totals of balance sheet (percent)*					
1954	100.0	100.0	100.0		100.0	26.5	71.1	0.0	0.0	94.7	
1955	172.4	172.4	117.0	100.0	135.9	29.8	62.1	0.0	4.9	72.4	
1956	178.1	178.0	176.0	224.0	166.6	19.2	69.8	1.1	7.3	71.5	
1957	171.3	171.3	201.9	329.1	153.1	15.9	69.2	0.4	9.9	60.1	
1958	317.3	318.2	214.0	263.0	172.2	28.9	61.6	0.2	7.4	57.5	
1959	406.3	406.3	238.5	214.0	179.4	31.7	58.7	0.1	5.3	58.7	
1960	723.1	723.1	263.1	363.4	219.4	44.9	47.2	0.0	6.8	67.7	
1961	920.3	920.3	232.0	429.7	228.3	51.1	41.2	0.0	6.9	60.7	
1962	2168.9	1301.7	−27.7	686.5	304.8	75.5	17.6	0.0	6.4	47.2	
1963	2615.7	1569.9	34.9	546.2	419.2	74.2	19.1	0.0	4.1	52.0	
1964	2777.5	1667.1	107.0	736.9	445.4	74.0	18.1	0.0	5.2	50.2	
1965	3348.0	2009.4	118.6	888.1	497.8	80.2	12.1	0.0	5.7	51.8	
1966	3219.4	2049.0	201.1	1666.9	519.6	75.3	12.4	0.5	10.4	52.3	20.5
1967	4391.7	2259.4	269.1	2606.3	665.9	65.0	23.3	0.6	10.4	43.3	22.4

[1]The difference in the corresponding entries in the index number series between IL and dollar terms after 1962 reflects the exchange-rate changes made in 1962 and 1967.
[2]"Discounts" represents the Bank of Israel's directed-credit accommodation, implemented by discounting a predetermined quota of promissory notes submitted by commercial banks.
[3]The "narrow" monetary base.
[4]Ratio of the value of a short-term government bond (MAKAM) to the monetary base.
Sources: Annual Report 1964, Table XXI-1, and corresponding tables in the last chapter of the Annual Reports that summarize the corresponding end-of-year balance sheets.

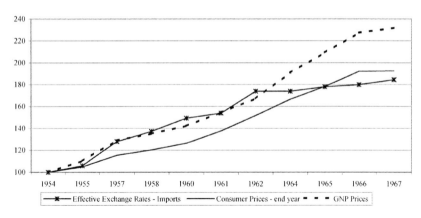

Figure 3.4. Prices and Exchange Rates, 1954–67 (1954 = 100)

unilateral receipts—reparation payments from Germany and the much weaker flow of U.S. government aid, which accounted for about 30% of the inflow in 1961—were expected to disappear by the mid-1960s.

This long-term forecast of the expected pattern of the balance of payments was reinforced by immediate microeconomic considerations related to relative prices and their effect on the emerging industrial structure of the rapidly growing economy. One of the main features of this price structure was emphasized by the widening gap between the formal exchange rate, which had remained at its 1954 level, and the effective exchange rates on foreign trade—exports and imports of goods and services. By 1961, the average effective import exchange rate surpassed the 1954 level by about 54% while the effective export rate had risen by 45% (table 3.2, figures 3.4 and 3.5). The difference between the two effective rates and the formal rate reflected, of course, a well-known feature of a multiple-exchange-rate system. The spreads between the rates applied to trade and those applied to transactions on capital and unilateral receipts account of the balance of payments inevitably created loopholes that encouraged the formation

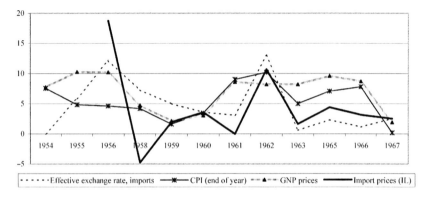

Figure 3.5. Exchange Rates and Prices, Annual Rates of Change (percent), 1954–67

of black (exchange) markets. The gap between the effective exchange rates on imports and on exports, 6% in 1961, was an expression of the entrenched preference of industries that manufactured import substitutes, reflecting the well-known Prebish growth strategy that the major South American economies had been adopting since the 1950s. The establishment of several automobile assembly plants during those years was a clear-cut indicator of this effect on Israel's emerging industrial structure.

The effective exchange-rate series represent estimates of weighted averages. In fact, however, the price structure, saddled with a labyrinth of duties, import quotas, and a host of devices that strove to establish a preference for this or that line of activity, created a maze that the business vernacular of the time described as "a thousand exchange rates." This generated more and more loopholes that created openings for abuse and had an inevitable long-term impact on the industrial structure.

The loss of economic bearings that occurred amid the repetitive raising of charges, duties, allowances, and similar devices pushed the Ministry of Finance and the central bank, both of which were in charge of macroeconomic policy, to the brink. By the third quarter of 1961, with the election campaign already out of the way, the idea of trying to recalibrate the system by applying one rate to all foreign exchange transactions, as the IMF had been suggesting unofficially for several years, gathered momentum. The long-term goal of such a move was to restructure the relative price setup and, among other things, tilt it in favor of tradables. The obvious technique to use in attaining this target was a formal devaluation of the Israel pound (IL) involving all transactions on the trade, unilateral, and capital accounts of the balance of payments. Indeed, the enormous gap that had evolved by 1961 between the zero rate of change in the official exchange rate, at which funds transferred on unilateral and capital account were converted into Israeli currency, and the rate of change in the domestic price level—a spread that in terms of GNP prices was more than 50% higher in 1961 than in 1954—finally convinced a dominant section of the political community that the monetary authority's argument was correctly reasoned. The politicians, too, acknowledged the unsustainability of a setup that imposed an implicit exchange-rate tax of more than 50% on households that transferred funds deriving from unilateral receipts over the general-government inflow of such funds, and on business and general-government transfers of funds on capital account.[8]

As long as the dominant components of the inflow of funds on unilateral and capital accounts were being received by general-government entities—for example, German reparations, Jewish fundraising, and proceeds of Israel Bonds—the widening implicit tax between say, the rate of change in the GNP price deflator and the formal exchange rate, was hidden in the general-government accounts. By 1960 and 1961, however, the inflow of *personal* restitution payments from Germany had climbed to about 33% of the total inflow on the unilateral payments account and immigrant transfers added another 11%. To mitigate the implicit tax effect on these two groups of households and, thereby, to ensure the maintenance of the inflow, recipients of personal restitution payments were granted special privileges that gave them a higher effective exchange rate than the formal one for a significant fraction of the transferred funds. Similar devices were applied to immigrant transfers, for example, allowing the newly landed to deposit one-third of their annual income from foreign transfers in a foreign-currency account and another fraction in a forex-indexed deposit.[9] Thus, by the end of 1961, the value of these deposits, denominated in foreign currency or indexed to the formal exchange rate that had been set back in 1954, had climbed to nearly 35% of the total outstanding volume of the monetary base. This had immediate implications, of course, since a substantial official devaluation would inflate that volume proportionately in IL terms. Thus, it was obvious to all that the expected capital gain from converting even a fraction of these deposits, and from the proportional increase in the value of the current inflow of these funds into Israeli currency, would inflate the monetary base considerably in one stroke. This consideration alone suggested a devaluation sooner rather than later.

This was clearly the mood and the declared attitude at both the Bank of Israel and the Ministry of Finance. The Ministry of Industry and Trade, however, was of a different mind. Pinhas Sapir, the minister and one of Israel's most dominant political figures, flatly opposed devaluation in the belief that it would hamper the industrialization drive that he had been orchestrating for almost a decade. Thus, he expressed his vehement objection to the idea and absented himself from the government meeting at which the motion to devalue the currency was to be resolved. Just the same, on the afternoon of Friday, February 9, 1962, the government passed the resolution to move the formal exchange rate from IL 1.80 to the dollar to IL 3.00.

This substantial change reflected the facts of life. By that quarter, the effective exchange rates on imports and exports were already 54% and 44% higher, respectively, than the nominal exchange rate that had been set in 1954. The rate of devaluation chosen, which would hike the relative prices of tradables and, thereby, improve the trade balance, allowed only a small upward change in the effective rate on trade and services account—the immediate raison d'etre of the whole exercise. However, monetary considerations related to the volume of deposits denominated in or indexed to foreign currency, which at the new nominal exchange rate would balloon instantly to 56% of the outstanding monetary base, coupled with the rapidly growing inflow of reparation payments, suggested moderation. A steeper devaluation might have inflated the supply of money even more. Thus, since any devaluation is expansionary by nature, both in the goods and services markets and in the monetary dimension of the economy, the small margin offered by the chosen exchange rate for a higher relative price of tradables plainly required strict application of the standing orders relating to such an occasion on the monetary front. These orders, of course, prescribed swimming against the current, that is, the restriction of monetary expansion.

MONETARY POLICY IN A STRAITJACKET

Therefore, a highly restrictive monetary policy was a sine qua non for success, since a major nominal devaluation would be implemented in a hostile environment for such a move. The economy was operating at if not beyond the frontier of its capacity. An unemployment rate of 3.6%–3.7% in an economy in which employment was growing at a 6.4% annual pace, as was the case in 1961 and 1962, underscores this reading of the situation (table 3.1). Furthermore, inflation expectations, which rise immediately in the wake of a major devaluation, were undoubtedly augmented by the 9% inflation rate in 1961, a highly unfavorable development on the eve of such a move.[10] Yet when the final decision to go ahead was made, information about both parameters—the rate of capacity utilization and the inflation expectations generated by economic events in 1960–61—was available to the central bank and the Ministry of Finance. The data cried out for highly restrictive macroeconomic policy measures on both the monetary and the fiscal fronts.

The practical steps taken by the Bank of Israel in 1961—raising the minimum reserve ratio of the banking system twice (in March and November) and adding in June another type of deposit to the list requiring the backing of liquid assets—were the first restrictive measures that the BOI had ever adopted at its own initiative. They were not successful in 1961, as noted; the effective liquidity ratio actually declined, thus amplifying the expansionary force of the multiplier, which rose from 1.60 to 1.68 (table 3.6). This immediate and frustrating outcome of the adopted measures reflected the availability of excess reserves in the asset portfolios of the commercial banking system and a built-in lag in the application of the higher required liquidity ratio, amidst vigorous demand for bank credit driven by accelerating inflation. With the legal interest rate capped at 11% while inflation ran at 9% and 10% in 1961 and 1962, borrowers had an all-out incentive to acquire bank credit at the going rates. Be this as it may, the law would have frustrated any attempt by the BOI to dry up the excess reserves of the banking system by moving forcefully on the selling side in the short-term capital market, if the central bank had a bond portfolio that would have allowed such a move. With almost no negotiable securities in its portfolio, however (table 3.7), and with the Ministry of Finance disinclined to approve the issue of the BOI's own debentures, the central bank found that its ability to maintain a restrictive selling position in the open market was sterilized ab initio.

The Bank of Israel *Annual Report* for 1961, published in May 1962, that is, after the February devaluation, refers to this state of affairs explicitly although not in headline terms: "The Bank of Israel actually has only one effective instrument for the implementation of monetary control: changes in [compulsory] liquidity ratios. . . .The Interest Law, however, reduces the option of using the interest rate as an instrument affecting the volume of credit, and the limited scope of the money market makes the absorption of purchasing power by selling securities less feasible. . . . It turns out that this instrument, although available to the bank, is not always sufficiently flexible. Since the implementation of changes in liquidity ratio entails a lengthy legal procedure, we were unable to issue the directive requiring higher liquidity ratios until the end of March 1961" (*Annual Report* 1961, p. 226).

This captures in a nutshell the dilemma that the central bank faced when it considered applying a tight monetary policy. It also describes the straitjacket within which monetary policy had to be implemented not only in the crucial 1961–63 interval but also for more than two decades down the road. The report suggests that an open-market policy was off-limits and that the restrictive move in March 1961 should have been made earlier. Had this been done, the monetary environment would have been in better shape to deal with the February 1962 devaluation. Furthermore, the reference to the length of the "legal procedure" was a tongue-in-cheek allusion to the requisite "consent" of the BOI Advisory Committee—the membership of which included representatives of farming and manufacturing interests and the chairs of the leading commercial banks—in the first round, followed by a second-round government approval of any change in the compulsory minimum liquidity ratio.

These phases could have been wound up in a negligible period of time if political assent had been forthcoming. It is evident that the latter phase, which in this case and later on was slow in coming, reduced flexibility in terms of the proper timing and the ability of the central bank to make a forceful (restrictive) move on the monetary front by applying the liquidity-ratio instrument and/or by wielding the open-market sales instrument in order to contain the expansion of the monetary base.

The rising momentum of monetary expansion in 1960–65 shows up clearly in the pattern of interest rates in the so-called "bill-brokerage market," where credit was "free" (not controlled).[11] The Manzli series of interest rates (table 3.8) show that rates in the bill-brokerage market declined from 17.7% in 1959 to 13.7% in 1962 even as inflation rose from 2.6% to 8.2% in terms of the GDP deflator and stayed in the 8%–9% range through 1966. Although interest rates in this market rose again to 14.5%–16.2% in 1964–65, they remained much lower than the nominal rates in 1957–59, when inflation rates were below 5% and declining.

A similar time pattern emerges in average commercial bank rates for "free" credit, which declined from 9.5% in the late 1950s and 1960 to 8.5%–8.8% through 1966. Rates on directed-credit balances and "government-financed credit" mediated by commercial banks were significantly lower, at 5%–6%, through 1966. Since these two tranches accounted for about 50% of total lending to businesses and households, the average real rate of interest on the total credit balance in 1960–65 did not exceed 1%–2%. Wherever firms and households obtained more than, say, 60% of their total credit balance through subsidized facilities, the real rates were actually negative.

The declining cost-of-credit series offers highly relevant insights on comings and goings in the money and bank-credit markets in 1960–65. Even though the standing orders for monetary policy called for a tightening in these markets after the price level jumped by 9% in 1961, and even more so in view of the major nominal devaluation early in 1962, the interest-rate series suggest that rates in 1962 moved in the opposite direction. This, of course, reflected the avalanche of monetary liquidity. While in the wake of the 10% growth rate in 1960–65 the demand for money expanded correspondingly—at, say, this rate plus the possibility of an extra 1%–2% per year due to the monetization process—the money supply burgeoned at almost twice this pace, at an average annual rate of 19% and 18% for the monetary base and M_1, respectively. These rates were also significantly higher than those in the 1955–59 period—13% and nearly 16% for the monetary base and M_1, respectively.

Table 3.8. Selected Interest Rates, 1955–73 (percent)

	Free Credit[1]			Directed Credit			
	Major Corporate Notes[2] (1)	Bill Brokerage[3] (2)	Banks[4] (3)	Gov. Deposits (4)	Banks (5)	Term Deposits (6)	MAKAM Net Rates (7)
1955	16.3		7.9	6.2		4.7	
1956	(19)		8.2	6.8		5.5	
1957	17.9		9.5	7.3		5.5	
1958	17.7		9.5	7.6		5.5	
1959	17.7		9.5	7.9		5.5	
1960	16.5		9.5	7.7		5.6	8.7
1961	15.1		9.3	6.5		5.6	8.7
1962	(13.8)	13.7	9.1	5.4		5.6	8.4
1963		13.8	8.8	5.1		5.7	8.1
1964		14.5	8.7	5.4		5.9	8.1
1965		16.2	8.8	6.1		6.0	7.7
1966		18.3	8.5	6.2		9.0	8.0
1967		16.8	8.8	6.5		8.9	6.6
1968		14.6	8.6	6.4		9.0	6.3
1969		15.7	—				7.2
1970			18.4				8.0
1971			18.8				8.8
1972			18.7				

[1]Free credit refers to two different variants of credit accommodated by commercial banks. The entries in Columns (1) and (2) refer to gray credit markets, in which the interest rate ceiling was evaded by the use of (questionable) legal loopholes. Column (3) shows credit accommodated by commercial banks from their own sources, at rates that were limited by the legal interest rate ceiling.

[2]The entries are averages for the year, based on data for several months each year. The entry for 1962 is based on a one-month entry only.

[3]The series through 1969 are annual averages based on full monthly data for each year and are an average of the rates charged by the commercial banks (en bloc) that operated in the bill-brokerage market. The abolition of the legal interest rate ceiling eliminated the bill-brokerage market. Accordingly, the entries from 1970 onward in Column 3 refer to the interest cost of "free credit" as distinct from subsidized credit, i.e., not credit accommodated under the directed-credit label or under the PAMELA label.

[4]Rates charged by commercial banks for non-directed credit.

Sources: Columns (1)–(4) and (6): Manzali, 1971, Tables 2, 3, 5, 11 and 21; Manzali 1977, Table 1; column (7): Sanbar-Bronfeld (1973), Table 10. p. 227.

The acceleration of the monetary expansion and its specific high rates meant that the requisite monetary-policy backing for the devaluation exercise in 1962, and the developments in its aftermath through 1965, was hardly forthcoming. The BOI's initiative in 1961 to move forcefully into the arena in an attempt to lessen the impact of the money multiplier was frustrated at first, as noted, by the banking system's rapid expansion of credit. Some of this reflected a significant increase in reserves; the large-scale expansion of development-budget credit merely added fuel to the conflagration.[12] When the BOI's move on the interim target—the effective liquidity ratios of the system—finally took hold in 1963, it was easily overwhelmed by the leap in the expansion rate of the monetary base to almost 38% that year, underscoring the central bank's inability to drain monetary liquidity from the economy (table 3.4).

THE MONETARY BASE:
THE INJECTION-DRAINING MECHANISM

Indeed, the monetary base—over the expansion rate of which the BOI had effectively no control—had been running the monetary show during the six-year period between 1960 and 1965. The average annual rate of expansion of this parameter during those years far outpaced that of M_1 and, at 19%, was almost 1.5 times higher than in the previous interval, 1955–59. This reading of events is supported by the comparative patterns of the base and of M_1 in 1955–59, during which time M_1 expanded at a somewhat higher rate than base money.

An understanding of the driving force of monetary-base expansion, a major factor in the provision of liquidity to the system in the second half of the 1950s and a dominant contributor to monetary inflation in the 1960s, requires an analysis of the interplay of its determinants. These may be identified and classified into three blocs that inject liquidity into, or drain liquidity from, the system: the central bank; general government, dominated by the central-government cash flow; and the "private" sector, which in the Israeli case included publicly owned utilities and businesses that sold products and services.

Israel's private sector had been draining liquidity from the system year in and year out from 1948 through 1961 due to its huge deficit on trade and services account. This outflow, entailing the conversion of domestic currency into foreign currency and the concurrent shrinkage of the monetary base, was only partially cancelled out until then by the unilateral account inflow of funds to households and a trickle of incoming funds on private-sector capital account (table 3.9).

General government, in contrast, had been injecting large liquidity flows into the system in each of these years and in some succeeding years in the 1962–67 interval. This was a reflection of the significant receipts of general government, in GNP terms and even more in terms of the monetary base, on unilateral and capital account from abroad, plus the credit accommodation by the BOI that was used to even out its cash flow. Finally, the BOI's credit accommodations of "nongovernment" entities at its discount window—effectively, its contribution to the subsidized directed-credit component of the outstanding credit balance of the commercial banking system, had been injecting liquidity into the economy every year between 1955 and 1966. These injections, however, were quite small compared with the injection/drainage effects of the two other sectors.

The Liquidity-Draining Role of the Private Sector
and Its Erosion

The private sector had a substantial draining effect on liquidity in the early 1950s and remained highly significant in this respect through, say, 1959. Its impact, however, was declining by the late 1950s due to a massive increase of the inflow of German restitution payments to eligible households. In the middle of the 1950s, these inflows were still minute relative to the deficit on trade and

Table 3.9. Monetary Injections and Inflation (normalized by monetary base at beginning of year, percent)

	BOI Injection[1] (1)	Private Conversion[2] (2) = (4) − [(1) + (3)]	Government Injection[3] (3)	M.B. Rate of Change (4)	Inflation (5)
1955	5.9	−169.3	199.3	35.9	4.8
1956	5.0	−164.9	182.6	22.6	4.6
1957	3.8	−84.1	72.2	−8.1	5.2
1958	−5.6	−49.4	67.5	12.5	4.2
1959	0.5	−39.1	42.9	4.3	1.6
1960	5.0	−20.5	37.6	22.2	3.4
1961	1.8	−33.6	35.8	4.1	9.0
1962	6.8	45.1	−18.4	33.5	10.2
1963	3.0	37.4	−2.8	37.5	5.0
1964	2.6	−11.8	15.5	6.3	4.4
1965	−1.8	38.2	−24.7	11.8	10.1
1966	3.2	−24.0	25.2	4.4	7.8
1967	3.1	−59.8	84.9	28.2	0.2
Avg. :1955–59	1.9	−101.4	112.9	13.4	4.1
S.D. :1955–59	4.7	62.3	72.3	16.9	1.4
Avg. :1955–60	2.4	−87.9	100.3	14.9	4.0
S.D. :1955–60	4.4	64.8	71.6	15.5	1.3
Avg. :1960–65	2.9	9.1	7.2	19.2	7.0
S.D. :1960–65	2.9	34.8	26.8	14.2	3.1
Avg. :1960–66	3.0	4.4	9.7	17.1	7.1
S.D. :1960–66	2.7	34.2	25.4	14.1	2.8

[1]BOI injection: change in bills discounted (the BOI component of directed credit) plus change in the "other accounts" item on its balance sheet, minus change in commercial bank term deposits on the (end-of-year) balance sheet of the central bank.
[2]Private conversions of foreign exchange, derived as a residual.
[3]Government injection: domestic injection plus foreign (sources) injection. The domestic injection is derived from Bank of Israel balance-sheet data. The foreign injection is derived from balance-of-payments data on unilateral (general government) receipts from abroad, minus the value of "government imports"—effectively, the cost of defense imports—interest rates, and net general-government funds transmitted on capital account.
Sources: Column (1), BOI injection: derived from Bank of Israel data—Annual Report 1964, Table XXI-1; Annual Reports 1965 and 1967, Table XXI-1—based on the annual balance sheets of the central bank, included in each Annual Report. Column (3), government domestic injection: Annual Report 1964, Table XXI-1, p. 39; Annual Reports 1965 and 1967, Table XXI-1. Government foreign injection: Annual Report 1960, Table XVI-1, p. 237; Table XVI-10, p. 252; and similar tables in Annual Reports 1959 and 1956. 1961 data: from Table III-3 (balance of payments) plus data on defense import, based on Berglas, 1983, Table A-1, p. 52 was substituted for data from XVI-10, the publication of which was stopped. For 1962–67: data from Annual Reports for these years, Table III-1 (Balance of Payments) and Berglas (1983) for data on defense imports. Columns (4) and (5): Table 3.4, Column (1), and Table 3.2, Column (5).

services account and the outstanding balance of the monetary base, for example, only 7% of the outstanding monetary base at the beginning of 1956. By 1960, however, the inflow of funds on restitution account verged on $100 million, four times the 1956 level and 50% higher than in 1958 (table 3.10). By then, the IL value of this inflow, at the official exchange rate, had climbed to about 30% of a much larger outstanding monetary base.

The base did not expand by the entire annual inflow of reparations payments because some of this inflow was not immediately converted into

Table 3.10. Unilateral Receipts and Private-Sector Net Conversions[1]

| | Private Sector | | General Govt. (3) | Unilateral Receipts, Total $ million (4) = (2) + (3) | PAZAK + TAMAM Deposits | | Net Conversions[2] (7) = (2) − (6) | I.L. Million | | Ratio of Net Conversions to MBt−1[4] (percent) (10) |
	Restitution Payments (1)	Total (2)			Balance (5)	Net Change (6)		Net Conversions[3] (8)	Monetary Base (9)	
1954	6	22	240	262	—	—	—	—	260.4	—
1955	19	54	157	211	0.7	0.7	53.3	95.9	353.8	—
1956	26	61	179	240	1.9	1.2	59.8	107.6	433.9	30.4
1957	45	82	163	245	8.1	6.2	75.8	136.4	398.7	31.4
1958	65	102	162	264	17.3	9.2	92.8	167.0	448.5	41.9
1959	98	101	150	251	41.1	23.8	77.2	139.0	467.1	31.0
1960	98	135	176	311	69.1	28.0	107.0	192.6	571.3	41.2
1961	111	156	196	352	112.6	43.5	112.5	202.5	594.5	35.4
1962	134	202	184	386	159.0	46.2	155.8	467.4	793.7	78.6
1963	139	231	160	391	187.7	28.7	202.3	606.9	1091.6	76.5
1964	134	230	105	335	230.7	43.0	187.0	561.0	1159.9	51.4
1965	113	211	117	328	287.3	56.6	154.4	463.2	1296.2	39.9
1966	110	194	98	292	339.7	52.4	141.6	424.8	1353.0	32.8
1967	123	207	314	521	405.1	65.5	141.5	495.3	1733.9	36.6
Avg.:1954–60	51	80	175	255	23	12	78	140	419	35.2
S.D.:1955–60	37	37	30	30	27	12	20	36	97	5.8
Avg.:1960–66	120	194	148	342	198	43	152	417	980	50.8
S.D.:1960–66	16	36	40	37	95	11	35	162	325	19.2

[1] Conversions of foreign into domestic currency.
[2] Conversions of foreign currency by private-sector household recipients of unilateral payments.
[3] Net conversion to IL: nominal dollar entries, Column (7), multiplied by the current official rate of exchange.
[4] Ratio of net conversions to monetary base at the end of the previous year.

Sources: Column (1): Sanbar-Bronfeld (1973), Table 8; 1964–67: Annual Report 1972, Table III-25. Columns (2)–(3): 1954–59, Halevi-Klinov (1968), Table App. 9, p. 242. 1960–61: Annual Report 1961, Table III-14. 1962–64: Annual Report 1964, Table III-13. 1965–67: Annual Report 1972, Table III-25. Column (5): Sanbar-Bronfeld (1973) Tables 4 and 9. Column (6): derived from Column (5). Column (8): product of the entries in Column (7) and the official dollar exchange rate. Column (9): Table 3.4.

domestic currency. To encourage recipients to transfer these funds but to refrain from converting them at once, they were granted a privilege: they were allowed to place a significant fraction of their receipts, at interest rates similar to those offered in Germany, in deposits in or indexed to foreign currency (PAZAK and TAMAM). Thus, in 1956–60 a sizable fraction of these inflows was not immediately converted. The quid pro quo, of course, was a rapid buildup of PAZAK and TAMAM deposits, from $2 million in 1956 to $70 million in 1960, creating a major monetary overhang in the longer run (table 3.10).

In the short term, the PAZAK-TAMAM option did reduce the immediate injection of liquidity. The 21% expansion of the money supply in 1960, however, was clearly the result of the major increase in the inflow of reparations payments from 1959 on. The upturn generated a 38% upturn in conversions into domestic currency even though the balance of forex-denominated and indexed deposits kept growing rapidly. This large increase in conversions in 1960, originating in reparations payments, offers the most reasonable explanation for the change of the impact of the private sector on the monetary base at the turn of the 1960s (table 3.9). The drastic decline in the drainage effect that the private sector had traditionally exerted since 1948 explains the much weaker depressant impact of the private sector on the size of the monetary base in 1960 than in 1959. In the latter year, the drainage effect of the private sector plummeted from 40% of the outstanding monetary base at the beginning of the year to only 20% at year's end.

The massive effect of the inflow of reparations money and, specifically, its rate of conversion into domestic currency on the pattern of the monetary base, recurred in 1961 but in the opposite direction. In 1961, the private-sector drainage of liquidity rose temporarily again to about 34% of the monetary base (table 3.9), mainly due to a drastic change in the behavior of households. Households now chose to place a much higher proportion of the current inflow in foreign-exchange-indexed deposits: almost 40% of the vastly increased inflow in 1961 as against only 29% of the smaller 1960 inflow (table 3.10). This change of preference clearly reflected rising expectations of a devaluation. Beham's estimates leave no doubt that the upturn in devaluation expectations in 1961 dampened conversions and, thereby, increased the rates of accumulation in these deposits and the potential size of the postdevaluation liquidity injection (Beham, 1968, pp. 45–52).

The slowdown in the rate of increase of the monetary base in 1961, to only 4%, changed abruptly in 1962–63. Indeed, the most significant development in the wake of the major 1962 devaluation was the dramatic turnabout in the impact of the private sector's net foreign-currency inflow on the volume of the monetary base in the succeeding period. The injection series in table 3.9 demonstrates this. In 1962, the effect was expressed in the first of a sequence of changes in sign from negative to positive—that is, from liquidity drainage by the private sector, as had taken place throughout the 1950s and in 1961, to liquidity injection. Thus, whereas in 1961 the international balance of payments of the private sector still had a negative effect on the potential growth of the monetary base at 34% of its balance at the beginning of the year, its effect on the base in 1962 was positive and enormous. Its potential effect on the balance of the monetary base was expansionary at magnitudes of 45% and 37% of the size of the base at the beginning of 1962 and 1963, respectively.

This change of tack, from a draining effect to an alternating injecting/draining role, did not reflect a sudden improvement in the private sector's trade and services account. The dramatic change in the significant though (temporary) positive impact of the private sector on the monetary base traced to the major incentive, offered to households by the 1962 devaluation, to realize the domestic-currency capital gain that their ownership of deposits in or indexed to foreign currency made possible. These deposits (in deutschmarks) paid 6% annual interest, a rate somewhat higher than that available in Germany.[13] The 66% nominal devaluation in February 1962, of course, gave all recipients of the current foreign-currency inflow a similar incentive to convert these funds into domestic currency immediately—with investment in housing an obvious case in point. The well-known lead and lag traits of devaluation expectations before the devaluation and their immediate demise afterwards were quite relevant to businesses as well—exporters, importers, and, of course, the banking system.

By virtue of the very size and rapid increase in the reparations inflow in the 1960s, the PAZAK-TAMAM deposits, which had become the dominant component of foreign-exchange deposits, called the tune on this score. After the March 1961 revaluation of the deutschmark, which increased the German currency's dollar and IL value by 5%, the IL value of the balance of the DM-indexed deposits climbed to 34% of the balance of the monetary base by the end of 1961. The 1962 devaluation raised the IL value of these deposits to 57% of the base in one go. Accordingly, the monetary discussion at the time referred to the IL value of the accumulation of households' forex-indexed deposits as a "monetary time bomb" (Barkai and Michaely, 1963). The quantitative monetary potential of an "explosion"—massive conversion of these deposits, as had occurred in the immediate wake of the 1962 devaluation—was a constant source of concern in the 1960s. Although the fixed exchange-rate regime was supported by strict foreign-exchange controls, an avalanche of conversions into domestic currency would generate price inflation anyway, forcing sooner rather than later another devaluation and, in turn, another upheaval.

The reasonable thing to do, it seemed, was to try to defuse the bomb by making the conversion of DM and DM-indexed deposits into IL less profitable. After the 1962 devaluation, the interest rate on these deposits was raised by 1 percentage point (to 7%) and banks were instructed not to release funds from the deposits before the end of their term. This, however, could make a difference only in the short run, if at all, and would have the countervailing effect of increasing the absolute size of these deposits and, in turn, their relative size compared with the monetary aggregates in the longer run. This, of course, would increase of the exposure of the monetary dimension of the economy to the decisions of the private sector about the composition of its financial assets. Ultimately, the private sector's influence on the time pattern of the monetary base and of M_1 would grow.

Monetary developments from the early 1960s onward sent this very message. The injection figures that determined the trend of the monetary base in the late 1950s and the 1961–66 interval underline the transition. In 1958–60, the private sector still *drained* liquidity from the system at an annual average of 36% of the size of the monetary base (at the beginning of each year). The drainage effect had been much stronger in 1955–57. In 1961–63, the private sector *injected* liquidity at an average annual rate of 16%, thus contributing to the expansion of the monetary base. In 1964–66, it made no contribution to the expansion of the base (table 3.9).

The significance of the private sector's impact on the size of the monetary base through 1966 transcended its growing relevance for the time pattern of the money supply. The severe variance of this impact, reflecting expectations of the timing of a possible devaluation, inevitably amplified uncertainty about the future pattern of monetary aggregates and, in turn, the future pattern of the domestic price level as against that of prices abroad.[14] Accordingly, it signified the rising influence of the behavior of the private sector on the workings of the macroeconomy. This novelty imposed an additional constraint on the running of macroeconomic policy. The authorities in charge of its implementation, especially the Ministry of Finance, were slow in coming to terms with it.

The Liquidity-Injection Pattern of General Government

From the very beginning (1948) until 1961, government injection was dominant in furnishing the economy with monetary liquidity. Government injection fueled the expansion of the monetary base by building up the central bank's portfolio of assets. This caused government debt to the BOI to grow and led to a buildup of the foreign reserves, which until 1957 were generally small and miniscule in terms of Israel's imports. (They grew rapidly thereafter; see table 3.7.) The buildup of these reserves during that time represented net transfers to general government on unilateral receipt account (German reparations, American grants, and Diaspora philanthropy) and transfers on capital account, such as the proceeds of Israel Bonds. Thus, in 1957 the government injection into the monetary base, although smaller than before, amounted to 72% of the base money balance at the beginning of that year. By 1960, the injection contracted even more, to 38% of a much larger monetary base. Even this rate of injection, however, was the main power behind the extraordinary 22% expansion of the monetary base that year.

The 1960 injection rate, while somewhat lower than that of 1959, was clearly not coordinated with what may have been an unexpected rapid increase in the inflow of funds on personal-restitution account. Thus, the inflationary expansion of the monetary base and the money supply that year, as M_1 ballooned by 21%, came as a surprise. If so, the corresponding change in the "price climate" that occurred in 1961, at the latest, was an act of force majeure, so to speak. In any case, even though by 1961 the major increase in the restitution inflow, the expansion of M_1 in 1960, and the inflationary surge were well-known facts of life, the government injection was still subjected to inertia, remaining at the same very high plateau of 1960 in terms of the relevant monetary base.

The pattern would soon change. An important feature of the effect of the 1962 devaluation was the novel degree of freedom that it afforded to fiscal policy.

This is demonstrated foremost in the change of sign of the general-government injection coefficient that year, from its traditional positive to negative. Thus, the general-government cash flow, for the first time in history, had begun to drain liquidity from the economy instead of injecting it. The drainage effect, expressed in terms of 18% of the monetary base, marked a quantitatively meaningful turnabout in comparison with the injection effect of general government a year earlier. Thus, 1962 was a watershed year, after which the impact of fiscal policy on the monetary sector was maintained through 1965. Indeed, the government injection series in table 3.9 carries a negative sign in three of the four years through 1965, instead of the traditional positive sign of the 1950s.

The negative government injection in 1962, expressed in the reduction of the outstanding government debt to the central bank, had in a sense the effect of an open-market sale. This drainage effect was implemented by a substantial reduction of gross government debt to the Bank of Israel, from more than 40% of total BOI assets in 1961 to about 18% of a larger total in 1962 (table 3.7). The drainage was financed by the windfall that the 66% devaluation had brought about in the general-government finances. In other words, the devaluation eliminated the implicit tax on the general-government inflow of foreign revenue on unilateral and capital accounts plus BOI interest receipts on account of investment of the foreign reserves. The corresponding rise in the annual flow of funds in IL terms and the IL capital gain on the BOI's foreign-exchange balances were used to cancel about 25% of the outstanding government debt to the central bank. As a by-product of this move, the potential expansion of the monetary base, corresponding to the drain of government debt from the BOI's balance sheet, was reduced. The government injection series in table 3.9 indicate that the change of sign in the contribution of government to the monetary aggregates in 1962 was not a nonrecurrent event. It showed that the role of general government in the mechanism that generated monetary liquidity had crossed a threshold that year: instead pumping liquidity into the system systematically, year-in and year-out, general government had taken on an alternating role, sometimes injecting and sometimes draining. However, while the dramatic change in 1962 reflected the shifting of an endogenous variable—the exchange rate—the drainage effect through 1965 was largely a reflection of significantly lower general-government receipts on foreign unilateral account and substantially higher defense imports, coupled with higher interest payments on the rising foreign debt.[15] This meant significantly lower net revenue on the general-government foreign income accounts. This important change of tack features clearly in the fiscal indicators representing the income-expenditure dimension of fiscal policy (table 3.11). The foreign surplus in 1961, at 3.5% of GNP, eroded rapidly—verging on zero by 1964 and slipping into the red by 1966. Foreign receipts on capital account over this period, not shown in the table 3.11 series, fluctuated. The comparatively stable elements were proceeds from sales of Israel Bonds, which sometimes declined but mostly generated an annual average net inflow of around $30 million in 1960–66.

Table 3.11. General-Government Fiscal Indicators (percent of GDP)[1]

	Expenditures			Revenues			Deficit (−)		
	Foreign[2] (1)	Domestic (2)	Total (3) = (1) + (2)	Tax (4)	Tax Plus[3] (5)	Unilateral[4] (6)	Foreign[5] (7) = (6) − (1)	Domestic (8) = (5) − (2)	Total (9) = (7) + (8)
1956	5.8	25.4	31.2		21.7	5.6	−0.2	−3.7	−3.9
1957	3.8	30.3	34.1	24.1	28.6	9.0	5.2	−1.7	3.5
1958	4.7	29.3	34.0	23.7	28.0	7.9	3.2	−1.3	1.9
1959	4.2	30.2	34.4	25.3	30.0	6.0	1.8	−0.2	1.6
1960	3.9	31.1	35.0	26.3	31.5	5.2	1.3	0.4	1.7
1960	2.6	26.0	28.6	25.6	27.9	6.1	3.5	1.9	5.4
1961	2.8	25.3	28.1	26.4	28.8	5.4	2.6	3.5	6.1
1962	4.1	24.9	29.0	26.6	28.7	5.9	1.8	3.8	5.6
1963	3.8	25.1	28.9	26.8	29.1	4.6	0.8	4.0	4.8
1964	3.3	26.5	29.8	27.8	30.3	3.5	0.2	3.8	4.0
1965	2.9	27.9	30.8	26.8	29.3	3.3	0.4	1.4	1.8
1966	3.0	30.8	33.8	28.1	30.8	2.7	−0.3	0.0	−0.3

[1]From 1960 onward, entries were based on the revised BOI series including changes in classification and definitions, as published in *Annual Report* 1999. The series refers to the income-and-expenditure dimension only and excludes fiscal operations in domestic and foreign capital markets.
[2]Foreign expenditure: the cost of government imports (mainly defense imports) and net interest payments on the foreign debt.
[3]"Tax plus" includes tax revenues, receipts on property account, receipts on interest account, and (from 1960) depreciation charges and nominal receipts on civil-pensions account.
[4]Unilateral receipts from abroad of government and other general-government institutions include German reparations and philanthropy from the Diaspora.
[5]Foreign deficit: unilateral foreign receipts of general government less the cost of general-government imports and net interest payments.
Sources: Column (1): for 1956–60, *Annual Report* 1961, Tables III-3 and VII-1, and similar tables in *Annual Reports* 1960, 1959, and 1956. Columns (2) and (6): *Annual Report* 1960, Table XVI-10, and similar tables in *Annual Reports* 1959, 1958. For 1961–66, the revised Bank of Israel series: *Annual Report* 1999, Appendix Tables V-1a and V1-b.

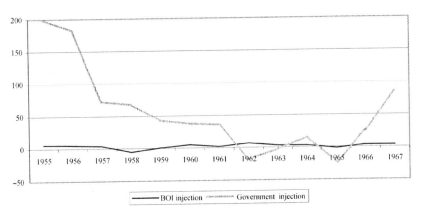

Figure 3.6. Government and BOI Injections

DETERMINANTS OF THE BOI's INJECTION RATES

During the BOI's first twelve years of operation, its contribution to the expansion of the monetary base was usually positive though small in comparison with the impact of the two other sectors (table 3.9 and figures 3.6–3.8). Its average annual contribution to the base during its running-in period, say, 1955–59, was 1.9% of the base at the threshold of each of these years. The coterminous government injection during that interval was 113% of the monetary base and the countervailing drainage by the private sector was 101%. The net injection of the three sectors combined, during that period of declining inflation, allowed the monetary base to expand by 13% on average.

The average annual expansion rate accelerated significantly in the next period, the six-year 1960–65 interval, a time of rising inflation. During these years, base money grew by 19% on annual average (17% if 1966 is included). While the average contribution of the BOI climbed to 2.9% (3.0% if 1966 is

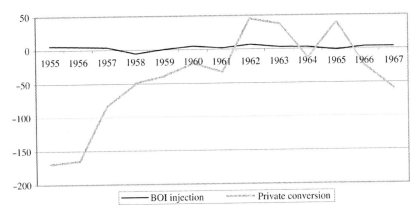

Figure 3.7. BOI Injection and Private Conversion

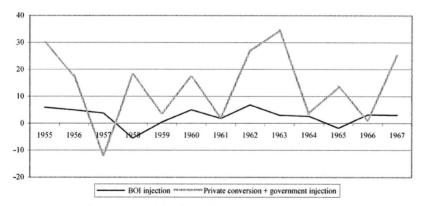

Figure 3.8. BOI Injection and Private Conversion + Government Injection

included), the average injection rate of the government "collapsed" to 7.2% (9.7% including 1966). Concurrently, the role of the private sector in the injection of liquidity made a highly significant turnabout, from 101% annual average drainage in the five-year period ending 1959 to annual average injection of 9.1% of the base-money balance at the threshold of each year (and 4.4% if 1966 is included in a seven-year sequence).

Thus, although in the first half of the 1960s the average impact of general government on the expansion rate of the monetary base was more than twice that of the BOI and even though that of the private sector was greater by a factor of about three, the significance of the BOI's contribution to system liquidity increased conspicuously in *relative* terms. In other words, the stance adopted by the BOI had a much greater effect on the momentum of monetary base expansion by that time than during the running-in period.

Under these circumstances, the BOI's injection rates in 1960 and again in 1962, at 5% and 6.8% of the balance of the monetary base at the threshold of each of these years, were highly questionable and inconsistent with its explicit statements in favor of "monetary discipline." The bank spelled out the practical meaning of this expression in its November 1960 means-of-payment report: a policy designed "to prevent the expansion of means of payment at a rate higher than GNP growth."[16] Its largest contribution to the expansion of the base, attained in 1962, was altogether inconsistent with its all-out support of the devaluation policy and its outspoken statements about the monetary restraint that the success of this policy required.

The BOI's relatively high injection rates in these two years, however, were hardly attained at its own discretion. The "discount" series that reflects its contribution to the directed-credit component, the portion mediated by the commercial banks, shows this clearly (table 3.7). The rapidly expanding foreign-reserve balances were another contributing factor in the expansion of base money. In 1960 and 1962, discounts grew at rates of 70% and 89%, respectively, and foreign reserves (in IL terms) by 78% in 1960 and, in the wake of the 66% devaluation in

1962, by a factor of two. Thus, although the bank's own declared marching orders signaled the need for monetary restraint from 1960 if not earlier, the BOI made a significant contribution to the expansion of the monetary base in 1960 and 1962—about 20% of the high rate of expansion of the base in both years.

Accordingly, the BOI had not sided with the "good guys." It did attempt to impose some restraint on discount-window accommodation by manipulating—in fact, delaying—the full 22% "liquidity dispensation" for the commercial banks on account of the directed credit that they granted (Beham, p. 55). Ultimately, the volume of these BOI transactions, of course, represented the directed-credit quota set by the Ministerial Committee on Economic Affairs, which also determined the interest rate to be charged for these funds. The BOI played an advisory role in this matter; it promoted its views by jawboning the relevant political authorities, which were usually attentive to the countervailing lobbying of the manufacturing and farming industries. Since technically it was the BOI that implemented the policy, the central bank could manipulate it at its edges, but only by means of delaying tactics.

In theory, the BOI could have operated on the selling side of the open market, even without government approval, in order to countervail the imposed expansion of the discount-window purchases and the coterminous rapid increase of foreign reserves due to the rising tide of reparations payments and the effect of the 1962 devaluation. However, the composition of its asset portfolio through the third quarter of 1966 denied it the freedom to do anything of the sort. The balance of government debt on the books of the central bank remained substantial from 1962 to 1965, at roughly 16% of total assets (table 3.7). Since none of it was tradable, at that crucial time the bank had no available assets with which it could enter on the selling side into a money market that was narrow to begin with. Furthermore, even if the Ministry of Finance were forthcoming enough to allow the BOI to issue its own debentures—an option that the law explicitly vested in the BOI—the central bank could hardly use this instrument to stanch that monetary avalanche "since the Usury Law prohibits the use of changes in the interest rate as an instrument . . . and the miniscule scope of the money market limits the option of absorbing purchasing power by selling securities" (*Annual Report*, 1961, p. 226). This explanation of the BOI's impotence in this regard was buried in the review of the monetary system in the *Annual Report* that appeared after the February 1962 devaluation. Thus, although quite blunt, it did not make the headlines. Still, it was a highly reasonable description of the state of affairs that prevailed at that juncture and onward until 1966.

The Finance Ministry's refusal to grant the BOI instrumental independence, although never stated explicitly, was nevertheless its praxis for three decades. The ministry implemented this policy by dominating the "high ground," the Ministerial Committee on Economic Affairs. To award instrumental independence, the committee would have to approve the issue of BOI debentures or a surrogate for the same, such as Treasury bills (see the final section of this chapter), as a device for open-market operations. In addition, or at the very least, it would have to give blanket approval to BOI proposals for restrictive moves on commercial-bank liquidity ratios for the purpose of reducing the clout of the money multiplier. The BOI Law said as much. The requisite approval of the debentures option was withheld through 1966 and again from 1971 to 1985. Furthermore, although occasional approval of increases in liquidity ratios was given from 1961 on, it was usually accompanied by footdragging. The BOI's reference to the process of approving the March 1961 upward adjustment of liquidity ratios, indeed a new departure in policy, plainly had this in mind. In its *Annual Report* for 1961, the bank says, "It was found that the flexibility of application of this instrument by the Bank was insufficient due to the lengthy legal procedure required to make changes in liquidity ratios. . . . The measure could not be implemented before the end of March 1961" (1961, p. 226). This statement, which refers to the very first premeditated tight-money policy move, implicitly blames the Ministry of Finance for the unwarranted delay in its application.

The crux of the failure on the monetary front was that monetary policy from 1960 to 1965, effectively speaking, was unable to stanch the inflationary expansion of the monetary base and, in turn, of M_1. The acceleration of the expansion rates of money from 1960 on (table 3.4) made a predicable impact on the price level of an economy operating at full employment. Nevertheless, the BOI's policy in 1960–66 did have a smoothing effect on the monetary comings and goings. Its smoothing effect on the pattern of both monetary aggregates, the monetary base and M_1, is visible in the data and demonstrated graphically in the comparative injection graphs (figures 3.6–3.8).

The overall smoothing effect of the BOI's measures through 1985 is described in greater detail in part II, chapter 9 section M, and part III, chapter 16 section L.

AN OPENING TO AN OPEN-MARKET POLICY: THE 1966 MAKAM (TREASURY BILL) ACCORD

The monetary bent of the restrictive fiscal policy adopted in 1965 is reflected clearly in developments on the monetary front. It is shown in the steady decrease in BOI injections from 1963 on, including the first small drainage (negative injection) of the monetary base in 1965. It is also evidenced in terms of the multiplier, the instrument wielded by the central bank from the early 1960s as its only lever of control over M_1. The legal reserve ratios imposed in 1961 finally took hold in 1963, reducing the multiplier from 1.68 to 1.51 in the respective years. Another upward tug at the reserve ratio, implemented in 1963, lowered the multiplier again to only 1.46 by 1965, supporting the restrictive fiscal stance described above. By early 1966, it was clear that these measures had been on target.

In 1966, with a major economic slowdown in plain sight, the BOI lowered the reserve ratios, raising the multiplier somewhat and restoring its stance to a significant positive injection (figure 3.9). This was not only a warranted reaction to the slowdown, which commanded headlines by the middle of that year. Nor was it another smoothing action, designed to reduce the volatility of the rate change of the monetary base and, in turn, of the money supply. Although it also reflected these features, it marked a new departure: an attempt to wield

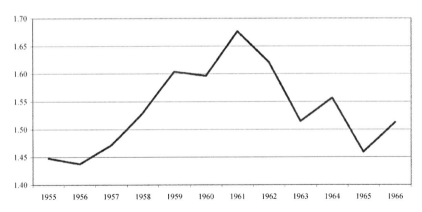

Figure 3.9. Money Multiplier, 1955–66

the main instrument that central banks use to control money markets: open-market operations.

The Bank of Israel Law, as noted, empowered the governor to be active in the open market. In practice, this required government approval, which for more than a decade had not been forthcoming due to the unavailability of the conventional instrument of a restrictive monetary policy, a meaningful stock of marketable short-term government paper. Although government debt accounted for much of the central-bank asset portfolio, hardly any of it was marketable through 1966. In fact, until that year the bank's balance sheet had not referred to marketable securities at all (table 3.7). At the time, such securities were a negligible fraction of the total asset portfolio (0.45%) and thus only 0.86% of the outstanding balance of the monetary base—hardly relevant for the task at hand.

The BOI was indeed free to engage in open-market operations on the other side of the market, that is, it could make purchases on the open market without government approval. To operate on the selling side, however, it needed approval to issue its own bonds, which as stated was not forthcoming. Potentially, however, an instrument that could serve this purpose was available in the money market by that time. In 1960, the government had begun to sell MAKAM (Treasury bills) to terms of 90, 180, 270, and 360 days, unindexed, using the proceeds in the way that it used receipts from sales of longer-term indexed bonds, to even out its cash flow. The outstanding balance of this stock, in terms of monetary aggregates, was nearly 15% of the corresponding monetary base in 1966. Thus, if the central bank had chosen to pursue an expansionary monetary policy—buying in the open market—it could have done so by the mid-1960s and possibly by 1964. In this case, the interest-rate ceiling would not have been an obstacle because the operation would have lowered the rates of return on these instruments, thus moving away from the ceiling. Between 1961 and 1964, however, it was obviously necessary for the BOI to operate as a seller, rather than as a buyer, in this market.

Aware of the asymmetry that kept it from selling on the open market without government approval, the management of the central bank might have been reluctant to operate on the buying side even when the state of the economy so warranted. In a paper contributed to the *Economic Review* in 1963, at the peak of the monetary inflation,[17] Dr. E. Lehman, manager of the Department of Issue in 1948–54, proposed that "the issue and management of short-term-loans [Hebrew acronym: MAKAM] be transferred to the BOI, thereby freezing the proceeds absorbed from their sale from the public" (Lehman, 1963, p. 58). For the time being, the authorities gave this proposal short shrift.

It was the severe economic slump in 1966, which climbed to the top of the political agenda in the first quarter of that year, that turned the tables. Now the Ministry of Finance was willing to submit the outstanding stock of MAKAM to the central bank's exclusive management and to give the BOI an additional unsold quota so that it could operate on the selling side of the open market if it saw fit to do so. This arrangement, fully consistent with Lehman's proposal, was consecrated on April 27, 1966, in an official document between the Government and the Bank of Israel known as "the Accord." To provide the bank with exclusivity in the short-term market, the government undertook not to sell securities of less than two years' duration and agreed that only a specified and small nominal sum of future sales of these securities by the central bank could be used to smooth its current cash flow. The rest of these sales would be used to reduce outstanding government debt to the central bank and, thereby, to affect negatively the size of the monetary base.

The accord might not have seen the light of day had the outstanding balance of MAKAM, which initially sold briskly, not collapsed by almost 30% in 1965, squeezing the Treasury's cash flow. With prices still rising at an average annual rate of around 7% in 1965 and at a nominal rate of 8.23% for twelve-month debentures, a real rate of return of about 1% was attainable.

Thus, the central bank, which came aboard late in 1966, moved into this market at an opportune moment. The inflation rate, still exceeding 12% during the first two quarters, plummeted to only 3% or so in the closing quarters of that year (both rates in annual average terms). At these inflation rates and with a 0.25% increase in interest (to 8.5% on twelve-month bonds) offered on new issues from June 1, 1966, the outstanding balance of MAKAM rose rapidly.

The monetary authority was aware, of course, that the action needed at this juncture, amidst the economic slump, was open-market purchases rather than sales. To compensate for the liquidity-draining effect of the sales of MAKAM in 1966, the BOI purchased other government paper from the banking system and, between November 1966 and February 1967, reduced the interest rate on MAKAM at issue to 7.5%, thus stopping the rise of the outstanding balance (*Annual Report*, 1966, pp. 331–32, and p. 454, table 21).

Most action in what may be described as the successful open-market experiment, however, occurred from 1967 on. By then, inflation rates had fallen to the 2%–3% range, offering enough leeway for restrictive operations on the open market within a legal framework that had left the Usury Law interest-rate ceiling in effect. The workings of the experiment are discussed in the next chapter. Nevertheless, 1966 may be viewed as a milestone year in the modus operandi of monetary policy—the year when the central bank acquired an instrument with which it could affect the monetary base, the major determinant of M_1.

Thus, for better or for worse, the first half of the 1960s may be identified as the period when the central bank made its first attempt to apply monetary policy, even though the effects of its actions were minor and belated. The first step was taken in 1961, in an attempt to establish control of the money multiplier by raising the liquidity ratios and expanding the list of liabilities requiring liquid reserves. The second step was the 1966 acquisition of the option to engage in open-market operations on both sides of the market. This, however, remained a limited option since it did not abolish the asymmetry of operating in the money market. It involved an effective quota constraint on MAKAM, set by the Ministry of Finance, for operations on the selling side. Nevertheless, although neither party to the Accord expected it when they signed this document in the summer of 1966, it emerged as a highly handy and effective instrument in 1967, as in the wake of the Six-Day War the economy swiftly returned to a robust growth trajectory, supported by large and rising budget deficits.

4

Monetary Policy in
a Mobilized Economy

THE FLOURISHING REAL ECONOMY, 1967–69/1973

The seven-year period between the Six-Day War (June 1967) and the Yom Kippur War (October 1973) marked the coming-of-age of the central bank in more than one sense. This was expressed meaningfully in an attempt to extend monetary policy into hitherto unexplored territory, the initiation and management of open-market operations. This novelty was introduced and tested in a propitious environment for the purpose: late in the last quarter of 1966, the trough of the 1965–67 slowdown.[1] Thus, the BOI acquired its first open-market experience during the recovery phase of what turned into the "seven good years" of the Israeli economy, a time of roaring prosperity. The experiment foundered in the overfull employment and accelerating inflation phase of the cycle from 1970 onward.

Growth Performance and the Balance of Payments

In the immediate aftermath of the Six-Day War—the third and fourth quarters of 1967—the system pulled out of its slump, which had been marked by an unemployment rate of more than 10%, and began to expand at rates that soon surpassed 10%. The average annual GDP growth rate during the eighty-one months ending on October 1, 1973, was almost 10%. Gross product of the business sector grew even faster. So did investment and consumption expenditure (table 4.1).

This long-term process was sustained by higher growth rates of resources available to the economy than of GDP. As resources increased by 11% on annual average during this period, the import surplus bulged again (figure 4.1).

Table 4.1. Real Economic Indicators, 1966–74

	GDP (1)	Domestic Resources[1] (2)	GDP per Capita (3)	Employment (4)	Unemployment Rate (5)	Imports (6)	Exports (7)	Import Surplus (6) − (7) = (8)
	Indices, 1966 = 100				*(Percent)*	*$ million*		
1966	100.0	100.0	100.0	100.0	7.4	1317.0	872.1	444.9
1967	102.3	103.7	98.3	95.7	10.4	1480.1	949.3	530.8
1968	118.0	120.9	105.8	104.3	6.1	1812.0	1132.0	680.0
1969	133.0	138.9	113.9	108.3	4.5	2188.0	1265.0	923.0
1970	143.2	154.5	114.6	110.2	3.8	2657.0	1374.0	1283.0
1971	159.4	166.4	116.7	114.1	3.5	3018.0	1823.0	1195.0
1972	178.9	178.2	123.2	119.8	2.7	3261.0	2129.0	1132.0
1973(9)	189.6	199.2	135.5	124.5	2.9	3416.0	2050.0	1366.0
1973	198.9	236.1	143.6	129.3	2.6	5325.0	2654.0	2671.0
1974	209.8	242.9	150.0	129.4	3.0	6844.0	3436.0	3408.0
	Annual average rates of change (percent)					*Annual averages*		
1967–69	10.0	11.6	4.4	2.7	7.0	1826.7	1115.4	711.3
1970–73/9	9.9	10.1	4.7	3.8	3.2	3088.0	1844.0	1244.0

[1]Real domestic Resources: GNP plus import surplus.
Sources: Columns (1)–(2) *Annual Report* 1999, Table Appendix II-1; column (3), Column (1) GDP series, and *CBS Annual* 1978, Table II-1 for population; columns (4)–(5) *CBS Annual* 1978, Table XII-1, p. 338; columns (6)–(7) *Annual Report* 1969, Table III-2, 1972, Table III-3, 1974, Table IV-2.

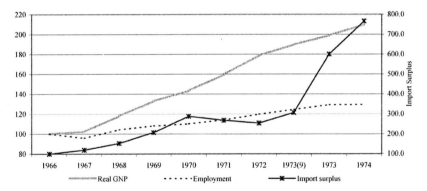

Figure 4.1. Real Aggregates—GNP, Employment, and Import Surplus, 1966–74 (1966 = 100)

By 1972, the import surplus in nominal dollar terms had nearly doubled relative to its earlier peak in 1964, which had prompted the government to launch the policy that resulted in the 1965–67 slowdown.[2] The 1972 import surplus and a fortiori its level during the three prewar quarters of 1973 underline, of course, the failure to approach, let alone to attain, the target that had been given top priority in the mid-1960s.

The rapid-growth process, which led to a deficit on the current account of the balance of payments, could not have been sustained without external sources of finance. To tap such sources, Israel turned to the U.S. capital market and was helped by the significantly growing inflow of unilateral payments from Jewish philanthropy and personal restitution payments from Germany. These, of course, injected liquidity into the system while the large deficit on trade and services account had the opposite effect. Thus, both sides of the equation had implications for the trend in the monetary base and the set of factors that determined it. The expansion rate of base money was inevitably affected by domestic factors: the vigorous expansion of net BOI credit to government plus discount-window contributions to directed credit, offset, as long as these continued, by the central bank's open-market operations. The impact of these measures, discussed below, may be traced on the central bank's balance sheet.

The Unemployment and Price Cycle

Figure 4.2 reveals a highly relevant feature of Israel's economic development during this seven-year interval. The contrasting cyclical trends in the country's unemployment and inflation rates may offer the best insight into the workings of the system and its growth pattern during that period. The unemployment rate peaked at over 10% in the first two quarters of 1967 (an interval that largely preceded the war). It then plunged to 3.8% by 1970, within the full-employment range (tables 3.1 and 4.1).

During those three years, the labor force had grown considerably due to the annexation of eastern Jerusalem and an upturn in annual average immigration rates to 30,000 as against only 12,000 in the years immediately preceding 1967.

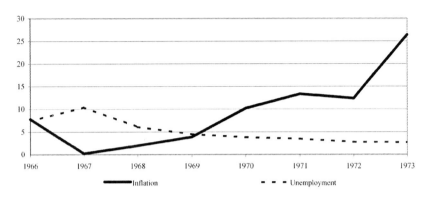

Figure 4.2. Inflation and Unemployment Rates (percent), 1966–73

Demand for labor, however, had grown so strongly that a rapidly increasing number of Palestinians also found work in Israel. Thus, the unemployment rate continued to decline—to 2.6% of the civilian labor force by the third quarter of 1973. This conflation of low unemployment rates and the growth rate of employment—by almost 12% per annum in the twelve quarters from Q4-1970 to Q3-1973—reflects a clear case of overfull employment.

The declining trend in the unemployment rate from its 1967 peak to the September 1973 trough had an obverse image in the price trend, as shown by every yardstick (table 4.2). Rates of change in consumer and (implicit) GDP prices and wages in 1967 marked the bottom of the inflation cycle. The abrupt decline of inflation rates to the vicinity of only 1% in 1967 ushered in a three-year period of price stability, in which prices rose at annual average rates of about 2% and nominal wages by about 3%. This very low slope of the price curve, shown clearly in figure 4.2, changed abruptly into a steep slope from Q4-1969 onward, as inflation surpassed 10% in 1970 and advanced to a somewhat higher level through 1972. In the first three quarters of 1973, a time when no one expected the "October 1973 surprise," inflation accelerated considerably, to an annual rate somewhat above 20% in CPI terms. A price explosion of this magnitude was a new experience after almost two decades of mild inflation—annual averages of 4% and 7% in the 1954–59 and 1960–66 intervals, respectively, and an even lower rate of 2% in the 1967–69 buildup to full employment.

As in the first transition from price stability to a significant inflationary environment at the beginning of the 1960s, the second transition to a (low) double-digit inflation climate in the early 1970s can hardly be ascribed to cost factors. Dollar import prices hardly budged during this time. The rate of change in the rising trend of effective exchange rates was much lower than that of 1968 (table 4.2). In any case, the vigorous rise in factor productivity dampened the cost-push effect of the exchange rate and the influence of nominal wages. The 24% improvement in factor productivity between 1966 and 1970 had a strong corresponding downward effect on unit costs, as the series in table 4.3 illustrates clearly. Furthermore, the price stability that prevailed in 1967–69, despite a devaluation of nearly 17% in late 1967, suggests that price expectations at the turn of the 1970s were not geared to an inflationary experience.

Table 4.2. Exchange Rates, Wages, and Prices, 1966–74

	Exchange Rates			Wages	Consumer		Prices					
		Effective						$		IL		
	Official (1)	Imports (2)	Exports (3)	Nominal (4)	End Year (5)	Avg (6)	Implicit GNP (7)	Import (8)	Export (9)	Import (10)	Export (11)	
Indices, 1966 = 100												
1966	100.0	100.0	100.0	100.0	100.0	100.0	100.0	100	100	100	100	
1967	116.7	102.5	109.2	100.4	100.2	101.7	101.9	100.0	98.1	102.5	107.1	
1968	116.7	115.0	110.6	104.7	102.1	103.8	104.8	98.0	97.1	112.8	107.4	
1969	116.7	117.5	110.9	111.1	106.1	106.4	107.3	102.9	101.9	121.0	113.0	
1970	116.7	123.1	122.9	121.1	116.9	112.9	116.0	103.9	101.0	127.9	124.1	
1971	140.0	141.8	138.0	141.0	132.5	126.4	130.7	106.9	104.9	151.5	144.7	
1972	140.0	—	—	160.6	148.9	142.6	149.2	113.7	112.6			
1973(9)[1]	140.0	—	—	199.3	180.4	175.9	179.5					
1973	140.0	—	—	204.8	188.2	171.1	216.7	145.6	138.5			
1974	200.0	—	—	278.9	294.0	239.1	293.0	200.2	163.3			

(Continued)

111

Table 4.2. Continued

	Exchange Rates				Prices						
	Effective			Wages	Consumer		Implicit GNP	$		IL	
	Official (1)	Imports (2)	Exports (3)	Nominal (4)	End Year (5)	Avg (6)	(7)	Import (8)	Export (9)	Import (10)	Export (11)
Annual rates of change (percent)											
1966	0.0	1.1	6.2	19.1	7.8	7.9	8.7	2.0	6.2	3.1	12.7
1967	16.7	2.5	9.2	0.4	0.2	1.7	1.9	0.0	-1.9	2.5	7.1
1968	0.0	12.2	1.3	4.3	1.9	2.0	2.8	-2.0	-1.0	10.0	0.3
1969	0.0	2.2	0.2	6.1	3.9	2.5	2.4	5.0	5.0	7.3	5.3
1970	0.0	4.7	10.9	9.0	10.2	6.1	8.1	1.0	-1.0	5.7	9.8
1971	20.0	15.2	12.2	16.4	13.3	12.0	12.7	2.8	3.8	18.4	16.6
1972	0.0	—	—	13.9	12.4	12.9	14.2	6.4	7.4		
1973(9)	0.0	—	—	24.1	21.2						
1973	0.0	—	—	27.5	26.4	20.0	45.2	28.0	23.0		
1974	42.8	—	—	36.2	56.2	39.7	35.2	37.5	17.9		
Annual average rates of change (percent)											
1967–69	5.3	5.5	3.5	3.6	2.0	2.1	2.4	1.0	0.6	6.6	4.2
1970–73/9	5.0	—	—	16.9	15.2	14.4	14.7				

[1]Annualized rate.

Sources: Column (1) *CBS Annual 1978*, Tables IX–13: X–2; columns (2)–(3) Amiel 1972, Table 2, p. 27; column (4): *CBS Annual 1972*, Table XII–27; columns (5)–(6) *CBS Annual 1978*, Table App. 2. p. 253; columns (8)–(9), *CBS Annual 1978* Table VIII–2; columns (10)–(11) Entries of imports and exports dollar prices, in columns (8) and (9), multiplied respectively by corresponding entries of effective import and export exchange rates, in columns (2) and (3).

Table 4.3. Real Exchange Rates, Real Wages, and Productivity, 1966–74

	Exchange Rate[1]			Terms of			Factor
		Effective		Trade	Wages[2]	Unit Cost[3]	Productivity[4]
	Official	Imports	Exports	Trade	Wages[2]	Unit Cost[3]	Productivity[4]
	(1)	(2)	(3)	(4)	(5)	(6)	(7)
Indices, 1966 = 100							
1966	100.0	100.0	100.0	100.0	100.0	100.0	100.0
1967	114.5	100.6	107.1	98.0	98.7	91.7	103.6
1968	111.4	109.8	105.6	99.0	100.9	89.3	110.4
1969	108.8	109.6	103.4	99.0	104.4	85.2	118.4
1970	100.6	106.2	106.0	98.0	107.3	81.0	124.3
1971	107.2	108.5	105.6	98.0	111.5	78.9	131.5
1972	93.8			99.0	112.6	74.9	138.8
1973(9)	78.0				113.3	72.9	140.1
1973	64.6			95.0	119.7	74.6	
1974	47.8			82.2	116.6	70.6	
Annual rates of change (percent)							
1967–69	2.8	3.1	1.1	−0.3	1.4	−5.2	5.8
1970–73/9	−8.5	—	—	—	2.2	−4.1	4.6

[1]Real Exchange Rates: Nominal rates deflated by GNP Prices.
[2]Real Wages: Nominal rates deflated by consumer prices.
[3]The series represents estimates for the ratio of nominal wages and nominal product per employee, as a proxy for the pattern of unit cost.
[4]Refers to the "private" (non government) sector only.
Sources: Columns (1)–(3) and (5) Table 5.2; column (4) *CBS Annual* 1978, Table VIII-2, p. 214; column (6) Nominal average product of labor according to GDP and employment series of Table 4.1, adjusted to nominal values by GDP implicit price series of Table 4.2, and nominal wage series entries of the same Table; column (7): 1966–69, *Annual Report* 1972, Table II-8, p. 24; 1970–1974, *Annual Report* 1974, Table II-9, p. 30.

What made the difference was the state of employment. Figure 4.2 emphasizes this by showing the intersection of the very low and declining unemployment curve and the still-low but rising price-level curve. This leaves no doubt that the primer for the inflationary eruption that followed—an escalation from near-zero annual rates to more than 20% within three years—must be traced to other factors. The onus for the takeoff of the accelerating inflationary process, which would take more than a decade to reverse, belongs to demand-side factors. These were dominated first by a highly expansionary fiscal policy, trailed by an accommodating monetary policy, both of which soon fed expectations of a rapidly rising pattern of the price level. These are the subjects of the analysis that follows.

THE EXPANSIONARY IMPETUS OF FISCAL POLICY

The comings and goings of the economy during the "seven good years," Q2-1967–Q3-1973, were clearly dominated by the rising impact of general government on the workings of the system. The main thrust of this development on the expenditure side materialized through 1969 and continued with less momentum until 1973. On the absorption side, the pattern was quite different: a modest rising trend through 1969 and greater momentum from 1970 onward. The tax and tax-plus (domestic) revenues series in table 4.4 makes this clear. In terms of the latter, broader, definition—which includes government receipts on property and interest account—state revenues climbed from 31% of GDP through 1966 to 36% in 1969, more than 42% in 1970, and 44% in 1972. The rising trend traced to the move of large groups of households into higher income-tax brackets due to rapid growth and also, from 1970, to the escalating rate of inflation. Israel's steeply progressive income-tax structure was relevant in this context. Higher tax rates, income-indexed social security contributions, and indirect taxation were also involved.[3]

This substantial rise in the ratio of tax revenues to social product was, of course, the obverse image of a much larger increase in the ratio of general-government expenditure to GDP. Domestic expenditure climbed from less than 30% of domestic product through 1965 to slightly over 30% in 1966, the slowdown year, and almost 42% in 1969, relative to a domestic product that had grown by 33% since 1966. Thus, real general-government expenditure ballooned by 80% in three years. By 1972, domestic expenditure had climbed to 48% of GDP. Similarly, foreign expenditure, which covered defense imports and interest on the foreign debt, climbed from only 3% of GDP in 1966 to 10%-plus territory by 1970 (table 4.4). This rate of increase in government activity meant that during the six years between 1966 and 1972, real general-government expenditure grew by about 2.8 times on domestic account and by 5.8 times on foreign account.

Most of the leap in expenditure, especially on foreign account, reflected the fact that during the first three of those "seven good years" the country was involved in a war of attrition that included actual combat along the Suez Canal and on its eastern border. Thus, the defense budget skyrocketed. The last four years of the period, through 1973, were a time of major efforts to rebuild the defense line along the canal and to rearm. The stable ratio of total budget expenditure at 59% of GDP in the three years through 1972 (table 4.4) shows that absolute defense expenditure had leveled off at the record 1970 plateau (Berglas, 1983, table A-1) after a second armistice along the Canal and the "Black September" affair in Jordan halted combat on these two fronts until October 1973.

The rising trend in both revenue and expenditure, with the latter rising at higher rates than the former, inevitably shifted general government from a pattern of surpluses on income and expenditure account (both foreign and domestic) in the first half of the 1960s to a rapidly rising deficit pattern from 1967 on.[4] The miniscule deficit in GDP terms in 1966, which in view of the severe economic slowdown was quite warranted, occurred mainly due to an external development, a decrease in unilateral receipts that shifted the external component of the total into the red. Thus, the expansionary impetus was provided by the government's domestic operations, which turned a domestic surplus of 1.4% of GDP in 1965 into domestic equilibrium (tables 3.11 and 4.4). This reflected, at least in part, a deliberate expansionary move on the expenditure

Table 4.4. General-Government Fiscal Indicators,[1] 1966–74 (percent of GDP)

	Expenditures			Revenues			Deficit (−)			Public Debt Ratio[6]		
	Foreign[2] (1)	Domestic (2)	Total (3)=(1)+(2)	Tax (4)	Tax Plus[3] (5)	Unilateral[4] (6)	Foreign[5] (7)=(6)−(1)	Domestic (8)=(5)−(2)	Total (9)=(7)+(8)	External (12)	Domestic (13)	Total (14)
1966	3.0	30.8	33.8	28.1	30.8	2.1	−0.4	0.0	−0.3	13.3	33.8	47.1
1967	3.3	34.2	37.5	26.6	29.4	6.2	3.7	−4.9	−1.2	15.4	35.9	51.3
1968	4.4	41.2	45.6	31.0	34.0	3.5	0.4	−7.3	−7.0	19	35.7	54.7
1969	5.1	41.6	46.7	32.8	35.9	3.7	−0.6	−5.6	−6.2	24.3	35.5	59.8
1970	14.6	44.4	59.0	38.7	42.6	3.7	−10.6	−1.7	−12.2	28.1	35.2	63.3
1971	11.3	47.7	59.0	42.9	46.5	3.0	−7.9	−1.1	−8.9	31.9	42.2	74.1
1972	10.7	48.2	58.9	40.2	44.1	3.9	−6.7	−4.0	−10.8	27.4	42.9	70.3
1973	19.6	54.0	73.6	40.4	43.7	15.5	−3.1	−10.5	−13.6	21.8	52.8	74.6
1974	14.8	60.1	74.9	43.6	47.2	8.0	−5.8	−12.8	−18.7	23.6	59.8	83.4

[1]Based on revised BOI series including changes in classification and definitions, as published in Report 1999. Refers to the income-expenditures dimension only, thus excludes fiscal operations—borrowing and foreign repayments and government lending and repayment flows in domestic capital markets.

[2]Foreign Expenditures: Cost of Government imports including defense imports, and net interest payments.

[3]Tax plus include: Tax revenues, receipts on property account, receipts on interest account, and from 1960 depreciation charges and nominal receipts on civil pensions account.

[4]Unilateral receipts from abroad by Government and other public sector institutions, includes German reparations, UJA donations, etc.

[5]Foreign Deficit: Unilateral foreign receipts minus cost of public sector imports.

[6]Bank of Israel estimates.

Sources: Revised Bank of Israel Series: *Annual Report 1999*, Table Appendix V1a and V1b.

side in fiscal 1966/1967, taken in response to an unexpectedly steep decline in the level of activity that had bumped unemployment rate up to 7.4% by the middle of that year (table 4.1)—twice the prevalent rate in the full-employment years (1960–65). Having become a headline issue, the upturn in unemployment carried obvious expansionary consequences for fiscal policy.

Thus, the Six-Day War was a fiscal watershed. After a decade, the economy performed a volte-face, switching from domestic and total budget surpluses on income and expenditure account to rapidly rising deficits on domestic, external, and total account. Outstanding war expenditure replaced the balanced domestic budget with a deficit of about 5% in 1967. The Diaspora, by now a traditional source of external revenue, increased its donations by 4% of Israel's GDP, generating a major surplus on general-government foreign account and holding the total deficit on income and expenditure account to a highly reasonable 1.2% of GDP. Although still highly significant in terms of the size of the economy, the reduced unilateral receipts of general government from 1968 onward, about 3.5% of GDP, pushed the total deficit to 6% of gross product through 1969 and into double-digit territory from 1970 on (table 4.4).[5]

With the economy operating at 90%–92% of capacity—the unemployment rate was 10% by the middle of 1967—the leap in government expenditure and the corresponding deficit were clearly warranted in terms of macroeconomic considerations. Through 1969, they hardly affected the price level. The vigorous increase in aggregate demand that the deficit generated had most of its effect on the quantity side, that is, on national product. By 1969, however, while the deficit had not yet surpassed 6% of GDP, the economy had attained full employment. It moved well past that frontier in 1970 and did so even more emphatically in succeeding years (table 4.1).

The rise of inflation, a universal phenomenon in the developed world in 1970—albeit at lower rates than in Israel—pressured the government to attempt to downsize its domestic deficit. Although the domestic deficit was cut substantially in the early 1970s (table 4.4 and *Annual Report*, 1972, tables VII-1 and VII-2), it was too little, too late. It was too late because the fiscal contraction was attained not by means of an immediate reduction in current government expenditure but by a major rise of tax revenue, which in the best case could reduce the bulging aggregate demand at a substantial lag. It was too little because it was applied to the ordinary (current) government budget irrespective of concurrent moves on the "other avenue"—the government capital account, that is, the monetary injection effected by means of the development budget. The huge government injection in 1970–71, shown in table 4.5 [and the related other injections (figure 4.3)], traced to an increase in government credit from the development budget, manifested in PAMELA deposits on the books of the commercial banking system. (See "The Impact of the 1973 Shock" in chapter 6 of this volume.) The escalation of inflation to annual rates of more than 10% in 1970 and 20% in the three quarters preceding the outbreak of war in October 1973 offers relevant evidence on this score. However, this prelude to Israel's great inflation cannot be traced solely to fiscal policy and its impact on monetary developments. Monetary policy seems to have been a joker in this game, and we turn our attention to this factor now.

Table 4.5. Monetary Injections and Inflation, 1966–74, Normalized by Monetary Base at the Beginning of the Year (percent)

	BOI Injection[1] (1)	Private Conversion[2] (2) = (4)−[(1) + (2)]	Government Injection[3] (3)	Annual Change of Monetary Base (4)	Inflation (5)
1966	3.2	−24.0	25.2	4.4	7.8
1967	3.1	−59.8	84.9	28.2	0.2
1968	−3.1	−31.7	51.1	16.4	1.9
1969	18.7	−61.5	40.9	−1.9	3.9
1970	4.6	−45.9	61.1	19.8	12.1
1971	5.6	−24.7	68.1	49.0	13.4
1972	18.9	28.0	−5.4	41.5	12.4
1973	23.3	−34.2	36.8	26.0	26.4
1974	35.0	−67.8	42.1	9.3	56.2
Avg.: 1967−69	6.2	−51.0	59.0	14.2	2.0
S.D.: 1967−69	11.2	16.7	23.1	15.1	1.9
Avg.: 1970−72	9.7	−14.2	41.3	36.8	12.6
S.D.: 1970−72	8.0	38.0	40.6	15.2	0.7

[1]BOI injection: change in bills discounted—BOI's component of "directed credit"—plus change in "other accounts," minus change of commercial Bank term Deposits, in BOI's end year balance sheet.
[2]Private conversion of foreign exchange derived as a residual.
[3]Government injection: domestic injection plus foreign (sources) injection. Domestic injection derived from Bank of Israel balance sheet data. Foreign injection derived from Balance of Payments data on unilateral (public sector) receipts from abroad, minus the value of "government imports" (the cost of defense imports), minus net interest payments plus net public sector foreign transactions on capital account.
Sources: Column(1): BOI injection. Derived from Bank of Israel Balance sheet data. *Annual Reports* 1967, Table XX1-1, *Report* 1968, Table XX-1, *Annual Report* 1970, Table XIX-1, *Annual Report* 1972, Table XVIII-1, and *Annual Report* 1974, Table XX-1. These tables are based on the annual balance sheets included in each *Annual Report*. Column (3): Government domestic injections: *Annual Reports* 1967, 1968, 1970, 1972 and 1974—the same tables used to derive column (1) BOI entries. Government foreign injections: Balance of Payment data in *Annual Reports*: 1967, Table XII-1; 1969, Table III-18, 1971, Tables III-17, and III-21; 1973, Tables III-20 and III-27, 1974, Tables IV-25, and V-4. Data on defense imports according to Berglas (1983). Columns (4)–(5). Tables 4.4 and 4.2, respectively.

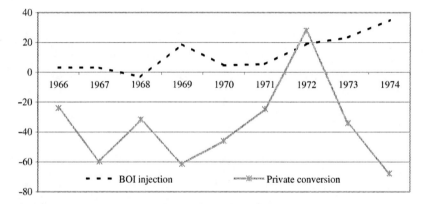

Figure 4.3. BOI Injection and Private Conversion, 1966–74

FROM STABILITY TO INFLATION: MONETARY AGGREGATES, CAPACITY UTILIZATION, AND PRICES

The pattern of the price level in terms of annual average rates of change (figure 4.4) suggests highly reasonable performance in the three-year period through 1969, as the economy moved from an excess-capacity, high-unemployment configuration from 1966 to mid-1967 to a full-employment level of activity by, say, 1970. The across-the-board stability in prices, despite a 17% nominal devaluation in November 1967, is underscored by the price indices.[6] This significant price stability amid rapid economic growth, however, changed tack abruptly in 1970, when annual price inflation leaped to 10% in CPI terms and from 2.4 % to 8.1% in terms of the implicit GNP price index. This level held fast through 1972 but accelerated past 21%, again in annual terms, in the three prewar quarters of 1973. Accordingly, one may define this 45-month period as the takeoff of Israel's "great inflation," which persisted through 1985, declining abruptly in the wake of the 1985 stabilization policy to rates in the 10%–20% range through the late 1990s.

Thus, monetary policy obviously failed in its mission to contain inflation. Admittedly, it had to operate in an environment of strong fiscal expansion and, from late 1969 on, of a very high rate of capacity utilization. The steeply rising curve of the rate of change of monetary aggregates—base money and M_1 from 1970 onward and the maintenance of strong M_1 growth through September 1973 (figures 4.5 and 4.6) offer a first approximation of the evidence in favor of this reading of events. The annual average growth rate of the monetary base and M_1 climbed from around 14% in the three years ending in 1969 to 32% and 24%, respectively, in the forty-five months ending with the outbreak of the October 1973 war. Thus, the expansion rate of M_1 outpaced the growth rate of the economy by a factor of about 2.5. This, of course, points to a highly expansionary monetary policy during that period. Although initiated in 1967, when the system had substantial spare capacity, it was maintained through the early 1970s, after the economy had clearly crossed the full-employment threshold (figure 4.2).

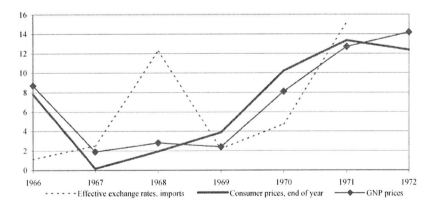

Figure 4.4. Prices and Exchange Rate, 1966–73, Annual Rate of Change (percent)

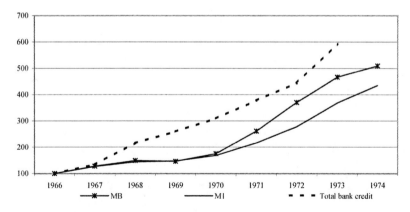

Figure 4.5. Monetary Aggregates, 1966–74 (1966 = 100)

The initial all-out expansionary leap of monetary aggregates in 1967, at annual rates of 28% and 26% for the monetary base and M_1, respectively, was an inevitable expression of unexpected expenditure related to the Six-Day War. These growth rates, however, were warranted in view of the specific macroeconomic context of that year. In the aftermath of the mid-1965–mid-1967 slowdown, when the supply of money had grown quite slowly—by less than 1% in 1966—and the unemployment rate had surged past 7%, even high rates of monetary expansion were reasonable due to their pump-priming effect. This assumes that the pace of monetary expansion would be slowed significantly as the recovery of activity proceeded. On the whole, this was the case in the following two years. Through 1969, the growth rates of the monetary aggregates plummeted, bringing the annual average expansion rates during the three-year recovery phase of the cycle, 1967–69, to 14% for M_1 and the monetary base (table 4.6). This only slightly surpassed the rate of increase in resources.[7] Consequently, prices during that time were almost stable despite the aforementioned 17% nominal devaluation in late 1967 (table 4.2 and figure 4.4) and even

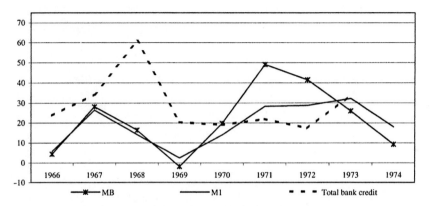

Figure 4.6. Monetary Aggregates, 1966–74 (rates of change, percent)

Table 4.6. Monetary Aggregates, 1966–74[1]

| | Monetary Base (1) | M₁ (2) | Outstanding Credit Balances | | |
			M₂ (3)	Banks[2] (4)	Total[3] (5)
Indices, 1966 = 100					
1966	100.0	100.0	100.0	100.0	100.0
1967	128.2	126.4	141.8	134.4	127.1
1968	149.2	144.4	174.7	216.2	156.5
1969	146.4	147.9	179.7	260.2	224.3
1970	175.4	168.6	255.2	309.7	284.8
1971	261.4	216.2	333.8	377.7	357.9
1972	369.8	278.3	436.6	443.4	424.8
1973(9)	422.5	333.4		546.2	596.2
1973	465.9	368.2	525.3	594.1	577.2
1974	509.2	434.4	575.8		
Annual rates of change (percent)					
1966	4.4	0.6	6.7	23.7	19.5
1967	28.2	26.4	41.8	34.1	27.1
1968	16.4	14.2	23.2	60.9	23.1
1969	−1.9	2.5	2.9	20.4	43.3
1970	19.8	14.0	42.0	19.0	27.0
1971	49.0	28.3	30.8	22.0	25.7
1972	41.5	28.7	30.8	17.4	18.7
1973(9)	19.0	26.4		30.8	53.8
1973	26.0	32.3	20.3	34.0	35.9
1974	9.3	18.0	9.6		
Avg.: 1967−69	14.2	14.4	22.6	38.5	31.2
S.D.: 1967−69	15.1	12.0	19.5	20.6	10.7
Avg.: 1970−73/9	32.3	24.3		22.3	31.3
S.D.: 1970−73/9	16.7	7.1		2.7	9.0

[1]End year balances.
[2]Total credit accommodated by the commercial banking system including the total outstanding "directed credit" balance, a component of which was BOI's quota—identified as discounts on the Central Bank's balance sheet.
[3]Total credit at the disposal of customers: credit balance of the commercial banking system (entries of Column 4), plus government credit intermediated by commercial banks and financed, by special PAMELA "government deposits for loans" with them.
Sources: Columns (1)–(3): 1966–69 Zanbar-Bronfeld, April-September 1973, Table (3), and (4), p. 7 and p. 9; 1970–74, *Annual Report 1974*, Tables XVII-4, p. 360 and XVII-6, p. 369 and a similar Table in *Annual Report 1973*; columns (4)–(5), *Annual Report 1968*, Table XV-IV, p. 279, *Annual Report 1970*, Table XIV-10, p. 275, *Annual Report 1972*, Table XIII-14, p. 312, *Annual Report-1974*, Table XXVII-10, p. 379.

as the "Vietnam inflation" began to take its toll, lifting prices in the United States and the European Community by 4%–5% on annual average through 1969.

The price data for the second half of the seven-year period elicit a totally different picture. Capacity utilization climbed rapidly and approached its limit as the labor market moved toward overfull employment. The average annual expansion rate of M_1, 24% from 1970 to the three prewar quarters of 1973, could not but stoke inflation in a system that was operating at if not beyond its potential.

INNOVATION IN AND EVOLUTION OF MONETARY POLICY

It was at this juncture that the BOI failed to deliver the goods, even though from the last quarter of 1966 it ostensibly possessed the two classical control instruments of monetary policy: control of the money multiplier and the ability to operate in the open market on the selling as well as on the buying side.

The political background of these developments is highly relevant. The major war effort, beginning in the middle of May 1967 and continuing with the war proper and its immediate aftermath, entailed the maintenance of an extraordinarily large standing army and, in turn, an immense allocation of real resources. The end of active hostilities in June 1967 was followed by three years of war of attrition and a major rearmament effort in the wake of the second cease-fire on the Suez Canal (August 1970). Consequently, defense expenditure skyrocketed—by a factor of 2.4 relative to 1966 by 1969 and by 3.0 in 1972, both in real terms (Berglas, 1983, p. 51). Traditionally, governments that face needs of this kind resort to inflationary finance, accommodated in one way or another by the central bank, thus leading to extraordinary expansion of the money supply. Developments on this score were even more complicated in the Israeli case due to the economy's dependence on enormous receipts of sources of finance on unilateral and capital accounts from abroad, over which the central bank effectively had no control. This, in turn, allowed the private sector to amass a major deficit on the dominant component of its external activities, the trade and services account of the balance of payments.

Accordingly, the study of monetary policy in that period involves an analysis of the liquidity injections and drains generated by fiscal policy, the "private" (nongovernmental) sector's foreign-currency transactions, and, finally, the BOI's efforts, such as they were, to cancel out the impact of these two sectors—their contribution—to the rapidly expanding supply of money. The central bank acted during most of this seven-year period by trying to use at least one of the two levers mentioned above, that is, to manipulate the size of the multiplier and to attempt—successfully at first and unsuccessfully from 1970 on—to control of the size of the monetary base. To analyze the BOI's open-market operations, however, we must first turn our attention to the statutory interest ceiling—the "Usury Law"—which remained on the books until 1970.

Track Clearance: Repeal of the "Usury Law"

Although formally at its disposal all along, an instrument that the BOI needed to operate on the selling side of the open market, if it chose to do so, was effectively vested in the central bank by the April 1966 "MAKAM accord" between the Ministry of Finance and the BOI (see "An Opening to an Open-Market Policy: The 1966 MAKAM [Treasury Bill] Accord" in chapter 3 of this volume). At this time, the 11% maximum interest rate allowed by law remained in effect. The meaningful reduction in inflation that followed, however—from almost 8% in June 1966 to around zero for the rest of that year and all of 1967 (table 4.2)—meant that the BOI's move into the selling side of the market, instigated in late 1966 with nominal yields to redemption of 7.68% on three-month MAKAM (short-term loan securities), almost 8% on six-month instruments, and even higher rates on twelve-month bills, proved highly attractive (Sanbar and Bronfeld, 1973, p. 227, table 10). Households were offered an additional implicit bonus due to the absence of a capital-gains tax, meaning that net yields on these (and other) capital-market instruments were equal to gross yields.

Thus, although the legal interest ceiling remained on the books, the BOI's move into the market proved successful at once. Accordingly, the maximum interest rate allowed by law was wholly irrelevant in the 1967–68 price environment. This was indicated in several significant reductions of nominal yields on MAKAM bills in 1967 and stable yields in 1968 while sales of these instruments in both years were brisk. Indeed, the balance of MAKAM held by the public was 83% higher at the end of 1968 than at the end of 1966 (table 4.7). The changing price-level environment in 1969, however, immediately drove net sales of MAKAM into the red,[8] leading to a turnaround of the rates at which these bills were offered to the public; the rates were raised from April 1969 on.[9] If yields continued to increase beyond the 7.75% level that twelve-month bills commanded in November 1969, they might collide with the de jure interest ceiling. The repeal of the ceiling in March 1970 eliminated this constraint and gave the BOI more freedom to tighten rates if required. It also eliminated at once the bill-brokerage market, which at that time was still the source of about 20% of total commercial bank credit. This removed an obstacle to the flow of funds from lenders to borrowers and facilitated open-market operations.

Furthermore, the repeal had a beneficial structural effect on the banking system by reducing (among other things) the legal uncertainties that had surrounded the workings of the bill-brokerage market. One immediate manifestation of its importance was the "unification" of interest rates that commercial banks charged for "free" credit, that is, the elimination of the dual lending interest structure that the banking system had maintained on credit from its "own sources" since 1960. The resulting average rate, although higher than that charged previously for loans granted from banks' "own sources," was lower than the rate on credit traded in the bill-brokerage market (AR [Annual Report] 1970, p. 9). Indeed, typical rates for bill-brokerage credit early in 1970, shortly before the abolition of the ceiling, were 17%–17.5% as against 10%–11% at major banks for their "free (nondirected) credit" tranche. The "unified" rate came to 15.5%–17% at the end of 1970, although many customers—firms and authorities that had strong bargaining positions and good collateral—did better (AR 1970, p. 277). Since the major leap of inflation had become a fait accompli by the end of that year, and for this reason had begun to affect price expectations, these end-of-year rates are of course not fully comparable with rates in the first quarter of 1970.

Table 4.7. Patterns of Selected Bank of Israel Asset and Liability Balances: 1966–77

| | Foreign Reserves[1] | | Net Government Liabilities | Discounts[2] | Monetary Base | Total | | | | MAKAM[3] | |
| | IL | Dollar | | | | Foreign Reserves | Government Liabilities | Discounts | Monetary Base | Ratio[4] | Index |
	(1)	(2)	(3)	(4)	(5)	(6)	(7)	(8)	(9)	(10)	(11)
Indices, 1966 = 100						*Ratios to totals on balance sheet (percent)*					
1966	100.0	100.0	100.0	100.0	100.0	75.3	12.4	10.4	4.4	20.5	100
1967	134.3	115.1	133.8	156.3	128.6	65.0	23.3	10.4	28.6	22.4	140
1968	124.5	106.7	446.6	172.2	153.5	57.6	28.2	11.2	19.3	24.5	183
1969	77.5	66.4	959.1	314.4	151.7	30.4	48.3	17.3	−1.1	23.4	173
1970	86.2	73.9	1337.8	385.0	180.1	26.8	53.3	16.8	18.7	23.5	208
1971	165.0	117.9	1862.1	493.9	268.8	33.7	48.8	14.2	49.3	17.2	266
1972	277.3	198.1	1744.2	763.6	379.9	42.8	34.5	16.5	41.4	13.6	277
1973(9)	362.3	258.8	—	—	434.1	—	—	—	19.0	12.9	305
1973	408.1	291.5	1741.5	1073.5	478.6	49.2	26.9	18.2	26.0	6.2	156
1974	270.5	193.2	2796.5	1829.1	—	24.5	32.5	23.3	—	2.7	56

[1]The differences of entries in index number series between IL and dollar terms reflect changes in the exchange rate.

[2] "Discounts" represents Bank of Israel accommodated "directed credits" implemented by discounting a set quota of notes submitted by commercial banks.

[3]Makam; short-term (government) loan.

[4]Ratio of value of outstanding Makam balance to monetary base.

Sources: All columns excluding column 11: Bank of Israel Balance Sheets, and corresponding Table 1, in chapter on "Bank of Israel activities" in the *Annual Report* of the BOI. Column (11): 1966–71 Zanbar-Bronfeld (1973), Tables 11; 1972–74 *Annual Report* 1972 Table XVIII-13; *Annual Report* 1973 Table XVI-11; and *Annual Report* 1974, pp. 482–83.

The Monetary Base: The Impact of Government and Private Sector Injections

Our reference to the 81-month period from 1967 to September 1973 as a time in which the economy was subject to inflation of the money supply captures events reasonably in view of the 20% annual average expansion rate of M_1. However, we may enhance our understanding of developments in the monetary dimension of the economy by dividing the period into two subperiods, 1967–69 and 1970–73, and studying the monetary comings and goings in each. In the first subperiod, M_1 and the monetary base expanded at nearly 14% per annum, a reasonable pace in view of the rate of capacity utilization and the growth performance of the economy. The second subperiod, however, when the monetary base and M_1 expanded at annual average rates of 32% and 24%, respectively, was obviously a time of extraordinary inflation of the money supply.[10] The climax of monetary expansion occurred in 1971, at the towering pace of nearly 50% (figure 4.6).

This rising trend of the monetary base—the major determinant of the supply of money—and the highly significant variance of its annual rate of change, from 1.9% in 1969 to almost 50% in 1971 (table 4.6), were determined largely by the interplay of government and private-sector injections and drainage during these years.[11] The interplay of these two sectors and, in turn, their impact on the (monetary) liquidity of the economy reverted to the 1950s pattern, in which the government sector injected liquidity into the system while the private sector operated as a draining agent. This feature applied to each and every year through 1960, whereas in the 1961–67 interval the two sectors alternated between injection and draining roles, usually in opposite directions (table 3.9 and figures 3.6–3.8).

The overall averages of the two sectors' injection rates underscore the opposing effects of the sectors on the money supply during this period. In the first subperiod, 1967–69, the government sector's average injection rate of base-money-creating assets climbed to 59% of the outstanding balance of the base at the beginning of each year. The countervailing drainage effect of the private

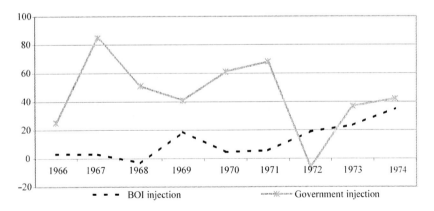

Figure 4.7. BOI and Government Injections, 1966–74 (percent)

sector in total terms (i.e., its net effect on trading and services account plus the net injection from its current and past unilateral receipts and its capital imports) generated net drainage of base-money-creating assets of about 51% on average relative to the same outstanding base money balance (table 4.5). In the second subperiod, 1970–72 (for which only data excluding the impact of the war are available), the annual government injection rate was lower but still enormous— 41% of the monetary base at the beginning of each year—and the drainage effect of the private sector declined much more steeply, to an annual average of 14%. Another interesting inference that arises from the data is the difference in variance of these two injection (and drainage) time series. The variance of the private-sector series, measured in terms of the coefficient of variation was significantly greater in the second subperiod in particular. The lag and lead effects of the timing of foreign-currency conversions performed largely by exporters and importers on trade account, and by the banking system on short-term capital account, is a well-known feature in countries that have fixed exchange-rate regimes even if they maintain extensive exchange controls. In the Israeli case, the lag-lead feature had an especially powerful effect because it could be implemented not only by professionals directly involved in foreign-trade transactions and by dealers in money but also by the large group of households that received restitution payments—a group that in 1970 took in an annual inflow of almost 4% of GDP (table 4.8). Furthermore, these households were allowed to place much of their annual reparations receipts in forex-denominated and indexed deposits, the cumulative value of which by 1970 had climbed to nearly four times the annual inflow of reparations payments that year. The accumulated volume of these deposits, which could be converted into domestic currency whenever their owners wished, soon became even more significant: in 1966, 75% of the size of the monetary base at the beginning of that year, and 113% of the corresponding parameter in 1970.[12]

The bunching of these private conversions into domestic currency, as occurred in 1970 and 1972, meant that these transactions alone potentially inflated the monetary base by nearly 43% and 59% in these two years, respectively. On the other hand, in 1969 the actual conversion ratio was lower than in the preceding year, although its potential effect on the monetary base—reflecting the ratio of the value of these foreign-currency deposits (in domestic-currency terms) to the base—was higher at the beginning of 1969 than in 1968. The blatant contrast between the two annual conversion rates, even though the potential was higher in 1969, reflects changes in expectations of a forthcoming devaluation. In 1969, devaluation was thought to be around the corner. These expectations were (temporarily) shelved in 1970 due to the government's decision to adopt a fiscal alternative to devaluation, the imposition of a 20% surcharge on imports (excluding "necessities") and a similar subsidy rate on exports (*Annual Report*, 1970, pp. 125–28, 348–50). The conversions that had been deferred in 1969 were compensated for in 1970 by a much higher conversion ratio than in 1968.

This explains the lower coefficient of variation, of the government and on the whole, and the much greater variance of the private sector's impact on the

Table 4.8. Unilateral Receipts and Private-Sector Net Conversions,[1] 1966–74

	Private Sector			Unilateral, Receipt Total $ Million	PAZAK-TAMAM Deposits			IL million		Ratio of Net Conversions to MBt-1[4] (percent)
	Restitution Payments (1)	Total (2)	General Govt. (3)	(4) = (2) + (3)	Balance (5)	Net Change (6)	Net Conversions[2] (7) = (2)−(6)	Net Conversions[3] (8)	Monetary Base (9)	(10)
1966	110.4	194.0	98.0	292.0	339.7	52.3	141.7	425.1	1317.1	32.8
1967	123.2	207.0	314.0	521.0	405.1	65.5	141.5	438.7	1694.4	33.3
1968	143.3	277.0	171.0	448.0	500.0	94.9	182.1	637.4	2021.1	37.6
1969	137.9	290.0	169.0	459.0	637.4	137.4	152.6	534.1	1998.4	26.7
1970	203.6	376.0	274.0	650.0	768.6	131.1	244.9	857.2	2371.6	42.9
1971	230.7	536.0	229.0	765.0	950.0	181.4	354.6	1138.3	3540.0	48.0
1972	291.5	683.0	368.0	1054.0	1112.1	162.1	520.9	2083.6	5004.0	58.9
1973	264.3	642.0	1530.0	2172.0	1431.0	318.9	323.1	1357.0	6303.0	27.1
Avg.: 1967–69	134.8	258.0	218.0	476.0	514.2	99.3	158.7	536.7	1904.6	32.5
	10.4	44.6	83.1	39.4	116.8	36.2	21.0	99.4	182.4	5.5
Avg.: 1970–73/9	229.8	531.7	290.3	823.0	1065.4	198.4	360.9	1359.0	4158.2	44.2
	44.0	153.5	70.9	208.2	281.2	83.0	116.2	524.6	1496.6	13.2

[1] Conversions of foreign into domestic currency at official exchange rate.
[2] Conversions of foreign currency by private sector recipients of unilateral payments.
[3] Net conversion IL: Nominal dollar entries, column (7), multiplied by the current official exchange rate.
[4] Ratio of net conversions to monetary base at the end of the previous year.

Sources: Column (1)–(3): Annual Reports 1972 and 1974, Tables III-25, and V-4, respectively; column (5) 1966–71: Zanbar-Bronfeld (1973), Tables 4 and (9); Annual Report 1974, Table XVII-7; column (6) Derived from Column (5); column (9) 1966–69: Zanbar-Bronfeld (1973), Table 4; Annual Report 1970–74; and Annual Report 1974, Table XVII-4.

size of the monetary base. It clearly reflects the more rapid and powerful response of business and households to exchange-rate changes and price expectations, inspired by the comings and goings of the real dimension of the economy and, particularly, by the current account of the balance of payments. The more flexible response of nongovernmental sectors to economic developments is a universal phenomenon. It had a strong impact on Israel's monetary arrangements due to the quantitatively significant inflow of foreign transfer payments to households that received restitution payments. Despite the considerable variance of each of these two series—the injection series of the government sector and the draining series of the private (nongovernmental) sector—their combined effect resulted in much less variance, evidently due to the sectors' opposing roles in the potential expansion of the monetary base.[13]

This splitting of six of the seven "good years" into two subperiods—1967–69 and 1970–September 1973—by using the crossing of the full-employment threshold around the beginning of 1970 as the dividing line, places in proper perspective the two sectors' combined effect on the potential expansion of the monetary base.[14] Thus, the annual average of their combined injection to the monetary base in 1967–69 was only 8% of the outstanding balance of the monetary base at the beginning of each of these years. The contrast between this and the combined impact of the two sectors on the (potential) expansion of the monetary base in the second subperiod could not have been greater. The annual average combined injection rate in the 1970–72 interval was 27% of the balance of the monetary base at the beginning of each of these years, a rate that seemed incongruous even amid very strong annual growth of nearly 10% during those years. In the preceding three years, the 8% combined injection rate fell short of the rate of economic growth, a result consistent with a stable price environment. This was evidently not the case from 1970 onward.

The BOI's Successful Experiment in Open-Market Policy and Its Demise

The dominant role of the monetary base as the determinant of the time pattern of M_1 and corresponding monetary aggregates was, as noted, a challenge that the BOI had faced from the very beginning. The central bank confronted this conundrum with even greater intensity from 1960 on, as its attempts to curb the momentum of monetary expansion in 1962–63 and again in 1965 by employing its leverage on the size of the money multiplier yielded results that were anything but encouraging.

In the 1967–69 interval, the BOI had to tackle the combined effect of the public- and private-sector injections of liquidity—8% of the balance of the monetary base at the beginning of the year. The bunched impact of these two sectors on the potential expansion of the base in the succeeding three-year subperiod, 1970–72, was altogether different, as stated: an annual average of 27% of the relevant balance of the base.[15]

This contrast in the two sectors' combined impact on the monetary dimension of the system called for central-bank intervention in the opposing direction. In the first triad of years, say through mid-1969, it is clear that the BOI should have acted in the money market by creating a net injection of liquidity in order to grease the wheels of the real economy (see, however, figure 4.7). The central bank's marching orders in the succeeding period, through the prewar quarters of 1973, should have placed it on the other side of the fence, that is, it should have attempted to effect a net drainage of the large excess liquidity inflow occasioned by the combined impact of the government and private sectors.

Thus, the 1966 MAKAM accord (discussed in chapter 3) came at an opportune moment. Signed during a severe slowdown of economic activity that argued in favor of an accommodative rather than a restrictive policy, it opened the gate to the money market and gave the BOI an instrument with which it could affect the size of the monetary base. The sale of MAKAM created a deposit balance on the BOI's balance sheet (table 4.7), indicating that by the end of 1966, several months after its first foray of MAKAM sales in the market, the BOI had increased the outstanding balance of these securities by 6% in terms of the size of the monetary base at the beginning of that year. This was a restrictive move indeed, since it reduced the potential expansion of the monetary base by that order in the context of what had been recognized by then as a major economic slowdown. Its immediate purpose, however, was technical—to establish a position in the relevant market. The BOI compensated for this draining operation by increasing its balance of other government debt ("domestic and foreign-currency advances" in terms of its balance-sheet jargon) and of "discounts."[16] Accordingly, the BOI's net contribution to system liquidity in 1966 was positive, at an injection rate of 3.2% of the outstanding monetary base required at that juncture (table 4.5). This level of injection, which just tilted the balance and provided for a small (4.4%) increase of the base, seemed quite justified under the circumstances.

Although the central bank operated on the selling side of the market rather than at the opposite pole, its action gave the discount window the required touch, indicating by the end of 1966 that the yield to redemption of forthcoming issues of MAKAM could be lowered with no detriment to the bank's ability to create larger outstanding issues of MAKAM. Thus, yields to maturity were reduced four times on short-term bills (3–6 months) and twice on longer-term instruments (12–18 months) between the end of November 1966 and the end of March 1967. Even so, the outstanding balance of all series increased in Q1-1967 and remained stable even when yields were lowered again in October 1967 by 1.75% and 1.46% on short-term and longer-term MAKAM (*AR 1967*, p. 505).

This sequence of reductions, which set rates (for October 1967) at 5.75%–6.25% on short-term and 6.75% on longer-term (twelve-month) MAKAM, clearly followed the market trend. Strong evidence of this was the spiking of interest rates in the bill-brokerage market in the last quarter of 1966 and their rapid and steep decline in 1967 and through Q4-1968 (tables 3.8 and 4.9). Thus, in the wake of the post–Six-Day War monetary expansion, the BOI was able to further reduce the relevant short-term rates and still increase the outstanding balance of MAKAM. This balance increased by 9% of the outstanding balance of the monetary base at the beginning of 1967 and by 9.5% of the much

Table 4.9. Nominal and Real Interest Rates, 1964–74 (percent)

	Nominal Interest Rate (Short-term Bank Credit[1]) (1)	Real Interest Rate[2] (%) (2)	Real Interest Rate on "Development" Credit (%) (3)	Real Rate of Return Gov. Bonds (%) (4)	Nominal Rate Return on MAKAM[3] (%) (5)
1964	16.00	11.5		4.6	—
1965	16.2	8.5	0.87	4.1	—
1966	17.9	9.4	0.18	4.4	7.70
1967	16.5	16.3	7.8	5.1	6.30
1968	14.3	12.1	6.0	6.2	5.80
1969	15.3	11.0	4.9	5.1	6.30
1970	17.8	7.0	−1.0	6.2	7.75
1971	18.6	4.6	−3.9	4.9	8.50
1972	19.0	5.9	−3.0	5.3	8.50
1973(9)	—	—	−13.8	5.6	8.50
1973	20.5	−4.7	—	—	8.50
1974	24.6	−20.2	−30.2	2.8	9.25

[1]The series represents average effective interest rates on "brokered bills" through 1969. From 1970 it represents the interest rate on the major fraction of short-term bank credit: the "free bank credit" which after the abolition of the legal ceiling on interest rates in March 1970 absorbed the balance of the "bill brokerage" component of what previously was definded as "free bank credit."
[2]Real rate: nominal rate (column 1) deflated by CPI.
[3]Rates (rounded) on 3-month bills. The entries represent annual averages if and when the (predetermined) set supply prices of these bills (sold at set discount) were changed within a given year. This occurred three times in 1966, four times in 1967—within which the 7.5 percent (discount) rate set at the end of 1966 was reduced to its all-time low of 5.75 percent; and finally three times in 1969 in which the rate was raised 7.75 percent in November. The 8.5 percent rate was maintained from August 1971 through October 1974.
Sources: Columns (1)–(4): Bank of Israel data bank. July 6, 1990; column (5) Zanbar and Bronfeld (1973), Table 10, p. 227, and Annual Report 1974, p. 482.

larger outstanding balance in 1968 (table 4.7). These sales on the open market were indeed the right moves—restrictive moves par excellence—at the right time. By reducing the potential expansion of the base at the rates cited, each year respectively through 1968, they held the annual average rate of monetary base expansion during these three years (1967–69) to only 14%.

Thus, in more than one sense, it is quite warranted to attribute the stable price level during the powerful upswing of the business cycle, from 1967 onward, to the BOI's success in wielding its newly acquired instrument with the proper impact on the restraining side of the divide. The zero sum of its net injection rates in 1967 and 1968—an injection of 3.1% of the monetary base in 1967 and a drain of 3.1% of the (larger) monetary base at the beginning of 1968—underscores the successful outcome of the BOI's attempt to hold the line in terms of monetary aggregates during that interval and in the entire 1967–69 period. Therefore, the subdued inflationary expectations during that period, occasioned by the relatively stable price level, did not negate the significant income-induced expansion of the demand for money, allowing rising national product to have its full positive income effect on the demand for monetary liquidity. It allowed the economy to absorb a 14% expansion rate of M_1 without a significant effect on the price level.

One can hardly say the same about the next period, a sequence of almost four years—from 1970 to September 1973. The BOI failed altogether in its mission to control the size of the monetary base. Apparently, however, this happened only in Q4-1973, when the outstanding balance of MAKAM bills collapsed by 47% in one go (table 4.7, column 11). Yet the declining pattern of the liquidity draining effect, although volatile, had first surfaced in the two closing quarters of 1969 and became dominant from 1970 on. The ratio of the MAKAM deposit balance to total BOI liabilities clearly suggests as much (table 4.7). The BOI's repeated attempts to save the day by making upward adjustments of rates—several times through August 1971—collapsed for good in 1972. By then, net MAKAM sales stagnated and came to only 1% of the outstanding monetary base at the beginning of that year—as against more than 8% in 1967 and still close to 5% in 1970.

The volatility of the declining trend in the ratio of net sales of MAKAM to the monetary base was inherently linked to the nominal at-issue yields offered to the public and to the rate of inflation, which fueled expectations and affected the corresponding pattern of market interest rates. As inflation surfaced again, the BOI's response to changes in the state of the money market in late 1969 and afterward was usually too little and too late. The changing climate in the financial markets, reflecting foremost the headlong recovery process that propelled the growth rates of GDP and of business-sector product to 15% and 19%, respectively, in 1968, generated commensurably increasing demand for credit. The latter effect began to pull interest rates upward in the middle of 1968, as shown clearly in bill-brokerage rates and the rapid upturn in outstanding credit in this market in the third quarter of that year (tables 3.8 and 4.10, and *Annual Report*, 1968, pp. 6 and 279–80). By 1969, rates were 1 percentage point higher than in 1968. The sluggish reaction of the BOI, which held yields at issue on MAKAM constant for almost twenty months (through April 1969), stopped the rising trend of MAKAM sales and explains the small negative level of net sales in 1969. In other words, at that critical juncture, as the economy was already operating at or quite close to its full-employment potential, the central bank switched from a (weak) selling to a buying stance in the open market. Thus, the BOI's open-market operations in 1969 affected the abrupt turnaround of its role, from an agent of liquidity drainage in 1968 to one of record injection in 1969, at almost 19% of the monetary base at the beginning of that year (table 4.5).

This is not to imply that the BOI's move in 1969 was altogether unwarranted at that point in time. The monetary base contracted slightly in 1969—the first absolute decline since 1957—mainly due to the doubling of drainage by the private sector and a significantly lower injection by government. By implication, a boost of liquidity by the BOI to maintain the level of the monetary base would have been in order. The injection that the BOI engineered in 1969 was plainly designed to hit this target. Accordingly, the BOI's slight open-market buying

Table 4.10. Banking System Aggregates, 1966–74

| | Bank Credit | | | | | | PAZAK + TAMAM Deposits[1] | |
| | Free | | | Directed Credit | Grand Total | Demand Deposits | | |
	Bank Resources (1)	Bill Brokerage (2)	Total (3) = (1)+(2)	(4)	(5) = (3)+(4)	(6)	IL-Index[1] (7)	$ (millions) (8)
Indices, 1966 = 100								
1966	100.0	100.0	100.0	100.0	100.0	100.0	100.0	339.7
1967	144.1	72.7	100.2	127.1	109.4	125.1	139.2	405.1
1968	205.9	63.3	118.2	149.3	128.9	143.8	171.7	500.0
1969	238.6	73.8	137.3	189.1	155.1	146.5	218.9	637.4
1970	408.3	2.1	158.6	231.6	183.7	167.4	264.0	768.6
1971	496.4	0.0	191.3	290.0	225.3	219.4	391.6	950.0
1972	567.3	0.0	218.6	351.8	264.4	287.5	363.3	881.4
1973/9	658.1	0.0	253.6	463.4	325.8	339.9	499.8	1212.6
1973	668.4	0.0	257.6	539.3	354.5	374.1	466.3	1131.4
1974	849.1	0.0	327.2	1034.6	570.5	440.9	816.0	1979.8
Annual rates of change (percent)								
1967–69	33.6	–9.6	11.1	23.7	15.8	13.6	29.8	514.2
1970–73/9	31.1	—	17.8	27.0	21.9	25.2	24.6	953.2

[1]I.L. Index of Pazak-Tamam deposits reflects also change in nominal exchange rates in the wake of devaluations.
Sources: Columns (1), (2), (3), (4), (5) 1966–71, Zambar-Bronfeld (1973), Table 6: 1972–74 *Annual Report 1972*, Table XIII-14; *Annual Report 1974*, Table XVII-10. Column (6) *Annual Report 1967*, Table XV-3, *Annual Report*, 1969, Table XIV-6, *Annual Report 1971*, Table XIV-5, *Annual Report 1973*, Table XIII-7, and *Annual Report 1974*, Table XVII-6. Columns (7) and (8): See sources to column 5 in Table 4.6 and note 1 to that table.

stance that year, reflected in the small contraction of the outstanding balance of MAKAM (table 4.7), was part and parcel of the BOI's significant injection package that year. The central bank implemented this policy by acquiescing in a major upturn in directed credit, increasing its discount-window facility by 83% and allowing the government's debt to the BOI to climb by more than 100% (table 4.7, columns 3 and 4). The increase in the latter parameter more than canceled out the hefty 38% decrease in foreign reserves from the BOI's asset portfolio—the obverse image of the increases in imports—civilian imports due to prosperity and defense imports due to hostilities on the frontiers.

Although the outstanding balance of MAKAM declined only slightly in 1969, the BOI's switch from a selling stance in the open market in 1968 to a buying stance in 1969 had quite an effect on the balance of the monetary base, from 6.7% drainage relative to the outstanding value of the base at the end of 1968 to 0.7% net injection. This was an inevitable market response to the perseverance of the price set for MAKAM back in October 1967 and, therefore, the prospective yield to maturity. This was so even though market interest rates, which had been declining since 1966, had bottomed out by Q2-1968 and were now rising. The Ministerial Committee on Economic Affairs initially shelved the BOI's proposal to raise at-issue yields on MAKAM and did not accept the necessity of this step for quite some time.

The second increase in yields (April and October 1969), supported by a substantial incentive to commercial banks to promote sales of MAKAM and/or to purchase these securities for their nostro accounts, did stanch the massive contraction of outstanding MAKAM balances that had been taking place since Q1-1969.[17] In view of the inevitable lag, the effect of the more substantial second raise of yields toward the end of that year appears in the 1970 entry of the series. Despite a meaningful change in inflationary expectations from, say, the third quarter of 1970, the positive-yield effect and the bonus to banks caused MAKAM sales to increase in 1970. The balance held by the public rose by 20% of the outstanding balance of the monetary base at the beginning of that year. All of this, however, merely held the ratio of outstanding MAKAM to the monetary base at the 1969 ratio (table 4.7, columns 10–11).[18]

This move, however, and the third and last gasp in the BOI's attempt to contain its contribution to the expansion of the monetary base—another increase in the yield on MAKAM, implemented in August 1971, to 8.50% and 9% on three-month and twelve-month instruments, respectively—marked the end of the story. The 27% increase in the outstanding MAKAM balance in 1971 helped to hold the BOI injection rate that year to 5.6% of the monetary balance. By that time, however, the injection rate on the BOI's account should have been zero if not negative. Indeed, the continuous and rapid contraction of the average duration of the portfolio of outstanding bonds from 1970 on, even though the total nominal value of outstanding MAKAM continued to rise through Q3-1973, amounted to handwriting on the wall for what was in the offing (*Annual Report*, 1977, p. 413).

The effect of the increasing outstanding nominal balances of MAKAM on the size of monetary aggregates, however, began to erode, as column 10 of table 4.7

shows emphatically. Thus, the ratio of outstanding MAKAM balances to the monetary base reached its all-time high in 1968 at about one-fourth and stayed at roughly this level through 1970. Down the road, the ratio skidded toward zero. By 1972, net sales of MAKAM had fallen to only 1% of the outstanding balance of the monetary base at the beginning of that year. This hardly made a dent in the BOI's record injection rate of 19%, which emphasized its loss of control of the monetary base. Indeed, the monetary base expanded that year by more than 40% for the second year in the row (table 4.5), marking the death knell of the open-market-policy experiment.

Despite repeated attempts by the new governor—Moshe Sanbar, who succeeded David Horowitz in the last quarter of 1971—the BOI lost the monetary-base battle due to its failure to persuade the minister of finance and, in turn, the Ministerial Committee on Economic Affairs, that monetary restraint was the order of the day. The level of economic activity, which by the middle of 1970 at the latest had clearly passed the threshold of full employment and capacity, should have sent the message by itself. In this context, the rapid rise of net government liabilities to the central bank, reflecting the corresponding fiscal expansion of its capital-account activity, generated an avalanche of base-money-creating assets. Thus, net government liabilities in 1972 were almost twice the 1969 level. The BOI's discounts—reflecting its contribution to directed credit—leaped similarly during that interval (table 4.7).

The refusal of the political community to face the monetary facts of life was firmly evidenced in the stance adopted by the Ministry of Finance, which controlled the tap of MAKAM issues. The ministry hardly accepted the necessity of even the August 1971 move on yields, which should have been made much earlier. It drove home its adamant refusal to let the BOI follow this track further by freezing MAKAM yields for the next two years, that is, until shortly before the Yom Kippur War, and onward. This explains the failure of the BOI on the injection front, underlined by its 19% injection of base-money-creating assets in 1972 and average injections of almost 10% annually during the overfull-employment period of 1970–September 1973. The average expansion rate of the monetary base during that period—32% in annual terms and even more if the first three quarters of 1973 are excluded—is an obvious case in point.

Despite its failure to stanch the onslaught of the combined net liquidity injection of the public and private sectors, it is clear that the BOI implemented a "first stage" smoothing operation of the expansion of the base during the period at issue here, as it had in 1954–66. Figures 4.7–4.8, describing the patterns of monetary injections by origin, demonstrate the much smaller variance of the BOI's injection rates than those of the two other sectors.

EPILOGUE

The verdict on the BOI's performance during the seven-year period between the Six-Day War and the Yom Kippur War would be quite positive if had it been the central bank's main mission to assure growth. The annual average growth rate during this period, verging on 10%, providing for annual per-capita growth of 4.6%, would warrant such an evaluation. However, the BOI's main responsibility apparently lies elsewhere. Its mission, spelled out in Section 3.1 of the BOI Law (1954), says as much: The central bank is "to promote, by means of monetary instruments, the stable domestic and foreign value of the currency."[19]

Table 4.2 and the corresponding figure 4.4, displaying the patterns of the price level and the exchange rate—mirror images of the "domestic and foreign value of the currency" to which the law refers—indicate that during the second half of the seven-year period at issue (1970–September 1973) the annual inflation rate advanced initially to 10%–12%, lingered there for three years through 1972, and made a second leap to somewhat beyond 20% in the three prewar quarters of 1973.

Admittedly, Israel's transition from a relatively stable price level in 1967–69 to an altogether different price environment was not totally incongruous with global market developments. The so-called Vietnam inflation, which surfaced in the United States in 1968 or so, ran at a 4%–5% pace through 1972. The OECD countries also experienced somewhat higher average rates. The U.S. inflation rate in 1973—a full-year rate, already affected by OPEC's oil-price coup in October, was 5.6% (in terms of the GNP deflator). Inflation rates in the EU and OECD countries that year were higher still. However, even the highest rate recorded, that in the United Kingdom, did not reach 10%. Thus, although the rise in dollar-denominated import prices did have a cost effect of, say, 1%–2% on Israel's price level in 1972 and 1973, this did not apply to the takeoff of inflation in 1970 or so. In any case, these exogenous cost effects were very small compared with the 12%–13% inflation rates that Israel experienced in 1970–72, let alone the 20%-plus price inflation that affected the activities of the economy during the three quarters preceding the altogether unexpected outbreak of war in October 1973.

Accordingly, the inflationary surge in 1970 and its working into the wheels of the economic system by 1971 were precipitated almost exclusively by endogenous factors. It goes without saying that the level of performance—the rate of capacity utilization—had a bearing on the country's inflationary turn and, subsequently, acceleration. This is shown clearly in figure 4.2, in which the price level series (in terms of the GNP deflator) is contrasted with the time series of the unemployment rate. The steady decline of unemployment from 10% before the 1967 war to the full-employment vicinity of 3.8% by 1970, and its further decline to the overfull-employment range of 2%–3% by 1973, coincide with an initial leap of inflation from around 3% in 1969 to 10% in 1970, lingering in the 12%–13% range in the succeeding two years, and finally accelerating rapidly to the 20%-plus range in the first three quarters of 1973, those preceding the war.

Although monetary policy does not operate in a vacuum, it is the obvious culprit at first approximation. Thus, the BOI may be blamed for the loss of control over the money supply. The annual average rate of M_1 expansion, 24% in the 1970–September 1973 interval in contrast to 14% in the three-year 1967–69 period, during which inflation was kept at bay, offers an obvious case for the prosecution. This is more than a retrospective judgment. In a newspaper article published as early as October 1971, based on data through June of that year, the doyen of Israeli economists, Don Patinkin, criticized the BOI overtly: "It's the mission of the central bank to prevent undesirable expansion of the money supply, not to write reports about it."[20]

Although aware of the implications of the process and formally, albeit not effectively, vested with both instruments that central banks traditionally use in such situations, the BOI failed to stanch the avalanche of money amid the full-employment and overfull-employment environments of these years. At the root of the matter, of course, was the total loss of control over the expansion of the monetary base, manifested in successive annual rates of expansion of M_1 that verged on 30% between 1971 and the three prewar quarters of 1973. This happened even though the MAKAM experiment, initiated in 1966, proved that the Israeli money market was already ripe for open-market operations by the central bank on the selling as well as on the buying side. The repeal of the legal ceiling on nominal interest in March 1970 created even more leeway for the requisite restrictive open-market policy. With double-digit inflation rates prevailing from 1970 on and affecting expectations in 1971 at the latest, the implementation of such a move clearly required an aggressive interest-rate policy.

The five BOI "means-of-payment reports," published between March 1971 and July 1973, occasionally carried proposals to shift to a higher spectrum of interest rates.[21] Hardly any such action of this sort was taken (*AR* 1972, p. 404). The final upward adjustment of yields on MAKAM, by 0.75 of a percentage point to 9%, was made in August 1971 after the political authority gave its reluctant approval at a lag of twenty-one months after annual inflation of more than 10%. From then on, the Ministry of Finance and, in turn, the ultimate authority on interest-rate policy, the Ministerial Committee on Economic Affairs, adamantly refused to give the BOI the requisite degree of freedom on prices and quantities in the MAKAM market, summarily depriving the central bank of the ability to pump out excess monetary liquidity.

This is why the BOI's injection rate leaped to almost 19% in 1972. This outcome reflected, to a great extent, the collapse of the MAKAM market, which involved a net repurchase of MAKAM that were up for redemption by the BOI. Accordingly, the central bank made a significant contribution to the 41% increase in base money that year. This development, which continued with greater momentum in 1973, seemed a reductio ad absurdum of the mission of monetary policy in an economy subject to a 10%–20% annual inflation rate.

Just the same, figure 4.8, which juxtaposes the BOI injection to the combined injections of government and the private sector, and figure 4.9, which conveys the time pattern of the multiplier and, thus, the mechanism of transmission from the monetary base to M_1, underscore the composite smoothing effect that the BOI had been creating on both planes:[22] the pattern of the monetary base during the brief 1967–70 period, in which the BOI was allowed to exercise control, and during the entire period, particularly the 1971–September 1973 interval, when its attempt to affect monetary policy was confined to the use of only one instrument, liquidity ratios as determinants of the size of the multiplier. The much lower variance of M_1 than of the monetary base,

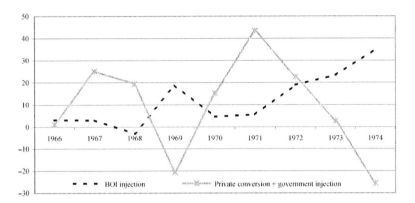

Figure 4.8. BOI and Private Conversion + Government Injection, 1966–74

particularly in 1970–73, shown clearly in figure 4.6, is presumably the best quantitative expression of what the government of the day "allowed" monetary policy to do.

This reading of relations between the BOI and the government, in which the central bank was allowed to tinker with but not to change the direction of monetary developments, was emphasized in the response of the first governor of the BOI, David Horowitz, to Don Patinkin's aforementioned criticism. Horowitz quoted from the preamble to the Bank of Israel Law (Section 3): "The function of the Bank is to manage, set, and direct the monetary system and to direct the credit and the banking system according to the economic policy of the Government." If so, the government of the day always held the upper hand in any disagreement with the central bank.[23] Since this exchange of views took place shortly before Horowitz's retirement after seventeen years in the governor's office, it may be interpreted as his message to his successor on the cardinal issue of relations between central banks and their governments. This kind of attitude was not inconsistent with the prevailing view in the industrialized countries.

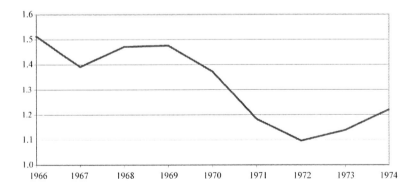

Figure 4.9. Time Pattern of the Money Multiplier

Table 4.11. Liquidity Ratios, Money Multiplier, and Credit Ratios

| | Liquidity Ratios (percent) | | | | Currency Deposit Ratio[3] (5) | Multiplier[4] (6) | Ratios (percent) | | |
| | Legal | | | | | | | | |
	Formal (1)	Net[1] (2)	Effective (3)	Calculated[2] (4)			Directed Credit[5] (7)	Bill Brokerage Credit[6] (8)	Govt. Credit[7] (9)
1966	65.0	40.0	44.5	45.6	60.6	1.51	34.4	40.3	17.1
1967	65.0	40.0	44.8	45.8	92.7	1.39	39.9	26.8	17.8
1968	65.5	40.5	43.2	43.8	75.4	1.47	39.8	19.8	16.9
1969	65.5	40.5	38.8	47.2	63.8	1.48	41.9	19.2	19.4
1970	65.5	37.5	38.2	52.3	75.8	1.37	42.5	0.5	20.4
1971	67.5	39.5	48.2	70.9	88.0	1.18	44.3	0.0	19.7
1972	72.0	44.0	57.4	83.9	83.4	1.10	45.8	0.0	19.8
1973(9)							48.9	0.0	21.8
1973	72.0	44.0	52.5	76.3	94.6	1.14	52.3	0.0	20.1
1974	72.0	44.0	50.0	68.6	74.7	1.22	62.4	0.0	18.9

[1]The difference between the formal and net legal minimum liquidity ratios represents the "recognized" maximum allowance from legal liquidity requirements for directed "credits" accommodated by banks to customers eligible for the privilege.

[2]Ratio of legally required liquid assets to demand deposits.

[3]Currency deposits ratios derived from series of currency and means of payment in Bank of Israel *Report*.

[4]Money multiplier calculated according to the well-known expression $\frac{1+cu}{re+cu}$, where cu and re are the currency deposits and currency banks effective liquidity ratios.

The "calculated" ratio of (column 4) was applied for the derivation of the money multiplier series.

[5]Ratio of outstanding directed credit balance to total commercial bank credit.

[6]Ratio of bill brokerage balance to total commercial bank credit.

[7]Ratio of (PAMELA)—total government credit mediated by commercial banks to total bank credit.

Sources: Columns (1)–(3), 1966–71, Zanbar-Bronfeld (1973), Table 6; 1972–74 *Annual Report* 1974, Table XIII-14; *Annual Report* 1974, Table XVII-10. Column (5) *Annual Report* 1967, Table XV-3, *Annual Report*, 1969, Table XIV-6, *Annual Report* 1971, Table XIV-5, *Annual Report* 1973, Table XIII-7, and *Annual Report* 1974, Table XVII-6. Columns (7), (8) and (9): See sources to Table 4.10.

However, a change of mind had surfaced among professional economists in the late 1960s. The "monetarist counterrevolution," underlined in Milton Friedman's presidential address to the American Economic Association (December 1969), was the beacon that illuminated this professional rethinking.

The Horowitz interpretation of relations between the central bank and the government, according to which the government wields ultimate authority over the monetary policy that the central bank implements—sometimes under the protest of its leadership—was more-or-less the law of the realm at the BOI until the late 1980s. By implication, monetary policy was effectively subjugated to fiscal requirements. This, of course, is the essence of "fiscal dominance," a term that surfaced in the literature in the closing decade of the twentieth century.

This vision of interdependence between the monetary authority and the government inevitably led to the sterilization of monetary policy, as the BOI was essentially confined to tinkering with the money multiplier (table 4.11) and could not do even this at its full discretion. Thus, most of the time (excluding the 1966–70 period), the Bank of Israel had only a slight effect on the positive slope of the money-supply trend—the annual rate at which the quantity of money grew. At best, it managed to reduce the variance of the curve that described the time pattern of monetary expansion.[24]

PART II

ISRAEL'S GREAT INFLATION: 1973–85

BRIEF OVERVIEW

Israel, like many other countries, endured a period of high inflation in the 1970s through the mid-1980s, its annual inflation rate escalating from 10% to over 400%. Before and after that period, the country had had rather low inflation rates (figure II.1). Econometric evidence suggests, and figure II.1 leaves little doubt, that inflation accelerated in the form of a step function (Liviatan and Melnick, 2001). Bruno's classification (1993) by stages shows much the same.

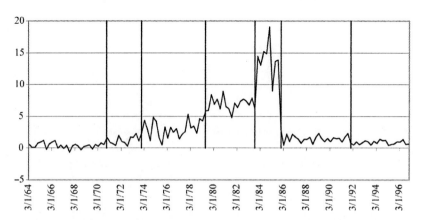

Figure II.1. Monthly Inflation in Israel, Q1 : 1964–Q4 : 1996 (vertical lines denote inflation subperiods)

Although inflation began to accelerate in 1970–73, the process unfolded to a divergent trajectory in the wake of the severe shocks that followed the October 1973 Yom Kippur War and energy crisis. Afterwards, inflation continued to accelerate until the middle of 1985, when the Economic Stabilization Program (July 1) lowered the annual inflation rate to a 20% plateau within six months after going into effect. The next step down, to annual inflation rates of 10%–12%, was reached only seven years later, in 1992. It was followed by virtual price stability from 2000 to the present writing, with the exception of 2002 (tables I.1–I.3).

The acceleration of inflation in the 1970s ruptured a pattern of relative price-level stability that had been maintained for a decade and a half. On the whole, Israel had kept its inflation under control for fifteen years since the mid-1950s. In Israel, as in many other developing countries, these fifteen years were a period of low fiscal deficits, low inflation, and strong growth under a regime of extensive financial repression. The low-inflation setting was pegged to the exchange-rate regime of the Bretton Woods system and collapsed with the collapse of that regime in the early 1970s.[1] Israel's economic regime, pegged to the nominal anchor provided by the Bretton Woods system and supported by conservative fiscal policies, suggests that the economy had been operating during that time within the framework of monetary dominance. The immediate causes of the acceleration of inflation in 1973 were the shocks of the Yom Kippur War and the energy crisis. While the October war was specific to Israel, the energy crisis was a watershed in the development of world inflation—a universal shock that generated global stagflation. The industrial countries responded to the shock by applying the monetary brakes; the major Latin American economies, in contrast, went over to an accommodative regime based on far-reaching indexation. By doing so, they transformed the original price shock into a long-term inflation shock. Israel, which had already established significant price indexation in its labor and capital markets, followed the Latin American lead and surrendered to a chronic-inflation regime. This behavior was inconsistent with its relatively high level of economic development and, particularly, the constraint imposed on small, open economies, both of which should point to a preference for low inflation (Romer, 1993).

The "chronic-inflation" regimes referred to here had very different characteristics from those of the better known hyperinflationary regimes that followed each of the world wars. By employing widespread indexation, these economies were able to safeguard real wages and also real tax revenues from the price-shock erosion that the so-called Tanzi effect brings about. Indeed, in Israel's case, both real wages and real tax revenues rose throughout most of the inflationary era (table II.1, table II.2, and figure II.2). Only toward the end of the inflationary acceleration (in 1984), as the annual inflation rate spiraled past the 400% level, was the economy subjected to Tanzi-style tax erosion.[2] However, the central bank's policies of de facto monetary accommodation, while managing to avert large-scale unemployment (table II.1), ushered Israel into a "lost decade," a time of economic stagnation and financial crises that lasted approximately from 1974 to 1985. While unemployment in Israel also climbed during

Table II.1. Growth (% annual) and Employment

Period	GDP Growth (1)	Population (2)	Growth of per Capita GDP (3)	Growth of Real Wage Rate in Business Sector (4)	Growth of Employment in Business Sector (5)	Unemployment (6)
1971–73	8.5	3.2	5.1	0.3	3.9	3.0
1974–79	3.6	2.4	1.2	3.3	1.2	3.4
1980–84	2.9	1.9	1.0	3.2	1.9	5.1
1985	4.5	1.8	2.6	−9.0	−1.2	6.7
1986–89	3.7	1.6	2.0	5.1	2.4	7.1
1990–94	6.1	3.6	2.4	0.1	5.3	9.8
1995–99	4.3	2.6	1.7	2.2	4.0	7.6
2000–04	4.3	2.6	1.7	2.2	4.0	7.6

Columns (1)–(5) percentage change, annual average. (6) percent of labor force, annual average.
Source: BOI.

Table II.2. Fiscal Aggregates (percent GDP)

Period	Public Sector Revenue (1)	Public Sector Exp. (2)	Domestic Deficit (−) (3)	Foreign Deficit (−) (4)	Total Deficit (−) (5)
1961–66	33.8	30.1	2.7	1.0	3.7
1967–73	45.8	54.3	−5.0	−3.5	−8.5
1974–79	62.1	77.3	−11.3	−4.0	−15.2
1980–84	60.2	72.6	−13.2	0.8	−12.4
1985	68.7	67.7	−6.5	7.5	1.0
1986–89	59.1	60.1	−3.6	2.6	−1.0
1990–94	52.0	56.1	−6.5	2.4	−4.1
1995–99	48.5	53.1	−5.7	1.2	−4.5
2000–04	47.8	52.3	−5.4	1.0	−4.4

Annual averages.
Source: BOI.

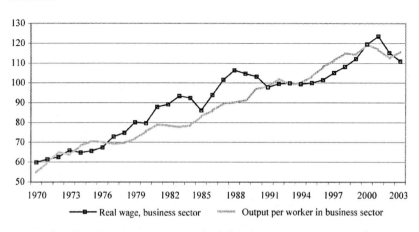

Figure II.2. Real Business-Sector Wages and Labor Productivity (1994 = 100).
Source: BOI.

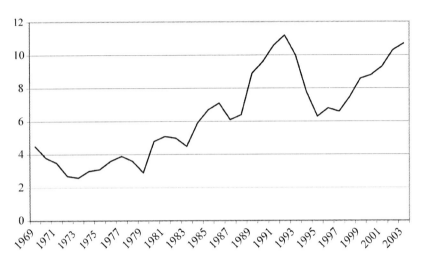

Figure II.3. Unemployment Rate (percent). *Source:* BOI.

the inflationary period, to about 5% of the labor force in the early 1980s (figure II.3), its level was significantly lower than that in the industrial world.

Israel's choice of a chronic-inflation regime traces mainly to highly significant changes in its political balance of power. Since the mid-1960s, the political scene, dominated by the Zionist Labor Movement for more than three decades, had been feeling the pressure of the drift of voters to the opposition, the right-wing Herut Party and its allies (subsequently and hereinafter the Likud). The Likud successfully mobilized the votes of lower income groups that felt they had been left out of the growth process. The Labor governments responded to the sense of shaky political ground by adopting populist fiscal and monetary policies—a process enhanced by the shock of the 1973 Yom Kippur War.

One of the cornerstones of these policies was the maintenance of full employment, a policy inherent to a state that promoted immigration and immigrant absorption and a traditional Zionist maxim. There were also domestic internal political reasons for this attitude, noted above. The shaky political situation prevented the hiking of interest rates, which could have raised unemployment. Even a temporary increase in the latter was considered to be politically risky. The other priority in the Labor governments' policies was an increase in transfer payments. Thus, transfer payments were substantially increased despite the major economic costs of the exogenous shocks from 1973 onward (table 6.1). These two factors effectively prevented the implementation of a restrictive monetary policy. The BOI was powerless to affect the situation due to effective control by the Ministry of Finance of the main instruments of monetary policy: open-market operations and the monetary multiplier (see chapter 2 in this volume). This economic policy stayed unchanged when the Likud came to power in 1977. The big change in the economic attitude of the political community and the government on this subject had to wait until the formation of the National Unity Government, which implemented the 1985 stabilization program.

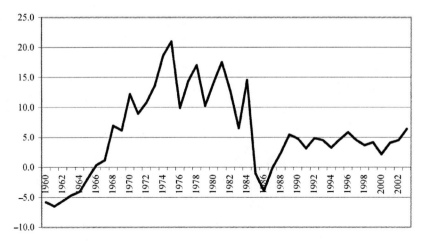

Figure II.4. Total General-Government Deficit (percent of GDP), 1960–2003.
Source: BOI.

The main economic features of the great inflation era were large general-government expenditures and correspondingly large fiscal deficits that caused the national debt/GDP ratio to swell (figures II.4, II.5, and II.7). However, the dissaving of general government was largely offset by private saving (figure II.6), implying that the Ricardian equivalence mechanism was working very effectively. If so, one may wonder what was driving inflation. To magnify the puzzle, we note that seigniorage as a percent of GDP was rather constant at around 2.5% throughout the inflationary period (table I.2), again in contrast to the typical scenario in hyperinflationary episodes. In principle, a rising rate of monetary expansion and a shrinking monetary base (relative to GDP) may result in constancy in seigniorage (the product of the two), as shown by Eckstein and Leiderman (1992). The basic question, however, remains unanswered: what was the driving force of the monetary expansion and the related acceleration of inflation?

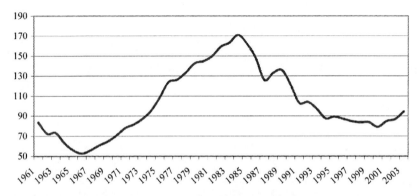

Figure II.5. National Debt Relative to GDP (percent). *Source:* Direct measure, 1983–2002: BOI; Calculated measure, 1960–82: Dahan and Strawczynski, 2001.

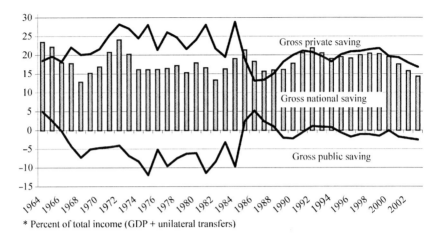

* Percent of total income (GDP + unilateral transfers)

Figure II.6. Gross National Saving Rate and Division between Private Sector and General Government. *Source:* BOI.

Part of the puzzle may be explained by a modified version of the "unpleasant monetarist arithmetic" model (Sargent and Wallace, 1981), related to the unsustainability of the growing government debt, which undermines economic stability. This sort of consideration seems to have become effective mainly in the 1980s. Indications from the interest rates on negotiable government paper[3] do not suggest a lack of confidence in the government's ability to pay back its debt in the 1970s.[4] Figures II.8 and II.9 show that real interest rates started to rise only in the 1980s.

Another related aspect of the inflation process was the low level of confidence in the government's willingness (and ability) to control inflation, in the spirit of recent models of policy games.[5] These models can explain monetary

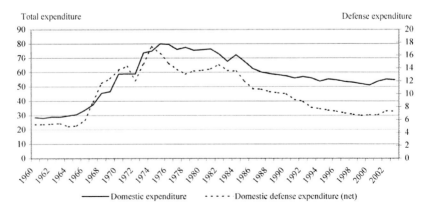

Figure II.7. Total General-Government Expenditure and Defense Expenditure (percent of GDP), 1960–2003. *Source:* BOI.

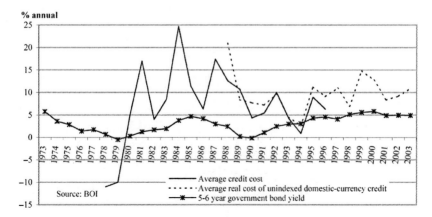

Figure II.8. Real Interest Rates (Average cost of credit and real yield on government bonds). *Source:* BOI.

policy when the basic macroeconomic setting is one of fiscal dominance,[6] a regime that lacks a nominal anchor and treats fiscal policies as being largely exogenous, with the role of responding to shocks assigned to the central bank, which turns the money supply into an endogenous process governed by discretionary considerations. Indeed, this reading of events was not far from reality in Israel's inflationary period.

The inflation era was also infested with persistent balance-of-payments problems. The 1970s were characterized by huge current-account deficits that sometimes climbed to 15% of GDP (figure II.10). They were essentially the result of an effort to keep the investment rate high by means of general-government credit, without the support of a corresponding high rate of national saving

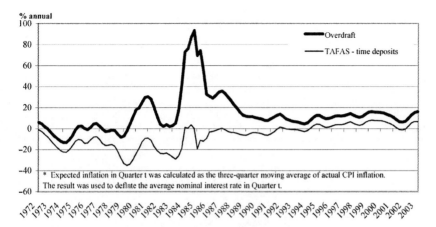

Figure II.9. Real Interest Rates on Loans and Deposits (quarterly data), Four-Quarter Moving Average. *Source:* BOI.

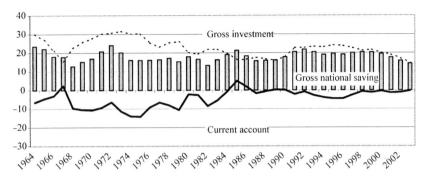

Figure II.10. National Saving, Domestic Investment, and the Current Account (percent of total income), 1964–99. Total income is GDP plus net unilateral transfers from abroad (calculated at the official exchange rate). GDP is based on the new SNA classification. *Source:* BOI.

(figure II.10). Since the U.S. government financed much of the external deficit, Israel did not drift into a Latin American–style external debt crisis. The highly fragile state of the external account,[7] however, played an important role in the inflation dynamics. Amid this shaky financial environment, external crises led to stepwise increases in inflation. Thus, the big jumps in inflation during the "lost decade" were associated with external crises in 1973, 1979, and 1983.

The government reacted to these negative BOP shocks by massive devaluations and hikes of public-sector prices, dealing severe shocks to the overall price level. These may be regarded as price shocks associated with the Pigou effect, which, in the absence of a nominal anchor, were transformed into jumps in the inflation plateau. Under the fiscal-dominance regime, which concerned itself with the solvency of general government and paid little attention to the level of inflation, there was never a serious effort to pull back inflation to its initial, pre-leap level. In the early stages of the process, the jump could have been reversed by a hike in interest rates. However, the aforementioned political considerations prompted governments to maintain persistently low interest rates in the 1970s to prevent an increase in unemployment and assure low-cost financing of their deficits. Thus, monetary policy was dominated by the fiscal and political considerations of the government, leaving no room for the actions of an independent central bank, despite the formal right of the BOI to take this course.

Despite the high ratio of investment to GDP, GDP growth was rather sluggish in the inflation era (table II.1 and figure II.11). This was partly due to the high rate of subsidization, which drove investment into inefficient channels. However, the growth rate of consumption was maintained at a higher level than that of output, thereby contributing to the increase in external debt.

This picture changed drastically upon the implementation of the 1985 stabilization program. The main structural change was the ability of the National Unity Government to eliminate the fiscal deficit and, by so doing, to stanch the increase in the national debt in the context of a fixed exchange-rate regime. The government also managed to change the rules of the game in its relations

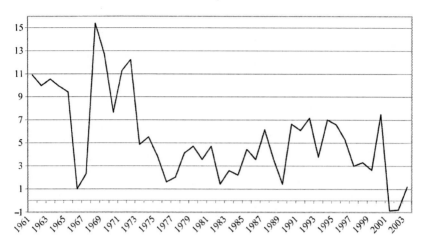

Figure II.11. GDP, Year-on-Year Volume Change (percent). *Source:* BOI.

with the household and business sectors. Finally, the move to low inflation in later years was strongly supported by the global trend toward price stability.

Our analysis of the inflation era starts with a capsule description of "financial repression," the characteristic feature of Israel's economic-policy regime in the 1950s and 1960s. To allow this section of the book to stand alone, the discussion repeats parts of the analysis in the first part of the historical survey (part I). Afterwards, we analyze the major shocks in 1973–74 and the rising momentum of inflation that forced the 1985 stabilization policy on a reluctant political community. We then analyze chronologically the stages of the inflation process as it evolved over time and evaluate some of its general features. The more technical aspects of the analysis are relegated to the mathematical appendices at the end of the book.

5

Financial Repression

ISRAEL'S "TRADITIONAL" MONETARY REGIME

It is important to realize that Israel entered its inflationary period after two decades of highly regulated financial markets. Government control of the capital market was almost total. Pension and mutual funds had to invest 95% of their total annual net inflow of sources in government bonds, mostly non-negotiable, that provided government with a cheap source of finance for its current expenditure. Thus, the government had no problem financing the fiscal deficits that it ran up in the late 1960s and early 1970s. Furthermore, the interest on *negotiable* government bonds was tax-exempt as against a 25% tax rate on interest paid by corporate bonds. This effectively channeled all available nondirected private-sector funds to government paper.

FINANCIAL REPRESSION: A UNIVERSAL ECONOMIC POLICY

This kind of regime was not specific to Israel. In one form or other, it was common practice in most developing countries at that time. Its label, financial repression (FR), was coined rather late in the season.[1] The literature offers two main explanations for the emergence and persistence of this regime. First, the restrictions imposed on the capital market increased the demand for domestic money and, thereby, enlarged the base of the inflation tax (Nichols, 1974; Sussman, 1991). The restrictions on investment in alternative liquid assets also tended to reduce the elasticity of demand for money with respect to inflation and thus facilitated the extraction of more inflation tax. Thus, FR could enable lower inflation for a given fiscal deficit. The imposition of low interest rates under FR was problematic for policymakers: it furnished the government with a source of cheap finance but dampened national investment by eroding the propensity to save.[2] Indeed, this was the main criticism of the FR regime by McKinnon (1973) and Shaw (1973), who pointed out that a market-determined interest rate would increase investment.

The second "benefit" of FR for the government was the following. By controlling the capital market, the government could direct economic activity, especially with respect to investment. For this purpose, the government discriminated against borrowing by private firms by means of taxation[3] and by controls on private bond issues. The latter restriction was implemented by vesting the control powers with a department of the Ministry of Finance that corresponded to the U.S. Securities and Exchange Commission. The government's rationing of cheap bank credit was another component of FR.

This rationale for FR requires some elaboration. The tendency to favor government intervention in economic affairs was widespread even in industrial countries. The dominance of the Keynesian view, which favored government intervention on the macroeconomic plane due to the inability of "market-managed" economies to overcome the crisis of the 1930s in the wake of their sluggish performance in the 1920s was a case in point. FR was also consistent with the dominant mindset in Western Europe at least through the 1950s, which, in the wake of the crisis and mass unemployment of the interwar wars, considered much greater government involvement in the economy a sine qua non for the maintenance of full employment. There was also a bias for low real interest rates because of the prevailing view, supported by Keynes, that the real interest rate in capitalist economies tended to be too high since people had a preference for liquidity as a result of uncertainty. The theoretical literature of the time abounded with models portraying monetary expansion as conducive to growth (e.g., Mundell, 1965). However, while all this supports a policy of monetary expansion at the macro level, it prescribes neither FR-style government intervention at the micro level nor a policy of taxing the financial sector in order to finance government deficits.

The last-mentioned features of FR were actually the result of the belief in many developing economies that only the government could direct economic growth efficiently. Such a belief may be warranted in countries that lack the infrastructure for a workable free-enterprise system. It has also been argued that FR might be advantageous as a substitute for an ordinary tax system in countries that lacked a satisfactory fiscal-revenue base and administration. These considerations, however, cannot be automatically applied across the board. Israel's Jewish community, for example, had an impressive pool of highly competent entrepreneurs and financial institutions that could form the nucleus of a market economy, which was prevented by FR. In fact, the pre-state Jewish economy grew at impressive rates in what could be described as a classical free-trade environment with minimal government intervention until the imposition of wartime controls in 1940. Israel adopted the FR system because it had inherited the basic framework of this system from the wartime Mandatory regime, which had been quite consistent with the statist philosophy of Israel's founding fathers and the Eastern European tradition of the interwar period. The difficulty in implementing more market-oriented macroeconomic policies in Israel stemmed from this statist outlook, which gained ground in Western Europe in the late 1940s and 1950s, and general-government control of the flow of foreign sources. This considerable flow was composed of unilateral receipts made up of Diaspora philanthropy, U.S. economic aid (which began in 1951), and German reparations (from 1953 onward).

Despite the shortcomings of FR, Israel had a strong case to make in having adopted it. For more than two decades (1950–73), its economy maintained high growth rates and relatively low inflation. Average annual per capita growth in the 1954–73 period, 5.5%, made Israel one of the "league leaders" in a rapidly growing global economy.

The fact that Israel was supported by a high ratio of unilateral transfers in terms of the major economic aggregates should not be overlooked. Nevertheless, it remains true that FR did not stand in the way of rapid growth and markedly efficient use of resources. The efficiency factor shows clearly in terms of the remarkable contribution of total productivity (the Solow residual) to the growth rate: more than 4 percentage points of 10%–11% annual real GNP growth in 1950–72 (Bruno, 1993). As noted, inflation during that time was also relatively mild. This was in line with global trends, as the Bretton Woods system of fixed (and adjustable) ERs sustained low inflation rates everywhere. Notably, the fixed exchange-rate setup of Bretton Woods pertained to the current account only; capital movements in Israel were governed by currency control involving specific exchange rates, a practice fully consistent with the domestic financial-repression regime. These phenomena—strong economic growth and low inflation rates—were linked by the noninflationary component of government finance, provided by growth-induced demand for money.

6

War and Oil Shock, October 1973–May 1977

The outbreak of the Yom Kippur War and the energy crisis in October 1973 left no doubt that the 1967–73 economic boom had ended and that Israel would be facing long-term economic and political difficulties. Indeed, this turning of the tide marked the beginning of a lengthy period of economic stagnation and accelerating inflation that would not end until 1985. In the estimation of Z. Sussman (1995), the total burden that these exogenous shocks imposed on the economy by 1979 (when the second oil shock struck) amounted to 15% of annual GNP. This emphasizes quantitatively the rate of deterioration in economic performance after the 1973 crisis.

We first discuss the effects of the crisis within the framework of short-term management of the initial shock (1974–75); then we focus on the succeeding period and the formulation of medium-term policy in 1975–77.

THE IMPACT OF THE 1973 SHOCK

The initial shock dealt the real economy a tremendous blow. Balassa (1984) estimates its effect in 1974–76 at 10.5% of GNP—not counting the domestic defense burden, which had risen for a number of years (table 6.1).[1] Between 1972 and 1974, the current-account deficit tripled in nominal dollar terms (from US$1.1 billion to US$3.4 billion and the basic account (the current-account deficit less long-term inflows) turned from a positive inflow of US$0.8 billion to a negative flow of US$1 billion. From then on, the balance of payments (BOP), problematic to begin with, became the number-one issue on the government's economic agenda. The economy somehow had to cope with this huge burden.

Table 6.1. Selected Items of Public Expenditures (percent GDP)

Period	Domestic Civilian Consumption (1)	Domestic Defense Expenditure (net) (2)	Transfer Payments (3)	Direct Subsidies (4)	Credit Subsidies (5)
1961–66	8.7	5.3	4.8	2.5	0.3
1967–73	9.6	12.5	9.2	4.4	1.6
1974–79	10.4	14.8	15.6	5.8	6.0
1980–84	17.1	13.8	11.6	5.5	3.9
1985	15.5	12.0	10.6	4.6	1.9
1986–89	15.6	10.5	12.3	3.0	1.1
1990–94	16.6	8.7	14.6	2.0	0.3
1995–99	20.0	7.0	13.7	1.0	0.1
2000–04	20.2	6.9	13.9	0.9	0.0

Annual averages.
Source: BOI.

The government's management of the crisis was influenced by domestic politics. The Labor-led Government that had been in office when the war began survived the elections that followed the cease-fire (December 31, 1973) but lost much strength and faced withering public criticism for having allowed Egypt and Syria to stage a surprise attack and for having made costly errors in the first stage of the war.[2] The government was also troubled by the acceleration of the long-term drift (since the early 1960s) of voters (specifically, of "Orientals," i.e., immigrants from Muslim countries) away from the traditional Labor establishment (Roumani, 1986). The government's readings of these omens suggested that its adjustments to the shocks had to have a minimum effect on unemployment.

This had far-reaching implications for the management of monetary policy. The policy was largely accommodative, reflecting (among other factors) the weak position of the BOI in the balance of constitutional and, particularly political, power. The accommodative nature of monetary policy was manifested in low short- and long-term interest rates (figures II.8 and II.9) and the avoidance of credit tightening (table 6.2 and figure 6.1). On the fiscal side, internal political pressure prompted the government to adopt a populist strategy of appeasing the dissatisfied population by applying novel and comprehensive social-welfare programs that entailed, in particular, a major expansion of transfer payments even as national income growth slowed considerably (table 6.1 and Bruno, 1993, pp. 30–34).[3]

The need to improve the balance of payments and the pressure to extend welfare-state reforms led to contradictory policies in the first two years after the crisis. There was an effort to apply fiscal restraint in some components of the budget in order to reduce the current-account deficit, but other components expanded. In the overall result, the fiscal deficit as a percentage of GNP continued to escalate and attained extraordinary magnitudes by 1974–75— 20% for the total deficit and 14% for the domestic deficit (*Annual Report*, 1995, pp. 316–17, 339–40). Steps to improve the current account included increases

Table 6.2. Growth of Nominal Variables by Period (percent annual)

Period	Nominal GDP (1)	CPI (2)	M1 (3)	M2 (4)	M3 (5)	Bank Credit (6)	ER (USD) (7)
1974–79	52.5	53.3	30.2	25.5	46.8	91.7	44.2
1980–84	190.0	200.3	121.6	162.9	194.7	233.9	209.4
1985	273.7	185.2	339.1	522.5	309.4	154.1	144.5
1986–89	32.4	18.2	77.7	62.8	28.8	37.1	7.5
1990–94	22.0	14.1	23.4	32.5	23.5	32.2	9.2
1995–99	13.3	7.1	10.9	25.1	19.7	24.4	6.9
2000–04	4.0	1.4	11.8	9.1	9.0	5.8	0.9

Source: BOI.

in the domestic prices of imports and exports by means of a universal levy on imports in 1974 and a major devaluation (40%) in November of that year. As a result, the price of imports relative to the price of domestic uses rose in 1974–75 and the relative price of exports started to improve in 1975 after an initial decline in 1974 (*Annual Report,* 1977, pp. 62, 81). This improvement also applied to the real exchange rate—measured by the dollar ER deflated by the ratio of Israel's GDP deflator to that of the United States (figure 6.2).

The other side of the coin (related to the effect of the real depreciation) was the erosion of real wages by these price shocks relative to output per worker (figure II.2) despite universal wage-indexation arrangements. (Formally, COLAs were paid twice a year.)

The overall effect of these external and internal developments was an increase of domestic inflation to an annual rate of around 40% in 1974–75. This acceleration was not out of line with the trend in global inflation, which accelerated due to the increases in the prices of energy and raw materials.

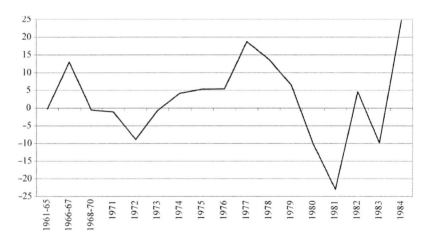

Figure 6.1. Changes in Credit/GDP Ratio (percent). *Source:* BOI.

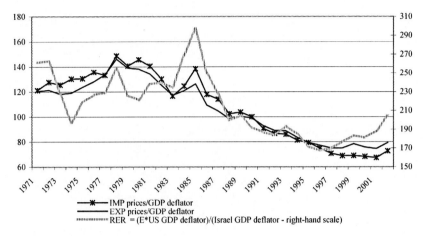

Figure 6.2. Real Exchange-Rate Measures (real depreciation—up), Index (1990 = 100)

Israel's inflationary leap, however, far surpassed that in industrial countries (where the inflation rate in 1974–75 reached 11%–13%), developing countries other than oil producers (17%–20%), and the rest of the Western Hemisphere (28%–37%), presumably due to the additional impact of the 1973 war. A contributing factor to this development was that Israeli inflation had been running at more than 20% in the three quarters preceding the outbreak of the war.

The rise to the 40% step in CPI inflation was fairly well synchronized with a large set of other nominal variables in the domestic markets, such as nominal wages and devaluation (on the latter see table 6.2). Nominal bank credit expanded more quickly than nominal GNP, signaling "easy money." Thus, total nominal bank credit increased by 48% and 53% in 1974 and 1975, respectively, as against 43% and 39% nominal increases in GNP, respectively (figure 6.1).

The perception of monetary permissiveness in 1974–75 is supported by additional indicators, such as real yields on government bonds and real interest rates on loans and deposits (figures II.8 and II.9). In contrast to the drastic rise of inflation from 10%–20% to a 40% plateau, the annual interest rate on directed credit, a very significant component of bank credit, increased only from 6% in 1972 to 10.5% in 1974 and 12.7% in 1975.[4] The formal reserve ratio had not been changed since 1972 and the money multiplier increased in 1972–75 (Barkai, 2002). Real rates on short-term deposits and bank credit were low and declining (figure II.9). The real yield to redemption on indexed government bonds was also low and falling during these years (figure II.8).

This does not mean that the BOI fully endorsed the monetary accommodation of inflation. After the initial period after the war, the governor, Moshe Sanbar, recommended an increase in interest rates and asked the Ministerial Committee on Economic Affairs for more freedom to bring this about. This by itself signaled the bank's resentment of its subordinate status, since the committee, of which the governor was a nonvoting member, normally kept such matters under its jurisdiction. The committee accepted the BOI's requests but only in a badly watered-down and belated form. Consequently, the increase in interest rates on directed credit and development-budget funding was not properly aligned with the acceleration of inflation. The central bank submitted to this under written protest. This episode is more informative than anything else about the BOI's weak political position and its inability to conduct an independent monetary policy.

As with every stepwise increase in inflation, the leap described here came with a surprise element. The decline in real (ex-post) interest rates on nondirected bank credit to severely negative real levels (minus 10%–15%) indicates as much. However, interest rates on government credit to businesses fell farther below zero and remained at that level much longer. (Barkai, 2002, table 4). Even in the fourth year after the initial shock in October 1973, eligible firms could obtain directed credit at real rates of –17% for investment and –13% for working capital, which says something about the stance of monetary policy in that period.

From a certain perspective, it is not so surprising that monetary policy was so accommodative in 1974–75, when inflation was dominated by the external supply shock. The BOI had not been able to apply monetary constraint in the early 1970s, when inflation was dominated by demand-pull factors. Under demand-pull circumstances, the monetary screws could have been tightened without entailing a tradeoff between inflation and unemployment. It is more problematic to impose a tougher monetary policy in response to a supply shock because the Phillips Curve tradeoff then comes into play. With economic policy constrained by the requirement that unemployment must not increase, there was no opening for the implementation of a restrictive monetary policy. As long as the BOI accepted this attitude toward unemployment, it had no latitude to make money tight. In fact, Israel did emerge from the 1970s with lower unemployment rates than those in the industrialized countries, but it had to pay the price in terms of lingering and accelerating inflation and long-term economic stagnation. Basically, this choice was dictated by domestic political instability and the corresponding vulnerability of governance.

VALIDATING INFLATION: THE CRAWLING-PEG REGIME

By 1975, the initial balance-of-payments shock had been partly absorbed. Various BOP indicators started to show positive signs. The trade balance showed some improvement in both nominal (dollar) and in real terms. The real exchange rate depreciated. Most importantly, long-term borrowing from abroad increased substantially, mitigating the need to rely on short-term capital (*Annual Report,* 1977, pp. 36–41). Thus, the time for medium-term adjustments in economic policy had come. On the fiscal side, the government (with Yehoshua Rabinowitz as minister of finance) cut the total and domestic deficits to 10% and 7.5% of GNP, respectively in 1976, half the 1975 levels (*Annual Report,* 1995, p. 330; figure II.4). In the nominal dimension, it replaced the Bretton Woods exchange-rate (ER) system, which prescribed discrete maxi-devaluations spaced over lengthy intervals, with a crawling-peg regime in which the crawl was set at around 2% per month. Under this regime, which ran its course from June 1975 to October 1977, the dollar ER depreciated (nominally) by about 30% in annual terms, resulting in real depreciation of the IL (figure 6.2).[5]

The changeover from maxi-devaluations to a crawl had the advantage of eliminating speculation and, thus, increasing stability. However, it had an adverse effect on inflation expectations. It signaled the government's validation of the new inflation plateau of 30%–40% by fostering expectations of a somewhat higher rate of devaluation, as indicated by the black-market premium on the official ER. Over the entire crawling-peg period, the real ER depreciated at an annual rate of 5.9% (Bruno and Sussman, 1979). The basic account of the BOP continued to improve gradually, from a $1 billion deficit in 1974 to a $38 million surplus in 1977 (*Annual Report*, 1977, p. 38).

On the monetary side, the expansion of nominal short-term bank credit outpaced the growth of nominal national income in 1975–77 (figure 6.1), although the excess was somewhat smaller in 1976. This shows that, on the whole, monetary policy was accommodative during the crawling-peg period. As noted above, the real interest rates on directed and development-budget-financed credit were strongly negative throughout this period.[6] In contrast, the real interest rate on nondirected bank credit recovered from its negative values in mid-1975 (figure II.9). The real short-term rates for lending (i.e., working-capital facilities) and deposits were higher during the crawling-peg period than in the preceding years. (The real working-capital rate rose from –13% in Q4-1973 to 2.5% in Q1-1975.) This is not necessarily a sign of tight money; it may simply mean that inflation expectations adjusted to the new inflation plateau. Indeed, annual CPI inflation continued at the 1974 level with a slight declining trend—40%, 39%, 31%, and 35% in 1974–77—as one would expect following the initial price shock.

Although policymakers may have thought at the time that cutting the fiscal deficit could improve the BOP situation *and* reduce inflation, it proved effective only in regard to the former. The announcement that the ER would crawl at a 30% annual pace left little doubt that the policy was geared only to improving the BOP and that disinflation had nothing to do with it. The BOP indicators did continue to improve during the crawling-peg period; in particular, the trade balance took a turn for the better in both nominal (dollar) and real terms (*Annual Report*, 1977, pp. 36–37). In this case, unlike other ER-based programs discussed below, the fixing of the rate of crawl was neither intended to set a nominal anchor for low inflation nor construed by the public as such. Irrespective of the authorities' intentions, the public interpreted it as a signal that the government viewed 30%–40% inflation as a new long-term plateau to which it would be committed from then on.

The fact that the government did not attempt to roll inflation back to the level preceding the BOP shock dictated the path of inflation in future years. It indicated that the government had no nominal anchor and was willing to validate the initial jump in inflation as a permanent feature of the price-level pattern. As we show below, however, the attempt to secure the ex-post inflation plateau was bound to fail, opening the way to further acceleration.

From a different perspective, we find that the inflationary potential of the fiscal deficit increased during this period due to the slowing of the growth rate, from 10.3% in 1968–73 to 2.6% in 1974–77 (annual averages). Thus, while the domestic deficit during this time was 7.3% of GNP, the *warranted*, non-inflationary deficit (with the ratios of money and national debt to GNP and the growth rate taken into account) was only 2.6% (Bruno, 1993, table 3.2). The difference, 4.7%, was still somewhat higher than the inflation tax, 3.9%. This suggests that the inflation potential, calculated in the context of a steady-state setting, remained higher than the actual inflation plateau. In view of these figures, our foregoing conclusion is reinforced: the possibilities of effective anti-inflation monetary restraint were very limited indeed.

7

The Liberalization Episode
of 1977–79

In October 1977, four months after its electoral victory, the new Likud govern-ment introduced a revolutionary liberalization program for the foreign sector. Although repealed in failure two years later, it had far-reaching effects on the inflationary process. In retrospect, it is clear that the liberalization was not backed by a proper supportive macroeconomic policy.[1] In fact, this liberaliza-tion attempt was not an organic part of the evolution of the economy and may be attributed mainly to the ideology of the liberal faction of the Likud Party. Hence, as suggested in the title of this chapter, the liberalization that ensued at this time was an episode only. The Likud, following its political priorities, initially handed responsibility for economic affairs to the erstwhile Liberal Party, which was liberal in the classical European free-trade tradition. Simcha Ehrlich, the Liberal Party leader who had ushered his movement into a union (or *likud* in Hebrew) with Herut, was given the Finance portfolio. The foreign-exchange liberalization began shortly afterward.

The main feature of the liberalization was a drastic change in the exchange-rate regime. The crawling peg was replaced with a pure float, thereby abolishing three decades of multiple exchange rates that differentiated specifically between the trade account and the unilateral-transfer and capital accounts. The unification of these exchange rates entailed a 43% devaluation by decree. Export subsidies, the special 15% levy on imports, and most restrictions on foreign-exchange transactions were abolished. From then on, Israelis could borrow abroad and hold deposits (up to $3,000) in foreign banks (Bruno and Sussman, 1979). Another important feature of the liberalization was the introduction of dollar-indexed demand and time deposits for residents (PATAM), which effectively became a close substitute for money. The main purpose of this step was to divert demand for "green" dollars, which might jeopardize the BOI's foreign reserve position, to deposits. (The commercial banks' required reserve ratio for these deposits was raised gradually to 100%.)

One of the main shortcomings of the liberalization strategy was its unwarranted implicit assumption that the foreign sector could be isolated from domestic macroeconomic developments. Such a proposition would be highly questionable for a large and relatively closed economy, not to mention a small and relatively open economy like Israel's. Thus, the liberalization policy required the application of supporting measures to the domestic sector of the macroeconomy. The measures at issue boiled down to fiscal retrenchment, and Mr. Ehrlich did push for it. The final say in the matter, however, resided with Prime Minister Menachem Begin, who favored a strong defense position and generous transfer payments to the lower-income groups whose votes had elevated him to the premiership (Stammerman, 1986). Since the prime minister was loath to compromise on these political principles, the finance minister's bid for a cut in the fiscal deficit was rejected (see Gross's essay in volume II).

On the labor front, the large initial devaluation led to wage hikes (including the advancement of COLA in January 1978), resulting in a substantial increase in real wages in both the private sector and general government during the liberalization process. In a related development, the real exchange rate appreciated (figure 6.2), reversing the trend that had been established in the crawling-peg period.

Monetary policy tried to cope with the risk of capital flight following the liberalization of the capital account and the absence of a corresponding attempt to impose fiscal constraint. At first, monetary policy accommodated the leap in inflation that the maxi-devaluation had caused, as the BOI's monetary injections between Q4-1977 and Q3-1978 strongly attest. During the liberalization period, real interest rates on financial assets and the short-term real interest rate declined, as did short-term interest rates on overdrafts. Bank credit to the public followed a similar pattern, rising by an astonishing 20% in Q4-1977. Inflation could not be contained in such a setting; indeed, the initial devaluation was eroded in the course of one year. At this stage of the process, the volume of dollar-indexed PATAM deposits increased by a steep 28% in Q4-1977. Gradually, these monetary assets became the leading component of domestic liquidity.[2] To stanch the monetary flood, the BOI finally tightened the monetary screws, starting in October 1978 and continuing through February 1979. Under the new regime of the liberalized capital account, this led immediately to large capital inflows that resulted in a hefty 30% real appreciation despite countervailing partial intervention in the foreign-exchange market. These developments, accompanied by deterioration in the trade balance, led rapidly to a partial retreat from the liberalization in early 1979. Various restrictions were imposed on capital mobility, including ceilings on foreign borrowing that were later replaced by a levy on capital imports.

In 1979, the aim of monetary policy changed from initial indifference to the real ER pattern to a deliberate PPP policy aimed at stabilizing ER value.

This policy, coupled with continued monetary tightness in the first half of 1980, led to real depreciation (Bruno and Sussman, 1979). The monetary-policy instruments used for this purpose shifted from the tightening of reserve ratios toward direct quantity control, that is, the targeting of the rate of growth of nominal bank credit by imposing bank credit ceilings.[3] The notion behind the scenes was to raise the nominal bank credit at a somewhat lower rate than the rate of inflation. Although this policy was quite effective in the short run in turning the real ER around, it could not (as one might expect) prevent the acceleration of inflation.

While the stance of monetary policy changed during the liberalization period, it could not be identified, on the whole, as tight. Thus, in 1978, the pilot year of the liberalization policy, the rate of growth of nominal bank credit (92%) exceeded by far the growth of nominal GNP (61%) (figure 6.1). Nevertheless, the corresponding figures toward the end of the liberalization episode in 1979, 90% and 85%, respectively, indicate some monetary tightening. This is consistent with the previous description and is also reflected in the path of interest rates on directed credit. The nominal (directed) interest rate for working capital in industry, for example, climbed from only 24% in 1977 and 1978 to 44% in 1979, following the leap of inflation. Another indicator of monetary tightness was the dollar interest rate on forex-denominated nondirected credit. In 1978 and through the first quarter of 1979, its annual rate was 10%–14%. For the rest of the year, the effective rate was raised to 25%–29% by the imposition of a 12% capital-import ("Tobin") tax. This again indicates that monetary policy was tightened as the retreat from the liberalization policy gathered momentum.

The impact of the liberalization on the inflation process deserves some comment at this stage. The basic fact is that the liberalization was not supported by a reduction of the fiscal deficit. Thus, in its pilot year (1978), the total fiscal deficit climbed to 17.5% of GNP while the domestic deficit stayed at 11%. In this case, there was certainly no reason to expect the inflation rate to decline. Furthermore, there was no commitment to a nominal anchor that would signal a government intention of bringing inflation under control.

In fact, some policy measures were taken that had the potential to fuel inflation expectations. First, the introduction of PATAM deposits undermined the nominal anchor of the economy and offered a reasonable explanation for the decline in demand for money, that is, unindexed domestic currency,[4] as several econometric studies indicate clearly.[5] The reduction in demand generated an increase in inflation down the road. Second, the policy of targeting the real exchange rate, introduced in April 1979, dealt another blow to the nominal anchor and made the economy extremely vulnerable to nominal shocks, such as those associated with devaluations resulting from external crises.

Finally, although the philosophy of capital-account liberalization was diametrically opposed to that of financial repression—the cornerstone of the economic regime since the establishment of the state—the new regime left the main elements of FR intact. For example, the highly significant component of directed

Figure 7.1. Ratio of Directed Credit to Total Bank Credit to Public (percent).
Source: BOI.

credit, the embodiment of FR, was not reduced until after 1980 (figure 7.1).
The BOI remained subordinate to the Ministry of Finance. The labor-market
regime and the dominance of the Histadrut persisted even after the new ruling
party took up the reins of government. Thus, only in respect to the exchange rate
regime was a measure of liberalization undertaken.

8

Early Attempts at Stabilization

The acceleration of inflation in the 1970s eroded some components of the financial repression (FR) regime. One reason for having applied FR to begin with, as noted, was the *intention* of increasing the demand for money and, consequently, broadening the base of the inflation tax. However, the rise of inflation, the prime motive for the introduction of money substitutes, depressed demand for money and, by so doing, made the inflation tax harder to "collect." Concurrently, the very slow adjustment of nominal interest rates on the private sector's debt to the government (which was unindexed until 1979) increased the implicit inflation subsidy that the Finance Ministry provided. Indeed, this subsidy rose to a daunting 6% of GNP in the late 1970s, exceeding the seigniorage component by far. In this sense, the "net inflation tax" had already become negative by the mid-1970s (figure 8.1). Thus, both the FR system and inflation became fiscally burdensome, not beneficial. Although this increased the incentive to stabilize the economy once and for all, political conditions in the late 1970s and early 1980s were still not ripe for such a drastic change in course.

THE TENURE OF YIGAEL HURWITZ AT FINANCE

In 1979, amid accelerating inflation, a deteriorating current account, and rising real wages, the government backtracked from its liberalization program. Various factors contributed to the acceleration of inflation that year. The first was the lagged effect of the monetary expansion in the previous year, precipitated by the money injection that the aforementioned rising fiscal deficit and capital inflow had set in motion. Second, the second oil shock (1978–79) caused import prices,

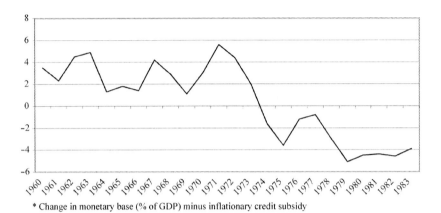

* Change in monetary base (% of GDP) minus inflationary credit subsidy

Figure 8.1. Net Inflation Tax (percent of GDP). *Source:* Meridor, 1987.

specifically of oil, to rise. Third, economic activity picked up due to expectations of a construction boom associated with the planned military redeployment in the Negev in the wake of the peace treaty with Egypt.[1] The same factors contributed to the deterioration in the external position. The rise in real wages was both a cause and an effect of the acceleration of inflation. The long-term instability that usually accompanies rapid inflation induced more frequent nominal wage adjustments, which, in turn, raised the inflation plateau—a well-known process in chronic-inflation economies.[2] Yigael Hurwitz, appointed as finance minister in late 1979, had to tackle all these problems.

The Hurwitz plan, implemented at the end of the year, took the form of a tighter fiscal stance based largely on cutting the subsidization of "essentials" (food, public transport) and eroding real wages. The erosion would flow from the hike in government-controlled prices and the accelerated rate of devaluation in the last quarter of 1979. In the event, the program failed to reduce the total fiscal deficit, but the subsidy cuts and real wage erosion generated pessimistic expectations, dampening domestic uses and, especially, private consumption. The finance minister's determination to stay the course earned him the nickname "I-Don't-Have-Any," after a statement he repeatedly made in public when asked to loosen the Treasury's reins.

While the Hurwitz program managed to stabilize the external position, it failed completely on the inflation front and actually contributed to its acceleration. A similar sequence of actions in Mexico and Brazil in the early 1980s—a temporary fiscal stabilization that included an actual cut in the deficit—had a similar outcome: an acceleration of inflation (Kiguel and Liviatan, 1988). This was explained at the time by the fact that these programs, including the Israeli one, were not committed to a nominal anchor. Furthermore, the real aim of these programs was to improve the balance of payments (BOP) rather than to reduce inflation. In fact, the rise in inflation, achieved by real wage erosion, was an instrument used to reach the BOP target.

The situation in Israel, however, ran into a more fundamental difficulty, a political one. Mr. Hurwitz was the finance minister in a Likud-run government;

his program, if successful, would have severely harmed the position of the Labor Party due to its negative effect on the major firms and other economic entities that were controlled by the Histradut. Thus, his stabilization program could not succeed politically as a unilateral step, especially with elections on the horizon. It turned out that a temporary cut in the deficit, which might be effective in stabilizing the BOP, could aggravate inflation due to the hike in government-controlled prices. The very poor credibility of the government's policy, associated with the absence of a nominal anchor, meant that the jump in the price level could easily transform into a long-term shock to inflation.

The failure of the Hurwitz plan to reduce the fiscal deficit suggests that the actual deficit surpassed the warranted one during the entire 1978–80 period. Bruno (1993, p. 48) estimates the excess at about 5 percentage points of GNP, constituting a substantial inflationary threat. It is therefore no wonder that the tightening of monetary policy in those years could not be effective in restraining inflation.

Mr. Hurwitz's policies toppled the economy into a growth recession in 1980. The GNP growth rate fell from 4.2% in 1979 to 1.8%. Real disposable income declined by 1.6%, private consumption by 3.4%, and real wages by 6.5%. The unemployment rate rose from 3% to 5%. These measures did lower the private import surplus from 14% of GNP in 1979 to 9% in 1980. Inflation, however, crossed the three-digit threshold, soaring from 78% in 1979 to 131% in 1980 and staying at the new plateau until the second half of 1983. The improvement in the current account and the turnaround of the basic account from negative to positive changed the policymakers' priorities by defusing the urgency of the current-account issue. In view of his failure to establish a national consensus around his policy, which had brought on a recession just as elections were approaching, Mr. Hurwitz, the second finance minister in the first Begin government, had to resign. He was replaced at the beginning of 1981 by Yoram Aridor, a critic of Mr. Hurwitz's policy who recommended an entirely different strategy in fighting inflation.

THE TENURE OF YORAM ARIDOR AT FINANCE

The new policy was predicated on tackling inflation from the nominal side. Initially, this strategy was implemented by lowering duties and purchase taxes on durable goods. These moves, applied on the eve of a highly sensitive political season—the 1981 elections—dampened inflation temporarily but had to be reversed a year later. Phase 2 of the Aridor policy, launched in the second half of 1982, aimed to slow the rate of devaluation to 5% per month while inflation ran at 7%. This was effectively an imitation (in a less extreme form) of the Tablita policy implemented in the Southern Cone of Latin America (Ramos, 1986). The Latin American version, however, failed whenever not supported by fiscal contraction, and only Chile among South American countries ultimately managed to stabilize inflation due to its consistent maintenance of fiscal discipline. Since Israel did not make the requisite fiscal adjustment, its program was doomed to failure ab initio.

Although sometimes identified as pure gimmickry, the "5% program," as Aridor's devaluation policy was called at the time, rested on a certain logic.

Although the conception appears mistaken in hindsight, it was difficult to refute as it was unveiled. Its conceptual framework rested on the notion that inflation consists of two components: a "core," related to the fiscal deficit, and a "bubble" occasioned by indexation, inertia, and other factors. This view was supported by the seeming absence of correlation between inflation and the fiscal deficit. Thus, inflation jumped to a new plateau in 1980 even though Finance Minister Hurwitz had tried, unsuccessfully, to bring about significant fiscal contraction. If one accepts this premise, one can make a case for tackling the "bubble" independently of the fiscal component, say, by slowing the rate of devaluation. Aridor followed this approach consistently by trying to synchronize all nominal variables, such as COLA and general-government prices, with the 5% target.

Admittedly, the concept of an inflation bubble is consistent with the way inflation is viewed in the modern theory of policy games, for example, Barro and Gordon (1983) in the context of a discretionary regime (see appendix D below). In retrospect, we know that Aridor's error can be traced to his assumption that the bubble component could be eliminated without change in the fiscal regime. Expressed in policy-game terminology, the policy assumed that the bubble may be eliminated in the context of a transition from "discretion" to "rules." Effecting "regime change," however, is not a simple matter. Presumably, it cannot be done in an economic environment where the government's weak fiscal stance brings the credibility of its anti-inflationary stance into severe doubt. In terms of the recent literature on dominance, one may state that Aridor was trying to set monetary targets under a regime of fiscal dominance that allowed the public deficit and debt to follow unsustainable paths.

The success of the "5% program" depended critically on the realignment of expectations with government policies. No such realignment occurred. In particular, real wages, which were supposed to remain neutral during the process, rose dramatically (by 10%) in 1981 and continued to escalate, albeit more moderately, in the following two years. The inflation rate did not budge, resulting in real currency appreciation (figure 6.2).[3] The current-account deficit ballooned from $0.8 billion in 1980 to $2.2 billion in 1982 (figure II.10).

In 1983, Aridor desperately attempted to solve the nominal-anchor problem once and for all by proposing full dollarization. This gambit, too, however, did not stand a chance in the absence of a major fiscal adjustment. The Ministry of Finance assumed that the mere commitment to dollarization would suffice to induce the government to implement the fiscal reform that was needed to make the scheme work. The government did not buy this logic. The whole program was swept away in the wake of a huge devaluation and the October 1983 stock-market meltdown known as the "bank-share crisis."

THE BANK-SHARE CRISIS AND THE ACCELERATION OF INFLATION

The bank-share crisis was closely linked to the failure of the "5% program." In the early stages of the 5% scheme, more than a year before the crisis broke into the open, the public distanced itself from dollar assets due to their low return (Brener and Rutenberg, 1987). As the program progressed and the current account deficit grew, however, devaluation expectations began to build up and the public switched to foreign exchange in lieu of bank shares, which through 1982 had been an attractive liquid (unindexed) asset due to the banks' dubiously legal support of their prices. Thus, it was the change in expectations that made the difference. At first, the banks attempted to continue supporting the domestic-currency price of their shares by taking foreign loans. As speculation about a pending devaluation persisted, however, they found it impossible to carry on this way. It was this that brought the crisis into the open.

To prevent the total collapse of bank shares and all financial assets traded on the Tel Aviv Stock Exchange, the government closed the exchange for two weeks or so. Afterwards, it stepped in to bail out the holders of bank shares and salvage the credibility of the banking system by guaranteeing a minimum price for the bank shares. This amounted to the virtual nationalization of the banking system and a substantial increase in the effective national debt. To give an idea of the magnitude of the increase, we should note that the market value of the bank shares fell from about one-third of annual GDP before the October 1983 crisis to 20% of GDP by the end of that year.

Immediately after the crisis, pursuant to its bailout program, the government bought up 4% of GDP in bank shares in order to stabilize their value at the minimum guaranteed price. The result of the monetization of these financial assets was partly reflected in a switch by the public from bank shares to foreign exchange and dollar-indexed PATAM deposits. This influx of liquidity facilitated the accommodation of the new inflation step that emerged in the wake of the crisis.

The bank-share crisis was the Israeli version of the debt crisis that afflicted Latin American economies in the 1980s when governments in that part of the world assumed responsibility for private *foreign* indebtedness. By implication, the "5% program" was shakier than it looked, since the public probably took into account the costs of the fiscal bailout. In terms of the "second-generation literature" of BOP crises,[4] one may say that the economy at that time entered the range of multiple equilibria, in which adverse expectations could trigger a financial crisis. The leap in the effective level of the national debt following the crisis and the future fiscal burden that this implied (Burnside, Eichenbaum, and Rebello, 1998) are enumerated among the factors that may explain the acceleration of inflation to over 400% in 1984.

During the year after the bank crisis, Aridor stepped down and the government took actions that amounted in many ways to the reversal of his policies. The new finance minister, Yigal Cohen-Orgad, replaced inflation fighting with stabilizing the balance of payments as the highest priority. Accordingly, he pursued a PPP exchange-rate policy and gave little thought, if any, to its implications for the rate of inflation. By Q4-1983, a 23% devaluation and a sharp hike of controlled prices of basic goods and services propelled inflation to a record 16% per month.

The BOI's monetary policy accommodated the initial jump in inflation, over and above the initial inflow of liquidity into the system, by increasing its discount-window lending. This policy had two goals in mind: to support the reduced bank-share prices, and to restore the liquidity that the collapse and rescheduling of the bank shares had drained from the economy.

Although this policy powered a leap in the inflation plateau—not only the price level—in 1984, it was effective (as usual) with respect to the balance of payments for several reasons. First, the price shock depressed real wages and domestic consumption. Second, the bank-share crisis reduced both the size and the liquidity of the private sector's financial assets. Third, the accelerated rate of devaluation managed to attain a small degree of real depreciation—about 4%—even though it was accompanied by a large stepwise increase in inflation.

Despite the improvement in the civilian current account (the deficit was cut by about $600 million) the foreign-exchange situation deteriorated because the public was unwilling to purchase new government debt and turned to foreign currency instead. In fact, the government deficit was financed predominantly by the sale of foreign exchange, a process that began effectively in 1983 (*Annual Report*, 1984, p. 265). This was an unprecedented fiscal development; over Israel's three-decade history, general government had always made a positive contribution to the reserves. The turnaround indicated that the large fiscal deficits could not be sustained much longer.

As ominous as this development was, however, it did not trigger a foreign-debt crisis of the sort experienced in Latin American countries, even when the gross foreign debt surpassed 80% of GDP in 1984. The structure of Israel's foreign debt was less susceptible to foreign speculative attack; most was long-term and owed to foreign governments (mainly the United States), holders of Israel Bonds, and international institutions. The short-term liquidity position was also in reasonably good shape, reflecting a balance between assets (mainly the foreign reserves) and liabilities (*Annual Report*, 1984, pp. 228–31). The lingering danger, however, was that the public might use its large stock of domestic bonds to mount an attack on the foreign reserves. This threat, which resurfaced in the early 1990s, would eventually be known in the popular discourse as the "sheqel mountain" issue.

Additional developments made the inflationary process unsustainable. The Tanzi effect influenced tax collection for the first time in 1984, when revenues (in real terms) declined for reasons partly related to the acceleration of inflation. Furthermore, the decrease in real wages despite monthly COLAs created the feeling that the indexation arrangements were collapsing. Finally, the new National Unity Government, established in September 1984, tried to protect the real exchange rate by resorting to a maxi-devaluation without a corresponding fiscal adjustment. This merely propelled inflation to even higher rates.

THE THIRD STABILIZATION ATTEMPT— THE "PACKAGE DEALS"

In response to the sense that inflation was about to spiral out of control, the new National Unity Government entered into an arrangement with the

Manufacturers' Association of Israel and the Histadrut that was termed the "package deal." The "deal" aimed to stop the wage-price spiral by imposing a freeze of wages and prices for three months starting in November 1984. Renewed twice—on February 1 and May 1, 1985—the package deals were the last attempt to stabilize inflation without a comprehensive program predicated on major fiscal restraint.

The set of package deals dented the inflation rate only in the first month of each of the three rounds, mainly due to the absence of a serious effort to impose pervasive and sustained fiscal reform. The new method was different from Aridor's policies in that freezing the exchange rate was not officially part of the deal. However, an attempt was made to create real depreciation by devaluing the currency at a higher rate than inflation (one may visualize this as a manifestation of dynamic inconsistency), resulting in an additional hitch.

However, inflation spun out of control, climbing to a monthly rate of about 20% in April 1985. With all previous attempts having failed, it became clear that a comprehensive stabilization program was unavoidable. It was postponed to July because of Histadrut elections in May, it being assumed that political support for such a program entailed the cooperation of organized labor in formulating and, particularly, implementing the stabilization effort.

INDICATIONS OF THE UNSUSTAINABILITY OF THE INFLATIONARY REGIME

One of the preconditions for the implementation of a stabilization policy is the conviction that the inflationary regime cannot cope with the emerging problems. Developments after the 1983 bank-share crisis, during which price increases escalated toward hyperinflationary rates, cast doubt on the ability of the indexation system to cope with inflation at such rates, which had never happened before. Real wages in the business sector eroded in 1984 and, as noted, real tax collection fell for the first time that year, partly due to the Tanzi effect (*Annual Report*, 1984). Furthermore, the public was unwilling to acquire new government bonds, forcing the government to finance its expenditures in a clearly unsustainable way, by selling dollars.

Finally, all previous stabilization attempts, based on partial measures, had failed. Isolated policies in the form of fiscal adjustment (Hurwitz), slowing the pace of devaluation (Aridor), and wage-price freezes of the National Unity Government's tenure (the package deals) were of no avail. All this convinced the policymakers and, later on, the public that the time was ripe for a comprehensive program with a traditional fiscal adjustment at its core. This awareness blossomed into action in the 1985 stabilization policy, to which chapter 10 is devoted.

9

General Features of the Overall Inflationary Process

The following chronological review of Israel's inflation process underscores the relevance of several general characteristics of inflationary onslaughts and the importance of elucidating them at this juncture of the discussion.

THE REAL ECONOMY AND THE COSTS OF INFLATION

Israel's "lost decade," 1974–84, was associated with very poor economic performance in terms of growth and productivity. The comparison with the boom years of 1967–September 1973 is highly instructive. The rate of real annual GDP growth plummeted from 11% in the earlier period to a mere 3.3% in 1974–84 (table 9.1). Total factor productivity in the business sector plunged from 6% per annum in 1967–73 to 0.7% in 1974–84 (Annual Report 1999, p. 266).

Despite the stagnation of output per capita, real wages continued to rise. It is especially noteworthy that the of real-wage in the business sector increased in the lost decade by more than 3% per annum (table I.1). The continued rise in real wages points to the existence of a basic "disequilibrium," or unsustainability, in view of the stagnation of gross domestic investment and total factor productivity in 1973–84 (*Annual Report*, 1984, p. 12). Further evidence of the unsustainability of the pattern was the 4.9% rate of increase in private consumption during the lost decade, as against 3.3% GDP growth (table 9.1), reflected in the doubling of the foreign debt/GDP ratio from 40% to over 80%. These developments did have a positive side: the oil crises, which caused worldwide stagnation, raised unemployment in Israel less than in industrial

Table 9.1. Real Resources and Uses

	Resources					Use of Resources					Uses	
		Business-Sector Product[a]	Imports[b]		Total Resources	Consumption			Gross Domestic Investment	Domestic Value of Exports[d]		
	GDP		Total	Civilian		Private	Total Public	Public Domestic[c]			Total	Domestic[e]
Annual Rate of Change (percent), 1961–99												
1961–66	8.6	9.0	10.1	9.7	9.0	8.9	10.4	9.7	6.4	12.2	9.0	8.3
1967–73	9.5	10.0	17.0	14.1	11.7	7.4	17.9	12.5	15.2	13.6	11.7	10.0
1974–84	3.3	3.2	2.3	3.9	2.9	4.9	0.3	2.1	-0.1	6.0	2.9	2.8
1985–89	3.8	4.9	4.0	4.7	3.8	6.0	0.1	0.4	0.1	5.7	3.8	3.4
1990–94	6.1	7.5	11.7	12.3	7.8	7.4	3.5	3.5	17.2	7.3	7.8	8.2
1995–99	4.1	4.9	7.0	7.0	5.0	5.0	2.3	2.0	3.9	8.3	5.0	4.1
2000–03	1.8	1.5	0.9	0.8	1.5	3.2	2.6	2.6	-8.4	3.7	1.5	0.8
Annual Rate of Per-Capita Change (percent), 1961–99												
1961–66	4.9	5.2	6.3	5.9	5.2	5.1	6.5	5.9	2.7	8.3	5.2	4.5
1967–73	6.0	6.5	13.3	10.5	8.2	4.0	14.1	8.8	11.5	10.0	8.2	6.5
1974–84	1.2	1.1	0.2	1.8	0.8	2.7	-1.7	0.0	-2.1	3.8	0.8	0.7
1985–89	2.1	3.2	2.3	2.9	2.1	4.3	-1.6	-1.3	-1.5	4.0	2.1	1.7
1990–94	2.3	3.6	7.7	8.3	3.9	3.5	-0.2	-0.2	13.0	3.4	3.9	4.3
1995–99	1.5	2.2	4.3	4.4	2.4	2.3	-0.3	-0.5	1.3	5.6	2.4	1.5
2000–03	-0.3	-0.5	-1.2	-1.2	-0.6	1.1	0.5	0.5	-10.3	1.6	-0.6	-1.2

[a]Excluding public services, nonprofit organizations, and housing services.
[b]Imports of goods and services (c.i.f.); excluding factor payments abroad and interest payments by general government to the rest of the world.
[c]Excluding direct defense imports.
[d]Exports of goods and services (f.o.b.); excluding factor payments from abroad and interest receipts of general government from the rest of the world.
[e]Domestic uses are equivalent to total uses (excluding direct defense imports) less exports.
Source: BOI Annual Report.

countries—but at the cost of long-term economic stagnation and galloping inflation.

In principle, there is a two-way relationship between inflation and growth, although the quantitative parameters of the correlation are difficult to establish. There is a theoretical argument that points to a negative effect of growth on inflation: a lower rate of growth reduces the noninflationary component of money creation, implying that a given fiscal deficit becomes more inflationary. By inference, the slowing of growth during the lost decade was equivalent to an increase of about 3 percentage points in the deficit/GDP ratio (Bruno, 1993, table 3.2).

Turning to the other side of this relationship (the effect of inflation on growth), we note first that inflation causes the financial sector to grow unnecessarily by absorbing sources that could be used more productively elsewhere, thereby hindering economic growth. In Marom's estimation, between 1970 and 1982 the share of the banking system in GDP climbed from 1.7% to 5%, for an increase of 3.3 percentage points, as against a 1.1 percentage-point (average) increase in selected OECD countries (Marom, 1987). Most of this additional increase, a sizable increment in cumulative terms, may be attributed to the inflation differential.

Another element of the cost of inflation, often mentioned in the literature, is the distortion that inflation inflicts on the relative price structure. A measure of this distortion is the standard deviation of the monthly difference between the Consumer Price Index and its components. Calculations by the BOI (*Annual Report*, 1984) indicate that the standard deviation almost doubled between the early 1970s and 1979–83. The standard deviation of monthly changes in the total CPI behaved similarly. While this finding points to a growing distortion in relative prices, it does not take into account the adjustment of the economy to these deviations.

Yet another cost of inflation is associated with the recurrent stabilization efforts that are made whenever the inflation rate accelerates or the balance of payments runs into difficulties due to partial disinflation policies. In the Israeli case, these policies caused excessive variance in private consumption in particular. Contractionary policies after the 1973 shocks, for example, slowed the growth rate of private consumption to zero in 1975, and similar policies later on drove the growth rates of consumption below zero in 1980 and 1984. However, we cannot estimate the excess of this variance relative to the counterfactual (i.e., the level that would prevail in a noninflationary economy).

The costs of inflation are not limited to the inflationary period itself. The increase in national debt as a result of the continuing deficits, for example, saddles the economy with a long-term burden. Although Israel's debt/GDP ratio has been declining since the 1985 stabilization program, the gross debt/GDP ratio in 2004 was 105%, only 4 percentage points lower than the average level in 1994–97 and 45 percentage points higher than the Maastricht benchmark of 60%. (The debt net of reserves stood at 88.4% of GDP in 2004, 2 percentage points higher than the 1994–97 average.) Evidently, then, the economy is finding this legacy of the inflation era harder to shed.

THE MONEY-SUPPLY PROCESS

During the inflationary period, 1974–83, seigniorage was generally stable at around 2% of GDP (table I.2), meaning that the increases in inflation and the money supply were not powered from the fiscal side. However, the annual rate of base-money growth increased dramatically, from 40% in 1974–77 to over 140% in 1981–83. Thus, the increase in the rate of inflation reduced the base money/GDP ratio during the inflationary period but engendered a proportionate increase in the rate of growth of the money supply. If so, one may describe the elasticity of the base-money supply (relative to GDP) with respect to inflation as unitary. This tautology, however, does not explain the force that drove inflation. Nor does the impressive presentation of Eckstein and Leiderman (1992), who derived the asymptotic constancy of the seigniorage ratio (which is empirically equivalent to unitary elasticity) from an optimizing representative-agent model, help us to answer the question. One may also argue that the growth of the money supply offset inflation expectations, which reduced the monetary base so as to hold the seigniorage ratio constant. If so, however, what force was driving expectations?

Our partial explanation of this puzzle hinges on the monetary regime that Israel applied during the lost decade: a fiscal-dominance regime that lacked a nominal anchor. This regime transformed nonrecurrent shocks to the price level (originating mainly in the balance of payments) into inflation plateaus, as described in detail above. The theoretical framework of policy games and the "unpleasant monetarist arithmetic" of the national debt can explain many of the monetary developments in this period. Only after the 1985 stabilization did monetary policy halt the automatic accommodation and restrain the growth of the money supply. This entailed a lowering of the seigniorage ratio, offset by a reduction in the fiscal deficit so as to keep general government solvent. These developments were reflected in a change in monetary regime from fiscal dominance to monetary dominance.

POLICY-GAME PERSPECTIVES OF THE HIGHER INFLATION PLATEAU

Theoretical developments in the area of policy games (see Barro and Gordon's seminal essay [1983]) may shed more light on the issues associated with the acceleration of inflation in 1974–77. With fiscal policy absolved of responsibility for supporting a nominal anchor, the path to coping with the precarious inflation situation by means of various monetary "tricks" was wide open. In this context, it is useful to distinguish between regimes of "discretion"—in which the policymaker has no commitment—and regimes of "rules," in which full credibility of the policymaker's behavior is assumed. As the status of the Labor-led governments became increasingly shaky from the early 1970s onward, the public realized that these governments would not take the chance of adopting policies that might induce unemployment and would not cut the fiscal deficit.

In fact, unemployment rates were much lower in Israel than in the industrial countries excluding Scandinavia, where they resembled Israel's. Israelis also took it for granted that the government had an overriding commitment to the maintenance of external solvency and the continuation of the inflow of imports. By implication, then, it would not risk the currency appreciation that usually accompanies stabilization programs.

In this environment, inflation and the nominal anchor seemed to be matters of secondary significance. As long as the current account of the balance of payments was sustainable and unemployment did not increase substantially, the government would be satisfied if inflation refrained from accelerating. Acceleration was viewed as a negative development because it might overwhelm the indexation arrangements and impair income distribution.[1] Accordingly, we may interpret the government's political weakness as implying that Israel had what Barro and Gordon would define as a discretionary regime.

It is also supposed that after the external shock in 1973–74 the government shifted its preferences from the maintenance of low inflation rates to the reduction of the current-account deficit. Within the discretionary framework, the government uses the nominal exchange rate to erode real wages in order to improve the trade balance while trade unions use the nominal wage as an instrument for preemptive strikes. The result is a wage-price spiral, which has no effect on the trade balance. An increase in the motivation to improve the BOP by devaluation, as happens during an external crisis, will only result in an increase in inflation.

In the equilibrium setup of the game, the inflation rate is a positive function of the trade deficit and the relative preference for a balanced external position. (See appendix A for a detailed presentation.) An increase in any of these factors, as may well have been the case in 1973, tends to increase the rate of devaluation and of inflation in equilibrium. This is the simple interpretation of the acceleration of inflation after 1973 from the point of view of policy games, assuming the absence of a nominal anchor, which could be supported by an appropriate fiscal policy. It also explains the linkage between the motivation to erode the real wage, in order to improve the BOP, and the increase in inflation in the case of a current-account deficit. The same argument applies to the attempt to orchestrate a real depreciation beyond the market-equilibrium level of the exchange rate.

Policy-game models may also provide some insight in the case of a policymaker who tries to maintain the current inflation plateau *irrespective of the absolute level of inflation.* In appendix B, we show that under the given assumption the policymaker will be unable to maintain the inflation plateau in a policy-game equilibrium. This resembles the situation during the crawling-peg period (1975–77), when the government accepted the inflation plateau that had emerged from the 1973 crisis.

In the course of Israel's inflation process, the inflation rate got "stuck" on a plateau several times and policymakers were content to leave it there. Each time, however, their efforts were frustrated in a manner similar to that described by the model in appendix B. Thus, inflation eventually jumped to a higher plateau.

In fact, a monetary regime that concerns itself only with *maintaining* a given inflation rate irrespective of the level of the inflation plateau may be regarded as one that has no nominal anchor. In this model, the policymaker is averse to *changes* in inflation rates but still has use for surprise inflation, especially in cases of balance-of-payments crises that entail large devaluations. Given these two motives, which the public perceives, the equilibrium outcome will be a persistent rise in inflation, as modeled in appendix B.

From a statistical point of view, this scenario entails a unit root in the series of inflation (since the policymaker's loss is related only to the *change* in inflation). This corresponds to a random walk with a positive drift in the inflation series, which may increase over time as the economy improves its ability to live with inflation by adopting higher degrees of indexation. Indeed, this property holds for the quarterly series of inflation in Q1-1974–Q2-1985, as appendix B shows in greater detail. If the drift increases over time (as seems to be the case in practice), then the inflation series moves quickly toward hyperinflationary territory. This evidently corresponds to the feeling in Israel before the mid-1985 stabilization.

If we assume that the policymaker uses surprise inflation tactics only when under stress (as in the case of balance-of-payments crises), then we obtain that the inflation plateau is constant in ordinary times and surges in times of crisis. This scenario fits the Israeli experience during the lost decade.

In contrast, the hypothesis of a unit root in the inflation series is rejected for the poststabilization period (after 1985). This is consistent with the policy-game model provided that the policymaker is concerned not only with the *change* in inflation but also with its *level*, as is the case, for example, in an inflation-target regime. From a statistical point of view, the latter regime implies a stationary inflation series given the drift term (which has been significantly negative since the stabilization), as has been indeed the case for inflation after 1985.

INDEXATION

Indexation is an endogenous and inseparable characteristic of the inflation process. It is only natural that people will try to protect themselves from the unexpected component of inflation. Monetary authorities that cannot eliminate the original sin, inflation itself, come under pressure to accommodate this need. Although the timing of changes in indexation arrangements may affect the dynamics of inflation, from a longer-term perspective indexation is endogenous to factors that govern the inflation process. It must be recognized, however, that indexation arrangements in chronic-inflation economies develop *gradually* and that every step in this development entails higher inflation because people learn to live with inflation. On the whole, then, inflation and indexation exist in symbiosis.

Liviatan and Frish (2003) analyze (indirectly) the relationship between indexation and inflation in the context of a discretionary regime. In this model, based on a representative agent with an infinite horizon, the discretionary policymaker has two conflicting goals. First, he wishes to provide optimal real balances, entailing an increase in real balances until their marginal utility falls to zero (the liquidity channel). Second, he wishes to erode the real value of initial financial wealth by raising the current price level through surprise inflation, in order to obtain a fiscal windfall (the erosion channel). The restraining factor to this policy is the potential damage that inflation may inflict on output and real balances. The equilibrium in such a model, involving positive financial wealth, entails the use of a monetary instrument in addition to the stock of base money. We assume this to be the interest on base money. Although each of these channels creates a link between initial wealth and inflation, in equilibrium the inflation corresponding to both channels has to be the same.

It turns out that as the output cost of inflation is reduced (by more indexation) the equilibrium level of inflation rises to extraordinary rates. In fact, in this model the reduction in the output cost of inflation is the most prominent cause of the rise of inflation. Moreover, as inflation accelerates due to this factor, the level of seigniorage does not increase and the real economy is affected very little. Thus, the nominal economy and the real economy are dichotomized—a situation that corresponds to Bruno's description of the great inflation in Israel (Bruno, 1993).

With this in mind, we turn to the empirical developments. The coverage of Israel's indexation arrangements expanded continuously as the inflation process advanced and contracted (albeit slowly) after the stabilization process began in July 1985.

Three major components of the economic system are usually, but not simultaneously, involved in broadening the scope of indexation: the labor market, the assets market, and the tax system. In all these cases, the connection with inflation is strongly evident. Wage indexation has a very long history in Israel. It began in 1942, in response to the wartime inflationary surge that was generated, among other things, by increases in commodities prices and the monetization of a fraction of the U.K. deficit in Palestine; it was implemented by means of the Currency Board mechanism. This effectively established identity between the Palestine pound and the pound sterling, as it did for the currencies of all dependency members of the sterling bloc. In the 1970–85 period, the indexation of wages to prices was strengthened by a progressive increase in the frequency of COLA. (In 1984, the frequency was monthly.) Israeli government bonds were indexed in the early 1950s. In the 1970s, indexation was extended to social insurance and the income-tax system. Long-term development loans to firms were indexed in 1979. Shiffer (2001) shows how all features of indexation intensified in the post-1970 period. Specifically, his overall measure of real-wage protection by means of indexation (taking account of both the percentage and the frequency of indexation) points to a continuously rising degree of real-wage protection as inflation increases.

In the assets market, the government was actively involved in the process of extending the coverage of indexation, especially by providing indexed money substitutes. Notably, however, even in the absence of such involvement the private sector would have found ways of indexing its financial assets by turning to foreign exchange. During the inflationary period in Latin America, both tendencies were visible: the public in Argentina and Uruguay held dollars while Brazilians kept their savings in indexed government bonds. In Israel, as in Brazil, the government opted for the indexation alternative by introducing PATAM deposits in 1977, partly in order to divert demand for "green dollars"— foreign currency in cash or deposits—to dollar-indexed domestic deposits. These considerations imply that while the introduction of the PATAM affected the timing of the acceleration of inflation, the acceleration would have taken place at some stage as long as the basic causes of inflation remained untreated. Nevertheless, it is clear that the government's policies in 1977 stepped up the process of asset indexation, a matter that deserves explanation.

Arguably, the government had an interest in introducing inflation-protected financial assets of some kind, be it PATAM or green dollars, even though such a measure would be detrimental to the demand for money and, thereby, to the base of the inflation tax. In fact, along with the introduction of PATAM the government liberalized the foreign-exchange market and made green dollars easier to obtain. Thus, one cannot say that the only motivation for PATAM was to deflect demand from green dollars.

One factor behind the initiative to introduce inflation-protected short-term financial assets had to do with the reduction in real liquidity due to the acceleration of inflation. The government had an interest in slowing this process even at the cost of a loss of seigniorage. After its retreat from foreign-sector liberalization in and after 1979, the government still continued to allow the creation of PATAM deposits, which soon dominated the stock of real liquidity. Thus, the level of the broader monetary aggregates (M_3), which include forex-indexed deposits, changed only moderately during the inflation process (figure 9.1). In this way, the damage to real liquidity, in the broad sense, was limited.

The introduction of indexed money substitutes such as PATAM is problematic for those who believe that the government instigates the inflation process in order to finance the fiscal deficit (the premise of inflation-tax models). The insertion of asset indexation into such a model means that the government is

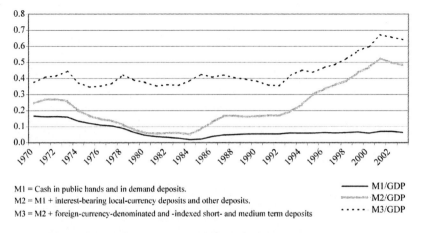

M1 = Cash in public hands and in demand deposits.
M2 = M1 + interest-bearing local-currency deposits and other deposits.
M3 = M2 + foreign-currency-denominated and -indexed short- and medium term deposits

———— M1/GDP
········· M2/GDP
· · · · · M3/GDP

Figure 9.1. Ratios of Monetary Aggregates to GDP. *Source:* BOI.

protecting the public against its own inflationary policies. Would it not be more reasonable to protect the public by creating less inflation? This ostensibly para-doxical behavior of the government, it turns out, may be rationalized in the context of lack of credibility. In this case, the policymaker does not have full control over the inflationary process and has to accommodate adverse expecta-tions. Thus, he has to strike a compromise between the need to preserve the real liquidity of the economy and the loss of seigniorage as a result of asset indexa-tion. (See appendix E, based on Liviatan 2002b.) In terms of the policy-game literature, this tradeoff is more relevant for a discretionary regime than for one driven by rules.

Another type of tradeoff is associated with the indexation of the tax system—a counter-Tanzi-Olivera effect. As Fischer and Summers (1989) note, such a policy has short-term advantages but tends in the longer term to raise the equi-librium rate of inflation and, thus, to be harmful. By implication, this area of indexation has an intertemporal tradeoff. A responsible government that attaches great importance to long-term considerations will not pursue such policies. Again, the intertemporal tradeoff is more relevant to a discretionary policymaker who has little concern for the future and does not have much control over the inflationary process to begin with.

DEFICITS, SEIGNIORAGE, AND INFLATION

One of the most puzzling features of Israel's great inflation was its relatively low level of seigniorage. Although the fiscal deficit was large, the money-creation component of deficit finance was relatively small. If inflation was generated by money creation for fiscal purposes, would it not have made sense to elimi-nate inflation by a small tax increase and, by so doing, to avoid the inflation problem altogether? The fiscal loss in this case would have been much smaller than the damage that the inflation caused. In the 1978–83 period, for example, seigniorage was around 2% of GDP. If this amount of money creation were accountable for the great inflation, would it not have been reasonable to elimi-nate inflation by raising taxes or cutting the primary deficit by this amount? After all, the primary deficit was cut by much more than that in the 1985 stabilization.

The same criticism may be expressed against a calculation based on an attempt to explain inflation by the ratio of "unwarranted deficit" (the deficit in excess of that warranted) to the money base. In the last year and a half of Israel's inflationary process, this excess was estimated at about 2.5% of GDP. If this were the source of the inflation, would it not have made sense to eradicate the inflation by reducing the deficit by this amount? If inflation were so easy to conquer, why was it necessary to go through all the hardships of the 1985 stabi-lization process, in which much larger fiscal cuts were made in order to reduce inflation to moderate levels? These queries suggest that the explanation of the great inflation is more complicated than the simplistic constructions proposed above. We connect the difficulty in conquering inflation to the difficulty in the transition from fiscal to monetary dominance.

PERSISTENT FISCAL DEFICITS, THE PUBLIC DEBT, AND THE UNPLEASANT MONETARIST ARITHMETIC

The entire inflationary period was characterized by large fiscal deficits that showed no particular trend over the years (*Annual Report*, 1995, pp. 338–40). The total deficit (internal and external) averaged 17% of GNP in 1973–84 (Bruno, 1993, and table II.2). Consequently, the national debt/GNP ratio grew steadily. The increase in the fiscal deficit in 1973–84 relative to 1967–72 was not related solely to the growth in defense expenditure, much of which was financed by an increase in U.S. aid. It is quite reasonable to trace it to an increase in transfer payments by 3.3–3.5 percentage points of GNP (Barkai, 1998, table A-1, p. 154). Indeed, most of the increase in the deficit between the two periods originates in this factor.

The increase in the fiscal deficit and its persistence in 1973–84 were originally the results of political pressure that induced the last Labor governments to appease immigrant and low-income voters. Fear of electoral defeat prompted these governments to adopt populist fiscal policies implemented by a major increase in transfer payments. Outlays on account of child allowances climbed with special vigor, from 0.84% of GNP in 1970 to 2.82% of GNP in 1976 (Barkai, 1998, table 8.1), the last full year in which Labor was in power. The Likud maintained the same policy when it took over in 1977. Not all welfare-state transfers, of course, are necessarily populist. However, as Bruno (1993) points out, what was appropriate in the boom years of 1967–72 became harmful in the stagnant years of the lost decade.[2] The size of the deficit far exceeded the "warranted deficit," that is, the non-inflationary deficit consistent with the rate of economic growth and the ratio of general-government debt plus base money to GNP.[3] The large fiscal deficits allowed disposable income and consumption to increase faster than GNP, resulting in a growing external debt/GNP ratio.

The growth of the total national debt from 80% of GNP in 1970 to more than 160% in 1984 had a much stronger destabilizing effect on the economy than anyone realized at the time. The inherent instability that such an increase in debt brought about is not felt in tranquil times but emerges as a threat at times of financial pressure, since there is always the possibility that the holders of its liquid portion, at least, might shift to foreign currency and cause a severe external crisis. The M_3 to GNP ratio (M_3 including foreign-currency deposits) climbed to the vicinity of 40%, far surpassing the foreign reserves, which were about 10% of GNP in 1980.

An increase in the debt/GNP ratio may be transmitted to inflation along several paths. Consider the long-term, perfect-foresight models. Under strict Ricardian equivalence, an increase in national debt that the private sector willingly absorbs in anticipation of future taxes should have no effect on the real economy or on inflation. In the Israeli case, the relevant data show strong indications of Ricardian equivalence. The simple correlation coefficient between public and private saving (as ratios of total income) was –0.84 in 1964–99 and –0.9 in 1974–84.[4] However, if the national debt grows faster than the real interest rate (adjusted for growth), it is an indication of insolvency of general government, that is, a signal that general government does not intend to pay its debt. Accordingly, Sargent and Wallace's seminal essay (1981) on the "Unpleasant Monetarist Arithmetic" places an upper limit on the size of the debt.[5] They suggest that if the national debt is following an insolvent trajectory and the public expects general government to eventually curb the increase, at least partly, by money creation, there may be inflationary implications for the years preceding the stabilization. This approach, based on long-term considerations, is attractive since it links the path of inflation with that of the stock of debt, which continues growing even if the annual flow of the deficit remains constant.

While this model is capable of explaining important features of the financial developments during Israel's inflationary era, it does not quite fit other features of the Israeli experience, as described immediately below.

SOLVENCY AND THE SUSTAINABILITY OF THE PUBLIC DEBT

A basic problem with the foregoing analytical framework in the context of our analysis is that the primary deficit in Israel did not remain constant during the inflation process, as it does in the Sargent-Wallace model. The primary deficit decreased substantially in the course of the process and the real interest burden of the national debt grew (table I.2). As a result of these contrasting developments, the operational deficit as a percent of GDP (table I.2, line 1) stayed within approximately the same range throughout the "lost decade."[6] It can be shown that a constant operational deficit may imply solvency of general government (McCallum, 1984; Tanner and Ramos, 2002). However, since Israel's operational deficit was not only positive but also large, the nondiscounted debt kept growing and reached alarming levels, causing the public to doubt the government's ability to service the debt. It is this aspect of the modified Sargent-Wallace model that is crucial in understanding the role of persistent fiscal deficits in the inflation process.

Tanner and Ramos (2002) show that when the primary deficit net of the inflation tax responds negatively to an increase in total fiscal liabilities (money plus bonds), then the public sector is solvent (provided this state of affairs continues indefinitely). This seems to be the case shown in table I.2. Thus, we may conclude that during the inflationary period the general-government sector seemed to be solvent, at least in the statistical sense. By this we mean that the conditions for solvency were satisfied in the observed period—which does not, however, guarantee that the observed relationship will last forever. Similarly, one may show that if the primary deficit net of seigniorage responds negatively to the size of the national debt (consisting of bonds only), then general government is solvent in the sense that the discounted value of its debt tends to zero as time tends to infinity.[7] Again, the series in table I.2 seems to satisfy these conditions, implying that the current stock of bonds equals the present value of all current and future adjusted primary surpluses, again assuming that the observed situation will last indefinitely (all in terms of ratios to GDP).[8] In this sense, then, Israel's general government appeared to be solvent throughout the inflationary period. Statistical solvency, however, does not prevent the nondiscounted debt from reaching unsustainable levels in the opinion of operators in the capital market.

Note that while solvency is expressed in terms of the present value of the discounted debt, regardless of its current size, the sustainability of the debt refers specifically to its current size. Just as a commercial bank may refuse to lend to a customer who keeps asking for more credit and is willing to pay a higher interest rate, so the public may impose credit rationing on the government by refusing to purchase more government bonds even at higher yields to redemption. Indeed, in Israel, even though the government raised the effective interest rate on its bonds by gradually making them more liquid and stabilizing their prices, the public stopped buying bonds in late 1983 and persisted in this behavior through 1984. Thus, the government had to sell foreign exchange to finance the fiscal deficit.

The foregoing sharp distinction between solvency and sustainability relates to what we called "statistical solvency," which refers to the observed period only. This concept of solvency is usually different from true solvency, which refers to the infinite future. There is no guarantee that the conditions for solvency in an observed period will be satisfied forever. Thus, while there may be no distinction between true solvency and sustainability, there may well be a divergence between statistical solvency and sustainability.

During Israel's inflationary period, the adjusted primary deficit (i.e., the primary deficit less seigniorage) was positive, while in a steady state the primary deficit as defined should become a surplus, assuming that the debt is positive. This switch may be performed if the negative relationship between the adjusted primary deficit and the stock of debt is maintained indefinitely (because in this case a large enough debt may turn the deficit into surplus). This, however, is not guaranteed by the observed negative relationship over a limited number of years. In fact, one may argue that the public did not consider the authorities capable of turning the adjusted primary deficit into surplus without a major change of policy. This may well be the underlying reason for the observed difference between the (statistical) solvency and sustainability.[9]

Recent formulations of "fiscal dominance" assign monetary policy to the role of ensuring solvency of general government under any fiscal policy.[10] The Israeli experience indicates that the monetary base was too small to perform this role during the inflationary period. Thus, fiscal policy assumed the task of keeping general government solvent. However, it kept the level of operational deficits too high, generating an excessive increase in the nondiscounted debt of general government. The latter seems to be the more significant indicator of the sustainability, rather than statistical solvency, of fiscal propriety. For the debt to be sustainable, the operational deficit must be held not only constant but also small. This, in fact, is the approach taken by the Maastricht criterion, which limits the national debt to 60% of GDP, a significantly tighter constraint than the mere requirement of (statistical) solvency. The government of Israel embraced this principle only when it adopted the 1985 stabilization policy.

The inflationary regime retained one crucial feature of the prevalent notion of fiscal dominance: the practice of responding to shocks by hiking prices, considered part and parcel of monetary policy. The price increases played the role of the Pigou effect (Patinkin, 1966) in a broader sense than in the usual formulation. Thus, the government responded to all balance-of-payment shocks during the high-inflation "lost decade" by creating price shocks of the type described above, eroding not only real balances but also real wages and subsidies. Although BOP crises are not directly related to fiscal solvency, the indirect link is clear: they may require bailout operations by the financial sector, which increase the fiscal deficits (Burnside, Eichenbaum, and Rebello, 1998). This scenario in the Israeli case, involving a major increase in the national debt, materialized only in the 1983 bank-share crisis. However, the potential of such an outcome existed in each crisis during that time. This aspect of fiscal dominance led to an economic regime that could not control the inflation process because it lacked a nominal anchor. Indeed, the use of price shocks in response to BOP crises was discontinued only after the 1985 stabilization.

MONETARY ACCOMMODATION AND CORE INFLATION

Monetary accommodation is an elusive concept. In inflationary economies, however, it usually means that the money supply allows inflation to be higher than the minimal rate needed to finance the fiscal deficit (which we shall call "core inflation" below). For example, a temporary external shock that would normally cause only an upward shift of the price level may evolve into a long-term increase in inflation under monetary accommodation, without any appreciable effect on the real fiscal deficit (appropriately defined). Thus, when we speak of a wage-price spiral, we mean an inflation path that is higher than core inflation.

The nature of the reaction of inflation to shocks provides an example of monetary accommodation. According to the conventional wisdom, the indexation mechanism allows a price-level shock to be translated into a shock to inflation. (See the analysis of this approach in Bruno, 1993, pp. 67–74.) This, however, entails monetary accommodation and is not necessarily reflected in a significant change in the fiscal deficit (see appendix D). In Israel, for example, as noted above, the seigniorage/GDP ratio (representing a form of deficit finance) was fairly constant at around 2% throughout the entire inflation process. Yet inflation leaped dramatically.

One simple example of monetary accommodation of inflation that has no fiscal implication is the case considered by Eckstein and Leiderman (1992), in which the Laffer curve does not have a downward sloping segment—a case that corresponds to the Israeli experience (table I.2). Here the empirical elasticity of the monetary base with respect to inflation is approximately unitary for a certain range of high inflation rates. In this case, core inflation will be the lowest inflation rate in the range in which demand elasticity is approximately unitary.[11]

Another case in which a rise of inflation may be supported by monetary accommodation with no significant effect on the real fiscal deficit occurs when the central bank pays interest on the commercial banks' reserves. This was standard operating procedure in chronic-inflation economies, including Israel's during the period at issue. In this case, a leap in inflation may be accommodated by an increase in the interest rate on reserves, with no appreciable effect (if any) on the real fiscal deficit of general government (see appendix D). The BOI gave this policy special priority starting in 1982, in order to strengthen the "sheqel base" in view of the pervasive shift to PATAM deposits.[12] In fact, in 1984 these interest payments came to a remarkable 0.8% of GDP (*Annual Report*, 1984, p. 266).

By paying interest on reserves, the BOI effectively returns some of the seigniorage that it collects due to the high inflation, thereby increasing the fiscal burden. For those who believe that governments deliberately orchestrate inflation in order to collect an inflation tax, the return of seigniorage by means of interest payments on reserves poses the same problem as the introduction of indexed money substitutes. This ostensible paradox, however, may be resolved if we consider it within the framework of a government that has only partial control over inflation (due to credibility problems, for example). In this case, the government has an incentive to offset the reduction of liquidity caused by high inflation even at the cost of a fiscal loss, as Liviatan and Frish (2006) show. (Appendix D formalizes this case in a somewhat different configuration.)

These examples establish the important point that the real fiscal deficit of general government cannot serve as an anchor for inflation. By implication, a nominal anchor is needed to control inflation. The examples presented above demonstrate that monetary accommodation may allow inflation to surpass core inflation significantly. Indeed, it is well known that fiscal solvency of the public sector may be consistent with various paths of inflation.

THE NEGATIVE INFLATION TAX

One of the most puzzling features of Israel's inflation era was the slow upward adjustment of the nominal interest rate on government "development credit." As a result, the implied inflationary subsidy of the enormous outstanding balance of credit of this type exceeded the seigniorage on money balances from the mid-1970s onward, rising from 4% of GDP in 1975 to more than 6% by the end of the 1970s, when new "development loans" were finally indexed (Meridor, 1987). However, since inflation continued to accelerate, the subsidy on the stock of the old development loans continued to rise and stayed above 6% of GDP in the early 1980s as well. Concurrently, seigniorage (the increase in the monetary base) remained in the range of 2%–2.5% of GNP. This phenomenon was sometimes referred to in Israel as a net "negative inflation tax."

Ostensibly, the government's behavior on this score seemed irrational. One way to rationalize it is to regard the inflation subsidy as intentional. After all, the government had to finance the domestic defense burden and was under political pressure to increase transfer payments to the private sector. In this context, the Ministry of Finance and even the BOI had an incentive to protect the level of investment of the private sector by subsidizing its capital outlays. This argument is not watertight, however, since it does not explain why the new loans were indexed in 1979 when inflation was on the rise.

An alternative approach is to regard the phenomenon as a form of the Tanzi effect, in which the government adjusts its nominal fiscal instruments at a lag. By implication, the acceleration of inflation caught the government by surprise, meaning that inflation was not deliberately planned as part of fiscal policy. This, however, still fails to explain why it took the government so many years to respond to the changing situation.

One possible explanation is that the policymakers (who are assumed to be discretionary) were uncertain about the nature of the increase in inflation expectations. Specifically, they were uncertain about whether the leap of inflation was temporary or long-term. If it were temporary, the government would not like to signal its acceptance of the rise in inflation by raising its interest rates. If we accept this explanation, we would conclude that the government indexed the new loans only after the continued acceleration of inflation became plainly evident.

A simpler explanation of the lengthy delay in indexing the development loans would refer to the uncompromising opposition of the business community to any increase in the interest burden. This, of course, reflected a short-term perspective, based exclusively on a cost consideration, that the successive finance ministers should have resisted. Only when a strong finance minister, Yigael Hurwitz, took office did the indexation of the loans go into effect.

Be this as it may, the negative inflation tax phenomenon is just another piece of evidence that the acceleration of inflation in the 1970s and 1980s was not orchestrated by the government for fiscal reasons but was rather the consequence of the loss of fiscal control. The fact that the elasticity of demand for base money seems to have been approximately unitary, at the relevant rates of inflation, points in the same direction. In appendix C, we show how an economy may position itself on the nonincreasing segment of the Laffer curve under a discretionary regime.

BALANCE-OF-PAYMENTS CRISES AND INFLATION PLATEAUS

Figure 9.2 suggests that the quantum leaps from one inflation plateau to the next occurred in conjunction with peaks in the civilian import surplus that

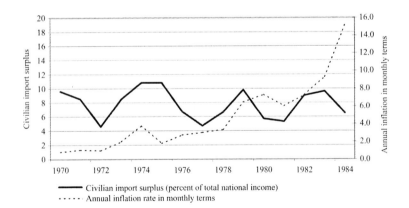

Figure 9.2. Civilian Import Surplus (percent of national income from all sources) and Annual Inflation (within years) in Monthly Terms. *Source:* BOI.

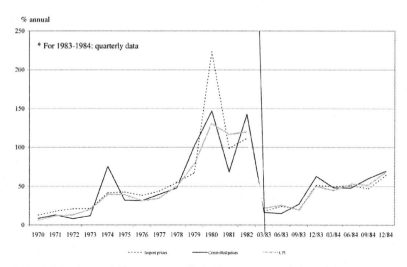

Figure 9.3. Rates of Change: Controlled Prices, Import Prices, and CPI.
Source: BOI.

signaled BOP crises.[13] The government reacted to these crises by making massive devaluations and sharply raising the prices that it controlled (figure 9.3) in order to create real depreciation supported by a temporary cut in the fiscal deficit. Indeed, as figure 9.4 shows, the increases in the import surplus were associated with reductions in the fiscal deficit. (In 1974, the reduction in the primary deficit came at a lag.) The same figures, however, show that the BOP crises were also associated with an increase in the inflation tax, reflecting the fact that the price shocks had been created by major devaluations and hikes in general-government prices. Thus, we have two opposing effects. Deficit cutting exerts downward pressure on aggregate demand and therefore tends to be deflationary. The price shock that accompanies a budget cut, however, raises

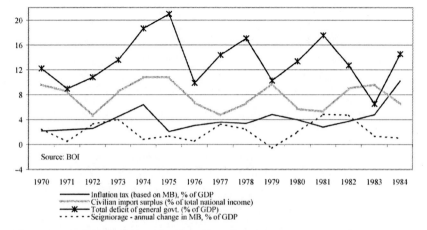

Figure 9.4. Import Surplus, Total General-Government Deficit, Seigniorage, and Inflation Tax (1970–84). *Source:* BOI.

costs and therefore tends to raise inflation. In chronic-inflation economies that have no nominal anchor, the latter factor tends to be dominant and results in a stepwise increase in inflation. In the Israeli case, the cuts in the fiscal deficit turned out to be temporary while the inflation shocks tended to be permanent.

Interestingly, this scenario runs contrary to the "twin deficit" model, which implies a positive correlation between internal and external deficits. In our view, a positive relationship between the twin deficits is more likely to occur when the immediate cause of the shock is the growth of the fiscal deficit, which involves an increase of aggregate demand. The opposite relationship obtains when the policy faces an unexpected balance-of-payments shock, which, in a small economy, raises costs and thus shifts the aggregate supply curve upward.

While the scenario described above indicates clearly that Israel's chronic-inflation regime was incapable of containing the inflationary impact of BOP crises, it does not imply that the path of causality always runs from the external crisis to inflation. The direction of causality plotted above was clearly of greater importance in the 1970s, when the twin energy crises (1973 and 1979) dealt all oil-importing countries a cost shock.

The jump in inflation associated with the 1983 crisis, in contrast, was predominantly homemade, resulting from the failure of Aridor's Tablita policies. Here the causality runs from unsustainable exchange-rate policies to a balance-of-payments crisis and thence to a leap in inflation. Since the unsustainability of the ER policy stemmed from its inability to reduce inflation in the absence of major fiscal reform, the jump in inflation can be basically attributed to the fiscal regime, that is, a fiscal-dominance regime, which paid insufficient attention to the need for a nominal anchor.

This description points to a scenario of endogenous cycles of alternating BOP crises and leaps in inflation, as in Rodriguez (1978). This is in fact what happened in Israel at least from 1979 onward. The BOP crisis that year led to a jump in inflation, which led to Aridor's Tablita, which in turn triggered the 1983 balance-of-payments crisis. Neither did the last-mentioned event mark the end of the chain, because Yigal Cohen-Orgad, Aridor's successor at Finance, implemented a PPP exchange-rate policy in 1984 to protect the balance of payments, invoking yet another round of inflation acceleration. Thus, the upward turn of the inflation path was partly associated with alternating government priorities in dealing with BOP crises and inflation. The 1985 stabilization program proposed, for the first time, to tackle both problems simultaneously.

FROM PRICE SHOCKS TO INFLATION SHOCKS

One of the features of Israel's inflation dynamics was the transformation of price shocks into inflation shocks. This phenomenon, it is commonly argued, occurs when strong wage indexation is in effect. Such indexation turns the economic model into a unit-root system, in which any shock has a permanent effect on inflation (Bruno, 1993, pp. 67–74). This argument sounds plausible but is flawed in that it implies a symmetrical reaction to both positive and negative shocks, which was clearly not the case in Israel. Thus, when Israel's terms of trade improved in the mid-1970s, the inflation plateau did not fall. Another weakness of the explanation is the absence of a positive drift in the unit-root system, which is needed to explain the rising trend of inflation.

A related view of the transformation of price shocks into inflation shocks is that the Israeli inflationary regime had no nominal anchor to which it was committed. Under these circumstances, a price shock that could have been stabilized by a rise in the short-term interest rate was converted into an increase in inflation because the monetary authorities were not allowed to raise interest rates lest they create a temporary increase in unemployment. In the absence of a commitment to a nominal anchor, the possibility of a price shock being transformed into an inflation shock became a real danger.

MONETARY POLICY UNDER FISCAL DOMINANCE

During the inflation era, the BOI was independent neither in setting inflation targets nor in the controlling its own instruments. The Ministry of Finance determined the amount of borrowing from the BOI ("printing money") and had a dominant influence on interest-rate policy. So what was the BOI "allowed" to do and what were the goals of monetary policy? To answer these questions, we analyzed the BOI's contribution to the monetary base and came up with some interesting results. It turns out that while the BOI did not attempt to affect the *trend* of money injection by the Finance Ministry, it was very active in attempting to reduce the *variance* around the trend. In other words, the BOI did not, and could not, attempt to change the course of inflation but rather confined itself to its stabilization. It accomplished this by means of considerable sterilization of monetary shocks that originated in general government and the impact of the "private" sector on the balance of payments through its transactions involving the foreign reserves.[14]

The behavior of central banks is usually analyzed in reference to their interest-rate policy, and this is the way we approached the problem in the previous sections. An alternative summary quantitative index is the "liquidity injection" by the central bank (CB). We applied this approach in chapter 3, where we used annual data. However, from 1974 the BOI calculates this statistic on a quarterly basis.[15] Let us restate briefly the conceptual framework of this approach. Broadly speaking, the BOI injection is the change in net credit from the BOI to the private sector (loans to banks less banks' nonreserve deposits with the BOI). By means of its liquidity injection, the BOI can affect the monetary base (MB). In fact, the change in the base is determined by three types of injections: that of the central bank (CB), that of general government (G), and that of the private sector, implemented by the sale of foreign currency to the BOI (F).

The relevant identity, derived from the balance sheet of the central bank, is $\Delta MB = \Delta CB + \Delta G + \Delta F$, where Δ denotes change, that is, injection of liquidity. Table 9.2 describes the quarterly liquidity injections of the three sectors, normalized by the size of the monetary base at the beginning of the relevant quarter. Alternatively defined, ΔMB is equal to the change in currency outside the BOI plus the change in the banking system's deposits with the BOI as

Table 9.2. Monetary Injections, Inflation, and Deficit

A. Injections Normalized by Monetary Base at Beginning of Quarter (percent).

Quarterly Data	BOI Injection (ΔCB) (1)	Private Conversion (ΔF) (2)	Government Injection (ΔG) (3)	Quarterly Change in Money Base (ΔMB) (4) = (1) + (2) + (3)	Quarterly Inflation (5)	Domestic Deficit** (6)	Change in M1* (7)
Q2:1973–Q4:1978	0.84	−12.68	18.55	6.70	8.62	28.72	6.82
Q1:1979–Q2:1985	−2.46	−55.39	84.67	26.82	29.09	109.87	23.14
Q1:1986–Q4:1994	3.93	−7.11	8.36	5.10	3.77	19.83	7.99
Q1:1995–Q3:2001	−14.97	17.00	1.94	3.97	1.33	18.22	3.17

*Normalized by beginning of quarter M1.
**Available from I:1977.

B. Injections Normalized by GDP (percent).

Quarterly Data	BOI Injection (1)	Private Conversion (2)	Government Injection (3)	Quarterly Change in Money Base (4) = (1) + (2) + (3)	Monetary Base* (5)	Domestic Deficit** (6)
Q2:1973–Q4:1978	0.53	−4.70	6.47	2.29	9.81	8.76
Q1:1979–Q2:1985	0.05	−4.42	6.27	1.91	2.91	9.36
Q1:1986–Q4:1994	0.77	−1.12	1.18	0.82	4.56	3.09
Q1:1986–Q4:1994	−2.20	2.52	0.19	0.51	3.96	2.56

*Quarterly GDP in Annual terms.
**Available from I:1977.
Source: BOI.

reserves against their domestic-currency deposits. Note further that ΔG—the change in the outstanding credit balance of the government with the BOI—is essentially the flow of net loans by the BOI to the Ministry of Finance, that is, the change in gross loans less the change in the government's deposits with the central bank and net of the contribution of the government to the foreign reserves of the BOI. ΔG also equals the domestic general-government deficit plus the change in net long- and medium-term government loans to the private sector.

Traditionally, inflation-tax models have focused solely on ΔMB (related to seigniorage) and paid little attention to its composition. The more recent literature, however, places stronger emphasis on separating out the policies of the central bank. Thus, Sargent and Wallace (1981) envisage general government as composed of two entities: the treasury, which determines the *size* of the fiscal deficit, and the central bank, which determines the *composition* of its finance. Similarly, the more recent policy-game approach of the Barro-Gordon type allows one to consider the central bank as having a different objective function than the government, leading to the implementation of a different policy, usually involving a tougher stance on inflation (Rogoff, 1985; Alesina and Tabellini, 1987). Within our framework, the Sargent-Wallace and Barro-Gordon conceptual construct is expressed by assuming that the central bank, by using its monetary injection, ΔCB, can offset some of the effects of the other two injections on this base.

Viewing this setting from the point of view of the recent distinction between monetary and fiscal dominance, we may say that the regime during Israel's "lost decade" was one of fiscal dominance in the sense that shocks to the monetary system were offset by monetary policy. The long-term path of inflation, however, was determined by the Ministry of Finance, which treated it like a source of finance for public expenditure—a form of behavior that the literature identifies as the inflation-tax aspect.[16] In the Israeli experience, any decrease in the base of the inflation tax was offset in the long run by an increase in the inflation rate, so that the real value of the inflation-tax receipts was maintained.

SOME STYLIZED FACTS ABOUT MONETARY INJECTIONS

Tables 9.2A and B describe the main features of the monetary injections in the course of inflationary developments in Israel over the past thirty years. The effect of these injections on the economy may be traced most effectively by partitioning this lengthy period into four successive intervals, two relating to the inflation era and two pertaining to the post-1985 stabilization. In this section we confine ourselves to the inflation era (mid-1973 to mid-1985) only; we address the post-stabilization era in part III. The inflation years were characterized by very large government injections relative to the monetary-base aggregate (table 9.2A). While inflation eroded the monetary base, the discretionary policymaker had limited control over the latter. Most of these liquidity injections were used by the public for purchases of foreign exchange from the BOI to finance the substantial current-account deficits and capital flight.

In fact, about two-thirds of the government injection, ΔG, was converted into (negative) ΔF during Israel's inflation period.

Table 9.2B shows that seigniorage as a percent of GNP (column 4) was fairly constant in the inflationary period, in spite of the tremendous increase in the rate of growth of base money. This suggests that inflation cannot be explained fully by the fiscal motive alone. Since inflation outpaced the increase in the monetary base throughout this period, the real monetary base contracted. This aside, the historical relationship between the rate of growth of MB and inflation was rather close (i.e., the two variables were cointegrated).

Since the BOI injection was very small compared with ΔMB, it could not affect the inflation trend significantly. Even if we take into account the spillover of government injections to the balance of payments (negative ΔF) which came to two-thirds of ΔG (considering the sum $\Delta G + \Delta F$), we obtain that in the second subperiod, Q1-1979–Q2-1985, the BOI's offsetting injection was only 10% of the net injection of general government. This, however, masks the BOI's intensive activity in two opposing directions, as the large standard deviation of ΔCB implies (table 9.3). It turns out that the BOI made an effort to sterilize each of these streams (the positive ΔG and the negative ΔF) separately, resulting in the large standard deviation of ΔCB. Below we discuss the rationale behind this behavior.

The sizable variation of currency conversions (in both directions), even with the spillover from the general-government deficit taken in account, shows that Israel never had a pure floating regime for any lengthy period of time. Neither, however, may we characterize the inflation period as the tenure of a strictly managed exchange-rate regime with perfect capital mobility. This is because under such a regime, by implication, demand for money depends solely on the foreign interest rate (plus the expected devaluation); thus, $\Delta G + \Delta F$ has to be sterilized completely by ΔCB. This did not occur; according to our calculations, the regression coefficient of ΔCB on $\Delta G + \Delta F$ was -0.55 in the early stage of the inflation era and -0.76 toward its end.

Figures 9.5–9.7 present the main features of Israel's monetary history since 1973 (all variables are expressed as percentages because they are normalized by the beginning of period MB). Figure 9.5 shows that liquidity injection by general government (through the government budget and development loans)

Table 9.3. Standard Deviations, Quarterly Data, Normalized by Beginning-of-Period Monetary Base

	BOI Injection	Private Conversion	Government Injection	Quarterly Inflation	Change in Monetary Base	Change in MI*
Q2:1973–Q4:1978	9.06	15.15	10.08	4.11	8.19	4.19
Q1:1979–Q2:1985	45.24	60.6	75.38	14.07	31.66	14.47
Q1:1986–Q4:1994	38.5	34.17	26.56	1.58	13.37	7.75
Q1:1995–Q3:2001	30.74	29.76	19.37	1.38	10.33	3.04

*Normalized by beginning-of-quarter M1.
Source: BOI.

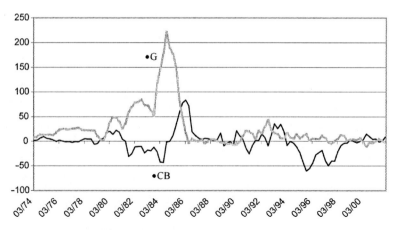

Figure 9.5. Government and BOI Injections, Percent of beginning of quarter monetary base. Four-quarter moving average. *Source:* BOI.

was a dominant characteristic of the inflation era, especially in the 1979–84 period. To offset (partly) the inflationary consequences of this injection, the BOI implemented a contraction of ΔCB.

Figure 9.6 shows that (negative) foreign-exchange conversion by the private sector dealt the monetary base another shock. Shortly before the stabilization in 1985, a significant outflow (capital flight) began due to a spillover effect of the massive monetary injection by general government: fears of repudiation of the large national debt accumulated during the inflation era. Figure 9.7 adding up the government and private-sector injections (ΔG + ΔF) and plotting them against ΔCB, shows that the main monetary shock during the inflation era was the one related to the fiscal expansion in 1982–84, which was associated with large fiscal deficits and the public's unwillingness to continue purchasing government bonds.

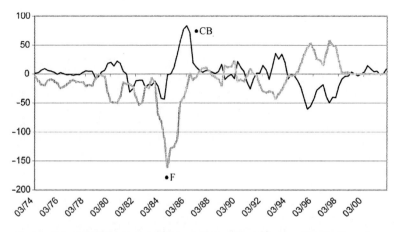

Figure 9.6. BOI Injections and Private Conversion, Percent of beginning of quarter monetary base. Four-quarter moving average. *Source:* BOI.

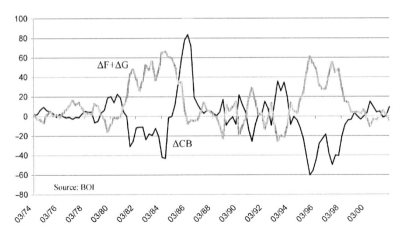

Figure 9.7. BOI Injections and Private Conversion plus Government Injection, Percent of beginning of quarter monetary base. Moving average of four quarters. *Source:* BOI.

The data relating to the monetary injections during the inflation era raise two questions: (1) To what extent did the BOI try to offset the large monetary injections that had brought on the inflation? In other words, did the BOI try to affect the trend of the monetary base? (2) What was the purpose of the BOI's major effort to intervene in the *gross* flows of the general-government monetary injection and the outflow of foreign exchange, when the *net* intervention was very small? In other words, why did the BOI intervene to sterilize both the inflows of liquidity from general government *and* the outflow through the balance of payments? Would it not have been more sensible to allow the injections from general government to find their way to the BOP naturally, without any intervention?

Let us consider the first question first. A more detailed analysis of the data than that provided here (Liviatan, 2002a) shows that in the first subperiod (1974–79) the BOI's injections were, on the whole, positive (see also table 9.2), so that on average the BOI provided no balancing response to the net injections represented by (ΔG + ΔF). Consequently, the monetary base continued to grow unabated at 6.7% per quarter. In the second subperiod, from 1980 through mid-1984, the stance of the BOI was contractionary but not contractionary enough in view of the large general-government injection. As a result, the growth rate of MB increased in a stepwise pattern, from 10% per quarter in 1976–79 to 20% in 1980–mid-1984. From the latter time until the stabilization of July 1985 the BOI apparently renounced any effort to stanch the monetary flood.

Turning to the second question, we note that while no serious attempt was made to offset the net injections given by (ΔG + ΔF), the BOI made a remarkable effort to sterilize ΔG and ΔF separately. This is clearly suggested by the regression coefficients (of the form ΔCB = $b_1 \Delta$F + $b_2 \Delta$G) in table 9.4, which indicate that the BOI sterilized 40% of ΔG and 56% of ΔF in the first subperiod and 75% and 100%, respectively, in the second subperiod. Since the *net* intervention of the BOI in both subperiods was negligible, why did the BOI not stay

Table 9.4. Regressing BOI Injection (ΔCB) on Other Injections (Quarterly Data), percent*

	C	Private Conversion	Government Injection	R2	DW
Q2:1973–Q4:1978	1.0387 (2.6781)	−0.5631 (0.1028)	−0.3959 (0.1544)	0.6040	1.6283
Q1:1979–Q2:1985	4.9392 (7.7609)	−1.0191 (0.1433)	−0.7540 (0.1152)	0.6956	2.0035
Q1:1986–Q4:1994	5.8179 (2.3252)	−0.8656 (0.0655)	−0.9614 (0.0843)	0.8904	3.0354
Q1:1995–Q4:2001	4.2461 (2.1410)	−1.0421 (0.0650)	−0.7752 (0.0999)	0.9129	2.9447
Q2:1973–Q2:1985	2.8958 (3.5965)	−0.9763 (0.1007)	−0.7143 (0.0782)	0.6796	1.9772
Q1:1986–Q4:2001	3.9013 (1.5677)	−0.9474 (0.0457)	−0.8974 (0.0659)	0.8931	2.9724
Q1:1995–Q1:1998	1.7293 (4.4393)	−0.9793 (0.0930)	−0.5948 (0.1474)	0.9288	2.2727

*Numbers in parentheses are standard errors.
Source: BOI.

outside this process? The apparent reason for this ostensibly unnecessary intervention was the central bank's wish to stabilize interest rates and the inflation rate by stabilizing the monetary base.[17] Thus the BOI, which was powerless to stop the monetary flood, confined itself to the stabilization of its variance.

Appendix F shows that a motive to stabilize the monetary base may be derived from a mean-variance model. The endogenous variables in this model are the sterilization parameters of ΔG and ΔF; these injections carried opposite signs throughout the inflation period. By increasing the degree of sterilization, it is possible to reduce the variance of ΔMB for any given expected value of ΔMB. This model may explain not only the high degree of intervention described above but also why the sterilization of ΔG was smaller than that of ΔF.

The economic rationale for reducing the variance of the monetary base is that this action stabilizes interest rates and output when the shocks originate in the money supply, as seemed to be the case during Israel's inflation era. As an additional step in this direction, the money multiplier may be used to stabilize the variance of M_1 for a given variance of monetary base. The standard-deviation series in table 9.3 underscores this by showing that the variance of M_1 is always smaller than the variance of monetary base. A similar feature—lower variance of M_1 than that of the monetary base—in the 1954–73 period is displayed by the series referring to the variance of these two monetary aggregates on the basis of annual data (chapters 3 and 4, tables 3.4 and 4.6).

PART III

THE EMERGENCE OF AN INDEPENDENT MONETARY POLICY AND MACROECONOMIC DEVELOPMENTS AFTER THE 1985 STABILIZATION

LANDMARKS ON THE ROAD TO PRICE STABILITY

In the wake of the 1985 stabilization policy, Israel gradually completed a lengthy process of restoring price stability. It made its moves within, and in response to, a universal process that embraced the full spectrum of industrialized economies. This part of the study describes the main features of the monetary and fiscal policies that Israel employed in the course of its disinflation process.

We begin by presenting an outline and analysis of the 1985 Stabilization Policy, which drastically transformed the rules of the game, and follow by offering a chronological survey of economic developments in the aftermath of the stabilization effort and an analysis of some general features of the disinflation process, starting with the main monetary developments.

The Israeli disinflation process, lasting about fifteen years was part of a global trend that stamped out inflation in both industrial and developing economies. The global upturn in inflation after the oil shocks of the 1970s and the collapse of the Bretton Woods regime was reversed in the industrial economies after the early 1980s and in Latin America since the early 1990s. Only Israel, among countries at its level of economic development, joined the Latin American group of "chronic-inflation economies" and maintained its "membership" in this group until 1985. This may be attributed largely to the internal political developments discussed in part II. Therefore, it is not surprising that with the establishment of the National Unity Government in 1984, Israel was the first member of the group to embark on a path of disinflation that followed the standards of industrial economies. The elimination of high inflation in the industrialized world and the pragmatic attitude of the Israeli authorities, who adjusted efficiently to these changes, were the most important factors in the success of Israel's disinflation process. The process started with a transition to moderate inflation, which became a fact of life by the second half of the 1980s.

The global eradication of inflation was accompanied by fundamental changes in the role of monetary policy and the status of central banks. Indeed, monetary policy assumed a much more independent role than it had been allotted by the tradition following World War II and through the late 1970s. In fact, it may be stated without much exaggeration that central banks in the OECD countries were leading players in the war on inflation. What is more, they played this role successfully, although their contribution to economic growth has been more controversial.

To say that central banks were the sole actors in this process, however, would be far from the truth. The disinflation process in the OECD countries proceeded on the basis of the principles of the Maastricht criteria. These, in turn, rested on a combination of fiscal and monetary measures that eventually delivered price stability.[1] On the fiscal side, these policies demanded the capping of the GDP/public-debt ratio, a limit to the size of fiscal deficits, and an inflation target (or, more generally, a nominal anchor). This strategy required a transition period, during which the fiscal and monetary authorities aimed to establish credibility in regard to their commitment to abide by these operating rules. The transition period lasted many years and took various forms. The strategy also entailed fiscal discipline, backed in some cases by specific legislation. Finally, the monetary authority was given freedom of action and tasked with the nominal component of the disinflation policy. Accordingly, central banks received both the de jure and the de facto independence that they needed for their part in the disinflation process.

With the growing integration of world capital markets ("globalization"), it became evident that the fixed exchange-rate regime, while an important component of the transition from runaway to moderate inflation, was unsustainable due to its vulnerability to speculative attacks. Accordingly, many disinflation processes took place within the framework of inflation-target regimes, with the central bank's interest rate as the main monetary instrument.

Israel followed the global trend by gradually giving its central bank greater independence. To do this, it liberated monetary policy from the constraints that had hobbled it during the three decades preceding the 1985 stabilization policy. This was reflected in greater freedom from fiscal intervention, greater independence in the use of conventional central-bank instruments, and greater influence on setting the goals of macroeconomic policies.

The road to "instrument independence," however, was bumpy and did not reach its end until the late 1990s. Only due to the major fiscal adjustment effected by the 1985 stabilization were the aforementioned measures feasible at all. They facilitated the reduction of inflation from more than 400% (annually) to a plateau of about 20% for five years or so starting in 1986. The next step, lowering inflation to international standards, was spearheaded by the BOI, which was quick to identify the global trend of disinflation and the implications of globalization.

The governors of the BOI contributed their share to the process. The "no-printing law," an instrumental measure in the disinflation process, was drafted during the governorship of Dr. Moshe Mandelbaum (in 1985) and was passed by the Knesset with his support, although he did not participate in the team that planned the stabilization policy. His tight monetary policy in the first few months of the 1985 stabilization period was a necessary condition for the successful conclusion of the initial stabilization stage. Members of the political community and even some officials at the Ministry of Finance criticized his policy, administered by the new Monetary Department that he had established, as too extreme. Professor Michael Bruno, Mandelbaum's successor, had been one of the chief architects of the 1985 program and a leading player in convincing the government that a comprehensive stabilization program was necessary. During his term as governor (from mid-1986 through 1991), he consolidated the moderate inflation step of 20% on the basis of the strategy of fiscal discipline and the exchange rate as a nominal anchor (conditioned on the behavior of nominal wages). As noted, this strategy worked well in reducing inflation from extreme to moderate levels but was problematic for the further effort to pull the inflation rate toward price stability.

Professor Jacob Frenkel, who succeeded Bruno as governor in 1991, was quick to identify the worldwide trend toward disinflation, which in the era of globalization required a more flexible exchange-rate system than had been applied to date. He also introduced in Israel the inflation-target regime that other countries had been using successfully and played a major role in transforming the BOI into a major player on the economic scene. His policies have been criticized for their cost in terms of recession and slow growth, even though real interest rates during Israel's final disinflation effort in the second half of the 1990s were not very different from similar rates in OECD countries. Dr. David Klein, before succeeding Frenkel in 2000, had been responsible for many monetary reforms, the most important being the elimination of directed credit in the second half of the 1980s. After his appointment, he adhered to the strategy of tough monetary policy and the decontrol of the capital account. By 2004, he had completed the liberalization of the foreign-exchange market by lifting the last vestiges of the currency controls that had been in effect for fifty-five years.

The 1985 stabilization policy was a watershed for the Israeli economy in many ways. Inflation fell dramatically (figure II.1), as is usually the case in exchange-rate (ER) based stabilizations, and progressed toward price stability in a stepwise fashion. The fiscal deficit was cut by about 10% of GDP (figure II.4) and stabilized at 4%–5% of GDP after an initial overshooting. The public debt/GDP ratio stopped rising and began to decline gradually (figure II.5). The external debt followed a similar pattern: the gross external debt/GDP ratio, which had tripled between the 1960s and 1984, returned to the 1960s level in 2000–2002.[2] The bloated general-government sector began to shrink. The current account of the balance of payments improved, mainly due to a decline in the share of investment (which was no longer subsidized) in GDP (figure II.10).

At the dawn of the twenty-first century, some of these trends have pointed in mixed directions. The public debt remains much higher than the Maastricht criterion of 60% of GDP. The downward trend in general government expenditures has leveled off (figure II.7). The GDP growth rate increased somewhat following the stabilization (figure II.11) but the unemployment rate also climbed, mainly due to mass immigration in the early 1990s (figure II.3). In 2001–3, growth slumped and unemployment rose amidst global recession and the Second Intifada (the Palestinian uprising in the occupied territories that began in late 2000). However, this trend has apparently been reversed in 2004. Mass immigration in the 1990s was also instrumental in blocking the upward march of real wages in the inflationary era (figure II.2). Real wages resumed their rising trend in the second half of the 1990s but slipped again in 2002–3 as a result of the recession. The real exchange rate appreciated during most of the 1990s but seems to have turned around during the recession in recent years (figure 6.2).

On the financial side, the real lending interest rate, which was high and moving upward before the stabilization, declined gradually when the stabilization era began and bottomed out in 1990–91 (figure II.9). Yields on long-term government bonds behaved similarly (figure II.8). After 1994, however, all interest rates climbed in the context of the tight monetary policy. This was part of the disinflation policy that persisted until the effective price stability was attained in 2000. From then to the present writing (early 2005), nominal and real interest rates have been declining, with a temporary reversal in 2002. The ratio of M_1 to GDP increased after the stabilization but never attained the ratios that prevailed at the beginning of the inflationary process (figure 9.1). Broader monetary aggregates, however, surpassed their prestabilization levels (reflecting "financial deepening"). The steep increase in M_2 since 1994 is a consequence of the high interest-rate policies.

The exchange rate was pegged initially to the U.S. dollar and then to a five-currency basket. The ER regime was gradually made more flexible. First, the narrow horizontal band introduced in 1989 gave way to a sliding band in 1991. The band was widened on several occasions, mainly by raising the upward-sloping ceiling that represented the depreciation constraint at which the BOI would have to intervene.

It was during the second half of the 1990s that inflation finally started its descent to price stability within the framework of the inflation-target regime that replaced the exchange-rate anchor strategy (figure III.1). The concurrent slowdown in economic growth and increase in unemployment contributed to the improvement of the current account and furthered the disinflation process. The recession in the late 1990s traced mainly to the tight money and the restrictive fiscal policy that tackled the twin sources of economic stress, inflation and the balance of payments.

The implementation of the tight monetary policy in the second half of the 1990s is reflected in the rise of nominal and real interest rates on BOI funds. Yields on indexed bonds behaved similarly (table III.1). In 2000–2001, Israel's inflation rate fell below the OECD average and its target range for future years, 1%–3% per annum, is considered price stability. The only blip occurred in early 2002, when recorded inflation spiked after the BOI slashed the key rate in December 2001.

Since 1997 through 2003, with the exception of 2000 (the year of the global high-tech bubble), the economy was in a state of recession and interest

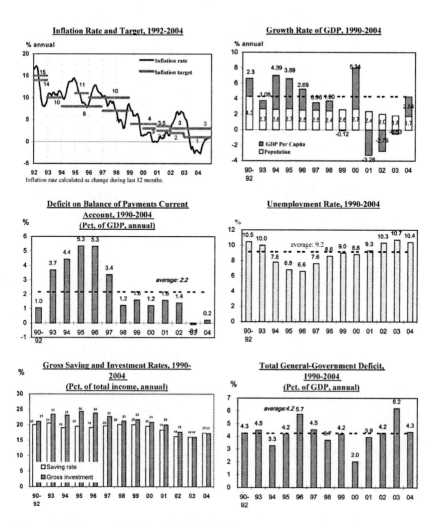

Figure III.1. Economic Indicators, 1990–2004

rates were considerably higher than the OECD average. CPI inflation in 2004 was 1.2% and inflation expectations twelve months ahead hovered in the middle of the 1%–3% inflation target range.[3] On the whole, the six-year experience through 2004 suggests that Israel has attained price stability, although the measured inflation rate reflects the state of excess capacity that is still with us. The disinflation process was completed under a regime of monetary dominance, meaning that the fiscal authorities have accepted and internalized the monetary targets of price stability and the regime that has become prevalent in OECD countries in the globalization era.

Has Israel paid a recessionary price for its disinflation? The data on the growth performance in 1985–90 answer in the negative. However, there is a stronger case for the claim that in the second half of the 1990s the reduction of inflation from the 10% step to OECD levels involved a cost in terms of subcapacity

Table III.1. Real Yield to Redemption on CPI-Indexed Bonds, Fixed Gross Interest (% annual)

	Years to Redemption					
	1	3	5	7	10	Slope
	(1)	(2)	(3)	(4)	(5)	(6) = (5)−(1)
1985	5.5	8.2	6.5	6.0	6.6	1.1
1986	4.0	5.7	5.8	4.2	6.4	2.4
1987	4.1	4.2	4.4	4.6	5.3	1.2
1988	2.5	3.2	4.1	4.2	4.5	2.0
1989	−0.8	0.8	1.6	2.0	2.4	3.2
1990	−0.1	0.8	1.3	1.6	1.9	2.0
1991	0.8	1.8	2.2	2.2	2.9	2.1
1992	1.8	2.4	2.4	2.5	2.7	0.9
1993	2.9	3.0	3.0	3.0	3.0	0.1
1994	2.8	3.0	3.1	3.1	3.3	0.4
1995	4.8	4.4	4.3	4.3	4.4	−0.4
1996	4.6	4.5	4.6	4.5	4.6	0.0
1997	4.5	4.2	4.1	4.0	4.1	−0.4
1998	5.6	5.4	5.1	5.0	4.9	−0.7
1999	6.4	6.0	5.6	5.4	5.2	−1.2
2000	6.8	6.4	6.0	5.7	5.5	−1.3
2001	5.3	4.9	4.9	4.9	4.9	−0.3
2002	4.6	4.7	4.8	5.0	5.2	0.6
2003	4.9	4.9	4.9	4.9	4.8	−0.1
2004	3.3	3.5	3.8	4.0	4.2	1.0

Source: Bank of Israel *Annual Reports.*

economic performance. The tight monetary and fiscal policies of the second half of the 1990s do seem to have caused a lingering state of recession (with the exception of 2000), helping disinflation along but at a high social cost.

This, however, is not the whole story. The massive BOI intervention, designed to sterilize the powerful inflow of foreign funds in response to the high interest policies of the second half of the 1990s, created a large stock of liquid assets at the public's disposal—the so-called mountain of sheqels, which constrained monetary policy in subsequent years. However, this was offset by the growing financial stability that better macroeconomic control made possible.

Since the end of 2000, two destabilizing developments have buffeted the economy: the collapse of the American stock exchanges—where the previous high-tech boom had found its outlet—and the outbreak of the Second Intifada. In both cases, the monetary and fiscal policies thwarted financial crisis by adopting a conservative stance that, admittedly, was reflected in an increase of unemployment. While the pace of disinflation and its related social costs may be a topic of criticism, there appears to be a consensus about the validity of Israel's integration into the global economy. By implication, the need to adopt the norms of the OECD macroeconomic regime and, in turn, to abandon the fiscal-dominance regime that characterized the inflationary decade appear to be matters of general agreement. Under fiscal dominance, as described in earlier sections of this study, monetary policy was subordinated to, and mobilized in the defense of, fiscal targets. The new regime that emerged in the 1990s was one of *monetary dominance*, which sets nominal targets (i.e., an inflation target) and requires fiscal policy to support it. In broad terms, the main features of Israel's new macroeconomic regime focus on the acceptance of something resembling the Maastricht criteria for the management of the economy. Thus, the BOI's tight monetary policy has had costs and benefits. On balance, the successful integration into the global economy and the continued effort to abide by international standards have improved Israel's financial stability since the 1990s.

The year 2004 may have marked the emergence from the recessionary trend that has characterized the Israeli economy since the mid-1990s (in the context of disinflation) and a stricter application of the OECD norms. GDP growth resumed, the fiscal deficit contracted (figure III.1), the negative debt dynamics ground to a halt, real public spending declined, and the long-term problems of the economy (e.g., pension reform) were addressed. All these favorable developments took place under a virtual price stability that may signal the beginning of a new era of growth in an environment of financial stability. We know from experience, however, that developments over one or two years do not necessarily affect the long-term trend. Much depends on significant progress in the peace process—which will allow Israel to reduce its defense burden—successful efforts to reduce poverty and inequality, and positive international developments.

10

The 1985 Stabilization Policy

As noted earlier, the 1985 stabilization, in contrast to earlier attempts, was carried out by a National Unity Government that commanded a massive majority in the Knesset (parliament). This government viewed the elimination of inflation as one of its main targets. At its helm as prime minister stood Shimon Peres, the leader of the Labor Alignment, representing the Labor Movement.[1] By his side, as minister of finance, was Yizhak Moda'i of the liberal wing of the Likud Party. They were assisted by the intellectual guidance of Michael Bruno (subsequently governor of the BOI) and the organizational skill of Emanuel Sharon, Director General of the Ministry of Finance, who took care of the implementation of the program. This team deserves the main credit for the success of the program, although some credit also goes to the economists of the BOI, the Finance Ministry, and academia.[2]

BASIC PRINCIPLES OF THE PROGRAM

The 1985 stabilization policy was based on several principles that would have lasting effects on the economy. The first was the establishment of fiscal balance and perseverance in fiscal discipline in future years, in order to make the reduction of the debt/GDP ratio feasible. The second principle was the necessity of dealing *simultaneously* with the balance-of-payments (BOP) and inflation issues within the framework of a nominal anchor. This course of action was also supposed to halt the wage-price-exchange-rate spiral and put an end to the use of surprise-inflation tactics. The third principle was the implementation of a drastic ("cold turkey") disinflation policy focusing on the macroeconomic dimension and leaving structural reforms to later stages of the process.

Let us consider the rationale of each of these principles. There is a virtual unanimous consensus among economists that long-term disinflation requires the establishment of fiscal balance. This requirement was noted both in academic writings and in BOI publications. The large fiscal deficit became particularly problematic in the 1980s due to the increasing difficulty of sterilizing the large monetary injections by selling government bonds. A related aspect of this problem was the growing difficulty of rolling over, let alone increasing, the internal debt. Difficulties in selling government bonds to the public surfaced in the second half of 1983 and intensified until the stabilization policy was launched in July 1985. By implication, the government had to finance its deficit by drawing on its foreign reserves—clearly an unsustainable course of action even though the current account of the BOP improved in 1984. Thus, financing the deficit by means of internal debt at 6.5%–8.7% of GDP in 1980–82 was replaced by sales of foreign exchange to the public at 6.6% of GDP in 1983 and 9% in 1984.

The government was well aware of the inflationary implications of switching the policy focus from the BOP to inflation and back. To deal with the BOP crises, it imposed large devaluations and hiked prices under its control sharply. These actions, in the absence of a nominal anchor, caused inflation to leap to a new plateau. Slowing the rate of devaluation to reduce inflation, in turn, led to overvaluation and a worsening of the BOP position, bringing on a BOP crisis and closing the vicious cycle. This motivated the government to favor a policy package that could tackle both problems simultaneously—a large cut in the fiscal deficit in order to reduce domestic demand and the adoption of a nominal anchor to control inflation. The anchor chosen, as in the initial stage of many other stabilizations, was the ER. Israel pegged its ER to the U.S. dollar at first but moved over to a currency-basket peg a year later.

This strategy was based on the realization that the fiscal deficit per se—or, more generally, the solvency of general government—did not constitute an effective anchor for inflation. There are many examples of chronic-inflation economies that caused an upward jump in inflation by tightening their fiscal policies due to an increase in government-controlled prices. The simultaneity of a (substantial) deficit cut and the pegging of the nominal exchange rate help us to identify a fiscal policy as being directed toward the disinflation objective and not toward the BOP target.

It was well understood that the government's noncooperative game with the Histadrut (the national federation of labor), in which the former set the nominal rate of devaluation while the latter reacted by effecting a preemptive wage increase, led only to a wage-price spiral. Accordingly, the pegging of the exchange rate was conceived as a unilateral cease-fire on the government's part. To protect itself against an uncontrolled increase in real wages, however, the government had to enter into a temporary wage-price freeze agreement with the unions. Since the unions were asked in this context to accept the suspension of the COLA arrangement, understandably they sought guarantees against real wage erosion by continuing inflation.

This, in turn, required the government to conclude a price-freeze agreement with the Manufacturers' Association of Israel as the representative of major private-sector employers. (Such an action also required the freeze of the ER). To make the program consistent, implying the synchronization of all nominal macro variables, the government negotiated a package deal (or a social pact) with the Histadrut and the manufacturers association for a wage-price freeze, which, as a quid pro quo, was formally protected by government controls. This was a short-run strategy, entailing a three-month suspension of the COLA arrangement and an agreed temporary reduction in real wages for about nine months, until March 1986.

This stabilization strategy, backed by the highly restrictive fiscal and monetary policies, succeeded impressively. The inflation rate plummeted from over 400% per annum to a plateau of around 20% within two quarters and stayed there, with some variations, through 1991. The "cold turkey" nominal strategy was not accompanied by significant structural reforms; these were deferred to some later date. Thus, the 1985 Israeli stabilization policy, unlike the stabilizations in Latin America in the 1990s, was purely a "macro" affair.

TIME PATTERN AND IMPACT EFFECTS

The first few years of the stabilization program may be analyzed from two perspectives: the effectiveness of the program in arresting inflation and its influence on the sustainability of the disinflation process in later years. The program succeeded from both points of view. It led to steep disinflation within two quarters—from 445% in 1984 to 29% (in annual terms) in Q4-1985—without any significant enforcement of price controls because the highly restrictive monetary and fiscal policy measures had created a state of excess supply, rendering the controls irrelevant from the economic standpoint (Blejer and Liviatan, 1987; Barkai, 1995, pp. 196–200).[3]

The excess supply may be traced to several factors. The large cut in the fiscal deficit dampened aggregate demand at first. This effect was supported by an extremely tight monetary policy, occasioned by the slow reduction of the nominal interest rate. The real interest rate on "free" (short-term) bank credit rose from 6% (in annual terms) in the first half of 1985 to 65% in the second half of that year. This real interest spread against foreign rates was sustainable due to the grave uncertainties associated with the disinflation program and because the long-term process of liberalizing the capital account had hardly begun. Along with the contraction of aggregate demand, these policies induced an increase in supply. An important channel of the latter effect was the incentive that the tight monetary policy gave to firms and even households to sell off their inventories of goods, in view of the high cost of behaving otherwise. Another channel of influence on supply prices was the (agreed) 10.6% cut in real wages in the business sector (*Annual Report*, 1985, p. 94).

As a result of these developments, the imports and trade deficit did not increase in the second half of 1985 and potential pressure on the exchange rate (arising from the current account), which could derail the program, was averted. Luckily, the external position was supported initially by the depreciation of the dollar (to which the exchange rate was pegged) against the European currencies, which stimulated exports to, and discouraged imports from, Europe. As it happened, soon after the initial depreciation the real ER of the NIS embarked on an appreciation trend that continued well into the 1990s (figure 10.1).

The fact that the government managed to muddle through the first stage successfully boosted the credibility of the program. A special U.S. grant of $1.5 billion (about 6% of GDP), spread over two years, which the government used only as a financial safety net, gave confidence an additional boost. A further benefit that enhanced the image of the economy was an improvement in U.S. aid in 1985: the conversion of U.S. loans, at an annual rate of $0.9 billion, into grants (Liviatan, 1988). These factors helped to enhance the credibility of the short-run sustainability of the ER policy.

It is usually hard to identify the factors that make a stabilization program credible in the longer term, since so much depends on speculation about its future course. The fact that the program established its credibility contributed to its long-term success. Ruge-Murcia (1995) argues that an econometrician may pronounce the program successful on the basis of monthly observations in 1982–87 of trends in government spending (which the 1985 stabilization slashed drastically), taxes, industrial output, and the paths of the nominal interest rates and inflation. One doubts, however, that this is sufficient without observation of the factors described above and, especially, without a long-term view of the economic consequences of the military pullout from Lebanon.

Another factor that may help to identify a long-lasting break with the past is a change in the rules of the game. One manifestation of this in the Israeli stabilization attempt was the government's attitude toward the financial strain imposed on firms that manufactured for the domestic market by the very high real interest rates that they had to face for a long stretch of time. During the stabilization era, unlike the practice in previous years, the government was

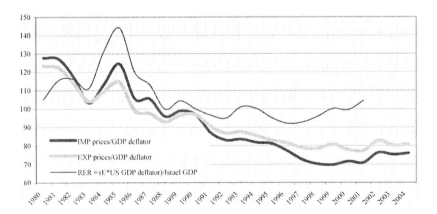

Figure 10.1. Measures of the Real Exchange Rate, 1980–2004

reluctant to bail out even firms that were on the verge of solvency. The most impressive evidence of this reluctance was the government's refusal to grant special treatment to Solel Boneh, a large and long-established construction firm owned by the Histadrut. This was an impressive change, especially since it took place even though the Labor Party sat in the National Unity Government and its leader served as prime minister. This had special significance along the lines of "Why Does It Take a Nixon to Go to China?" (Cukierman and Tomassi, 1994).

11

The Consolidation of Moderate Inflation, 1985–90

REAL WAGES, THE EXCHANGE-RATE ANCHOR, AND THE 20% INFLATION STEP

Comparing the high-inflation period of 1974–84 with 1986–89, one observes a drastic reduction of the fiscal deficit—from 15% of GDP in 1974–79 and 12% in 1980–84 to a mere 1% in the 1986–89 (table II.2). Most of the decrease can be traced to a cut in defense expenditure, facilitated by the withdrawal from Lebanon. As a result, the actual deficit fell below the "warranted," that is, noninflationary, level (Bruno, 1993, table 3.2) and the debt/GDP ratio started to decline.[1] This is the pattern that monetary-dominance require in cases where the initial debt is unsustainable (see appendix G). However, the annual inflation rate did not fall to international levels and remained at a plateau of 18%–20%, suggesting that the stabilization program suffered from a residual credibility problem.

One of the factors that undermined the credibility of the exchange-rate policy in the medium term and that, for this reason, may explain the 20% inflation step was a statement by the government that the commitment to the fixed ER was not absolute but depended on the "good behavior" of wages. This induced employers to accommodate wage demands in the hope that the government would spare them from the consequences by devaluing the currency. The government did devalue the NIS on several occasions, but at a lower rate than expected: once in January 1987, in two steps in late 1988, and at a small rate in June 1989. The cumulative devaluation through the end of 1989 was 32% against the dollar and 54% against the basket of currencies. Cumulative inflation was much higher during that interval, at nearly 20% per year.

The resulting real appreciation and recession undermined the sustainability of the disinflation.

Even though the devaluations were coordinated with the trade unions, which agreed to sterilize them from the COLA, real wages kept rising beyond the increase in labor productivity by force of adverse inflation expectations (figure II.2). Since this suggests that the rise in real wages was out of equilibrium, this wage movement created inflationary potential since the erosion of the real wage by a reduction in *nominal* wages was obviously unlikely to occur. Thus, while the social pact was able to keep real wages in check during the initial phase of the stabilization, it failed to do so in the medium term.[2]

A related aspect of the increase in real wages had to do with the likelihood of precisely such an increase when the government renounces devaluation as an instrument of real wage erosion in a noncooperative game.[3] Indeed, the initial strong cooperation between government and labor diminished as time passed.[4]

The behavior of real wages was strongly influenced by the consumption-driven business cycle that ensued in 1986–89. Thus, GDP and private consumption increased at annual rates of 4.8% and 11.9% in 1986–87 and by only 2.1% and 2.2%, respectively, in 1988–89 (*Annual Report*, 1990, pp. 12–13). Real wages in manufacturing grew by 13% in the first two years of the cycle and by only 2.5% in the last two years. The cyclical rise in real wages may have fueled expectations that the recession that emerged in 1988–89 would be redressed by a rise in inflation.

This kind of business cycle was characteristic of ER-based stabilizations in Latin America, regardless of whether they were eventually successful or not (Kiguel and Liviatan, 1992). This phenomenon seems to be consistent with contrasting views about the credibility of a stabilization program. Thus, Calvo and Vegh (1993) trace the consumption boom to lack of credibility in the program while Bruno and Meridor (1991) hold the opposite view. There is probably some truth to both sides, which lead to the same results. Be this as it may, the business cycle and the associated rise in real wages, coupled with the rise of unemployment in 1988–89, may have undermined the credibility of the exchange-rate peg and, thereby, contributed to the rigidity of inflation expectations at the 20% step.

When we consider the 20% inflation plateau from a historical perspective, we should probably bear in mind that global inflation was not yet fully under control at the time. Furthermore, the very possibility of stamping out chronic high inflation by a program of the Israeli type was not clear. In the historical context of the 1980s, it was quite reasonable to take any kind of disinflation with a grain of salt.

THE INCIDENCE OF BUSINESS TAXATION AND THE MONOPOLISTIC FEATURES OF ISRAELI BANKING

One of the main difficulties in the first few years of stabilization was a decline in the profitability of the business sector. Although the consumption boom mitigated this effect somewhat, it began to bite severely in the recessionary phase (1988–89). One aspect of the problem was the increase in the real unit cost of labor, which may be directly attributed to the basing of the stabilization on the exchange-rate peg.

Several other features were adverse to the business sector. One was the increase in the sector's tax burden. The net rate of taxation on nonwage income increased from 11% in 1982–84 to over 20% in 1986–1989, even though the formal tax rates did not rise. The increase in the effective tax rate traces to the "reverse Tanzi effect," a well-known phenomenon that surfaces whenever a disinflation process takes hold. Disinflation hurts business more than labor since business, by its very nature, is much more adept than labor at manipulating the timing of its tax payments in the event of high inflation rates. This calls for an adjustment of the tax rates once the rate of inflation declines substantially. The government did implement a tax reform in 1987 but desisted from the effort in subsequent years.

Another contributing factor in the low profitability of the business sector was the lingering high ex post interest rates on bank credit. Although many stabilization programs encounter this phenomenon due to credibility problems, its occurrence in Israel can be traced to an additional factor: the dominance of the two largest banking groups, which invested the banking system effectively, if not formally, with cartel features in the provision of short-term credit to business. Although the BOI pressured the banks to lower their interest rates, the process was slow. It was mainly during the downturn of the business cycle that the real short-term lending rate began to show a substantial decline, to 11%–12% in annual terms. These negative influences, including the recession, reduced the business sector's rate of return on capital to 10%–11% in 1988–89, somewhat below the rate before the stabilization program.

It should also be noted that the recessionary phase of the post-1985 business cycle (1988–89) was aggravated by the First Intifada. This factor, however, could not affect the Israeli economy badly because of the miniscule size of the Palestinian Territories' economy compared with Israel's and the small proportion of Territories workers in total Israeli employment. The Territories themselves bore the brunt of the damage of the First Intifada because of their severe dependence on the Israeli economy. The Second Intifada (the "shooting intifada," which began in late 2000), however, would affect Israel more seriously.

MONETARY INSTRUMENTS AND RISING COMPETITIVENESS

Since the "no-printing law" absolved the BOI from the need to finance fiscal deficits, the central bank strengthened the focus of monetary policy on price stability. In fact, in a strict interpretation of monetary dominance, the only purpose of monetary policy should be the assurance of a credible nominal anchor. In practice, however, monetary policy during the period in question also paid attention to the state of the real exchange rate, the monopolistic behavior of the banking industry, and the state of the business cycle.

In the aftermath of the 1985 stabilization, the BOI needed the ability to conduct an independent monetary policy, including the possibility of sterilized intervention. In particular, speculative attacks on foreign reserves are likely in the early stages of stabilization. The BOI needed monetary instruments to stave off such attacks, for example, the one that did occur in 1988.[5] This task, coupled with the need to stabilize shocks to the monetary base in an environment of controls on capital flows, entailed sterilized intervention.

A major reform that enhanced the option of an independent monetary policy was the phase-out of directed credit in the second half of the 1980s. To start moving along this route, the BOI adopted a technique that effectively expanded its arsenal of monetary instruments. Since the available stock of MAKAM (Treasury bills) for open-market operations was limited and tightly controlled by the Ministry of Finance, the central bank took its first step down this path by introducing a monetary-loan facility for commercial banks. From then on, banks could borrow at the BOI's discount window but faced a stepwise rising curve of interest rates, each step representing a quota of funds offered at that rate. This instrument gave the BOI what amounted to a facility for open-market operations.

These measures increased the BOI's ability to manage an independent monetary policy. The effectiveness of the central bank's policies in the realm of finance, however, was constrained by additional factors. The monopolistic structure of the commercial banking system allowed the banks to maintain a wide and rigid margin between their lending rates and the BOI rates and, similarly, between their lending and borrowing (deposit) rates. To mitigate the impact of this market failure, the BOI applied the medium-term strategy of pressuring the banks to cut their lending rates. At first, it went about this by moral suasion and later supported this move by inviting the nonbanking private sector to participate in "monetary loan auctions" that would compete with commercial banks in lending terms.[6] Indeed, these operations lowered real interest rates on overdraft facilities dramatically, from 40% in 1987 to 10% in 1990. Other interest rates followed suit.

Evidence of increased competitiveness in the banking sector was the narrowing of the spread between interest rates on short-term credit (overdrafts) and deposits by 1992–93. The central bank's measures improved the efficiency of the transmission mechanism from the interest on monetary loans to short-term interest rates on commercial banks' unindexed loans and deposits.[7]

Another major change in the realm of monetary instruments was the dramatic contraction of legal reserve requirements on bank deposits. In this respect, Israel followed the global lead. Note, however, that the change was facilitated by the reduction of the fiscal deficit and, in turn, less need to charge an inflation tax by means of reserve requirements. This measure also reduced the incentive of disintermediation, that is, the recourse of borrowers and lenders to nonbanking financial markets, and thereby increased the BOI's grip on the banking system.

THE MONETARY AND FISCAL POLICY MIX

While the main task of monetary policy during this period was to support the exchange-rate anchor, it could not be indifferent to the state of the business cycle.

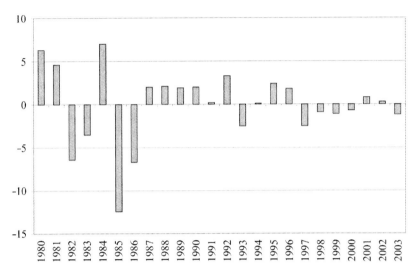

Figure 11.1. Fiscal Impulse as Percentage of Potential GNP. *Source:* BOI.

The recession of 1988–89 is a case in point. In response to the recession, the BOI implemented an accommodative monetary policy; after developments in 1989, it allowed the monetary aggregates to adjust freely to the upturn of demand for money in 1990 (*Annual Report*, 1990, p. 9). The policy of easy money during the recessionary phase was reflected in the negative real interest rate on monetary loans to commercial banks and the decline in yield curves of indexed bonds, with a steeper reduction of the yield on bonds with short terms to redemption (table III.1).

The fiscal stance during the 1988–90 recession was mildly countercyclical in an active sense. Thus, the measure of the fiscal impulse according to the IMF definition (referring to the structural deficit) was positive but relatively small (figure 11.1 and Dahan and Strawczynski, 2001, p. 401). The fiscal policy, however, was *passively* countercyclical. It allowed the deficit to increase fully in response to the slowdown in activity and let the automatic stabilizers operate without interference. Tax revenues decreased by more than 4 percentage points of GDP in 1989 and the measured fiscal deficit climbed to 6% of GDP even as the *structural* (cyclically adjusted) deficit remained fairly constant (Bruno and Meridor, 1991). This contrasts with the fiscal conservatism that governments of Israel have exhibited in recent years.

12

The "Russian Immigration Wave" and the New Inflation Step, 1990–94

MASS IMMIGRATION

Economic developments in the first half of the 1990s were dominated by mass immigration from the Former Soviet Union. The influx began shortly before the beginning of 1990, continued at a rate of nearly two hundred thousand a year for the next few years, and added up to three quarters of a million by the end of the decade (augmenting the 1990 population of the country by 17%). Since the analysis of the full economic implications of this major event falls outside the scope of this study, our discussion confines itself to the macroeconomic effects of the mass immigration and, specifically, its impact on the disinflation process.

LABOR-MARKET EFFECTS

The immigration wave had a direct stimulating effect on demand, resulting in a boost to investment and economic growth. Concurrently, it generated excess supply by bolstering the stock of labor. Thus, the decline in real business-sector wages precipitated by the 1989 recession continued even more vigorously (figure II.2) and the unemployment rate climbed from 6.4% of the civilian labor force in 1987 to 10.6% in 1991 (figure II.3).[1] The unemployment rate remained at this high level for another two years and thereby exerted downward pressure on the annual inflation rate, which plunged discontinuously in 1992 from 18%–20% to 10%–12%, where it would stay for the next four years (figure II.1).

The immigration wave also had a contributory effect on the ongoing erosion of the power of the Histadrut. The low-inflation environment reduced the importance of COLAs and national wage agreements, which the Histadrut had been handling for more than four decades as the representative of hired labor. Thus, the labor federation's grip on the labor market weakened (Artstein, 2002). Indeed, since 1987 there had been no wage agreements at the national level. Arguably, then, the rising decentralization of the labor market, which reduced the clout of the Histadrut, facilitated the stepwise reduction of inflation. In effect, both processes occurred simultaneously.

FISCAL POLICY

The government assumed responsibility for two needs related to the mass immigration: the newcomers' immediate requirements and infrastructure for the rapidly growing population. Thus, the total fiscal deficit ran at a relatively steep 4% of GDP in the first two years of the immigration wave (figure III.1). To convince the public that the poststabilization fiscal discipline would be maintained, the government shepherded through the Knesset a deficit-reduction law that specified a predetermined schedule for the reduction. It backed this undertaking by securing an agreement with the U.S. government to guarantee $10 billion in loans to be raised in the American capital market to finance investment in housing and infrastructure. If one excludes the additional public expenditure related to the immigration wave from the deficit by regarding it as temporary, the fiscal stance in 1990–92 was actually contractionary.[2] Later on, however, and particularly in 1994–95, fiscal policy became expansionary mainly due to liberal wage agreements in general government. This action, by increasing the more permanent elements of the deficit, was inconsistent with the requirements of "fiscal consolidation." In any case, the government did not manage to cut the deficit as envisaged (according to the legislation, the deficit was to be eliminated by 1995) but kept it from increasing over time (table 12.1). To reconcile the inconsistency between its commitment and reality, the government announced every now and then a new declining path of the deficit. Such an approach could not but undermine the credibility of fiscal policy. On the positive side, however, it may have prevented the return to the high deficit rates that characterized the inflationary era.

MONETARY POLICY

Although formally the government adopted the inflation-target regime at the end of 1991, the BOI continued in 1990–94 to use the exchange rate as the monetary anchor. However, in order to eliminate some constraints to monetary policy, it refined the exchange-rate regime in the direction of greater flexibility. The first measure of this sort was the introduction of an exchange-rate band in January 1989, replacing the point exchange rate. The band was initially horizontal and quite narrow: ±3% of the decreed rate. In December 1991, the BOI replaced this instrument with an upward-sliding band. Its crawl was set at an annual rate of 9%, which corresponded, more or less, to the difference between the inflation target and the relevant foreign inflation rate. The band was widened to ±5% at that time and again on several subsequent occasions until it came to 30% by the end of the 1990s. The main widening move was implemented by raising the upper limit of the band, that is, the line denoting the highest possible rate of depreciation of the NIS before the BOI would intervene firmly. The rationale for the shift to a sliding

Table 12.1. Deficit and Total Expenditure of General Government, 1993–2003 (percent of GDP)

	1993	1994	1995	1996	1997	1998	1999	2000	2001	2002	2003	2004
Total government deficit ceiling (excluding BOI)	4.7	3.8	3.9	3.7	3.0	2.8	3.1	3.6	1.8	3.9	3.0	4.0
Actual total government deficit (excluding BOI)	2.5	2.3	4.3	4.2	3.3	3.2	3.3	0.7	4.4	3.8	5.6	3.9
Total general-government deficit (excluding BOI)	5.0	3.6	4.6	6.0	4.3	4.1	3.4	1.3	3.9	5.0	5.3	4.7
Tax burden	38.7	39.5	40.0	38.6	39.2	38.2	38.5	39.8	39.7	39.0	38.1	37.9
Total general-government expenditure	56.1	53.8	54.8	54.5	53.2	52.6	51.8	50.4	53.0	54.3	52.9	51.1

Source: Central Bureau of Statistics and BOI caculations.

215

band was to avoid the recurrent speculative attacks that occurred whenever the market anticipated a realignment of the horizontal band.

Through the end of 1993, monetary policy continued trying to lower the high interest rates that had been prevalent since the 1985 stabilization. Concurrently, however, it had to hike the key rate occasionally in order to support the maintenance of the ER band. In the last quarter of 1991, for example, expectations of an ER realignment led to a speculative attack. However, the BOI did not budge and absorbed the shock by allowing its interest rate and the exchange rate to rise (within the band). After the attack subsided in early 1992, the BOI swiftly brought the key rate back to its previous level. Basically, the central bank continued to rely on the ER as the nominal anchor during this period and allowed the interest rate only a supporting role. The motivation for the easy-money policy was to overcome the rigidity in interest rates associated with the commercial banks' monopolistic behavior and, thereby, to stimulate economic activity in support of the absorption of the mass immigration.

THE NEW INFLATION STEP

In late 1991, as noted, the annual inflation rate collapsed to a lower step of 10%–12%. Again, however, the BOI was slow in reducing the nominal interest rate on its monetary lending, causing the real interest rate on its funds to rise. It was in this passive manner that the BOI supported the transition to the lower inflation step. Fiscal policy, too, played a supporting role in this additional phase of disinflation.[3] The stepwise reduction of inflation was also aided by a decline in the dollar prices of imports in 1991.

Apparently, however, the main support came from the decline in wage inflation due to excess supply in the labor market. In fact, wage inflation had begun to slow during the 1989 recession and continued to slump in 1990–93 (*Annual Report*, 1997, p. 94). Furthermore, nominal wage inflation, unlike CPI inflation, declined gradually and did not share the discontinuous feature of stepwise reduction (figure 12.1 and Liviatan and Sussman, 2002).

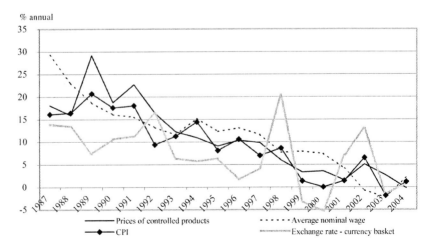

Figure 12.1. Rates of Change: CPI, Currency Basket Exchange Rate, Prices of Controlled Products, and Nominal Wages (percent annual). *Source:* BOI.

13

Monetary Developments in the Second Half of the 1990s

THE CHANGE IN MONETARY STRATEGY IN 1994

Monetary developments in 1994 dealt a serious blow to the notion that the disinflation process could proceed on the basis of the exchange-rate band as the nominal anchor, supported indirectly by the interest-rate policy in case of speculative attacks. Until then, it was the BOI's strategy to continue lowering the nominal key rate in tandem with the pace of disinflation. This concept was supported by moves to liberalize the financial market and the stepwise reduction of inflation at the end of 1991. This strategy was considered by the BOI to be part of the long-term trend of rate-cutting in the wake of the 1985 stabilization and part of the ongoing liberalization of the capital markets. The downward trend of nominal rates fit into the ongoing process of closing the spread between domestic and foreign interest rates.

Accordingly, the inflation target for 1994 was set in mid-1993 at 10% and the upward crawl of the ER band was lowered to 6%. Concurrently, the BOI's nominal interest rate was reduced by 2 percentage points. The BOI did not regard the new inflation target as radical, since the inflation plateau had fallen to 10%–12% in 1992 and solidified at this level by the middle of 1993.

These measures, however, badly misjudged actual developments in the coming quarters. In 1994, the inflation rate climbed to 14.5%. The resurgence of inflation led to a reassessment of the monetary strategy because it could not be blamed on the exchange rate. After all, the exchange rate had stayed within the band and did not endanger its bounds. The resurgence of inflation indicated that the exchange-rate band could no longer serve effectively as an anchor for the price level in the short run.

What might explain this deviation of inflation from the ER path? The main factor, it appears, was the expansionary monetary policy of the BOI itself. The central bank had lowered the interest rate on its funds prematurely—as it would on several future occasions. Indeed, the real (ex-post) interest rate on BOI funds fell from 2.3% in 1992 to zero in 1993. This reflected the extraordinary expansion of monetary aggregates, as both the monetary base and M_1 grew by about 30% in both years (year on year). At the time, the BOI did not realize that this constituted an *excess* supply of liquidity, which gravitated to the stock market and resulted in a boom. The bull market, delivering a real rate of return of 27% on shares in 1993, diverted funds from the foreign-exchange market. This explains how the monetary expansion could have raised the inflation rate without causing a faster rate of devaluation. Although the stock market crashed in early 1994, the lagged effect of the earlier monetary expansion sufficed to raise inflation far above its target for that year.

These developments precipitated a fundamental change in the strategy of the BOI, leading to a new strategy that the central bank has essentially maintained ever since. The cornerstone of this strategy is the *direct* use of the interest rate to assure the attainment of the inflation target, as opposed to the roundabout method of supporting the exchange-rate anchor. Although the inflation-target regime does not prefer one specific instrument to another in principle, the interest rate does have a leading role to play in practice. The uniqueness of the Israeli version of this regime is that the exchange-rate band continued to exist after the inflation-target regime had been introduced. This may have led to occasional inconsistencies in monetary policy, as the authorities learned the hard way. To overcome the inconsistency, the trend in subsequent years was to make the exchange-rate-band regime more flexible by means of widening, mainly at the upper bound.

Israel's abandonment of the exchange-rate band anchor was part of a global trend toward more flexible exchange-rate regimes in the wake of the financial crisis in Mexico, a country that in December 1987 had patterned its stabilization policy on the Israeli prototype. The attack on the Mexican peso in December 1994 made it clear that the conflation of a fixed exchange-rate regime and fiscal balance do not suffice to ensure financial stability in the globalization era, due to the absence of a lender of last resort in foreign currency ("dollars"). The financial crises in Asia in the second half of the 1990s amplified the global trend toward abandoning fixed exchange-rate regimes. Although the need to flexibilize Israel's exchange-rate regime in the era of globalization seems self-evident in retrospect, matters were not so clear at the time. In fact, some senior economists at the BOI continued to adhere to the old concept of a fixed (or managed) exchange rate as the nominal anchor.

The transition to the new monetary regime began hesitantly in late 1993 and proceeded more firmly toward the end of 1994. At first, the nominal interest rate on BOI sources was raised in tandem with inflation, leaving the real rate unchanged. The real rate finally rose in the last quarter of 1994. The change in policy was reflected in slowing the expansion of monetary aggregates, especially at the end of the year. The disinflationary effect of this move was manifested at a lag, in the following year.

MONETARY DEVELOPMENTS: OVERALL PERSPECTIVE

Having described the transition to a new monetary strategy, we now consider the matter from an overall perspective. Since 1994, the BOI's main policy instrument has been the interest rate on its monetary loans to the banks, announced on a monthly basis. As the monetary loans dwindled over time due to the high interest policy, which attracted capital inflows, the BOI switched to a different main instrument: the interest rate that it paid on the fixed-term deposits that commercial banks placed with it. This was another device that the BOI had contrived to circumvent the Finance Ministry's control of the quota of Treasury bills (see chapter 3), the short-term government paper that the BOI was allowed to use for the management of its open-market policy. The BOI's overall strategy was indeed one of "tight money," but the policy evolved in several stages that deserve elaboration.

Initially, as noted, the high interest rate policy attracted large capital inflows that pushed the NIS-forex ER toward the floor of the crawling band, reflecting the limit of the "permissible" appreciation of the NIS. In fact, for lengthy periods in which the lower part of the band constituted an effective constraint to the movement of the ER, the economy functioned practically as if under a rigidly crawling ER regime with capital mobility. Consequently, between 1995 and 1997, the high domestic interest rates generated enormous forex inflows that the BOI had to sterilize. This led to the reshuffling of the net public debt from foreign to domestic. It also inflicted increasing losses on the BOI (the "quasi-fiscal deficit"), since the central bank was paying higher interest on the fixed-term deposits that commercial banks placed with it (adjusted for depreciation) than the interest it earned on its foreign reserves. This cost was estimated at 0.33% of GDP in 1997.

Then came an unexpected development: another decline in inflation in the middle of 1997, prompting the government to slash its inflation target in 1998 from the 7%–10% range to 4% for 1999. In response to the disinflation and the economic slowdown that had ensued by then, the BOI cut its key rate by 1.5 percentage points in mid-1998. However, before the economy could adjust to the lower inflation level, the Russian stock-market crash in 1998 triggered a global financial crisis that led to a speculative attack on the NIS and, in turn, to severe depreciation. The BOI responded to this unexpected development by raising the key rate dramatically—by 4 percentage points. In the event, the downward path of the inflation *target* was not affected by the shock; this had a stabilizing effect on expectations. Furthermore, the disinflation process during these years was supported by large autonomous—that is, unrelated to interest differentials—capital inflows for real and financial investment in Israel, which had a downward effect on the ER.

THE BEHAVIOR OF INTEREST RATES

Let us now consider in greater detail the path of interest rates and the question of sterilized intervention.

The tight monetary policy that was implemented since late 1994 reversed the downward trend of real interest rates that had characterized the money market since the 1985 stabilization. The BOI's nominal and real interest rates had been rising since 1994 and other interest rates behaved similarly (figure 13.1, figures II.8–9, and table III-1). To illustrate the change in the stance of monetary policy between the two halves of the 1990s, one need only note that the average annual real interest rate on the monetary loan of the BOI increased from –1.3% in 1990–94 to 5.7% in 1995–99.

The pattern of the rate hikes tells an interesting story about the evolution of the stance of monetary policy. There were three major hikes of the BOI's interest rate in the 1990s—in 1994, 1996, and 1998 (figure 13.1).[1] Each was implemented in response to jumps in inflation. (Note the *announced* interest-rate changes in figure 13.1.) This marked a major departure from the prevalent pattern during the inflationary period, when there had been no attempt to rein in inflation after the initial shock. Note also that the increase in the nominal rate on these occasions surpassed the upturn in inflation, which implied an increase in the real rate. The increase in the *real* interest rate corresponded to the optimal rule in central banks' behavior models, such as that derived by Clarida, Gali, and Gertler (1999)—the model that we shall call CGG.

THE INTEREST SPREAD AND THE STERILIZATION OF CAPITAL INFLOWS

The tight monetary strategy was associated with the creation of a considerable spread between NIS and forex interest rates in 1995–97, both with and without account taken of depreciation expectations (figure 13.2).[2] Since the calculation of depreciation expectations is problematic, we also calculated the real interest spread on the assumption that real depreciation expectations were zero—a PPP assumption (figure 13.3). Again we see that the real spread widened with the changeover to the tight monetary strategy in 1994. These calculations are based on the interest rate on deposits, but similar behavior is observed in the case of short-term loans. Thus, the widening spread became a general feature of the financial markets in the short term. This meant an increase in the risk of taking a loss on a financial portfolio composed of both domestic and foreign net assets, possibly leading to bankruptcies and thereby harming financial stability.

Although the creation of the spread was part of the disinflation strategy, it was not easy to maintain because of the liberalization of the BOP capital account. As is well known, in a small open economy with capital mobility, an attempt to raise domestic interest rates may be self-defeating if not harmful in the longer term.

In the Israeli case, the commitment to the exchange-rate band created an additional difficulty by fomenting inconsistencies between the band and the inflation-target regime. Basically, *the interest rate that was needed for the targeting of disinflation exceeded the rate required to keep the effective exchange rate within the band.* Therefore, the tightening of monetary policy pushed the exchange rate toward the floor, that is, toward the "appreciation limit," of the exchange-rate band (figure 13.4), in a process that was reinforced by exogenous capital inflows. The commitment to the exchange-rate band forced the

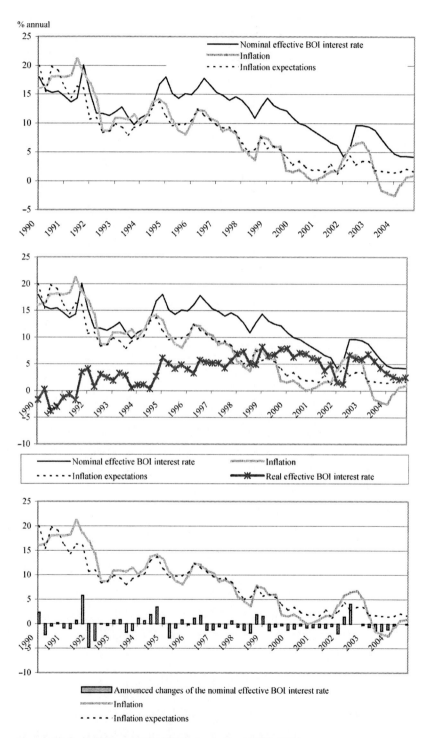

Figure 13.1. Inflation and the BOI Interest Rate, 1990–2004

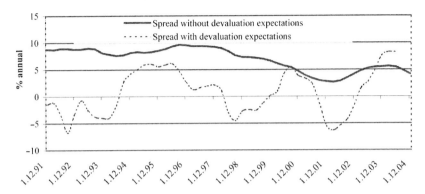

Figure 13.2. Spread of Short-Term Nominal Interest Rates on Assets, With and Without Devaluation Expectations (eight-quarter moving average). Expected devaluation calculated as $[(E_{t+2}/E_t)^2 - 1]$, where Et is the exchange rate in quarter t

BOI to intervene in the market and purchase huge amounts of foreign exchange. Accordingly, the foreign reserves ballooned from $5 billion to around $20 billion in just three years. The cumulative increase amounted to 15% of GDP.

This, however, was not allowed to affect the monetary base due to its potential harmful effects on inflation targeting. Hence, the BOI implemented a policy of massive sterilization of capital inflows, reflected in a drastic reduction of domestic credit (figure 13.5), as measured by the difference between the monetary base and the foreign reserves. Thus, the net external debt (gross debt less foreign reserves) plummeted to 2.3% of GDP in 2002 while gross foreign debt rested at 47% of GDP.

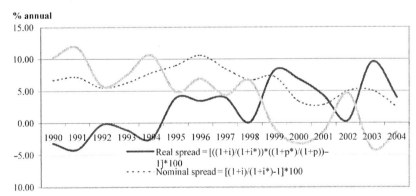

Where i = nominal interest rate, p = inflation (December–December)
*Denotes U.S.

Figure 13.3. Real Spread on Assets Ex Post (eight-quarter moving average)

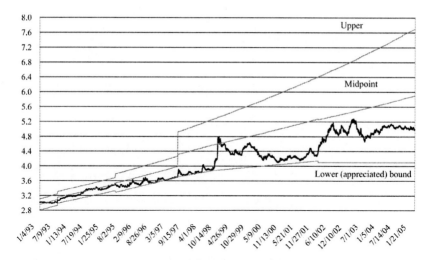

Figure 13.4. NIS-Currency Basket Exchange Rate. *Source:* BOI.

The capital markets responded to these developments with increases in external borrowing (because the interest spread made it cheaper to borrow abroad) and short-term NIS assets (because the tight monetary policy had made them more profitable) (figure 13.6). The relevant ratios of these variables, however, stabilized after one or two years. (The ratio of foreign borrowing to total bank credit stabilized in 1997.)

A possible explanation of the stabilization of the capital markets is that the increase in foreign exposure in the early stage of the tight-money policy raised the domestic risk premium on the exchange rate, bringing the uncovered interest parity into balance. This is consistent with the theory that the risk

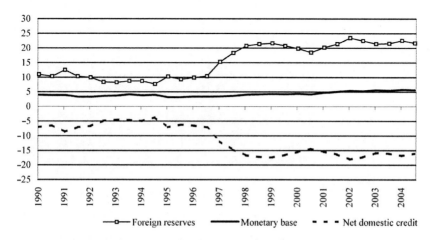

Figure 13.5. Monetary Base, Foreign Reserves, and Net Domestic Credit (percent of GDP). *Source:* BOI.

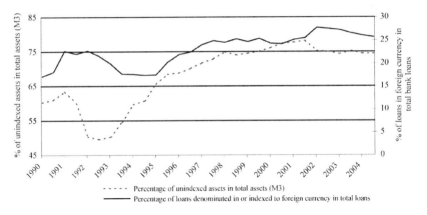

Figure 13.6. Loans Denominated in Foreign Currency (or Indexed Thereto) in Total Bank Loans and NIS-Denominated Assets. *Source:* BOI.

premium depends on the composition of the portfolio between domestic and foreign assets and liabilities (Krugman and Obstfeld, 1994).

If the uncovered-interest-parity argument holds, the interest spread adjusted for depreciation expectations would be equal to the risk premium on the exchange rate. Therefore, we may use the average spread, adjusted for our estimate of expected depreciation, as a measure of the risk premium. Our calculations show that for the entire period from Q4-1994 to Q2-1998 (before the Russian financial crisis began), the risk premium relative to the U.S. dollar was about half the nominal interest spread during the tight-money-policy period.

Notably, however, the risk premium (measured in these terms) has been decreasing since 1997, with the exception of the temporary interval following the crisis in 1998 (figures 13.2 and 13.3). This may be associated with the increased level of long-term capital inflows (figure 13.7) that, while largely

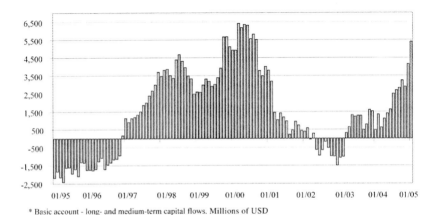

* Basic account - long- and medium-term capital flows. Millions of USD

Figure 13.7. Long-Term Activity in Foreign Exchange: Sales(+)/Purchases(−), Cumulative-12 months. *Source:* BOI.

independent of the short-term interest differential, were not independent of the macroeconomic regime. Exogenous inflows such as these tend to reduce the risk premium by increasing the foreign-exchange component of the private sector's financial portfolio (insofar as the central bank does not sterilize them). This represents the other side of tight monetary policy, that is, the salutary effect of the efforts of Israel's macroeconomic policymakers to adopt international standards that induce long-term capital inflows. The mitigating effect of the U.S. government's loan guarantees, which applied to a significant fraction of Israel's capital inflows, worked in the same direction. The guarantees may have been the main reason for the fact that Israel's sovereign rating did not change during the 1990s.[3]

These developments indicate that internal monetary policies had no significant adverse effect on Israel's country risk. In fact, the sovereign interest spread, an indicator of country risk, reacted only to the attack following the Russian crisis of 1998 and not to the homemade crisis that was created by the sharp rate cut by the BOI in December 2001 (figure 13.8). Notably, sovereign

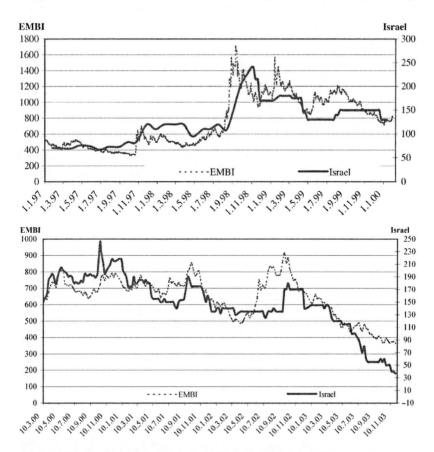

Figure 13.8. Sovereign Spread (Israel and Emerging Markets). Yield spread relative to U.S. Long-term government-guaranteed. Basis points. *Source:* EMBI—J.P. Morgan. Spread on Israel—Salomon Smith Barney.

risk refers to "dollar loans" to Israel, which are free of the exchange-rate risk that clings to NIS loans. It should also be noted that sovereign loans are of higher quality than ordinary loans. Thus, the effect of internal monetary-policy shocks seems to apply mainly to the ER risk and less to the sovereign risk.

Figure 13.8 suggests that the tight-money disinflation policy created a risk-premium cycle that lasted from 1994 to the middle of 1998. This period should probably be treated separately from developments in later years. We may speculate that had the Asian and Russian international currency crises of 1997–98 not occurred, Israel might have completed its disinflation process by 1997 or 1998. As it happened, however, the external shocks caused unexpected jumps in inflation and raised the risk premium temporarily. The shocks also tilted the BOI's monetary policy in a more conservative direction. Thus, the first stage of the new strategy, inaugurated in 1994, seemed to be completed by mid-1998, after which time Israel entered a second stage during which it had to deal with an environment of international financial crises. Thus, a basic question that requires elucidation (and is addressed in the next section) is whether the tight monetary strategy adopted in 1994 made Israel more vulnerable to financial crises and, by do doing, harmed the economy's financial stability.

INDICATORS OF VULNERABILITY AND FINANCIAL STABILITY

It turns out that despite the adverse impact of the tight monetary policy on the risk premium, as noted above, various indicators show that Israel's financial stability did not deteriorate in the second half of the 1990s.

A popular way to evaluate financial stability is by constructing a financial-volatility index based on the sum of the coefficients of variation of three (inter-related) variables—the nominal exchange rate, the central bank's nominal interest rate, and the foreign reserves. The intuition is that if, for example, the ER is kept constant then the foreign reserves will vary (since they will absorb the shocks) and if the exchange rate is flexible then the reserves will be stable and the exchange rate will absorb the shocks. Thus, the index would register the overall stability. The results of this calculation (table 13.1) show, somewhat surprisingly, that the country was more stable financially in 1995–2001 than it had been in 1989–94. The volatility of GDP was also lower in the more recent period. According to this indicator, the tight monetary policy brought greater financial stability to the Israeli economy even though it could have had the opposite effect. As noted, a possible explanation for the increased financial stability in the 1990s was the recognition in global capital markets that Israel's economic regime had made substantial progress toward monetary dominance, a necessary feature for survival in the era of globalization.

The downside of these developments is that the improvement in financial stability in the second half of the 1990s was attained at the cost of growth. Moreover, the "mountain of sheqels" that had formed during the massive sterilization of capital inflows, coupled with the liberalization of the BOP capital account, crimped the BOI's rate-cutting freedom in subsequent years due to fear that a possible attack on the NIS would precipitate a financial crisis. As the literature noted long ago (Friedman, 1953), a flexible exchange-rate regime is a

Table 13.1. Indexes of Volatility

	Monthly Data				Quarterly Data	
	Nominal Exchange Rate %, CV (1)	Total Reserves Minus Gold %, CV (2)	BOI Effective Interest Rate %, CV (3)	Index of Financial Volatility % (4) = (1) + (2) + (3)	Volatility of Nominal GDP %, CV	Volatility of GDP vol. (1995 = 100) %, CV
1989	4.49	5.98	14.01	24.47	6.09	1.48
1990	1.87	7.33	10.49	19.69	6.71	2.90
1991	6.10	7.94	24.24	38.27	10.33	4.96
1992	4.69	10.98	10.99	26.66	4.49	1.42
1993	2.74	14.61	11.74	29.09	6.63	4.45
1994	0.86	8.86	19.51	29.23	7.80	3.27
1995	1.46	6.88	10.17	18.51	4.60	2.42
1996	2.12	10.08	7.20	19.40	4.81	1.50
1997	2.61	13.42	3.91	19.94	4.25	1.54
1998	6.60	1.86	12.89	21.35	4.27	1.92
1999	1.96	1.65	6.96	10.57	4.44	3.67
2000	1.04	1.74	8.19	10.98	4.42	3.27
2001	1.68	1.84	11.54	15.06	1.56	0.39
1989–94	3.46	9.28	15.16	27.90	7.01	3.08
1995–2001	2.50	5.35	8.69	16.54	4.05	2.10

CV - Coefficient of variation = SD/Average.

major deterrent to a speculative attack on the currency. Israel made considerable progress in this respect by gradually widening its exchange-rate band in an upward direction, the direction that is vulnerable to an attack. By taking this pragmatic approach, Israel avoided the trap that snared Mexico and the East Asian economies, which concurrently adhered to a fixed exchange-rate regime and promoted capital-account liberalization.

14

The Real Economy Background

DWINDLING IMMIGRATION AND THE LABOR MARKET

The immigration wave, which began at two hundred thousand persons in 1990 (about 4% of the population), subsided to fifty to eighty thousand per year in the second half of the 1990s. Initially, mass immigration reduced the capital/labor ratio in the business sector, depressed real wages, and raised the unemployment rate from 8.9% during the 1989 recession—high to begin with—to 11.2% in 1992. Real wages declined by 3 percentage points during the same period. The resulting deflationary shock in the labor market was instrumental in creating the stepwise decrease in inflation in 1992.

However, the previous equilibrium was reestablished during the 1990s, mainly due to a continuous stream of investment that brought the capital/ output ratio in the business sector back to where it had been (*Annual Report*, 1999, p. 45, figure). By 1995, the unemployment rate had returned to the 1987–88 level (6.3%) and real wages in the business sector had returned to their late 1980s plateau. The increased rate of investment that supported this process was financed largely by the $10 billion in U.S.-guaranteed Israeli government bonds that were sold in the U.S. capital market. Therefore, this major investment effort had a limited effect on the disinflation process. The absorption of the immigrants went more smoothly than had been expected, although the process was hampered by the mismatch between the immigrants' previously acquired skills and those required in the new economic environment.

THE BALANCE-OF-PAYMENTS PROBLEM

As a result of the immigration wave and the expansionary fiscal policy after 1992, the BOP current account exhibited deficits that climbed from $1.1 billion in 1990–92 to $6 billion in 1995 (figure III.1). Despite the increase in investment, national saving as a proportion of national income (from all sources) decreased by 5 percentage points between 1991 and 1995 (*Annual Report*, 1998, p. 227), implying that the upturn in the current-account deficit was not fully backed by investment. The government considered this an unsustainable situation despite the U.S. loan guarantees. Consequently, the balance of payments became the number-one macroeconomic problem toward the mid-1990s. Now, however, unlike the inflationary era, the problem was not redressed by massive devaluations, lest this cause inflation to reignite.

ECONOMIC GROWTH AND THE FISCAL DEFICIT

The deterioration of the BOP coincided with a surge of economic growth that proved to be unsustainable. Thus, in 1994–95 GDP growth exceeded 4% per year in real terms and the fiscal impulse turned from a negative value in 1993 into a positive one in 1995 (figure 11.1, based on the methodology of Dahan and Strawczynski, 2001). The main reason was a liberal increase in general-government wages during the premiership of Yitzhak Rabin. It was this form of growth that undermined the sustainability of the process.

It was in 1994 that policymakers became aware of the emergence of the twin-deficit phenomenon, that is, the simultaneous growth of the fiscal and current-account deficits (figure III.1).[1] When a new Likud government came into power in 1996, this realization led to a turnaround in the stance of fiscal policy. In the second half of the 1990s, tight monetary *and* fiscal policies contributed to the slowdown of economic activity, which, in turn, had a decisive effect on the disinflation process.

15

Moving toward Price Stability

RECENT DEVELOPMENTS ON THE INFLATION FRONT

The new monetary strategy that was adopted in late 1994 started the rate of inflation down the road to price stability. The first phase of the policy was completed around the middle of 1998. By that time, inflation had been resting at a plateau of around 4% for a year. Thus, some economists consider mid-1997 the time when the target of price stability was attained. The last phase, beginning in late 1998, was subjected to several major shocks that could not, however, blur the picture of movement toward price stability.

The first of these shocks was the collapse of the Russian stock exchange in August 1998, preceded by a drastic domestic interest rate cut in July. This fortuitous timing caused the exchange rate to leap in October. This upturn was translated into a leap of inflation during 1998 and year-on-year in 1999. The BOI had to raise the key interest rate drastically to pacify the capital market and restore confidence in its commitment to price stability.

These events were soon followed by the global high-tech boom in 2000, which abetted a surge in Israel's GDP growth rate, and a major inflow of capital imports, related mainly to the sale of Israeli high-tech companies to major U.S. firms. The bursting of the high-tech bubble and the beginning of the intifada caused investment and tourism to collapse in the two closing quarters of 2000 and quickly brought on a sharp recession. Monetary policy managed to preserve financial stability despite these shocks, albeit at the cost of high real interest rates and a high rate of unemployment for most of the period through 2003.

It was initially thought that the target of price stability had been attained by 2000, since CPI inflation rates in the three-year 1999–2001 interval were

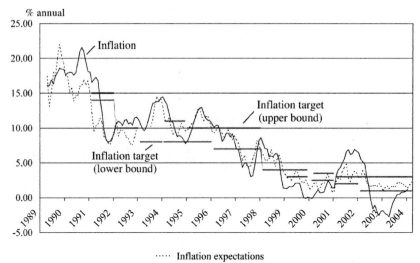

Figure 15.1. Inflation Expectations, CPI, and Inflation Target. *Source:* BOI.

1.3%, 0.0%, and 1.4%. Indeed, inflation was below expectations (as measured by capital-market data) and below the official inflation target (figure 15.1). In 2000–2001, the BOI gradually lowered the key rate at the rate of 0–0.3 percentage points per month, as prescribed by the strategy of the new governor, David Klein. Within the framework of this policy, the nominal key interest rate fell from around 12% in early 2000 to 5.8% at the end of 2001, still implying a real interest rate of about 3% (all in annual terms). The spread between the BOI and Fed interest rates narrowed considerably during this period (figure 15.2).

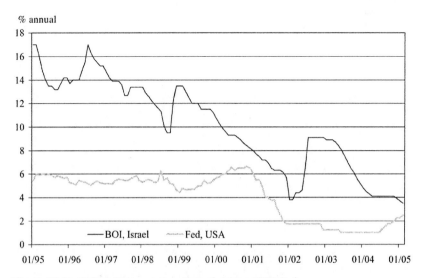

Figure 15.2. BOI-Fed Interest-Rate Spread. *Source:* BOI, Fed.

The downward path of inflation was blurred by a monetary shock associated with a sharp rate cut, from 5.8% to 3.8%, in December 2001. The steep rate cut was part of an unofficial deal with the Prime Minister and the Ministry of Finance, in which the Government committed itself to stringent fiscal belt-tightening and accepted a request that the BOI and its six previous governors had been seeking since 1966—virtually total instrument independence. Formally, this involved a technicality only: the Ministry of Finance agreed to lift the quota of MAKAM—short-term bonds that the BOI used for open-market operations (see chapter 3). Until then, the Finance Ministry had set the quota and used it to crimp the central bank's freedom of action. Now the government also agreed to widen the exchange-rate band by lowering its floor and turning it into a flat line instead of one that crept upward at the rate of 2% per year.

On the whole, this package, designed to implement a policy of "fiscal tightness and easy money," coupled with increased exchange-rate flexibility, gave the BOI full instrument independence de facto if not de jure. In respect to dealing with the recession, this seemed to be in principle a step in the right direction. As it happened, however, it was premature, partly because of uncertainty about the government's ability to deliver its part of the deal and partly due to underestimation of the risk premium that was needed to keep the "mountain of sheqels" from leaving the country. Yet, the public perceived this step as an infringement of the central bank's independence because it entailed a drastic rate cut that clashed with the BOI's previous stance.

The BOI had not foreseen these difficulties. The immediate result was a precipitous depreciation of the NIS against the dollar and a consequent leap in CPI inflation to almost 7% in the first seven months of 2002, corresponding to an annual rate of about 12%. The unexpected inflationary surge, mimicking the surprise-inflation effect in the Barro-Gordon model, eroded real wages and created real depreciation. The BOI responded to the inflationary spurt by sharply hiking its interest rate by more than 5 percentage points by the middle of 2002, in what may be viewed as an "error correction." Its behavior was definitely influenced by the government's delay in honoring its commitment to tighten the fiscal belt, a move that did not begin until April 2002. The central bank's highly restrictive measures, raising the key rate from 3.8% to 9.1% within only seven months, underscored its significantly enhanced independence. They also had a strong effect on inflation expectations, which fell abruptly to the target range of 1%–3%. Actual inflation followed at a lag, in the closing quarter of 2002.

The results of the stepwise reduction of the BOI rate in December 2001 resembled the October 1988 shock in terms of depreciation, inflation, and the subsequent increase in the key rate. Despite all these upheavals, however, there is no mistaking the fact that Israel has basically attained price stability in recent years, as the data for 2003 and 2004 make clear.

The BOI's inflation reports indicate that inflation in 2003 dropped to *negative* 1.9% and that inflation expectations twelve months ahead (as measured by capital-market indicators) fell to about 1% in November and December of that year. Indeed, actual inflation in 2004 was only 1%. In response, the BOI began again in 2003 to lower the key rate gradually—to 4.5% in February 2004 and

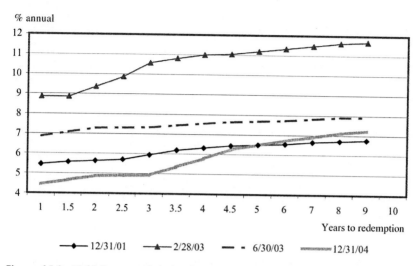

Figure 15.3. Yield Curve on Unindexed Bonds, December 2000–July 2003.
Source: BOI.

only 3.5% in early 2005, much lower than the December 2001 level (both rates in annual terms). With inflation expectations running at around 1.5% in January 2005, the real ex ante interest rate was about 2%. The real yield curve for indexed bonds for December 2004 stabilized below the December 2001 level (at about 4%) and the nominal yield curve for bonds of up to five years to redemption exhibited lower interest rates than in December 2001 (figures 15.3 and 15.4).

These developments give further indication that the financial events of 2002 were an aberration that may obscure the trend. *Therefore, we suggest that the developments up to December 2001 and from the last quarters of 2002 through*

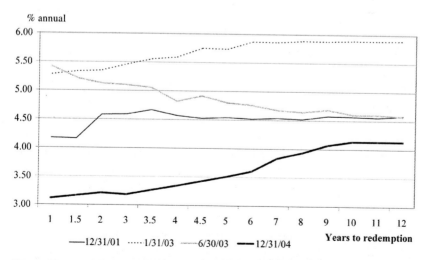

Figure 15.4. Yield Curve on CPI-Indexed Bonds, December 2000–July 2003.
Source: BOI.

2004 are those of relevance for future years. In 2004, the various measures of inflation (inflation in the past year, inflation expectations to one year ahead, and the inflation target) converged, giving evidence of stationarity (figure 15.1). These developments were accompanied by a drastic contraction of the sovereign spread for Israeli bonds, surpassing that of emerging markets generally (figure 13.8b). Thus, one has good reason to view the economy as having attained price stability, albeit within a framework of a jittery capital market (in view of developments in 2002) that tends to overreact to changes in nominal policies due to the country's inflationary heritage and the (still) very high debt/GDP ratio.

THE INFLATION-TARGET REGIME

The long road to price stability started with the 1985 stabilization program, which established the basic principles of fiscal discipline and the need for a nominal anchor. As noted, the original anchor, the ER, was replaced in 1994, effectively, by a more general inflation-target regime. From then on, the key interest rate played a more direct role in controlling inflation. Strictly speaking, the inflation target had been introduced as part of the implementation of the crawling ER band in 1991. Only with the introduction of the tight monetary policy at the end of 1994, however, did it become a practical policy guide.

Until 2000, the government set the inflation target for the coming year only, although the BOI recommended a multiyear target. In principle, the target reflected a consensus between the government and the BOI about the desired inflation path. During the regime's initial run-in years, the targets were not aggressive and reflected mainly the perceived inflation plateau (figure III.1). In practice, the target regime had two main implications. First, it was meant to influence the public's expectations and serve as a guidepost for various economic agreements, especially those related to wages. Second, as far as monetary policy was concerned, it served as a warning that the BOI would treat any deviation of inflation from its target as a significant and politically acceptable input for interest-rate policy.

Since 1995 (except for 1999), the inflation target has been expressed in terms of a range rather than a number. At first, the upper bound of the range was considered the more significant indicator. As an indication of the nonaggressive stance of the disinflation policy, when inflation surged in 1994 the upper limit of the range for 1995 was set at 11% as against the single rate of 8% in the previous year. The behavior of the lower bound of the target also reflected the nonaggressive stance; it stayed at 8% in 1995–96 and was reduced gently, to 7%, in 1997–98.

The stance of monetary policy took a more aggressive turn in 1998. In view of the apparent stepwise reduction of inflation in the second half of 1997, from an annual plateau of 10% to one of 5%, the inflation target was reduced drastically in mid-1998 from 7%–10% for 1998 to 4% for 1999. The unexpected external financial crises in August and October 1998 did push the (average) annual inflation rate that year to 8.6%, leading to pressure on the government to adjust the inflation target upward. The Government vacillated but the BOI, insisting that the crisis reflected a *price-level* shock rather than a shock to inflation, argued that this was no reason to change the target, which was forward-looking. The path of inflation after the shock vindicated the BOI's position by falling to just over 1% during 1999. Thus encouraged, the (new) Government set the target for 1999–2000 at 3%–4%, with the BOI's endorsement (figure 15.1).

The BOI played an active role in these developments. Just as its premature 1.5 percentage-point rate cut in mid-1998 contributed to the severity of the unexpected October crisis, so did its cumulative 4 percentage-point rate increase following the crisis help to pacify the capital market. The BOI's policy of not intervening in response to the steep 20% depreciation that occurred during the crisis also abetted the stabilization of the financial system. (Notably, the exchange rate never reached the upper limit of the band.)

One way to interpret the BOI's tough stance after the financial crisis is by arguing that the central bank intended to orchestrate a reduction in actual inflation so that the government would find it easier to adopt a low inflation target. Indeed, since 1999 inflation has been undershooting the targets consistently. This misalignment soon became the topic of considerable criticism of BOI policy. In view of the low (zero) rate of inflation in 2000, the government set the inflation target on a declining path: 2.5%–3.5% for 2001, 2%–3% for 2002 and 1%–3% for 2003 onward, with the last-mentioned figure construed as price stability. This target range remains in force at the present writing.

16

General Features of the Disinflation Process

RULES IN THE SERVICE OF PRICE STABILITY

Modern monetary disinflation strategy is based on rules that strive to ensure the attainment of price stability. The Maastricht criteria are an example of such a set of rules. In fact, the Israeli rules associated with the goal of price stability are patterned after these criteria, at least conceptually.

The first rule was the aforementioned "no-printing law," which enjoins the Bank of Israel from lending money to the Ministry of Finance. This legislation severed the link between the BOI and the financing of the fiscal deficit and forced Finance to risk an increase in interest rates if it chose to finance the deficit by issuing bonds. Thus, it restricted the Finance Ministry's ability to amass deficits. By excusing the BOI from having to maintain low interest rates on the national debt in order to help finance the fiscal deficit, it also contributed to the creation of monetary-policy independence.

The second rule was the 1991 Reduction of the Deficit Law, also mentioned above. Although this statute was never implemented as planned, it has helped to contain the deficit at about 4% of GDP on average since the early 1990s. From the 1985 stabilization until that time, the steep reduction in the defense budget and the high-growth years that followed lowered the debt/GDP ratio considerably. This process, however, stopped in the mid-1990s.

The third rule was the inflation target. Supposedly, the target regime reflected a consensus between the government and the BOI, the purpose of which was to lower the target over time until the attainment of price stability. Responsibility for managing the inflation target was entrusted to the central bank, which implemented a tight (overly tight, according to some critics) monetary policy to attain the goal. Due to the inflation-target regime, the BOI could mobilize political support to raise its interest rates and had to desist from the surprise-inflation tactics that had been so common in the inflation era. Thus, the inflation-target regime helped the monetary-policy regime to evolve from one of discretion to one of rules.

These rules recognize the importance of keeping the deficit and the national debt (as ratios of GDP) low, in accordance with accepted international standards and in keeping with the evaluation of the capital market and, especially, the credit-rating companies. The rules also recognize the importance of having a nominal anchor—practically speaking, the inflation target—after the commitment to price stability gathers some credibility. In fact, these rules, which attempt to emulate the Maastricht criteria, are interconnected and may be considered part of a system designed to deliver price stability. In appendix G, we show that the inflation target and the market-dictated limit on the national-debt ratio restrict the size of the fiscal deficit. In particular, a low national debt and a low inflation target require a low fiscal deficit (for consistency). Thus, the fiscal deficit should not exceed the growth of the (warranted) national debt plus the level of seigniorage implied by the inflation target.

WHY DO REAL AND NOMINAL INTEREST RATES RISE (TEMPORARILY) IN DISINFLATION?

One simple explanation for the increase in real interest rates in disinflation is that the real rate reflects the unexpected decline in inflation (as the result of a disinflation program) while the nominal rate changes little because people do not believe in the commitment to disinflation. This relates to *ex post* real interest rates. In Israel, however, where we have estimates of inflation expectations, we know that *ex ante* real interest rates rise as well. Furthermore, the above theory does not explain why nominal interest rates, too, usually rise in the early stage of disinflation.

Let us state at the outset that no model of rational expectations can explain the rise of the real interest rates in disinflation under conditions of full information and full credibility. To explain the phenomenon, then, we have to look for various forms of lack of credibility or asymmetric information. Lack of credibility can enter the system along different channels.

In this context, it is useful to distinguish between models in which money is endogenous and those in which money is exogenous in the sense of its being a policy variable. Modern formulations use a reaction function of the central bank in terms of its interest rate, treating the money supply as endogenous (e.g., Taylor, 1993; Clarida, Gali, and Gertler, 1999; Woodford, 2003). In these models, the money market is actually redundant since the money supply accommodates demand with infinite elasticity. Hence, the model consists typically of an IS equation, a Phillips Curve, and a Taylor equation that expresses the response of the central bank in terms of its interest rate.

Let us consider the widely held belief that the reduction of inflation rates around the world in recent years is associated with the transition from a regime of discretion to one of rules. It is easy to see that in the CGG model this is associated with a reduction in expected inflation, but since the nominal interest rate decreases by the same amount the real interest rate is unchanged. However, when the transition from discretion to rules is not credible, the public continues to believe for some time that the regime has not changed. Consequently, nominal wages continue to rise at a faster rate than inflation. The central bank may view this as a supply shock that raises inflation and reduces output. The optimal response in this case is an interest rate hike that will ease inflationary pressures at the cost of greater unemployment. (In this case, the Phillips Curve tradeoff is unavoidable.) This will raise the ex ante real interest rate, which is the instrument for reducing demand. It also requires the central bank to raise its nominal key rate.

The empirical question is whether a credibility problem existed in the case at hand. Since credibility is not directly observable, we examined this problem for Israel in an indirect manner by comparing inflation expectations twelve months ahead as observed four quarters earlier ($\pi^e[-4]$) with the realization of inflation during this period, that is, during the past twelve months (π). Thus, $\pi^e(-4)$ and π relate to the same time span.

The results show that inflation expectations were well above the realization of inflation in all periods (table 16.1, column 2).[1] We take this as evidence of the existence of a credibility problem, since people were systematically surprised by the low level of inflation. (This outcome is still consistent with rational expectations under lack of credibility.)

The formulation of the Taylor equation focuses on the difference between inflation expectations and the inflation target (π^T), which in Israel was usually set for a calendar year. We found no significant difference between the two (table 16.1, column 5). However, when we compared the inflation target announced four quarters earlier, $\pi^T(-4)$, with the realization of inflation during these four quarters, π, we found that the former exceeds the latter consistently (table 16.1,

Table 16.1. Difference among Measures of Inflation

	$\pi - \pi^e$ (1)	$\pi - \pi^e(-4)$ (2)	$\pi - \pi^T(-4)$ (3)	$\pi - \pi^T$ (4)	$\pi^e - \pi^T$ (5)
Q1:1992–Q2:2004	0.13 (0.42)	−0.99 (0.75)	−0.87 (0.73)	0.02 (0.65)	−0.11 (0.49)
Q1:1995–Q2:2004	−0.4 (0.42)	−1.44 (0.76)	−0.95 (0.73)	−0.27 (0.65)	0.14 (0.36)
Q1:1998–Q2:2004	−0.59 (0.60)	−1.73 (1.0)	−1.8 (0.87)	−0.92 (0.82)	−0.34 (0.36)
Q1:2000–Q2:2004	−0.67 (0.84)	−1.46 (1.33)*	−1.37 (1.05)	−0.92 (1.07)	−0.25 (0.32)
Q1:1995–Q2:1998	−0.11 (0.25)*	−1.31 (0.92)*	0.5 (0.73)	0.5 (0.76)*	0.37(0.74)

All calculations are based on quarterly data. The items in the table are quarterly averages, Figures in parentheses are standard errors of these averages. π denotes inflation in the past 12 months; π^e denotes inflation expectations to 12 months ahead; π^T is the midpoint of the inflation target, available from 1992:1, π^e (−4) denotes expectations four quarters (one year) earlier; and similar notation applies for the inflation target. The standard errors of the means of the differences are corrected by the Newey-West formula for serial correlation. Since there is a built-in serial correlation of at least three quarters, in the case of few observations, when the formula above did not detect three autocorrelations, we forced it upon the calculation (this is indicated by an asterisk beside the standard error).

column 3). We construe this as evidence of an attempt by the BOI to target a lower inflation rate than the one agreed within the framework of the inflation-target regime. (This interpretation concurs with the thesis of N. Sussman in volume II.) This represents, in a manner of speaking, disbelief on the BOI's part in the government's commitment to price stability or, at least, to the pace of achieving it.

Another possibility is that central banks react asymmetrically to deviations of inflation from the target, that is, they respond more aggressively to positive deviations than to negative ones. For example, Sussman (volume II) finds that the BOI responded vigorously only to inflation that exceeded the upper bound of the target. Cukierman and Muscatelli (2003) provide a theoretical basis, as well as empirical evidence from other countries, for an asymmetric reaction of the central bank to deviations of inflation from target. Basically, this is also a reflection of lack of credibility because it stems from fear that an overrun of the target will lead to a panic, that is, the belief among the public that inflation is spinning out of control. By implication, the central bank will raise its interest rate in the medium term even though the average deviation of inflation from the target is zero.

An entirely different form of lack of credibility or information asymmetry arises in a case where the central bank uses the supply of base money as a policy variable and allows the interest rate to be determined endogenously. The rationale here is that in the course of disinflation, the central bank does not want to create the impression that it is continuing to finance the fiscal deficit by printing money. Therefore, it proceeds *gradually* to the new steady state, which is characterized by lower inflation. If we add "sticky prices" (á la Calvo) to this, we find that real money balances are rigid in the short run and that so is the nominal interest rate. When inflation expectations decline in the course of disinflation while the nominal interest rate remains rigid,[2] the real interest rate is bound to increase. As the economy proceeds to the new steady state, the nominal interest rate will decline and the money supply will rise. This scenario may be derived from a forward-looking model or of an ordinary IS/LM model (see appendix H).

One may extend the foregoing IS/LM model to an open economy by applying the contours of Dornbusch's overshooting model, which is based on the idea that the exchange rate is more flexible than the domestic price level, which is assumed to be sticky. As the money supply contracts in the course of a money-based stabilization, the nominal exchange rate appreciates more than the price level declines, causing real appreciation and expectations of real depreciation that will raise the real interest rate. (This is modeled formally in Liviatan, 1980.) We show later that this model works quite well in the Israeli experience.

THE THEORETICAL BASIS OF THE INFLATION-TARGET REGIME

The theoretical basis of the inflation-target regime has been set forth in numerous articles, the best known of which are Svensson (1997), Taylor (1993), and

Clarida, Gali, and Gertler (1999). In these theoretical models, which usually consist of the three equations mentioned above—an IS equation, a Phillips Curve, and a Taylor rule—money responds endogenously to the interest rate set by the central bank.[3]

In Svensson's model, the current interest rate of the central bank can affect only *future* inflation[4] (current inflation is predetermined) due to the existence of lags in the monetary transmission mechanism. Similarly, the current real interest rate affects activity only in the next period. According to the Svensson model, the central bank's interest rate is determined optimally in the framework of a loss function, which is based on the deviation of future inflation from target and, possibly, on the state of unemployment. In Svensson's view, the central bank sets its current interest rate to minimize the deviation of its own inflation prediction from the target. In this model the nominal interest rate of the central bank affects future inflation negatively, implying a negative relation between the key rate and inflation expectations.

Importantly, the model does not determine the inflation target itself and, therefore, says little about the disinflation trend. According to Clarida, Gali, and Gertler, the model refers only to deviations from a trend that is determined outside the model. One may relate the evolution of the trend to the building of credibility by the central bank in models where money is endogenous or to some version of Dornbusch's "overshooting" model (see chapter 17) in exogenous-money models.[5]

In terms of the recent literature on dominance, one may say that the inflation-target strategy supports a *regime* of monetary dominance that is conducive to low inflation. Under such a regime, the interest-rate policy strives to safeguard price stability by keeping the nominal anchor on track. In particular, inflation targeting supports a monetary regime in which *the central bank renounces the option of surprise inflation*, thereby laying the foundation for a rules regime. As the Barro-Gordon models show, the shift from discretion to rules is capable by itself of reducing inflation. If one believes, as we do, that the abandonment of surprise-inflation tactics was an important factor in the global disinflation of recent years, then the very fact that central banks followed the inflation-target regime may explain much the success of the disinflation.

One of the implications of the Svensson model is that an increase in actual inflation relative to the target should induce the central bank to hike its nominal key rate by more than the increase in inflation. The Clarida-Gali-Gertler model arrives at the same conclusion but replaces actual inflation with inflation expectations, so that the ex ante real key rate has to increase in response to a positive gap between inflation expectations and the inflation target. Woodford (2003) shows that this kind of reaction is required for the convergence of the economic system.

The level of unemployment (or the output gap) should also influence the central bank's interest-rate policy. Since the state of unemployment influences inflation expectations, this is the case even if the loss function of the central bank is not based explicitly on unemployment.

An important implication in Clarida, Gali, and Gertler is that, generally, the convergence toward the inflation target should be gradual rather than immediate. An immediate move is optimal only in the absence of cost-push elements or when the state of unemployment is of no concern whatsoever. Since the presence of cost-push elements is uncertain, the gradualist approach must emanate from monetary policy. Uncertainty about the parameters of the model reinforces this cautious attitude.

THE MONETARY TRANSMISSION MECHANISM IN ISRAEL

After Israel adopted the inflation-target regime in the early 1990s and implemented it strictly since 1994, economists, especially at the BOI, have tried to determine whether the theoretical implications of this regime are consistent with the data. Some of the most important empirical monetary regularities are reported in Bufman and Leiderman (2001). One of them is the lagged effect of monetary expansion on inflation. It was found that the correlation between M_1 growth and inflation is highest when money is lagged by two quarters. We extended Bufman and Leiderman's analysis, which referred to the 1990–96 interval, through 2002 and found a similar pattern with possibly longer lags. We also extended their diagrammatic analysis that related M_1 growth (at an eight-month lag) to inflation and confirmed their finding of a positive relationship between these time series. This is consistent with Friedman and Schwartz's finding, in their famous monetary history of the United States (1963), that money affects output first and prices only later. It also squares with the assumption of the Svensson-Taylor models, which refer to lags in the monetary transmission mechanism.

Another important empirical regularity found is that an increase in the key interest rate (nominal and real) negatively affects the rate of growth of M_1. Combining this finding with the previous result, we infer, in a conclusion consistent with the Svensson model, that the BOI's interest rate affects inflation at a lag. An additional implication of this behavior is that an increase in the nominal key rate should reduce current inflation expectations, which are supposed to reflect the foregoing mechanism.

The structure of monetary transmission may be affected by the role of the exchange rate if the ER is free to move within a wide band. Thus, if the central bank does not intervene in the forex market, then its rate hike may give rise to capital inflows, which, by causing appreciation, may depress inflation along this channel.[6] This mechanism may speed up the transmission from the key rate to inflation. This channel in Israel was studied by Gotlieb and Ribon (1997) and Djivre and Ribon (2000). The latter study claims that the interest-rate effect through the ER channel is indeed immediate but tends to be short-lived because the ER adjusts rather quickly to changes in the asset market. Thus, from a monetary-dominance perspective, the ER channel provides the BOI with an instrument for a quick realignment of inflation with its target and, in turn, allows the central bank to demonstrate its commitment to price stability. Therefore, a flexible ER regime is conducive to the establishment of inflation-target credibility by the application of central-bank monetary policy.

Another empirical regularity, reported by Leiderman and Bar-Or (2000), is that the passthrough from the exchange rate to prices tends to be affected by the phase of the business cycle—strong in booms and weak during recessions. This finding seems to be robust, suggesting that a rate cut during recessions may generate effective real depreciation for some time.

ECONOMETRIC EVALUATION OF THE PERFORMANCE OF THE BOI

Recently it has become much the fashion to explain and evaluate the performance of central banks by using some version of "Taylor equations." These equations relate the central bank's interest policy to the deviation of inflation from target and to the state of unemployment. An important implication of the theoretical models discussed above is that the central bank, when faced with an upturn in inflation expectations, should raise its nominal interest rate in excess of the increase in the inflation rate in order to bring about a real interest increase (the "stabilizing" rule). Furthermore, the central bank should adjust the key rate in the direction opposite that of the change in unemployment, although the intensity of the rate change should depend on the bank's preferences. Clarida, Gali, and Gertler find that the behavior of the Fed has changed dramatically since the late 1970s (the Volcker-Greenspan era) and the parameters of the Taylor equation have changed in the direction suggested by the model.

Elkayam (2000) performed a similar calculation for Israel, basing it on the fact that Israel stated its inflation target explicitly as a guide to the BOI's monetary policy. The equation was estimated for quarterly data from Q3-1992 (shortly after the target was implemented) to Q3-2000. His estimating equation, which assumes interest-rate smoothing, shows that the BOI behaved in the recommended manner, that is, the reaction coefficient of deviations of inflation expectations from the target led to more than a 1 : 1 response on the BOI's part. Elkayam also presents the deviations of the key interest rate from the fitted rate. The deviations have tended to be positive in recent years, indicating a toughening of the policy stance.

The estimation of the Taylor equation seems to be affected strongly by the choice of period, time unit, and estimation method. For example, N. Sussman (volume II), applying the Clarida-Gali-Gertler statistical method to monthly data for the entire 1990s decade, finds that the BOI's reaction to deviations of inflation expectations from the implicit target in Israel was milder than corresponding estimates for major global economies. The coefficient of reaction during the 1990s was below unity in Israel and greater than one in the major economies. Sussman also finds that the inclusion of the *official* target brings the reaction coefficient slightly closer to unity. This leads him to conclude that the BOI pursued a zero-inflation target in the second half of the 1990s, notwithstanding the announced target. The main contribution to aggressiveness in the reaction to the straying of expected inflation from the target, Sussman says, is traced mainly to the observations preceding 1994. After the 1994 watershed in monetary policy, the degree of aggressiveness became rather slight and the "action" came from the BOI's reaction to "crisis situations" in which inflation vaults over the upper bound of the target range. Sussman also points to an increase in the effect of persistence of the interest-rate policy. However, the main channel to disinflation, according to Sussman, is the high real interest rate that the BOI charges for the use of its funds, which affects aggregate demand and is also associated with appreciation.

In a recent comprehensive econometric study of the BOI's reaction function, Melnick (2002) uses monthly data that reach back to July 1993, when the BOI began to announce its official key rate. He finds that foreign interest rates affected (positively) the BOI's rate by means of the uncovered interest parity—in addition to the deviation of inflation expectations from the inflation target—and that forward-looking models outperform models based on past inflation. He concludes that the BOI followed a strict inflation-target regime (ignoring the business cycle) rather than a flexible one.

Another way of using the Taylor methodology is by adjusting the equation that seemed to describe the behavior of the Fed to the Israeli data. We experimented with the coefficients that, according to Taylor (1993), worked well for the United States, as a criterion for the performance of the BOI. The equation that we used for this purpose is

$$i = \mathrm{inf} + g(\mathrm{gap}) + h(\mathrm{Edp}{-}\mathrm{dpT}) + \mathrm{rf}$$

where i is the annual interest rate of the BOI (denoted BOIEF in the figures), "gap" denotes the difference between (the log of) actual and potential outputs, Edp denotes inflation expectations, dpT denotes the inflation target, and rf is a measure of the real equilibrium interest rate, which can be estimated in various ways. In some versions of the Taylor equation, the annual inflation rate during the past twelve months is used for inf, and in alternative versions one may use inflation-expectations data (if available). Given the alternative ways of estimating inf and rf, we chose several representative versions, which are presented below.

Figure 16.1a shows the application of the Taylor equation with $g = h = 0.5$ (the parameter values that Taylor used); figure 16.1b does the same with $g = 0$ and $h = 0.5$. In both versions of the figure, inf represents inflation in the past twelve-months. The data for rf were taken from the real yield to redemption on short-term indexed bonds. These figures indicate that, in the 1990s, the BOI adjusted its interest rates broadly according to the Taylor rule, although these rates were lower than those predicted by the Taylor rule in 1993–96 and higher than the predicted level in 1998–2001. This is consistent with the view that the BOI has toughened its monetary stance in recent years.

Figures 16.1c–d show the same calculation with inf representing *expected* inflation, as calculated from capital-market data. In these figures, rf represents the nominal yield to redemption of twelve-month BOI paper (MAKAM/Treasury bonds) deflated by the corresponding inflation expectations (as above). The lesson from this experiment is that the BOI's policy may be better approximated by ignoring the effects of "gap." For example, the Fed's policy function during the 2001 recession would point in the direction of a drastic rate cut, such as the one that Fed actually performed, while the BOI pursued its policy

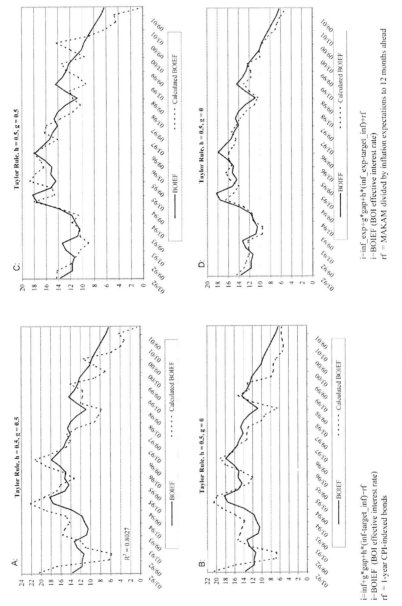

i=inf+g*gap+h*(inf-target_inf)-rf
i= BOIEF (BOI effective interest rate)
rf = 1-year CPI-indexed bonds

i=inf_exp+g*gap+h*(inf_exp-target_inf)+rf
i= BOIEF (BOI effective interest rate)
rf = MAKAM divided by inflation expectations to 12 months ahead

Figure 16.1. Taylor Rule and the Interest Rate of the BOI (% annual).

244

of gradual and rather mild cuts. Statistically, this version yields the highest correlation, $R^2 = 0.94$, among the alternatives with which we experimented. This provides further corroboration for the belief that, toward the turn of the twenty-first century, the BOI tightened its monetary stance beyond the standards that guided the behavior of central banks in the industrial economies.

A SUMMARY OF "AGGRESSIVENESS" INDICES

The foregoing analysis of the econometric measures associated with monetary policy may be viewed as an attempt to measure the aggressiveness of monetary policy in pursuit of its goals. These measures include the medium-term level of the real interest rate and the central bank's response (in terms of the key rate) to deviations of expected inflation from target and the deviation of actual inflation from the upper bound of the target range. These measures also estimate the policy response to economic recession and the persistence of tight monetary policies over time.

Despite the differences among the various studies in coverage and specification, we may point to some general conclusions. The evidence reviewed above points to the tendency of the BOI, in the 1990s, to adopt the norms of industrial countries' central banks in the sense of taking an aggressive monetary-policy stance toward inflation. Furthermore, by and large, the BOI became more aggressive in the second half of the 1990s. The first manifestation of the change in aggressiveness is represented by the rate hiking that occurred in the second half of the 1990s. The second aspect is evidenced in the drastic increase in the real BOI rate in response to crisis situations; in these cases, there can be no doubt that the BOI acted according to the Clarida-Gali-Gertler principles. The third aspect is the diminishing influence of the recession on the BOI's interest-rate policies. The fourth phenomenon is the growing persistence, or smoothing, of interest-rate policies. During the 1990s as a whole, the BOI's interest rate reacted positively to the rise of inflation expectations above target. One doubts, however, that the reaction was strong enough to qualify as an expression of aggressiveness.

Another aspect that seems relevant in measuring the aggressiveness of monetary policy is the role of the inflation target. As the disinflationary policies of the government and the BOI gained credibility, the inflation target increasingly became a guide to inflation expectations. The BOI, aware of this fact, tried to acquire more influence on setting the target, which was supposed to reflect a consensus between itself and the Treasury. After the surge in inflation that followed the Russian crisis in 1998, for example, the BOI insisted that the drastic reduction of the inflation target earlier that year not be altered (as the government was prone to do). The acceptance of the BOI's stance in this matter was a decisive factor in shaping the course of inflation in the years to come; it gave the BOI something of a "license to kill" with its interest-rate policy.

THE DYNAMICS OF RATE CUTS

It is clear that long-term disinflation should be accompanied by a similar reduction in nominal interest rates. It appears, however, that the way the rates are cut is also important. Recent experience shows that the BOI accomplishes more by lowering its rate gradually than by slashing it in one drastic stroke. This corresponds to the conclusion of the Clarida-Gali-Gertler essay, which discusses the advantages of gradualism in the conduct of monetary policy at moderate and low inflation rates.

The empirical evidence on this issue refers to the BOI's sharp rate cuts in mid-1998 and late 2001. In both cases, the early experience of moderate reductions spared the capital market from turmoil. In particular, the gradual reduction adopted by Governor Klein since the beginning of 2000, at a rate of 0.2%–0.3% per month, managed to keep inflation low (even below target) and augured Israel's move, at long last, to price stability. However, the BOI's drastic move—its immediate 2 percentage-point rate cut, from 5.8% to 3.8%, in December 2001, in the context of a package deal with the government—had a dramatic effect on the financial sector, causing the exchange rate and both the inflation rate and inflation expectations to leap in the following months. To protect its own credibility and that of the disinflation process, the BOI had no choice but to react aggressively by hiking interest rates sharply.

THE INDEPENDENCE OF THE CENTRAL BANK

Although the BOI obviously played a central role in the disinflation process after the 1985 stabilization, it did so without a formal change in its original charter, which was drafted in the early 1950s and legislated in 1954. The most significant legislative change, approved in 1985 as part of the stabilization program, was the "no-printing law," actually an amendment to 1954 Bank of Israel Law that repealed the section allowing the BOI to accommodate the government in order to even out its cash flow. Governments had been making extensive use of this option—the tapping of central bank credit—for three decades as a source for the financing of substantial fiscal deficits.

In 1997, the government appointed a special commission (the Levin Commission) to reformulate the BOI Law. To date, the commission's report and recommendations have not been discussed by the government or ratified by the Knesset. The main stumbling block is the recommendation to redefine the target of monetary policy. Under the 1954 law, the BOI was to strive for price stability *and* a high level of employment; the commission recommended the specification of price stability as the principal target.[7]

Although the BOI Law was not rewritten, the government's attitude toward the central bank was strongly influenced by a change that occurred in the industrial countries' concept of central-bank independence. Many countries entrusted their disinflation processes to their central banks, and Israel was no exception. A test case surfaced in 1994 when the BOI shifted to a tight-money strategy within the framework of the inflation-target regime. Although the government set the target and only coordinated its decision with the BOI, the degree of toughness of the response to inflationary shocks was left to the BOI's discretion. The Finance Ministry's criticism of the BOI policy was that the central bank had violated the BOI Law by reacting in a way that reflected the pursuit of the disinflation target irrespective of the effect on unemployment. Despite this sort of criticism, none of the governments that have served since the mid-1990s have taken active measures to crimp the growing effective independence of the central bank.

This ostensible paradox (notably, the government has to approve the appointment of the governor) may be rationalized by invoking the theory of dynamic inconsistency. Thus viewed, the government used the BOI to tie its own hands.

It is well known, however, that a central bank can be "too independent" in the sense of not being sufficiently sensitive to the state of unemployment or the balance of payments—the so-called "Rogoff central banker" issue. This effect may induce the government to place the central bank under some restrictions. In Israel, one of the main manifestations of this attitude relates to the width and slope of the exchange-rate band. According to the current arrangement, the BOI is free to manipulate the exchange rate within the band but cannot change the parameters of the band without the consent of the government. This constrains the BOI because a high interest-rate policy would push the exchange rate toward the bottom of the band and force the BOI to sterilize the resulting capital inflows, to the central bank's embarrassment. The issue is deadlocked. The BOI, favoring a floating ER, has demanded the elimination of the bounds of the band (effectively, the lower bound). The Ministry of Finance has argued that this step would cause the currency to appreciate but noted that this outcome could be avoided by lowering the key rate. Moreover, a rate cut strong enough to trigger depreciation would lift the ER away from the floor of the band and create an effective float. Again, the issue remains unresolved. It is clear, however, that in a cooperative solution one anchor only—the inflation target—would definitely suffice.

The BOI is hobbled not only by the lack of target independence but also by the lack of instrument independence. The parameters of the band are just one example. Until December 2001, the BOI was also constrained by a ceiling on the issue of its "own" short-term bonds to absorb money from the system. We noted earlier that to circumvent this restriction the BOI utilized a legal option that allowed it at first, from 1988 onward, to offer "monetary loans" to commercial banks and later to sell interest-bearing deposits to them. The latter is evidently a less efficient way of conducting monetary policy than regular open-market operations. In December 2001, the Government finally agreed to let the BOI take another step toward instrument independence by lifting the ceiling on the issue of its own short-term paper.[8]

FISCAL DISCIPLINE AND OECD NORMS

The most important feature of the 1985 stabilization was the elimination of the enormous fiscal deficit, which averaged 13% of GDP in 1980–84. The low-deficit regime that ensued, coupled with monetary conservatism, were the cornerstones of the gradual convergence to price stability.

In the early 1990s, however, the low-deficit policy that had been instituted became unsustainable. A substantial increase of public expenditure was needed to absorb the masses of immigrants from the former Soviet Union. As pointed out earlier, the government treated the resulting increase in the deficit as temporary and communicated this message to the public in 1991 by enshrining in legislation a path of decreasing fiscal deficits over time.

The Reduction of the Deficit Law refers to the central-government budget only. The relevant economic concept, however, is *general* government (or the "public sector," as it is often called in Israel). As it turned out, the total deficit of general government (as a percent of GDP) did not decrease during the 1990s; it averaged 4.5% in 1990–94 and 5% in 1995–99. Another indicator of fiscal discipline is the behavior of the deficit over the business cycle. As economic activity surged in 1993–94, the government used the increased tax absorption to finance additional expenditure. This behavior, although consistent with the Reduction of the Deficit Law, amplified the cycle and introduced an asymmetry that slowed the reduction of the debt/GDP ratio.[9]

This procyclical policy also increased the current-account deficit and, in later years, induced a fiscal contraction (figure III.1). The Likud government that took office in 1996 blamed its Labor predecessor for the need to redress the balance-of-payments position by applying the fiscal brakes. The use of higher tax revenues at times of economic growth to finance an increase in government expenditure does add to the economic expansion in the short run but has negative effects on growth in the long run. In future years, this lesson was internalized in the management of Israeli fiscal policy. Thus, when an economic boom took place in 2000, the tax revenue generated by higher income was used to lower the fiscal deficit of general government from 4.8% of GDP in 1999 to only 2.8%, resulting in a significant reduction of the debt/GDP ratio.

Although there were additional indications of tougher fiscal discipline (Zeira and Strawczynski, 2002), the overall fiscal performance in the 1990s and during the 2000–2004 interval was hardly satisfactory. The general-government deficit in 2004 was 5.1% of GDP in Israel as against the OECD average of 1.1%. Moreover, whereas the rate of decrease in the fiscal deficit during the 1990s was rapid in the OECD countries, Israel followed an ambiguous pattern in the 1990s. During the past decade, according to comparisons performed by the BOI, the OECD countries reduced their general-government fiscal deficits by 4.2% of GDP while Israel did not reduce its deficit at all. The difference cannot be explained fully by the deeper Israeli recession, since Israel also made less progress than the OECD in cutting its structural deficit. Note also that the measured deficit in Israel is based on the *real* interest cost of the national debt as a component of total general-government spending, while in the OECD it is based on nominal cost. Thus, the difference between Israel and the OECD group in respect to real deficits is even greater than the raw figures suggest.

Two other criteria for the evaluation of performance of fiscal policy are commonly used: the evolution of the ratios of debt and of general-government expenditure to GDP. Although these ratios did trend down gradually until the middle of the 1990s, they stabilized afterwards at higher levels than those prevailing in the OECD and increased in the first few years of the twenty-first century. In 2004, however, the ratios leveled off due to the tougher fiscal policy and the resumption of growth. Gross national debt in 2002 and through 2004 still exceeded annual GDP as the OECD countries moved toward the Maastricht criterion of 60%. The size of Israel's general-government sector, measured in terms of the public expenditure/GDP ratio, resembled that of the highest-ranking OECD countries and in 2004 surpassed the OECD average by 6 percentage points of GDP. This is particularly troubling because general government crowds out the private sector, the presumed locomotive of economic growth. The larger the general-government sector, the higher the level of taxation is needed. This cannot but have a distortionary effect on the growth potential of the economy (Lavi and Strawczynski, 1998).

The fiscal adjustment needed to redress these deviations from the OECD standards has been the leading problem in Israeli macroeconomic policy in recent years. The absence of progress on this score has made the BOI reluctant to reduce its interest rate more aggressively than it has. In the first half of the 1990s, the primary fiscal surplus more than sufficed to cover the interest burden adjusted for growth (mainly due to the high rate of growth), allowing the national debt/GDP ratio to decline.[10] In the second half of the decade, the primary surplus and the interest burden adjusted for growth were more-or-less balanced, so that the debt ratio remained fairly stable. In 2001–3, for the first time since the 1985 stabilization, negative debt dynamics were observed, presumably reflecting the recessionary state of the economy during those years.

These adverse developments took a turn for the better in the second half of 2003 and, especially, in 2004. The government cut its real expenditure two years in a row, an unprecedented event since the 1985 stabilization. This, coupled with the resumption of growth, allowed it to lighten the tax burden without increasing the deficit. In 2004, in fact, the government met its deficit target and the BOI met its inflation target. This highlights the relationship between the fiscal effort and the BOI's interest-rate policy. Specifically, the fiscal policy in 2004 allowed the "fiscal tightness and easy money" stance, which failed in 2002, to succeed.

The role of the international capital market in imposing fiscal discipline on Israeli policymakers cannot be overstated. This explains why in 2002 and 2003 the government had to amend the budget in mid-year to contain the growth of the fiscal deficit. Although such action seems unsound from the standpoint of budget procedure, it underscores the difference between political wishful thinking and the constraints imposed by the global capital market. The second of the two adjustments, implemented by Finance Minister Netanyahu on the basis of a spending cut rather than a tax hike, appears to have been highly effective in restoring fiscal balance because it conforms broadly to the principles of fiscal consolidation (Alesina and Tavares, 1998). It also addresses long-term fiscal issues such as pension reform and sets real general-government spending on a path that limits its growth to 1% a year, thus lowering the share of spending in GDP over time. In addition, the plan sustains the sharp cutbacks in transfer payments that have already been made. One doubts, however, whether this policy of reducing expenditure can persist in view of its medium-term negative implications for the welfare state. Furthermore, it depends

largely on the resumption of global growth and leaves doubt about the outcome if external conditions worsen.

STABILIZING THE EXTERNAL POSITION

Comparison of figure 16.2 with figure 9.4 reveals the main difference between
the high-inflation era and the period following the 1985 stabilization: in the
latter period, inflation was not used to deal with BOP problems. This is underlined not only by the stability of the inflation-tax curve but also by the fact that
the general-government deficit (as a percent of GDP) has been much more
stable since 1989 than before the stabilization, when it was allowed to rise and
was then cut drastically by inflationary measures whenever BOP problems
arose. Thus, the government's efforts to abide by the deficit-reduction rules
had an indirect positive influence on inflation. Furthermore, the existence of
the inflation-target regime ruled out the use of surprise-inflation measures—
the creation of large devaluations to erode real general-government wages or the
imposition of steep increases in general-government prices—to cut the deficit.

For example, an upturn in the import surplus in 1994–96, blamed at the
time on the increase in the fiscal deficit in those years, was handled by a mix of
tight monetary and fiscal policies without resort to inflationary measures as
in the past. The combination of the deficit-reduction rule and inflation
stanched the process that transformed price shocks into inflation shocks, as
had been common before 1985.

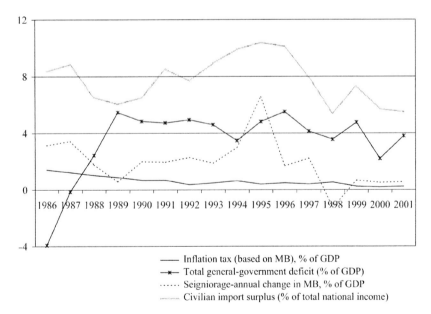

Figure 16.2. Import Surplus, Total General-Government Deficit, Seigniorage,
and Inflation Tax. *Source:* BOI.

THE COST OF DISINFLATION

Conventional wisdom has it that the reduction of inflation has future benefits that can be attained only at the cost of a recession in the present. In cases of ER-based stabilization, however, the picture seems to be more complicated. In many such cases, especially in chronic-inflation economies, drastic disinflation tended to generate a business cycle kindled by a consumption boom (Kiguel and Liviatan, 1992). Israel was no exception. After the 1985 stabilization, a very brief period of rising unemployment was followed in 1986–87 by a boom in consumption and GDP—unemployment falling from 7.5% of the labor force to less than 6% and GDP in 1987 growing by 6.2%—and a recession in 1988– 89.[11] Since the GDP growth rate was somewhat higher over the entire cycle (1985–89) than in 1980–84 (3.8% as against 2.9%), one might argue that the disinflation involved no macroeconomic cost at all. Of course, we do not know what would have happened in the absence of the stimulating effect of the mass immigration boom that began in 1990. We do know from the experience of ER-based stabilizations in Latin America, however, that there is no clear evidence of an overall cost of disinflation when the entire cycle is examined.

In money-based stabilizations, in contrast, the initial recessionary effect appears quite often (Calvo and Vegh, 1993, and *World Economic Outlook*, 2001). This is usually explained in terms of the rigidity of expectations and wage setting. Israel felt the bite of this process when it adopted a tight monetary strategy in late 1994. The recessionary effect of this policy was amplified by the implementation of a tight *fiscal* policy in 1996 to deal with balance-of-payments problems. Consequently, the unemployment rate surged from 6.6% in 1996 to 8.9% in 1999.

It is hard to unravel the separate effects of monetary policy, fiscal policy, and immigration on the paths of inflation and economic activity. However, the authors of econometric studies seem to have been rather adept at predicting the path of inflation in the second half of the 1990s, both within and outside the sample period.[12] The main explanatory variables in the disinflation that occurred at that time the second half of the 1990s were unemployment and the interest rate. It is clear that unemployment was influenced by the BOI's tight monetary policy, but thus far it has not been possible to estimate the separate effect of this policy as against that of other influences (especially the fiscal impact). The real interest rate and unemployment are estimated as having contributed about 30% apiece to the reduction in inflation between 1996 and mid-1998, and the former seems to have been the dominant factor since it also operated through the latter.[13]

The cost of disinflation must be weighed against its benefits. In the globalization era, consistent convergence toward the OECD standards or the Maastricht criteria may avert an external financial crisis. A deviation of inflation from international standards may be construed as evidence of some kind of irregularity in the economy. When capital flows so easily from country to country, it does not pay for a foreign investor to invest resources in an effort to determine the real causes of inflation (see Calvo and Mendoza, 1995); it is cheaper simply to move the capital to another haven. Similarly, convergence toward the OECD standards may attract capital inflows such as funds from long-term savings institutions. Thus, the name of the game in macroeconomic policy changed in the 1990s from full employment to financial stability.

The fact that Israel sidestepped the financial crises that plagued the Asian Tigers, Russia, and Brazil may be credited largely to the conservative monetary and fiscal policies that the BOI and the government, respectively, had been implementing since the mid-1990s. Similarly, the large foreign capital inflows in the closing years of that decade would not have materialized without the aforementioned conservative policy measures and the consequent improvement in Israel's credit rating. The payoff for Israel's monetary conservatism was its rapid acceptance as a respected member of the global economic club. Although the value of this benefit is difficult to quantify, there is a growing consensus in Israel that this integration was unavoidable even if the short-term costs in terms of unemployment were high.

MONETARY INJECTION AFTER STABILIZATION

Some Stylized Facts

Table 16.2, an extension of table II-6, describes monetary injections in the last three decades of the twentieth century (through 2001). The focus here is on the post-1985 stabilization period. (For developments before 1985, see chapter 9.) General-government injections into the monetary base were small in the two subperiods ending in 2001, 1986–94 and 1995–2001. During the latter subperiod, however, the private sector created a sizable injection by selling foreign exchange, reflecting the high interest-rate policy during that interval. Thus, massive sterilization of short-term capital inflows was needed. That this was done is reflected by the strong negative association between the BOI's monetary injection (resulting in negative ΔCB) and the net sale of foreign exchange by the private sector to the BOI (ΔF) after 1994. Since the exchange rate rested near the bottom of the exchange-rate band for a considerable time in the second half of the 1990s, the economy was effectively operating under a crawling exchange-rate regime. The virtual eradication of inflation in the 1995–2001 subperiod may be imputed largely to the BOI's tight monetary policy, reflected by the large negative ΔCB during that time.

The Monetary Story in Pictures

Figures 9.5–9.7 in part II present the main features of Israel's monetary history since 1973. Again, the focus here is on the poststabilization period. After the 1985 stabilization, the monetary injection from general government (ΔG) behaved quite regularly due to the 1985 "no-printing" amendment, which forbade the BOI to finance the deficits of the government (although the government could use its deposits with the BOI for the same purpose—a

Table 16.2. Monetary Injections, Inflation, and Deficit

A. Normalized by Monetary Base at the Beginning of Quarter (percent).

Quarterly Data	BOI Injection (ΔCB) (1)	Private Conversion (ΔF) (2)	Government Injection (ΔG) (3)	Quarterly Change in Money Base (ΔMB) (4) = (1) + (2) + (3)	Quarterly Inflation (5)	Domestic Deficit* (6)	Change in M_1** (7)
Q2:1973–Q4:1978	0.84	−12.68	18.55	6.70	8.62	28.72	6.82
Q1:1979–Q2:1985	−2.46	−55.39	84.67	26.82	29.09	109.87	23.14
Q1:1986–Q4:1994	3.93	−7.11	8.36	5.10	3.77	15.02	7.99
Q1:1995–Q4:2001	−14.97	17.00	1.94	3.97	1.33	16.76	3.17
Q2:1973–Q2:1985	−0.91	−35.34	53.63	17.38	19.48	90.78	15.48
Q1:1986–Q4:2001	−4.34	3.44	5.55	4.65	2.70	15.52	6.02
Q1:1995–Q1:1998	−36.41	36.61	3.85	4.05	2.01	12.15	3.15
Q2:1998–Q4:2001	3.61	0.00	0.29	3.90	0.75	19.64	3.20

*Available from Q1:1977.
**Normalized by beginning of quarter M_1.

B. Normalized by GDP (percent).

Quarterly Data	BOI Injection (1)	Private Conversion (2)	Government Injection (3)	Quarterly Change in Money base (4) = (1) + (2) + (3)	Monetary Base* (5)	Domestic Deficit* (6)
Q2:1973–Q4:1978	0.53	−4.70	6.47	2.29	9.81	8.76
Q1:1979–Q2:1985	0.05	−4.42	6.27	1.91	2.91	9.36
Q1:1986–Q4:1994	0.80	−0.87	1.18	1.12	4.56	3.09
Q1:1995–Q4:2001	−2.07	2.43	0.98	1.33	3.96	2.56
Q2:1973–Q2:1985	0.28	−4.55	6.36	2.09	6.31	9.22
Q1:1986–Q4:2001	−0.49	0.58	1.07	1.21	4.30	2.86
Q1:1995–Q1:1998	−5.19	5.23	1.44	1.47	3.43	3.35
Q2:1998–Q4:2001	0.63	0.00	0.57	1.21	4.45	1.82

*Available from Q1:1977.
Source: BOI.

matter that evoked controversy). In the poststabilization era, there were two major shocks associated with private-sector conversions of foreign exchange that were sterilized by the BOI (figure 9.6). First, monetary policy went through a period of laxity in 1993, reflected in a capital outflow—a negative ΔF—that was offset by a positive ΔCB. The tight monetary policy that went into effect in late 1994 induced a large wave of capital inflows in response to the large NIS-forex interest spread, while movement of the exchange rate (ER) was restricted by the floor of the exchange-rate band. To restrain the expansionary effect of the forex conversions on the monetary base, the BOI implemented a mass sterilization policy (noted above), manifested in a sharp decrease in ΔCB in 1995–97.[14]

Figure 9.7 combines the injections of both sectors, government and private ($\Delta G + \Delta F$), and plots the result against the BOI injection (ΔCB). This shows that there were two major shocks in the monetary history of Israel—one related to the fiscal expansion in 1982–84 relative to the shrinking monetary base, and one related to the capital inflows resulting from the tight monetary policy in 1995–97. In both cases, the BOI pulled ΔCB downward, that is, drained liquidity in order to offset the overall expansionary impact of the two sectors' behavior on the monetary base. The monetary contraction in both episodes resulted, predictably, in an increase in real short-term interest rates. The difference between them is that in 1982–84 monetary policy was tightened in the context of large fiscal deficits, while in the second case the tight monetary policy was applied under relatively strong fiscal discipline that belonged to an explicit effort to lower inflation to single digits. Only in the latter case, that is, under a monetary-dominance regime, could a tight monetary policy be effective in reducing inflation. Note further that ΔCB expanded considerably, that is, that a significant central-bank injection took place, in the stabilization year (1985). This was due to the shift from dollar-indexed resident deposits (PATAM) to the unindexed NIS base in response to the highly significant downturn of inflation. By definition, this shift implies an increase in both the monetary base and the central-bank injection. However, it had no inflationary implications because it originated in an increase in demand for money induced by a steep drop in inflation expectations.

The Invariance of the BOI Injection Function after 1985

The BOI continued to pursue its policy of sterilizing monetary injections from different sources in the poststabilization period. The striking feature of this era is that the BOI's injection function remained much the same as in the preceding high-inflation period. For example, the sterilization parameters of the estimating equation for the high-inflation period (Q1-1979–Q2-1985) and the period after 1995 are almost identical (table 9.4). Since the capital flows were almost totally sterilized, the dominant factor in the slowdown of the growth rate of the monetary base was the major decrease in the general-government injection.

Since inflation was reduced drastically after 1985, the reason for the persistence of high sterilization coefficients remains puzzling. We do not have a fully satisfactory explanation for the existence of this phenomenon during the entire period. One possible reason is that the BOI pursued a managed exchange-rate policy during most of the period. This explanation is also valid for the period after 1995, in which the exchange-rate band was widened considerably, since the ER spent most of that time near the floor of the band. Since nearly full capital mobility was the dominant feature of that era, the demand for money was probably strongly influenced by foreign interest rates. In the extreme case of a fixed ER regime with full capital mobility and a fixed demand curve for money, all capital flows are sterilized because the demand for domestic money is determined by the global interest rate.

This explanation, however, is irrelevant for the 1998–2001 period, because by then the BOI had stopped intervening in the foreign-exchange market and the exchange rate had moved away from the floor of the exchange-rate band. Our computations indicate that although the system was already verging on a pure float at that time, the BOI still sterilized most of the general-government injections. This calls for a different explanation from the previous one, at least for that period. The alternative explanation seems to be related to the policy of stabilizing the monetary base to avoid volatility in domestic interest rates.

STRUCTURAL REFORMS

Disinflation programs in emerging markets are often accompanied by structural reforms. Such reforms may help to establish credibility in the persistence of the macroeconomic measures. From a broader perspective, market-oriented reforms may signal the acceptance of the industrialized countries' economic regime, that is, the "OECD model," which leaves no room for inflation. In this case, disinflation becomes just one component of a broader policy package of fundamental economic change. This tends to reduce the marginal cost of disinflation as such. This type of linkage between disinflation and structural reforms was observed in Latin America and Eastern Europe during the 1990s. In Israel, the structural-reform process lagged significantly behind the macroeconomic stabilization. Thus, while the macroeconomic stabilization in 1985 was drastic, the reform process was gradual. This is one explanation of the sluggish pace of disinflation in Israel, as noted above.

Although structural reforms definitely offer significant support for stabilization programs, in terms of their time frame they may correspond more to inflation than to growth. Thus, it seems quite reasonable to take a cautious attitude toward the possible effect of reforms on growth.

Despite the gradual evolution of the reform process in Israel, the economic philosophy of the country's policymakers is believed to have changed drastically upon the implementation of the stabilization program (Ben-Bassat, 2002). Their basic conception of the role of government in the economy changed from pervasive intervention to a view of the private sector as the engine of growth. The change was reflected in the increased share of the business sector in GDP, from 59% in 1984 to 67% in 1998, and in the reduction of general-government expenditure from 67% of GDP in 1980–84 to 52% in 1994–98 (Ben-Bassat, 2002).

The public's internalization of this change in mindset is the basis of the disinflation process. As the change gradually took hold in the Israeli public mind, the disinflation process became irreversible, as it had in Latin America and Eastern Europe. Although the disinflation was stepwise, the undercurrent toward a new economic regime always flowed. The actual policies, reflected both in macro measures and in structural reforms, helped to internalize the new economic philosophy.

The inherent feature of the Israeli reform process (Ben-Bassat, 2002) was its focus on the financial sector, where it was supported or initiated by the BOI. In other sectors, especially that of "natural monopolies" (except for communication), market-oriented reforms were meager until recent efforts by Finance Minister Netanyahu. More significant effects were brought about by the long-term trade-liberalization agreements that Israel has been initiating since the 1960s. The financial-sector reforms, on which we focus here, mark a retreat from the financial-repression system that was prevalent in the inflationary era. They interacted sym-biotically with fiscal policy, being facilitated by the drastic cut in the fiscal deficit and helping to consolidate the new fiscal regime.

One of the financial-sector reforms was the cessation of using the reserve requirements of the banking system as an instrument of monetary policy. It was the elimination of the inflationary finance of the fiscal deficit that made this possible. The reserve requirements, still ranging from 32% on demand deposits to 84% on forex and forex-indexed deposits in 1987, plunged (pur-suant to the global trend) to 10% in 1990 and to 3%–6% from 1994 onward. Another feature of financial repression was the requirement of all institutional investors—mutual funds and pension funds—to invest some 90% of assets managed in earmarked government bonds that provided the government with a relatively cheap source of finance for its deficits. Since 1987, the government has reduced gradually this requirement (except for pension funds), to only 40% on average (Ben-Bassat, 2002).

Other features of the financial reform were the elimination of tax discrimi-nation against corporate bond issues, which opened that market to private firms, and an increase of the proportion of marketable government bonds in the portfolio of institutional investors. Last but not least was the elimination of the banking system's directed-credit component, the main tool of government intervention in financial markets before 1985 and an inherent element of the financial-repression regime.

The liberalization of the forex market was one of the most important financial reforms (see Michaely, volume II), with significant macroeconomic implications. The failed liberalization in 1977 made it clear that macroeco-nomic stabilization must precede the liberalization of foreign-currency trans-actions (Blejer and Gotlieb, 2002). In this process, deregulation of the business sector and capital imports (as against exports) was given priority. The process was concluded by 1998, with minor exceptions that were finally eliminated at the end of 2004, when the BOP capital account was liberalized. By enhancing Israel's integration into the global economy, the liberalization process imposed fiscal discipline on the Ministry of Finance and the political community in the spirit of monetary dominance. Integration into the global economy allowed Israel to reap the benefits of tapping external resources and improved financial diversification. As is well known, however, it also made the country more vulnerable to imported financial crises.

In 2003, the new government (again, Likud-based) took important steps toward addressing long-term fiscal problems. Its actions included financial reforms, most importantly an agreement that reformed the pension system. This act had direct implications for the credibility of general-government solvency and exerted an indirect effect on the credibility of the monetary-dominance regime. The pension reform is based on the principle of actuarial balance, to be attained by gradual increases in members' contributions and the retirement age. An important element of the reform is the reduction of the subsidy that pension funds have been receiving by means of guaranteed interest rates, much higher than those paid by the government in the bond market, on nonnegotiable earmarked government bonds. The reform gradually reduces the funds' holdings of these government-subsidized bonds; ultimately, 70% of their assets will be invested in negotiable bonds.

COUNTERCYCLICAL POLICIES

The attitude of economists toward countercyclical macroeconomic policies has come a long way in the past fifty years. The Keynesian prescription of government intervention is now viewed skeptically, after the global stagflation phenomenon in the 1970s supported the "monetary revolution" led by Milton Friedman. According to another recent view, fiscal expansion may turn out to be contractionary because of its crowding out of investment and, possibly, of consumption (Alesina and Perrotti, 1995). Furthermore, the globalization regime places constraints on the independent macro policies of individual countries. These considerations have brought the issue of the credibility of fiscal policy to the fore. In particular, economies with a poor record on fiscal policies tend to be very cautious in this matter, in order to avoid suspicion about the maintenance of fiscal discipline. The key question regarding this issue is whether increases in spending during recessions are followed by spending cuts during upturns. Thus, during the financial crises in the second half of the 1990s, East Asian countries that had good fiscal records took some expansionary fiscal measures while Latin American economies (e.g., Brazil and Mexico) adopted a more conservative stance due to their inflationary history.

A change in Israel's attitude toward countercyclical policies became observable as the disinflation process progressed and as the country's integration into the global economy intensified. During the 1988–90 recession, the authorities allowed the automatic stabilizers to operate and the fiscal impulse (following the IMF definition) was systematically positive although not large (figure 11.1). Monetary policy was also supportive in the sense that real interest rates kept falling. From 1997 on, as the disinflation process reached its final stages, a dramatic change of mind took place. Now, amid contractionary fiscal *and* monetary policies, the economy slid into recession exclusive of 2000, the high-tech bubble year. During this period, the implementation of countercyclical policies seemed to threaten the strategy of disinflation and of financial stability. In this context, the BOI stressed Israel's deviations from the OECD standards and the absence of a long-term fiscal strategy, which forced the authorities to tighten macroeconomic policies even in the midst of recessions.

The issue resurfaced in 2001–2, as the domestic recession worsened and the United States and other OECD countries did adopt active countercyclical monetary and fiscal policies. People began to doubt the wisdom of a passive policy stance as Israel wallowed in a protracted recession occasioned by Palestinian terror and, particularly, the global economic slowdown. While the government has recently increased public investment, the problem of countercyclical policies remains controversial.

FISCAL DOMINANCE AND MONETARY DOMINANCE

Israel's transition from its inflationary period to the poststabilization era involved economic-regime change. In the former period, monetary policy was dominated by fiscal requirements set forth by the Ministry of Finance; in the latter period, the policy assumed a leading role. This may be linked to the recent distinction in the economic literature between fiscal and monetary dominance.[15] This distinction does much to explain the transition from the inflationary economy of the "lost decade" to the economic environment of relative price stability in the wake of the 1985 stabilization. In part II, we dealt with these concepts to explain the inflationary period. Here we return to this analytical framework (at the cost of some repetition) to study the convergence to price stability.

Fiscal dominance (FD) is defined broadly as a regime in which fiscal policy is set exogenously and monetary policy ensures the solvency of general government in the sense that general government's current stock of financial assets (bonds plus money) is equal to the present value of primary fiscal surpluses (plus the inflation tax). FD proposes to attain its goals by changes in the current price level (the Pigou effect) and by the inflation tax. Monetary dominance (MD) is just the opposite. It assumes that monetary targets such as price stability are set exogenously and that it is the role of fiscal policy to ensure the solvency of general government, for example, by adjusting the path of the primary deficits.

Thus, MD is a regime that pursues a nominal target of price stability and is backed by a fiscal policy that takes care of balancing the general-government accounts. According to this definition, fiscal authorities should cooperate with the monetary authority in the process that eventually attains the goal of price stability. Under an FD regime, such as that adopted in the inflationary era, there are fiscal targets (general-government expenditure, deficits) but no nominal target, leaving the balancing of the general-government accounts to monetary policy.

To express these ideas with greater precision in the context of a perfect foresight model, the intertemporal budget equation of the public sector, imposing the non-Ponzi game condition, may be specified as follows:[16]

$$M_0/(P_0Q_0) = PV(T-G) + PV(im)-b_0$$

where $M_0/(P_0Q_0)$ denotes the initial value of real money balances (M, P, and Q stand for nominal base money, the price level, and real output, respectively), PV stands for present value, (T–G) denotes primary surpluses (taxes minus noninterest expenditure), im is the inflation tax (m denoting real balances and i the nominal interest rate), and b_0 denotes the initial value of the stock of indexed bonds (all expressed in ratios of GDP). Under fiscal dominance, the inflation tax, PV(im), is used as a source of finance for the fiscal deficit, while under MD the inflation tax reflects the monetary authorities' nominal target (which usually entails a fiscal cost relative to FD). Most importantly, under fiscal dominance, a disturbance to this equation should be offset by the Pigou effect (a change in P_0) and the inflation tax PV(im), while under monetary dominance the equilibrium is restored by PV(T–G).[17]

Two examples will help to clarify the implications of the foregoing statement. Suppose that G (government expenditure) increases, meaning that the right-hand side of the above equation decreases. Under an FD regime, the balance is restored by the Pigou effect and the inflation tax, while in MD the balance is restored by an increase in taxes (T). In another example, consider a worsening of the current account (a negative external shock). Assume also that the shock is internalized by general government, which takes responsibility for the external debt of the private sector. In such a case, this may be considered an increase in b_0. Under FD, this will be balanced by the Pigou effect and the inflation tax, while under MD the balance will be restored by an increase in the primary surpluses, with no need for any adjustment of prices.

The Israeli experience does not quite fit the foregoing classification. In the inflation era, the increase in the national debt was too large to be offset by the Pigou effect or by the inflation tax. Thus, the fiscal authorities had to reduce the primary deficits in order to prevent general-government insolvency. This tended to stabilize the level of the *operational* deficit (the primary deficit plus real interest payments on the national debt) during the inflationary period. A constant operational deficit may support the solvency of the national debt if this deficit, and seigniorage, remain constant indefinitely despite increasing debt. We may state equivalently that the solvency of the national debt depends on the permanence of the observed negative relationship between the primary deficit (minus seigniorage) and debt (see appendix G). However, in practice we observe only a limited number of years, and we have to base our considerations of solvency on the observed period only. In part II, we referred to this kind of conditional solvency as "statistical solvency" (based on the observed period only), which may differ from *true* solvency (based on an infinite horizon) if the public does not believe in the permanence of the observed relationship. In this case, the capital market may place a ceiling (b') on the warranted level of the national debt, just as a commercial bank may ration credit to a customer who keeps asking for more. Any level of debt in excess of this ceiling (b') is regarded as unsustainable in the long term. We may think of a sustainable path of b(t) as one that converges toward a steady-state value of b, say b*, which does not exceed b'. (This is shown formally in appendix G.)

While the theoretical models were based on the concept of general-government *solvency*—referring to the transversality condition on the discounted debt[18]—the Maastricht criterion was expressed in terms of an absolute level of national debt relative to GDP, that is, in terms of *sustainability*. The constancy of the operational deficit may ensure the statistical solvency of the national debt but does not ensure sustainability. This is especially the case when the operational deficit is so large as to raise doubts about whether it can be maintained in the future. This is precisely what happened in the inflationary era in Israel, where the large operational deficit raised the national debt to unsustainable levels—more than 160% of GDP in 1984, exceeding the Maastricht criterion by more than 100 percentage points.

The operational deficit, which was held approximately constant during the "lost decade," led to a path of debt that could potentially be stabilized at three or four times the annual GDP (Liviatan, 2003). However, this possibility, although "statistically solvent," was construed by the capital market as unsustainable. Absent a strong commitment to a nominal anchor, an unsustainable path of the national debt implies a financial crisis down the road, involving a jump in inflation. This is why a sustainable path of the national debt is essential for the success of any disinflation program.

Note also that during the inflation period the government reacted to BOP stresses by administering price shocks, that is, by using the Pigou effect as an equilibrating mechanism—a feature of FD.[19] In Patinkin (1966), the use of the Pigou effect did not endanger the monetary system because the model was based on belief in a basically noninflationary environment, in which a jump in the current price level would not generate a rise in future inflation. However, since the regime during the lost decade operated without a nominal target, the price shocks were readily transformed into inflation shocks.

This practice was discontinued after the 1985 stabilization, as reflected in the rejection of a unit root in the inflation series. We performed an ADF test on the quarterly inflation series from Q1-1986 to Q4-2001 and obtained an ADF statistic of −10.42, while the rejection of the hypothesis of a unit root in the inflation series at the 1% level was −4.11.[20] This clearly refutes the hypothesis that the poststabilization inflation level was a random walk after allowing for a *negative* linear trend, which confirms our view of the poststabilization era.

In the post-1985 period, the introduction of the inflation-target regime and the Finance Ministry's recognition of its role in securing not only statistical solvency but also sustainability—in the sense of taking into consideration the absolute level of the national debt as a percent of GDP—shifted the economic regime toward monetary dominance. The empirical evidence in support of this observation is based on the fact that the authorities maintained relatively low operational deficits in order to prevent an increase in the national debt and maintained *positive* primary surpluses, as are required for general-government solvency.[21] Additionally, as noted above, the government avoided the use of price shocks in dealing with balance-of-payments stresses. Where such stresses were unavoidable, as in the case of the speculative attacks on the currency in October 1998, the policy was to adhere to the preannounced path of inflation targets. To this end, the BOI raised the short-term interest rate whenever actual inflation exceeded the target rate in a threatening manner. Although this policy obviously carried the risk of creating short-term unemployment,[22] it was instrumental in bolstering the credibility of the nominal anchor. The size of the positive fiscal impulses (according to the IMF definition), which became more conservative during the second half of the 1990s, gives further evidence of the fiscal authorities' internalization of their role in supporting the price-stability strategy. The *nominal* wage decrease during the 2003 recession also points in this direction, underscoring the fact that the economic regime had shifted to monetary dominance.

The emphasis on sustainability and the absolute level of the national debt (as a percentage of GDP) established a relationship among the inflation target, the warranted level of the national debt, and the operational deficit, as in the set of Maastricht criteria.[23] In particular, setting a low inflation target requires a low operational deficit. This explains the effort—not always successful in specific years—to keep the operational deficit small. A precise relationship among the inflation target, the warranted debt as dictated by the capital market, and the operational deficit is derived in appendix G. The conclusion is that the operational deficit should not exceed seigniorage, which depends on the inflation target, plus the growth of debt occasioned by economic growth. The two legislative acts, deficit reduction and "no printing," may attain any inflation target that is consistent with the above relationship.

International developments in the 1990s with respect to inflation had an important influence on the shift toward monetary dominance in Israel. The unmistakable trend toward greater central-bank independence and the adoption of the inflation-target regime were major factors in the entrenchment of MD in Israel. On the fiscal front, the acceptance of the Maastricht principles in regard to fiscal deficits and the national debt was instrumental in shaping Israel's fiscal policies during that time. The BOI indirectly supported the restrictive fiscal stance by moving ahead consistently with the forex-market liberalization, thereby imposing fiscal discipline by means of the capital flows and the assessments of international rating companies, which became increasingly important to Israeli policymakers as the globalization era progressed.

17

The International Perspective

INFLATION, DISINFLATION, AND GROWTH

Israel's disinflation is part of a global trend of reducing inflation after the inflationary acceleration occasioned by the energy shocks of the 1970s.[1] In Latin America and the former Soviet Union, disinflation played a role in a much more significant economic transformation. In southern Europe, it was part of the adjustments required for joining the European Monetary Union. That Israel would join this worldwide trend was inevitable.

Inflation and disinflation processes around the world are usually considered in the context of growth performance, since poor performance on growth may provide an incentive to disinflate in the expectation that this action will be rewarded with faster growth. Since we know that growth patterns differ widely among countries—there is no general tendency for convergence of per capita GDP[2]—we compared Israel with various groups of countries that are of special interest. They include the G7 countries and those of the European Union (representing the winning OECD model), southern European countries that joined the EMU and resemble Israel in their stage of economic development, the former chronic-inflation countries of Latin America, Asian Tiger countries that have exhibited continuously strong growth performance, and the Australia–New Zealand duo, representing Western-style economies that are relatively isolated from the big economic blocs of the United States and the European Union.

Our computations compare per capita GDP growth rates,[3] per-capita GDP levels relative to the United States, and (median) inflation rates in terms of simple averages of country groups in various recent periods since 1960 (table 17.1).

Table 17.1. Inflation and Growth

A. Consumer Median Price Inflation (% annual, simple country average)

	1960–73	1974–85	1986–95	1996–02
(A) Seven major OECD countries	3.95	9.16	3.20	1.67
(B) European Union	4.52	11.46	4.48	2.10
Euro zone	4.35	11.68	4.69	2.16
(C) Southern Europe	4.81	18.35	8.72	3.00
(D) Australia & New Zealand	3.47	12.34	5.28	2.46
(E) Latin America	19.35	73.56	159.24	7.47
(F) Asia	2.56	8.47	4.96	2.44
(G) Israel	6.69	97.56	16.72	5.44

Source: IFS.

B. Per Capita GDP Growth (% annual, simple country average)

	1960–73	1973–85	1985–99	2000–03
(A) Seven major OECD countries	4.5	2.0	2.0	1.4
(B) European Union	4.5	1.6	2.6	1.8
Euro zone	4.9	1.6	2.8	1.9
(C) Southern Europe	6.5	1.2	2.5	2.0
(D) Australia & New Zealand	2.6	0.8	1.6	2.2
(E) Latin America	2.7	0.6	1.8	−0.2
(F) Asia	6.3	4.4	4.5	2.2
(G) Israel	5.1	1.0	2.3	−1.0

Source: Penn World Tables Mark 6.1.

C. GDP Per Capita, Relative to the United States ([U.S. = 100], simple country average)

	1960–73	1974–85	1986–99	2000–03
(A) Six major OECD countries	70.0	75.0	74.7	71.1
(B) European Union	66.5	69.0	69.8	71.8
Euro area	61.9	66.5	68.4	71.3
(C) Southern Europe	48.3	55.0	53.9	54.1
(D) Australia & New Zealand	86.8	76.5	69.3	68.6
(E) Latin America	32.0	29.8	25.3	23.4
(F) Asia	21.4	28.7	37.3	50.6
(G) Israel	51.0	54.3	53.5	48.7

Source: Penn World Tables Mark 6.1.
Definition of country groups: Southern Europe—Greece, Italy, Portugal, and Spain; Latin America—Argentina, Brazil, Chile, Colombia, Mexico, Peru, and Uruguay; Asia—Korea, Malaysia, Philippines, Singapore, Taiwan, and Hong Kong.

Although Israel joined Latin America in the club of chronic-inflation countries during its inflationary period (1974–85), its income level surpassed the Latin American standard by far. In all these chronic-inflation countries, growth performance was weakened considerably during the lost decade—in absolute terms, in comparison with the past, and relative to the industrial countries— and inflation accelerated powerfully. This certainly gave these countries good reason to adopt an economic model of the OECD type. The results for the post-1985 period show that the change resulted in an impressive reduction in inflation toward the end of the century in what had become the former chronic-inflation countries. As for growth, 1986–99 income-level data pointed to improved growth performance in Israel (growth rates comparable to those in the OECD countries but less than those in the Asian Tigers) and also, although to a much smaller extent, in the Latin American members of the group. Developments during the first three years of the new millennium show that all these countries (including Israel) adapted poorly to the shocks that were the hallmarks of these years.

Another comparison of interest for Israel is with the group of southern European countries that enjoyed cooperation with and support of the major bloc, the European Union, of which they were part. The results for 1986–99 show that Israel grew during these years at a rate comparable to that of southern Europe, although Israel failed to cope well with the shocks of the new century. It is also noteworthy in this context that Israel has had a specific shock to cope with in recent years, that of the intifada that broke out in October 2000. It is difficult to say how things would have looked had Israel faced a more tranquil environment.

To investigate Israel's path to price stability further, we compared the development of per capita GDP in Israel with the average in southern Europe and the European Union.[4] Israel's relative position, it turns out, began to deteriorate in 1996, before the Intifada began (figure 17.1) and corresponding to the

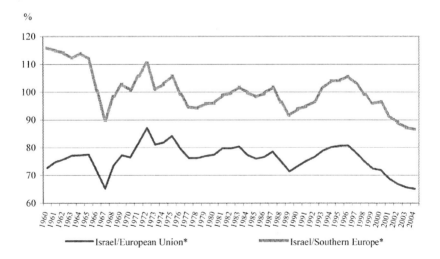

Figure 17.1. Relative Per Capita GDP

time when Israel introduced tight fiscal and monetary policies to deal with its balance-of-payments and inflation problems. It seems, then, that the economic recession that has been dampening economic growth in Israel in the past seven years is somewhat attributable to domestic policies related to the pace of the macroeconomic adjustment. This makes it even harder to determine the extent to which Israel's economic performance improved in the long run after the 1985 stabilization. In the absence of stronger evidence, it seems reasonable to take the average growth performance in 1986–99 as an indication of the impact of the changes that took place after the 1985 stabilization. The resumption of growth in 2004 and indications of its continuance in 2005 lend some support to this view. Thus, from a long-term perspective, the recession in 2001–3 may be offset by a boom in years to come.

The pros and cons of adopting the OECD model cannot be judged solely on the basis of the observed growth performance. A fundamental reason for embracing the new regime was the danger of being out of line with financial developments in the industrial countries in the globalization era.

Whatever the reason, the elimination of inflation in the world was part of the changeover to the new economic regime, which lent credibility to the disinflation process and reduced its costs. As a result, the transition to low inflation in the 1990s was made rather swiftly. Argentina and Brazil reached single-digit levels in the course of three years after stabilizations in the 1990s. In Peru, the process was longer at about six years. The disinflation process in Mexico progressed to single digits after six years but was interrupted by the 1994 currency crisis. The fact that Mexico's inflation has now settled into the single digit range proves that the disinflation process, unlike the experience in Latin America in previous decades, is irreversible.

COMPARISON WITH DISINFLATION PROCESSES IN INDUSTRIAL ECONOMIES

Since 1992, when the Israeli inflation plateau fell to 10%–12%, the reference point on inflation has shifted increasingly to the performance of Europe and the United States. In the second half of the 1990s, the standard for price-stability performance was expressed more often in terms of the Maastricht convergence criteria as a guide to what a normal monetary regime should look like. This was underscored recently when two prime ministers, Ehud Barak of the previous (Labor-led) government and Ariel Sharon of the incumbent (Likud-led) one, endorsed the Maastricht criteria as the guidelines for monetary and fiscal policy. This means that Israel has accepted, in principle, the OECD model of the macroeconomic policy framework. Now that this is the standard, it seems quite reasonable to compare the OECD's disinflation process with Israel's.

To perform the comparison, the seventeen OECD countries for which data on all relevant variables for the entire period are available were sorted into four groups: southern Europe (Portugal, Spain, Italy, and Greece), northern Europe (Norway, Sweden, Finland, and Denmark), other Europe (Germany, France, Austria, Belgium, and the Netherlands), and the rest, marked as "Non-Europe" (the United Kingdom, Japan, the United States, and Canada). More detailed data than those in table 17.2 show that, generally speaking, the disinflation process in the OECD started around 1980 and seems to have been completed by 1995–97, when inflation fell to low single digits. Thus, the process lasted fifteen to seventeen years. The Israeli experience was much the same in this respect, as the disinflation process starting from the moderate inflation level established in 1986 seems to have been completed by 2000–2001.

Table 17.2 shows the behavior of the real interest rates of OECD central banks during the disinflation process. It is evident that as inflation declined throughout the period starting around 1980, the real interest rate first increased and then decreased during the 1990s (figure 17.2). Since 1986, inflation in Israel has followed quite closely the path of inflation in southern Europe at a lag of about five years. The real key rate on BOI funds did not become positive until 1995–99, but then it reached an average of 5.7%, resembling the rate in southern Europe in 1990–94.

In all cases, the initial stage of disinflation was associated with an increase in *nominal* key rates, which were reduced in subsequent years (table 17.2). Data for individual years (1995–97) show that this was also the case in Israel.

An important and invariable feature of the disinflation process in the OECD countries was an increase in unemployment rates. We observe the same in Israel if we compare the 1975–84 decade with the post-1985 stabilization. The troubling thing about this phenomenon is the hysteresis of unemployment, that is, its failure to retreat after the completion of the disinflation process.

Although the downturn of the real interest rate toward the completion of the disinflation process may be predicted by the monetary model alone (as in Liviatan, 1980), actual disinflation in the OECD was associated with a distinct *fiscal* effort in the second half of the 1990s (table 17.2). This policy, which in the OECD may have helped to consolidate low inflation by establishing credibility in the permanence of the reduction in monetary growth, has not been implemented in Israel. This may indicate some imbalance in the Israeli process.

THE OECD DISINFLATION PATTERN AND ITS IMPLICATIONS FOR ISRAEL

The crucial point is to visualize the *pattern* of disinflation in the OECD countries, as illuminated by the foregoing data, and to consider its possible implications for the disinflation process in Israel. The first stage included the most important feature of monetary policy in the OECD disinflation process: the raising of real interest rates, usually from negative to positive levels. This stage involved an increase in unemployment and, sometimes, real appreciation of the currency. Once inflation was brought down, the fiscal adjustment went into action, mainly in the form of a cutback in public expenditure. In the final stage of the process, the ratios of fiscal deficit and national debt to GDP are lowered, as are the inflation rate and the real rate of interest of the central bank. It is believed that Israel has entered this final stage with its recent efforts to put its fiscal house in order. Time will tell.

Table 17.2. Economic Indicators, OECD Groups and Israel[1]

	Southern Europe	Northern Europe	Other Europe	Non-Europe	Israel
Inflation[2] (% annual)					
1975–79	17.90	9.75	6.60	9.74	52.72
1980–84	18.01	9.58	6.52	6.71	200.30
1985–89	10.49	5.24	1.94	3.66	18.22
1990–94	8.60	3.18	2.89	3.04	14.14
1995–99	3.44	1.61	1.54	1.77	7.13
Nominal interest rate[3] (% annual)					
1975–79	11.15	7.93	6.45	8.88	
1980–84[4]	18.41	9.42	7.76	9.45	
1985–89	15.24	9.07	6.16	6.67	17.17
1990–94	14.21	8.14	6.71	5.09	12.61
1995–99	8.54	4.51	2.67	3.40	13.19
Real interest rate[5] (% annual)					
1975–79	−5.61	−1.60	−0.11	−0.70	
1980–84[4]	0.49	−0.10	1.19	2.94	
1985–89	4.41	3.63	4.17	3.50	−1.12
1990–94	5.24	4.84	3.60	2.39	−1.30
1995–99	3.96	3.17	1.21	1.93	5.73
Real effective exchange rate[6]					
1980–84	93.61	102.90	93.07	107.29	98.30
1985–89	96.72	105.17	92.42	107.29	97.69
1990–94	105.15	103.87	94.45	104.75	99.74
1995–99	102.82	98.49	95.69	103.42	106.96
Primary deficit of general government[7] (% of GDP)					
1980–84[4]	3.24	0.29	1.52	1.26	7.04
1985–89	1.54	−2.82	−0.47	−0.47	−5.48
1990–94	−0.89	3.38	−0.22	2.13	−0.36
1995–99	−3.22	−3.97	−2.59	−1.66	0.82
Unemployment rate[8]					
1975–79	4.93	3.52	4.99	5.26	3.42
1980–84	9.90	4.61	8.15	7.47	5.06
1985–89	12.98	4.01	8.39	6.92	7.04
1990–94	12.33	8.03	7.42	6.94	9.84
1995–99	12.15	8.09	8.51	6.08	7.74

[1]Definition of country groups: Southern Europe—Greece, Italy, Portugal, and Spain; Northen Europe—Norway, Sweden, Finland, and Denmark; Other Europe—Austria, Belgium, Germany, France, and the Netherlands; Non-Europe—UK, Japan, Canada, and United States.
[2]The inflation rate is calculated as CPI change during the year.
[3]Nominal interest rate for Israel–the average cost of montary loan, for other countries–the discount rate, central banks' interest rates (line 60 in IFS).
[4]The average for Israel in 1985–89 is 1988–89.
[5]Real interest rate–the calculation is ex-post, during the year.
[6]*Source:* IFS, line 99.
[7]Source for Israel: Bank of Israel *Annual Report,* for other countries: OECD *Outlook.*
[8]Source for Israel: Bank of Israel *Annual Report,* for other countries: IFS, line r67.

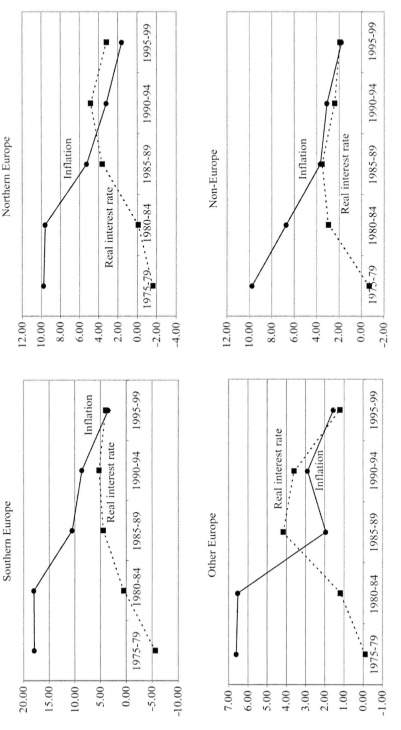

Figure 17.2. Inflation and Real Interest Rate (% annual).

An interesting issue related to the process of returning to price stability in the world was the choice of a regime of monetary and fiscal rules instead of some version of the gold standard. Several reasons for this may be offered. First, the collapse of the Bretton Woods system, a surrogate for a gold standard, undermined the credibility of a fixed exchange-rate regime. Second, it has been proved empirically that a rules regime can deliver price stability with no need for linkage to some metal or foreign currency.[5] Moreover, a rules regime is more efficient than a fixed exchange-rate regime because it allows monetary policy to adjust itself to the state of the business cycle within the framework of the Taylor Rule. Third, many small economies in the EMU effectively operate under a fixed exchange-rate regime as part of the EMU and the euro system. Last but not least, a fixed exchange-rate regime without a lender of last resort in "dollars" is vulnerable to speculative attacks.

The aforementioned pattern of OECD disinflation calls for some comments. The cycle in real interest rates, including the upward bulge in the medium term, may be explained in various ways. In chapter 16, we offered several explanations, all of which involve credibility considerations. All the aforementioned models treat money as endogenous and the key interest rate as the policy instrument. Thus, the nominal interest rate rises in order to raise the real rate.

Taking a more traditional course, one may assume that the central bank engineers a monetary crunch in the disinflation process, meaning that money is not fully endogenous. In addition, we have the usual assumption of sticky domestic prices. This approach is traditional in the sense that it proceeds from money to interest rates and not the other way around, as is common in contemporary models. If in the course of disinflation the central bank restricts the expansion of the money supply, then the real interest will rise (see appendix H).

DORNBUSCH'S OVERSHOOTING MODEL AND THE ISRAELI EXPERIENCE

The monetary-crunch mechanism may be generalized to an open economy along the lines of Dornbusch's (1976) "overshooting hypothesis" (appendix H). When the rate of monetary growth is reduced in the context of a money-based disinflation, the nominal ER reacts more strongly than the domestic price level, which is usually stickier (Liviatan, 1980). On impact, this causes real appreciation and expectations of real depreciation, which in turn induces (under rational expectations) an increase in the real interest rate. These developments are associated with economic recession. The theoretical model predicts that the real ER will depreciate before the disinflation process is completed, thereby offsetting the initial appreciation.

How does this model square with the Israeli disinflation experience? In Israel, real appreciation occurred in the second half of the 1990s, corresponding to the hike in the real key rate (table 17.3). This is in line with the overshooting model. Other things being equal, we may now expect a process of real depreciation. Some evidence to this effect is presented in figure 10.1.

Tables 17.3 and 17.4 allow us to examine macro developments at the beginning of the tight-money phase (1995–97) and the consolidation of low inflation

Table 17.3. Monetary Contraction in Disinflation

| | Pct. Change (annual) | | | | | Unemployment Rate (%) | MAKAM[2] | Inflation Exp.[3] | Real Interest Rate of MAKAM[4] | |
	MB (1)	M₁ (2)	CPI[1] (3)	Exchange Rate (basket)[1] (4)	Nom. GDP (5)	(6)	(7)	(8)	Ex-ante (9)	Ex-post (10)
1991	19.77	28.72	18.98	12.45	28.23	10.60	14.90	15.71	−0.81	−4.08
1992	12.95	22.40	12.15	10.55	20.57	11.20	12.22	9.63	2.59	0.07
1993	30.58	23.63	10.94	11.86	15.67	10.00	11.68	9.05	2.63	0.75
1994	25.16	19.73	12.30	7.78	21.45	7.80	13.20	12.88	0.32	0.90
1995	−1.15	4.08	10.12	4.69	16.64	6.80	16.12	10.06	6.06	6.00
1996	21.75	16.13	11.27	3.34	16.97	6.60	15.99	11.24	4.75	4.72
1997	17.60	13.27	9.02	4.51	13.05	7.50	14.08	9.18	4.90	5.05
1998	24.90	11.96	5.43	9.39	10.51	8.60	12.29	6.15	6.14	6.86
1999	14.03	9.56	5.25	8.74	9.08	8.90	12.39	5.30	7.10	7.14
2000	12.86	11.04	1.13	−5.18	9.49	8.80	9.32	2.63	6.69	8.18
2001	16.45	14.08	1.11	1.97	1.50	9.30	6.80	1.90	4.90	5.68
2002	12.63	16.00	5.68	14.14	3.33	10.30	7.26	3.29	3.98	1.59
2003	3.16	0.61	0.73	0.74	1.68	10.70	7.13	2.13	5.00	6.41
2004	8.14	17.94	−0.40	2.90	4.99	10.40	4.38	1.74	2.64	4.78
Average										
1991–94	22.11	23.62	13.68	10.66	21.48	9.90	13.00	11.50	1.18	−0.59
1995–97	12.73	11.16	10.14	4.18	15.55	6.97	15.39	10.16	5.23	5.26
1998–2004	13.17	11.60	2.70	4.67	5.80	9.57	8.51	3.31	5.21	5.81

All changes and interest rates are % annual.

[1] Past twelve months.

[2] Nominal yield on short-term Treasury bills (% annual).

[3] Inflation expectations to 12 months ahead (capital-market data).

[4] Nominal interest rates deflated (a) by inflation expectations to one year ahead (ex-ante) and (b) by inflation in past 12 months (ex-post). Real rates are calculated as $((1+i)/(1+\pi) - 1)$, where π is inflation and i is the nominal interest rate. Columns (1)–(4) were computed as average of quarterly data that measure the change in the past twelve months.

Table 17.4. Supplemental Data for Table 17.3

	π − π^e1 (1)	π^e − π^T2 (2)	Pct. Change (annual) M2 (3)	Pct. Change (annual) Real GDP (4)	Ratios to GDP (%) MB/Y (5)	Ratios to GDP (%) M1/Y (6)	Ratios to GDP (%) M2/Y (7)	RER (1990 = 100)^3 EXP.P/GDP_def_israel (8)
1991	3.27		33.44	6.09	3.54	5.22	16.49	0.93
1992	2.52	−4.87	18.60	7.15	3.32	5.31	16.23	0.89
1993	1.89	−0.95	30.17	3.77	3.76	5.67	18.33	0.89
1994	−0.58	4.88	53.39	7.01	3.84	5.55	23.04	0.83
1995	0.06	−0.44	31.21	6.59	3.26	4.95	25.91	0.79
1996	0.03	2.24	27.11	5.22	3.39	4.90	28.14	0.76
1997	−0.16	0.68	26.45	3.49	3.52	4.91	31.44	0.74
1998	−0.73	−2.35	19.36	3.74	3.98	4.98	33.95	0.73
1999	−0.04	1.30	21.75	2.47	4.16	5.00	37.90	0.77
2000	−1.50	−0.87	20.08	8.02	4.29	5.07	41.55	0.74
2001	−0.78	−1.10	17.29	−0.90	4.92	5.70	47.99	0.73
2002	2.39	0.79	2.33	−0.73	5.35	6.38	47.48	0.78
2003	−1.40	0.13	1.67	1.29	5.43	6.30	47.48	0.77
2004	−2.14	−0.26	4.01	4.28	5.59	7.07	47.03	
Avg. 1991–2003	0.50	−0.10	23.297	4.094	4.059	5.379	31.994	0.80
SD	1.990	2.279	13.343	2.944	0.747	0.510	11.809	0.07
Avg. 1991–94	2.182	−0.906	33.899	6.008	3.616	5.439	18.523	0.88
SD	1.724	3.792	14.471	1.563	0.235	0.210	3.151	0.04
Avg. 1995–97	−0.021	1.161	28.258	5.099	3.390	4.920	28.496	0.76
SD	0.979	1.036	2.577	1.552	0.132	0.023	2.785	0.03
Avg. 1998–2004	−0.360	−0.330	12.356	2.316	4.690	5.570	42.724	0.75
SD	1.880	1.460	9.180	3.122	0.668	0.823	5.635	0.02

[1] π − π^e is the difference between inflation in the past 12 months and inflation expectations to 12 months ahead.

[2] π^e − π^T is the difference between inflation expectations and the inflation target. Avg. and SD in (1) and (2) are from quarterly data. The others are from annual data. The Avg. and SD in (1) and (2) are from quarterly data. The others are from annual data. The Avg. and SD refer to mean and SD to individual observation, not to means.

[3] Real exchange rate (RER)—ratio of export prices to GDP deflator (index). Columns (1)–(3) were computed as averages of quarterly data.

in later years (1998–2004). During the first period, the rate of growth of the money supply, in terms of M_1 and the monetary base, fell dramatically as compared with 1991–94 and as compared with inflation, which declined moderately. The rate of growth of these monetary aggregates in the first period also dropped below the rate of growth of nominal GDP, as reflected in decreases in the ratios of the monetary base and M_1 to GDP. All of this points to a monetary crunch during the initial phase of the disinflation process, precipitating an increase in the real interest rate. Concurrently, the pace of depreciation fell behind the rates of money supply–growth and inflation, a development consistent with "overshooting." The rate of real GDP growth also slipped. The only variable that seems inconsistent with the model is unemployment, which decreased in these years. Notably, however, 1991–94 was the period of mass immigration from the former Soviet Union, and it took some time for the labor market to absorb the immigrants. Thus, the Israeli experience with disinflation seems consistent with some features of the overshooting model.

During the 1998–2004 period, a time of external and internal shocks, inflation plunged again to a mere 2.7% (on annual average) and inflation expectations declined to a somewhat lesser extent. Currency depreciation accelerated during this period, in response to the financial shocks of October 1998 and December 2001. Although the average real interest rate remained high, it declined in 2001–4 and, particularly, in 2004, as the model predicts. Thus, Israel's real interest rate followed the inverted-U path that was characteristic of the OECD. An indication that the monetary crunch continued in the second period was the tremendous increase in the M_2/GDP ratio during that period, which may be related to the persistence of the high interest rates. However, M_2 growth slowed considerably in the last two years, in tandem with the reduction of interest rates. These developments indicate that the phase of monetary crunch and high real interest rates is coming to an end.

Generally speaking, Israel's disinflation experience has followed the OECD pattern with the exception of one important aspect: fiscal consolidation, which the OECD countries performed in the final stages of disinflation and that has been absent in Israel until recently. Nevertheless, the policies pursued by the Ministry of Finance starting in mid 2003, suggest that the government has been making a serious effort to implement the kind of fiscal consolidation that the major OECD countries invoked in the second half of the 1990s.

Appendix A: Devaluation in the Framework of a Non-Cooperative Game

Consider the following objective function of the policymaker (Cukierman and Liviatan, 1990):

$$V = -[(1/2)B^2 + (a/2)\pi^2] \qquad (A1)$$

where B is the trade balance and π is devaluation (and inflation), so that

$$\pi = (e/e_{-1}) - 1 \qquad (A2)$$

where e denotes the nominal ER and e_{-1} is e in the previous period. B depends negatively on the real wage $w = (W/e)$, where W is the nominal wage rate, because an increase in w reduces the supply of output (Y) through the relation $Y = d_0 - dw$ where the parameter d is positive $(d > 0)$.

Consider a one-period game in which the trade unions set W initially and the government sets e (and hence π) later. In equilibrium, expected π must equal actual π. In this discretionary game, the government sets e in view of a given W so as to maximize V in (A1). This is denoted by e(W). The trade unions set W on the basis of expected e, which equals e(W), so as to obtain their optimal real wage (denoted w^*). By implication,

$$W = w^*e(W) \qquad (A3)$$

from which we obtain the equilibrium W.

In equilibrium (in which actual π equals expected π), inflation is determined by

$$\pi(1 + \pi) = (1/a)d(1 - C)w^*(-B),   \tag{A4}$$

where C is the marginal propensity to consume. B is defined as $B = Y - C(Y - T) - C_0 - G$, where T and G are the parameters that represent taxes and government expenditure. C_0 is a constant.

It follows from (A4) that in equilibrium the rate of inflation, π, is a positive function of the trade deficit $(-B)$ and of $1/a$, which indicates the relative preference for a balanced external position. An increase in any of these factors will increase the rate of devaluation and inflation in equilibrium. The same argument applies to the attempt to orchestrate a real depreciation of the exchange rate above its market equilibrium level (which may be related to an increase in $1/a$).

Notably, in this model the increase in $(1/a)$ will not result in the actual improvement of the BOP. It will lead only to an increase in inflation. (This is the analogue of the inability to affect the natural rate of unemployment by surprise inflation in equilibrium of the Barro-Gordon model.) In this case, it is obvious that a "package deal"—a cooperative solution—may arrest the wage-price spiral. Notably, however, in an extended model where labor (and not only the government) is averse to a rise in inflation,[1] we may obtain that the increased preference for the BOP position will lead not only to an increase in inflation but also to an erosion of the real wage.

Appendix B: The Futile Effort to Maintain the Inflation Plateau

Here we show that when a discretionary policymaker tries to preserve a given inflation plateau *irrespective of the absolute level of inflation*, he/she will fail in a policy game equilibrium.

Consider the following objective function:

$$V = -(a/2)(\pi - \pi_{-1})^2 + b(\pi - \pi^e), \quad a, b > 0 \qquad (B1)$$

where π^e denotes expected inflation (π). Here the policymaker is averse to a *change* in inflation ($\pi - \pi_{-1}$) irrespective of the inflation level but may benefit from surprise inflation ($\pi - \pi^e$). In a discretionary regime, we first maximize V w.r.t. π, holding π_{-1} and π^e constant and then equating the latter with π. This yields ($\pi - \pi_{-1}$) = b/a, which means that inflation will accelerate at a constant rate in equilibrium despite the policymaker's wish to prevent this.

This model entails a unit root because ($\pi - \pi_{-1}$) is constant (possibly with a random element). Furthermore, since b/a is positive, this implies a random walk with a positive drift. The term may increase over time as the indexation mechanism moves closer to perfection. Indexation may reduce b, the effectiveness of surprise inflation, but may also make the policymaker more immune to changes in inflation, which means a reduction in a.

We tested this hypothesis for quarterly inflation in Q1-1974–Q2-1985 using the standard Augmented Dickey-Fuller (ADF) test with the aid of the Eviews software, allowing Eviews to determine the number of lags automatically.[1] We assumed that the drift increases over time (an exogenous constant and a linear trend in the test equation), leading to four lags of ($\pi - \pi_{-1}$) and an adjusted R^2 of 0.52 in the test equation. In this case, the ADF test statistic obtained (-3.68)

still exceeds the critical 1% value (-4.17) for the rejection of a unit root in the inflation series, that is, the possibility of a unit in the inflation series is not rejected at the 1% critical level, but it is rejected at the 5% level. So the results are not clear-cut. The linear (positive) trend appeared to be significant but the constant (still positive) was not.[2] The hypothesis that the *change* in inflation ($\pi - \pi_{-1}$), has a unit root was rejected at the 1% level.

On the basis of this experiment, it seems that we cannot rule out the hypothesis that the quarterly ($\pi - \pi_{-1}$) series was stationary during the inflationary period, with a positive drift that rose over time. Note that the existence of a unit root and a positive linear trend in the test regression (with ($\pi - \pi_{-1}$) as dependent variable) implies a *quadratic* trend in the inflation (π) series, meaning that inflation quickly escalated toward hyperinflation.

The above behavior applies to the inflation era. In contrast, the hypothesis that π has a unit root was rejected at the 1% level for quarterly inflation in the post-stabilization era (Q1-1986–Q4-2001). This contrast may also be explained by the foregoing model. Thus, if we add to (B1) a term $c\pi^2$ ($c > 0$) to reflect the policymaker's concern with the *level* of inflation (and not only with its rate of change) while keeping b/a constant,[3] we will obtain in equilibrium a stationary series for inflation. This is the statistical characterization of the difference between the two regimes.

Appendix C: The Possibility of Being on the Inefficient Segment of the Laffer Curve

Consider the following model of public finance (Cukierman and Liviatan, 1990). Seigniorage R is given by

$$R = DM/P = (DM/M)(M/P) = \mu L(\pi^e), \quad \mu = DM/M \qquad (C1)$$

where D is the time derivative operator. In a steady state, $\mu = \pi^e = \pi$. In the short run, we assume only $\mu = \pi$. We define the policymaker's objective function as:

$$F = \delta R - \varphi(\pi^e, \pi) = \delta\pi \, L(\pi^e) - \varphi(\pi^e, \pi), \quad \delta > 0 \qquad (C2)$$

where $L(\pi^e)$ is the demand function for real base money and φ represents the loss from π^e and π. We assume that φ is separable and that the first- and second-order partial derivatives of φ are positive (as in Barro and Gordon, 1983).

Suppose that π^e is set at the beginning of the period (reflecting wage contracts) before π is known. To obtain the discretionary equilibrium, we first differentiate F w.r.t. π, treating π^e as given and then equate the two. In the first stage, we obtain the first-order condition:

$$\delta L(\pi^e) - \varphi_\pi(\pi^e, \pi) = 0 \qquad (C3)$$

and then set $\pi^e = \pi$. It is easy to see that an increase in δ will increase π in equilibrium. Hence, for a large enough value of δ we may reduce L to the range of larger-than-unitary elasticities of L w.r.t. π^e, that is, to the downward-sloping segment of the Laffer curve. If the latter curve does not have a downward-sloping segment because the demand curve has unitary elasticity for high inflation rates, then inflation can rise on the flat segment of the Laffer curve without any increase in seigniorage. It may be verified that this cannot happen in a "rules regime" where we assume that $\pi^e = \pi$ at the optimization stage.

Appendix D: Interest on Reserves and Core Inflation

In inflationary economies, it was common practice for the central bank to pay interest on commercial banks' reserve requirements. This was in fact one of the main forms of monetary accommodation that can be used to illustrate two features of chronic inflation, the implications of monetary accommodation and the concept of core inflation.

We explore these issues within the framework of a one-period loss function under stationary conditions. The net inflation tax (NIT) is given by $[(\pi - R)h]$, where π denotes actual inflation and we assume (without loss of generality) that R is the interest rate paid directly on monetary base h, which is assumed to be identical with means of payment (money).[1] We assume that h is composed solely of bank reserves. We prefer, for simplicity's sake, the use of NIT rather than of net seigniorage, defined as $(\mu - R)h$ where μ is the rate of expansion of base money. This remark pertains only to the optimization stage, whereas in a stationary equilibrium NIT is of course identical with net seigniorage, which in turn is equal to the operational fiscal deficit.

We shall assume that in each period the policymaker has full control over actual inflation and will use it accordingly as a policy instrument at the optimization stage. Monetary expansion μ is then adjusted endogenously to satisfy the money market equilibrium. The simplest way of thinking about real money balances within the framework of a one-period model is as a variable factor of production of output. The demand for real balances will then be a negative function of expected inflation.

Although the government can produce money at no cost, it may not try to reach the satiation level, at which the marginal product of real money balances is zero. The basic reason for this statement is that by restricting the use of money the government can collect seigniorage and reduce other distortionary taxes. Even in the case of lump-sum taxation, there are still compliance costs associated with the enforcement of ordinary taxes, so that the satiation point of real balances cannot be optimal (contrary to Friedman's Rule).[2]

Denoting $x = \pi - R$, we obtain that NIT $= xh$. Here h is assumed to be a negative function of the real cost of holding money, which is given by $r + x^e$, where $x^e = (\pi^e - R)$ and π^e is expected inflation. Under the assumption that the real interest rate (r) is constant,[3] we may consider h as a negative function of x^e. It follows that in a rational-expectations equilibrium ($\pi = \pi^e$) we have NIT $= xh(x)$. In the absence of shocks, the latter equilibrium is also a steady-state equilibrium.

The policymaker's liquidity target, h^*, may be set as equal to $h(-r)$ with $x = -r$, according to Friedman's optimal quantity of money, where the alternative cost of holding money is zero, or as equal to some lower value.[4] Within this construct, we consider the inflation tax a substitute for other distortionary taxes, implying that the policymaker is interested in collecting more NIT by raising inflation as long as this behavior outweighs the cost of inflation.

Assume that the loss function of the discretionary government is given by

$$L = (\alpha/2)(\pi - \pi^*)^2 - J(\pi - \pi^e) + (\beta/2)[h(x^e) - h^*]^2$$
$$- \gamma xh(x^e); \quad J, \alpha, \beta, \gamma > 0^5 \qquad (D1)$$

Here π^* is the inflation target in the discretionary regime. We assume that π^* equals the equilibrium value of x in the discretionary regime, to be denoted x^*. From the definition of x we derive $\pi = x^* + R$. *Given that R is non-negative*, we see that $\pi^* = x^*$ is the minimal π given x^*, which is obtained when $R = 0$. Alternatively, π^* may be interpreted as the minimum inflation rate that corresponds to the fiscal needs. Since it may be shown that x^* is independent of the optimal π, π^* will be taken as exogenous at the optimization stage in the discretionary regime. In *equilibrium*, of course ($\pi - R) = x = x^e = x^*$ must obtain.

The last term on the right-hand side of (D1) is NIT, which (for simplicity's sake) enters the loss function linearly with a negative coefficient (as explained above). Finally, $J(\pi - \pi^e)$ represents the benefit gained when the discretionary policymaker creates surprise inflation to stimulate employment, as in Barro and Gordon (1983).

We assume that the discretionary policymaker cannot commit on inflation but can commit on the interest rate on reserves. In a discretionary regime, we minimize (D1) w.r.t. π and R, taking π^e as given (the optimization stage), and then equate the latter with π. The first-order conditions, w.r.t. π and R, are given respectively by:

$$\pi = \pi^* + J/\alpha + (\gamma/\alpha) h(x^e) \qquad (D2)$$

and

$$\beta[h(x^e) - h^*]h' = \gamma h(x^e)(1 - \eta), \quad h' = (dh/dx^e), \qquad (D3)$$

where η is the elasticity of h with respect to its argument. (D2) shows that the inflation bubble $(\pi - \pi^*)$ consists of two components: a fiscal component associated with the contribution of surprise inflation to seigniorage $[(\gamma/\alpha) h(x^e)]$ and an employment-related component (J/α).

Assume that the solution of (D3) in terms of x^e is unique. If the elasticity η is less than one, then by using the fact that $h' < 0$ we obtain that $h < h^*$, meaning that the policymaker compromises on his liquidity objective because of the negative effect of R on NIT. If $\eta = 1$, or if there were no fiscal considerations $(\gamma = 0)$, then $h = h^*$ (as in the Friedman solution).[6]

Note that (D3) determines x, being equated to x^e independently of π. (Optimization w.r.t. $x = x^e$ is equivalent to optimization w.r.t. R.) We take this solution of x as the value of x^*, which we may interpret as the "core inflation" of the discretionary regime. If so, the equilibrium value of R is given by $J/\alpha + (\gamma/\alpha) h(x^*)$. This follows from $\pi = \pi^* + J/\alpha + (\gamma/\alpha) h(x^e)$, $\pi = x^* + R$ and $\pi^* = x^*$ (in equilibrium). Thus, R reflects the incentive to use surprise inflation tactics in order to raise employment and net seigniorage. Alternatively, we may use R, derived in the manner shown above, to determine π by $\pi = x^* + R$.

Appendix E: The Paradox of Indexed Money Substitutes

It has been a widely accepted view among economists that inflationary finance can be helped by reducing the substitutability between money and other financial assets. This is the rationale for imposing financial repression, which prohibits the holding of foreign exchange and other money substitutes (Nichols, 1974). Empirical evidence about the positive effect of financial repression on the demand for money in the 1960s is presented in Fry (1988, p. 15).

Developments in chronic-inflation economies in the 1970s, however, point to the opposite pattern of behavior. Specifically, a universal feature of government behavior was to introduce indexed money substitutes despite the implied damage to the inflation tax. Thus, in 1977 the government of Israel introduced dollar-indexed deposits, which dominated broad money. Similar developments took place in Latin America (Galbis, 1979). By so doing, the government shot itself in the foot. The explanation of this paradoxical behavior is the subject of this appendix.[1]

The explanation is based on the distinction between discretion and rules. In the discretionary regimes that were characteristic of the chronic-inflation economies in the 1970s, the loss of credibility in monetary policies forced governments to regard inflation as being partly *exogenous*. In this case, the government felt that it had to "protect" the economy against the harmful effects of inflation on domestic liquidity, *even at the cost of a loss in revenues*. This was the rationale for introducing indexed money on a large scale. Under a rules regime, the behavior is quite different.

Suppose we have two types of money—h, representing conventional real money balances, and x, representing indexed money substitutes. Assume a

282

constant-return-to-scale production function of liquidity services Q with partial derivatives Q_{ij}:

$$Q = Q(h, x), \quad Q_h, Q_x > 0, \quad Q_{hh}, Q_{xx} < 0, \quad Q_{hx} < 0$$

where $Q_{hx} < 0$ indicates that we are dealing with "rival" factors of production. We consider x a fixed factor the supply of which is determined by the government. The demand function for h is determined by $Q_h(h, x) = \pi^e =$ expected inflation. (Without loss of generality, we ignore the real interest rate.) The aggregate demand function for h, say $h(\pi^e, x)$, depends negatively on π^e and on $x(h_j < 0$ for $j = \pi^e, x)$. We may then regard Q as a function of π^e and x, say $Z(\pi^e, x)$. We also assume that $Z_x = Q_h h_x + Q_x$ is positive.

Consider the following one-period loss function of the discretionary policymaker: [2]

$$L = (1/2)\pi^2 - J(\pi - \pi^e) + (\beta/2)(Q - Q^*)^2 - \gamma\pi h \tag{E1}$$

where π is inflation and Q^* is the policymaker's liquidity target. We assume that h is also the monetary base, so that πh is the inflation tax. The latter negatively affects the loss function since it is a substitute for other distortionary taxes. The policymaker hates inflation but may benefit from surprise inflation (through J) along the lines of Barro and Gordon (1983). We assume that π and x are policy instruments while the rate of monetary expansion adjusts endogenously to maintain equilibrium in the money market. To keep things as simple as possible, we assume that the real interest rate on x is zero and that there are no government bonds.

In the discretionary regime, we minimize L w.r.t. x and π, treating π^e as given, and then equate the latter with π. The first-order conditions are:

$$\pi = J + \gamma h, \text{ and} \tag{E2}$$
$$\beta(Q - Q^*)Z_x - \gamma\pi h_x = 0 \tag{E3}$$

so that, in equilibrium, $\pi > 0$ and $Q < Q^*$. We can now calculate the slopes of the relation between π and x from the two equations above. In this calculation, we impose the equilibrium condition $\pi = \pi^e$ on (E2) and (E3). It is easy to see that π is a decreasing function of x in (E2). This is depicted by curve AA in Figure E1. It may be shown that under reasonable assumptions the slope in (E3) will be positive if (γ/β) is sufficiently small, meaning that the relative concern for liquidity is sufficiently large. Using this assumption, we draw the curve that corresponds to (E3) as BB in Figure E1.

It may be seen that an increase in J will shift the equilibrium point from E to F, implying that both inflation and indexed money will increase. This suggests that a large J, which presumably characterized discretionary chronic-inflation economies, is the basis for their large reliance on money substitutes.

Under a regime of credible commitments, $\pi = \pi^e$ identically and justifies setting $J = 0$. It may be shown that inflation tends to be lower under a rules

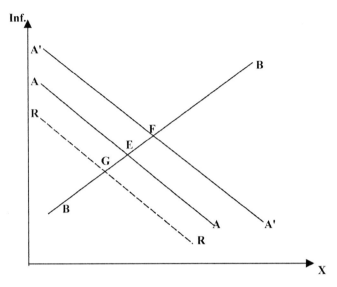

Figure E1. Inflation and Money Substitutes (X)

regime than under discretion for a given value of x and the other parameters. By implication, the AA curve of the rules regime (depicted by RR in figure E1) should be lower than the corresponding curve under the discretionary regime (even with J = 0). The equilibrium in the former regime is then represented by a point like G. Thus, in a rules regime we obtain both lower inflation and a less indexed money. *The latter may well be reduced to zero if its introduction involves a fixed cost*, as in Guidotti and Rodriguez (1992).

Appendix F: Monetary Policy under Fiscal Dominance

THE ECONOMETRIC MODEL

To construct our estimating equations for the money-injection function, we use the following identity (see definitions in the text):

$$\Delta MB = \Delta CB + \Delta G + \Delta F \tag{F1}$$

assuming that

$$\Delta MB = C + a_1\Delta G + a_2\Delta F + u \tag{F2}$$

where a_j ($j = 1, 2$) are non-negative parameters indicating the central bank's wish to prevent the pass-through of monetary injections to the money base. In the equation above, C is a constant and u is a random disturbance. We can treat the case of $a_j = 1$ ($j = 1, 2$), that is, $\Delta MB = \Delta G + \Delta F$, as a benchmark case of full monetary accommodation by the central bank. Substituting (F2) in (F1), we obtain

$$\Delta CB = C - (1 - a_1)\Delta G - (1 - a_2)\Delta F + u \tag{F3}$$

which is our basic estimating equation. Under complete sterilization we have $a_j = 0$ ($j = 1, 2$) so that the coefficients of ΔG and ΔF will be minus one.

In a fixed ER crawl regime with capital mobility, the demand for money will depend on the foreign interest rate plus expected devaluation so that ΔMB

should be (approximately) equal to the current inflation rate. In this case, the regression coefficient of ΔMB on $(\Delta G + \Delta F)$ should be zero, implying that the coefficient of ΔCB on $(\Delta G + \Delta F)$ should be -1. Since in a pure float the central bank does not intervene in the foreign-exchange market, there is no sale of foreign exchange to the central bank $(\Delta F = 0)$. The regression coefficients of ΔF on ΔG should be zero. If a certain fraction (λ) of ΔG is converted regularly to (negative) ΔF in order to finance the current account deficit of the private sector, and if otherwise the regime is a pure float, then we should expect $(\Delta F - \lambda\Delta G)$ to have zero variance.

The results for the inflationary periods confirm neither of these cases. The regression coefficients of ΔCB on $(\Delta G + \Delta F)$ are -0.55 for the first period and -0.76 for the second, significantly below unity. The correlation of ΔF and ΔG is far from perfect, indicating that the variance of $(\Delta F - \lambda\Delta G)$ is substantial. Thus, the two extreme cases are rejected for the inflationary period.

Sterilization

We first estimate the equation

$$\Delta CB = C + b_1\Delta G + b_2\Delta F \tag{F4}$$

If $C = 0$, then the b_i's are estimates of $-(1 - a_i)$. The results for the different subperiods show that C is not significant in the inflationary period, so that the (negative) b_is are usually estimates of the sterilization coefficients $(1 - a_i)$ of the BOI with respect to monetary injection from the public sector and from capital inflows (table 9.4). The results indicate that in the first period the BOI sterilized over one-third of ΔG and over one-half of ΔF, and in the second period (when inflation jumped to a higher plateau; see table 9.2) ΔF was sterilized completely $(b_2 = -1)$ and ΔG by three-quarters. It also seems that the degree of sterilization increased as the inflation plateau rose. Was the tendency to fully sterilize ΔF after the 1970s completely accidental? We will show below that there was an economic basis for this policy.

In view of the data in table 9.2, the findings reported above raise the question of why the BOI had to intervene so intensely, through ΔCB, in the process of foreign outflow originating in the monetary injection from general government. If we take the outflow of capital, related to ΔG, as an independent process, then a passive policy on the BOI's part, with $a_i = 1$, would still result in approximately the same spillover of ΔG to ΔF and lead to the same ΔCB and ΔMB (table 9.2A, lines 1–2). Thus, if the central bank were interested only in the level of the rate of monetary expansion, it could possibly attain the realized rate of ΔMB without any sterilization at all. If so, why did it adopt such an aggressive sterilization policy?

A possible explanation is that the BOI could reduce the *variance* of short-term interest and inflation rates by applying an active sterilization policy. Absent active intervention, the leakage from ΔG to ΔF would have required a prior reduction of domestic real interest rates or an increase in domestic inflation, which the BOI tried to avoid. This is a reasonable conclusion in view of the fact that the money injections were very large compared with the monetary base. Liviatan (2002a) shows that this view can be supported by empirical evidence.

The a_i coefficients may be derived from an optimizing model. Suppose that the ΔMB function is given by:

$$\Delta MB = a_1 \Delta G + a_2 \Delta F + u \tag{F5}$$

where a_i are non-negative and u is a random variable. There is a spillover from ΔG to ΔF given by λ, so that[1]

$$\Delta F = AF - \lambda \Delta G \tag{F6}$$

where AF is random and unrelated to ΔG. Inserting F6 in F5, we obtain[2]

$$\Delta MB = \beta \Delta G + (a_2 AF + u), \quad \beta = a_1 - \lambda a_2 \tag{F7}$$

The expected value of (F7 is $\beta E\Delta G$ and its variance (V) is $V(\Delta MB) = \beta^2 V(\Delta G) + a_2^2 V(AF) + V(u)$.

It can be seen that if $V(\Delta MB)$ for a given $E\Delta MB$ is minimized, $a_2 = 0$ and $a_1 = (E\Delta MB / E\Delta G)$. More generally, we define the loss function of the CB as

$$L = (E\Delta MB - \Delta MB^*)^2 + \gamma V(\Delta MB), \quad \gamma > 0 \tag{F8}$$

which is a function of a_i. This loss function assumes that the central bank cannot deviate (with its $E\Delta MB$) too much from the needs of the treasury to finance the deficit, as indicated by the target value ΔMB^*. Given this constraint, the central bank wishes to reduce the variance of ΔMB as much as possible. Optimizing w.r.t. the a_i parameters, which are determined prior to the realization of the random shocks, we obtain

$$a_2 = 0 \text{ and } a_1 = (\Delta MB^*/E\Delta G)/[1 + \gamma V(\Delta G)/E\Delta G^2] > 0. \tag{F9}$$

The first result is intuitive.[3] In view of the expression for $V(\Delta MB)$, the central bank can minimize the variability originating from AF (say, foreign shocks) by setting $a_2 = 0$, which implies that the offset coefficient $(1 - a_2) = 1$, as appears to be the case empirically after 1979. (F9) shows also that $(1 - a_1)$ is smaller than 1, as is the case empirically. Note also that a larger variance of ΔG is associated with a higher offset coefficient $(1 - a_1)$, which is again consistent with the data for the inflationary period.[4]

A more detailed analysis in Liviatan (2002a) shows that the BOI's sterilization policy was not related to the level of inflation during the two subperiods in question. This indicates that the BOI tried neither to influence the trend of inflation nor to redress its underlying causes but rather to stabilize its variance.[5]

Appendix G: Solvency and Sustainability

A simple example may illustrate the ideas stated in the text relating to these concepts. The time-pattern stock of government bonds at any moment of time is given by

$$Db = (r - n)b + (pd - \mu m) \tag{G1}$$

where b is the stock of (indexed) government bonds, m is real balances (identical to base money), μm is seigniorage (μ being the rate of expansion of money base m), and pd is the primary deficit (all expressed as ratios of GDP), r is the real interest rate, and n is the rate of growth. D denotes the time derivative operator. Note that seigniorage can be expressed as $\mu m = Dm + (n + \pi)m$, where π denotes inflation, so that adding Dm to both sides of the Db equation yields

$$Da = (r - n)a + (pd - im) \tag{G2}$$

where im is the inflation tax ($i = r + \pi$ being the nominal interest rate) and $a = m + b$ is the public's financial wealth. To simplify matters, let us denote $pd - \mu m \equiv pd_b$ and $(pd - im) \equiv pd_a$, and assume that $(r - n) \equiv \rho = $ constant. Using this notation, we express (G1) and (G2) as

$$Db = \rho b + pd_b \quad \text{and} \quad Da = \rho a + pd_a.$$

To derive a sufficient condition for the solvency of b, we assume that pd_b decreases linearly with b according to $pd_b = k - \beta b$, where k and β are constants (the latter is positive). We may then write (G1) as

$$Db = (\rho - \beta)b + k \tag{G3}$$

which may be solved in terms of time (t) to yield

$$b(t) = b^* + (b_0 - b^*)e^{(\rho-\beta)t} \tag{G4}$$

where $b^* = -k/(\rho - \beta)$.

Assuming that $\rho > 0$, we see that the discounted value of $b(t)$, $e^{-\rho t}b(t) = e^{-\rho t}b^* + (b_0 - b^*)e^{-\beta t}$, tends to zero as t tends to infinity, which implies solvency of b. If $(\rho - \beta) < 0$, then $b(t)$ converges to a steady state (b^*),[1] and if $(\rho - \beta) > \phi$, then $b(t)$ grows indefinitely (if $(b_0 - b^*) > 0$) but b remains solvent. In the foregoing cases, the debt grows more slowly than the interest rate ρ. These considerations still hold if pd_b is initially positive in the observed period (as was the case in the Israel's inflation era), since it is bound to turn negative as b increases over time.

In practice, we observe the behavior of the economy over a limited time span only. If during this period we find that pd_b is negatively related to b, we assume that the general government is solvent. The text refers to this labeled as "statistical solvency." True solvency, however, requires the maintenance of the aforementioned negative relationship *indefinitely*—a scenario that may not be considered realistic absent a major stabilization effort. This gives rise to a distinction between statistical solvency and *sustainability*, the latter referring to the level of the *undiscounted* debt, $b(t)$, as a precautionary measure against the risk that the negative relationship between b and pd_b will desist. This is specifically relevant where in the observed period pd_b is positive, in which case the transition to a negative pd_b (which is required for solvency if b is positive) may not seem credible in the absence of a major adjustment that may involve an inflationary shock. Formally, the β parameter may not be a positive constant (at least in the eyes of the public) but may fall to zero when b increases sufficiently. In the latter case, the system becomes insolvent, a state that we term "unsustainable."

Sufficient conditions for a sustainable path of $b(t)$ are as follows: (1) $b(t)$ has to converge to a steady state b^*, and (2) $b^* \leq b'$ (the upper bound of b). In terms of (G3) and (G4), it means that $(\rho - \beta) < 0$ and $-k/(\rho - \beta) \leq b'$.

During Israel's inflationary period, both the operational fiscal deficit (od) and seigniorage (as a percent of GDP) were fairly constant. To analyze the implications of these features, we write the evolution of b as $Db = \rho b + [(od - \mu m) - rb]$, where $(od - \mu m) = k$ in our former notation and $r = \beta$ provided r is constant. In this case, the steady-state value of b is $b^* = (od - \mu m)/n$. This expression may be calculated directly, yielding a debt/GDP ratio of about 3 to 4 in the inflationary period, much more than the actual ratio in 1984 (1.6), let alone the Maastricht criterion (0.6). In view of these figures, we may conclude that the debt was unsustainable.

Thus far, we have dealt only with the equilibrium of the general-government sector. In full equilibrium for the economy, we must ensure equilibrium in the private sector as well. In particular, the public must willingly maintain the value of m in the foregoing equations in accordance with its demand function.

The simplest way to introduce this requirement is to assume that the utility function of the representative agent is logarithmically separable into consumption (c) and money (m). In this case, the demand function for money is given by m = c/i, so that when c is constant the inflation tax is also constant. The dynamic equations, assuming that the operational deficit is a constant (as it was in the Israeli experience), are:

$$Db = -nb - \mu m + od \quad \text{and} \quad Dm = (\rho + \mu)m - c \quad (G5)$$

In a perfect-foresight model, r and c can be assumed to be constant (as in Liviatan, 1984) and the system is always solvent provided that od is constant, unlike the Sargent-Wallace (1981) model, in which only the *primary* deficit is constant. In this kind of model, solvency and sustainability are one and the same. However, in practice, where we do not encounter perfect foresight, we have only statistical solvency (as defined above), which does not ensure sustainability. In this case, we assume that the capital market can impose an upper limit on b, say b', beyond which there can be no long-term solution. Wherever b exceeds, b', we speak of unsustainability in the longer term.

The simplest case to consider for the application of this model is one in which there is an inflation target (π^T), so that $\pi = \pi^T$. Since in this case the demand for money is given by c/(r + π), we obtain a constant m, that is, Dm = 0 in (G5) and μ = n + π^T. Consequently, seigniorage (μm) is a constant equal to c(n + π^T)/(r + π^T). In this case, b(t) converges to (od − μm)/n. If, for example, sustainability requires an upper bound, b', then the sustainable path of the inflation target requires the condition S(π^T) + nb' $\geqslant$ od, where S denotes seigniorage. (For more detail, see Liviatan, 2003.) This means that an inflation target must be consistent with the operational deficit and the constraint on the national debt, as in the Maastricht criterion.

Appendix H: The Real Interest Rate in Disinflation (with Predetermined Money Supply)

The increase in the real interest rate during a disinflation process, which proved to be a robust empirical regularity, requires explanation. There are alternative explanations of this fact, as noted in the overview. In this appendix we present an explanation of the phenomenon in the context of the monetary crunch that is often used in money-based disinflations. We assume that in disinflation, the central bank, not wishing to be suspected of expanding the money supply in order to finance fiscal deficits, expands the money supply gradually. We assume that only in the event of this type of conservative behavior does the announcement of a stabilization program dampen inflation expectations. We also assume that the price level exhibits temporary rigidity, á la Calvo. This implies that real balances are momentarily rigid and that, consequently, the nominal interest rate is momentarily rigid as well.

It follows from these assumptions that when expected inflation falls as result of the announcement of a disinflation program, the real interest rate must rise. To take a simple example, suppose that money demand is expressed by

$$m_t - p_t = -\gamma i_t \quad (\gamma > 0), \tag{H1}$$

where m_t and p_t are the logs of the money supply and the price level in period t, and i_t is the nominal interest rate, which equals $r_t + \pi_t^e =$ the sum of the real interest rate and inflation expectations. Since the real money supply $(m_t - p_t)$ is momentarily rigid, a decrease in inflation expectations must raise the real interest rate.

292   Appendices

We may derive additional implications from this construct by assuming a forward-looking model with perfect foresight. Then it is easy to see that (H1) implies

$$\Delta i_t = (1/\gamma)(\pi_t - \mu_t), \tag{H2}$$

where $\mu_t = \Delta m_t =$ the growth rate of the money supply. Suppose that disinflation means a reduction in the long run μ, from μ_0 to μ_1. Then, if inflation lags behind μ the nominal (and real) interest rate will rise, which is consistent with the observed behavior.[1]

The behavior of the real interest rate in disinflation may be explained within the framework of the more conventional IS/LM setting. This model is formulated first for a closed economy, but below it is shown how it can be generalized to an open economy in the spirit of Dornbusch's overshooting hypothesis (following Liviatan, 1980).

The (continuous-time) model is composed of four equations:

$$\varphi y - \lambda i = m - p \tag{H3}$$
$$y = k - \sigma(i - Dp) \tag{H4}$$
$$Dp - \mu = \beta (y - y^*) \tag{H5}$$
$$Dm = \mu, \tag{H6}$$

where y is output and * denotes the long-run (steady-state) $D = d/dt$ (the time derivative). As before m is the log of nominal money balances (which are assumed to be predetermined), p is the log of the price level (which is assumed to be sticky), so that Dp denotes inflation (which equals expected inflation) and i is the nominal interest rate. Thus, the real rate is $r = i - Dp$ and μ is the rate of money expansion, which is assumed to be a constant policy parameter. (All other parameters are positive.) Note that in the long run, where $y = y^*$, we obtain $Dp = \mu$, $r^* = (k - y^*)/\sigma$ (the natural rate), $i^* = r^* + \mu$ and $(m - p)^* = \varphi y^* - \lambda(r^* + \mu)$.

Disinflation is a reduction in μ to, say, μ_1. The first requirement of a conservative central bank (CB) is that it does not raise m according to $(m - p_0)^* = \varphi y^* - \lambda(r^* + \mu_1)$, assuming that p is momentarily fixed (according to the sticky-prices assumption). Given this constraint, the difference between the long-term and the current stock of real balances is

$$(m - p)^* - (m - p) = \lambda(I - i^*) - \varphi(y - y^*). \tag{H7}$$

It can be shown that

$$(y - y^*)(1 - \beta\sigma) = -\sigma(i - i^*), \tag{H8}$$

where we assume that $(1 - \beta\sigma) > 0$, meaning that an increase in the interest rate reduces output. We also have

$$-(y - y^*) = \sigma(r - r^*) \tag{H9}$$

It follows from the last three equations that a decrease in m by open-market operations, with μ held constant, will raise the nominal and real interest rates. Although this will also reduce inflation, the reduction will be temporary if μ remains constant.

It follows from the above equations that

$$(r - r^*) = [(m - p)^* - (m - p)]/[\varphi\sigma + \lambda(1 - \beta\sigma)]$$
$$= [\varphi y^* - \lambda(\rho^* + \mu) - (m - p)]/[\varphi\sigma + \lambda(1 - \beta\sigma)], \qquad (H10)$$

implying that the real interest rate (in excess of the natural rate) depends on the difference between the long-term and the current (short-term) stocks of real balances. Thus, for a given set of parameters, $(r - r^*)$ depends negatively on $(m - p)$ and μ, so that a reduction in μ will raise the real interest rate r. The spread $(r - r^*)$ will be eliminated gradually as the real balances converge to their long-term value. It also follows from the last three equations that the nominal interest rate is determined by $(m - p)$ and μ. Although the central bank uses the nominal interest rate as its policy instrument, this model views it as being determined by more basic factors, that is, by $(m - p)$ and μ.

It may also be shown that inflation is determined by

$$Dp - \mu = -\sigma\beta(r - r^*), \qquad (H11)$$

which implies that, on impact,

$$\partial Dp/\partial\mu = 1 + \sigma\beta\lambda/[\varphi\sigma + \lambda(1 - \beta\sigma)] > 1. \qquad (H12)$$

This means that for a given reduction in μ, inflation will decrease on impact by more, which is necessary for the convergence of real balances to the new steady state. Thus, $D(m - p) = \sigma\beta(r - r^*) > 0$ along the convergence path. The larger the reduction in μ, the lower inflation will be and the more the unemployment rate will rise. A more conservative CB will reduce μ more, reflecting its preference for low inflation. This is the second aspect of CB conservatism.

Suppose i is increased by open-market operations while μ remains constant. This will create a recession (y will fall) and r will rise. According to (H11), inflation will fall. The reduction on the left-hand side of (H11), however, means that the real balances increase and return to their original position. Hence, an increase in the nominal interest rate that is not accompanied by a permanent decline in μ can reduce inflation only temporarily.

As the real balances converge toward their steady-state level, the real interest rate will decline to the natural rate and output will increase to its full-employment potential.

This model may be generalized to an open economy by following Liviatan (1980), an extension of Dornbusch's overshooting model based on the idea that the domestic price level is more rigid than the nominal ER. This entails the introduction of a new variable—the nominal ER—and two new equations, the uncovered interest-rate parity and an expectation-formation equation for depreciation. Once these changes are made, it may be shown that a permanent reduction in μ will cause on impact an appreciation that involves (under rational expectation) expectations of real depreciation and an increase in the real interest rate above the natural rate along the path of convergence to the new equilibrium.

Notes

Overview

1. The Bretton Woods system, in which members of the "club" adopted a set of fixed exchange rates, was clearly designed to function as a surrogate gold standard. Thus, it was basically a monetary-dominance arrangement.

2. This point is discussed in greater detail below. The theoretical foundation of this technique of securing price stability is set forth in Woodford (2003).

3. 5714 denotes the year according to the Jewish calendar.

4. Throughout this study, in both its volumes, GNP figures are used up to approximately 1973 and GDP as well as GNP series appear from then onward. This reflects the statistical conventions in the two periods.

5. Excluding 2000, the year of the global high-tech bubble.

Chapter 1 Emergence of the Monetary Texture and Macroeconomic Developments, 1948–54

1. See Keynes (1913), pp. 1–44.

2. Profits from Currency Board investments were channeled to Revenue of Palestine and a Crown Agents Reserve Account (Ottensooser, 1955, p. 159).

3. See data on U.K. government current expenditures and central government capital accounts in 1920–38 in Feinstein (1976), tables 12, 33, and 34, and in Howson (1975), tables 4A and 4B. The last-mentioned table shows that the budget was in surplus between 1928 and 1938, and that the British government redeemed debt out of revenue year in and year out between 1921 and 1938. The volume of these redemptions, however, was negligible in terms of the major real and nominal aggregates of the United Kingdom.

4. Szereszewski's estimate of the average annual rate of increase in domestic sources available to the economy—probably a more suitable variable to posit vis-à-vis the

expansion rate of M_1—sets the rate at 10.1% in 1931–39 and 12.3% in 1927–39 (Szereszewski, 1968, table 9, p. 62). Even this, however, falls far short of the expansion rate of M_1.

5. The bank runs in 1935, 1938, and 1939 traced to public scares generated by the Abyssinian War, the Munich Conference, and the eve of the outbreak of World War II, respectively. A government guarantee of credit from "foreign banks," if necessary, was discussed in 1938 after the Munich crisis. The government guarantee was to be given to the main "foreign banks" operating in Palestine, i.e., Anglo-Palestine Bank, Ottoman Bank, and Barclays Bank. The first-mentioned was the British-incorporated flagship of the Jewish and Zionist financial sector; the last-mentioned, the PCB's agent in Jerusalem, inevitably earned a good commission for its services. The high primary and secondary reserve ratios maintained by Anglo-Palestine Bank and the larger banks in the Jewish sector, in the range of 40%–45%, allowed the banking system to weather the storm with few serious casualties (Heth, 1994, table A-8, p. 25).

6. Redemption facilities only—i.e., conversion into blocked sterling accounts— were still available after June 1, 1948, in London. However, even if the Palestine Currency Board had made a currency-issue facility available, the facility would have meant that an expansion of the new state's monetary base would have required the surrender of foreign currency—effectively, U.S. dollars—for investment in a blocked sterling account at a nominal interest rate approximating zero.

7. These two "major policy issues" were specified and spelled out in a letter appended to the covenant.

8. This account follows E. Kleiman's detailed and fascinating survey of the ebbs and flows of the discussions and negotiations that finally settled the question of "what currency for the Jewish State?" as he felicitously put it (1977, pp. 216–45). See also Ottensooser's brief account, which describes the matter in its essentials (1955, pp. 108–15).

9. The PCB portfolio at the end of 1944, to which we refer, also included a sprinkling of Dominion and British Colonial issues (*Statistical Abstract of Palestine*, 1944–45, p. 87, tables 10–11).

10. By that time, practically all Palestine pounds in the department's portfolio had been converted into (blocked) sterling balances and were therefore included in the Gold and Foreign-Exchange Assets line in its balance sheet.

11. The Szereszewski series refers to midyear data. For the 1936–39 interval, this is the preferable series in view of the date on which World War II began. An approximation of the currency circulation series, derived from the source of table 1.1 and referring to outstanding currency balances as of March 31 of each of these years, suggests that currency in circulation grew by 1.8% per annum in 1936–39 and 37.4% in mid-1939–45.

British military expenditure in Palestine was formally counted as "export revenue" of Palestine. This practice and the impossibility of acquiring countervailing imports from sterling bloc countries or other foreign sources had obvious implications for the outstanding volume of Palestine currency.

12. The Fed (New York) rate of discount was 1.50% in 1949—1% less than the 2.56% rate in 1933 and 0.5% lower than the rate during the war. Rates below 2% were maintained through 1954 (*Economic Report of the President*, 1976, p. 238). The United Kingdom had much the same experience during that time: the 2% bank rate set in 1932 was still in force in 1945. It was considered a new departure when raised in June 1951 to 2.5% by Butler, the Chancellor of the Exchequer in the incoming Conservative government (Hutchinson, 1968, p. 104). The Fed also initiated a similar policy that year.

Similar rates were applied throughout Western Europe and in the dominions of the British Commonwealth. The (West) German discount rate in the early 1950s was significantly higher at almost 4%.

13. The well-known confrontation between the management of the Fed and President Truman in the first quarter of 1951 is a case in point. It resulted in the March 1951 "accord" that effectively granted the U.S. central bank the freedom to move toward a restrictive monetary policy.

14. Both the National Income data and the budget data were of much better quality from 1950 than in 1948 and 1949. Nevertheless, the entries for these years provide reasonable information in terms of comparative magnitudes.

15. Direct taxes during the Mandate period—on output, property, and income (the last-mentioned introduced in 1942)—generated only 28% of total revenue. The main tax sources of revenue were customs and other indirect taxes. Total tax revenue was only 10%–12% of GNP (Metzer, 1998, p. 181, table 6.2 and p. 185, table 6.3).

16. The annual expansion rate of currency in circulation was slightly lower than the pace of almost 50% shown in table 1.5, which pertains to currency held by the public and excludes currency held as reserves by the banking system. Including the reserves, the rate of increase during that time was 48.7% (Israel Central Bureau of Statistics, 1954–55, table XXIII-2).

17. The Examiner of Banks did not issue an official definition of the assets that should be identified as bank reserves until November 1950. According to the definition, such assets included Treasury bills and 3% in (compulsory) bank loans from "financial institutions." Although effectively applied only in 1951 and not in other years, the "effective monetary base" series (table 1.5) includes entries of these series for the entire 1948–54 interval.

18. The well-known query from Hugh Gaitskell, Chancellor of the Exchequer, to David Horowitz, later the first governor of the Bank of Israel, when they met in November 1950 to negotiate the release of the remaining sterling balances, speaks for itself. Gaitskell said, "If we release the whole of the balances left with us in 1951, what are you going to do in 1952?" (Horowitz, 1975, p. 78).

19. Note that the money supply grew at an annual average rate of 37% if all forty-three months from May 1948 are counted. During the war months, which included at least the first quarter of 1949, national product and imports, particularly civilian imports, actually declined. This, of course, suggests that the monetary inflation had an even greater impact on prices than that implied by the money and production data cited in the text.

20. Although the entries pertain to an index of land prices in central Jerusalem only, they are supported by seven series of real-estate prices in seven districts in Tel Aviv and its suburbs, which rose by factors of 1.5–2.7 (Borochov, 1965, p. 351).

21. This is not to imply that the manufacturing nominal wage series is fully representative of labor-market developments in that period. However, since this series refers to a large—probably the largest—segment of hired labor in the country, it presumably offers a reliable indicator of comings and goings on the wage front that affected nonimmigrants but not recent immigrants.

22. The name of the ministry, "Supply and Rationing," clearly reflects the state of mind during and immediately after the world war and not only in Israel. By 1951, however, rationing and price controls were already on their way out in the United Kingdom, West Germany, and the Low Countries. In 1950, they were still maintained for some goods and services in Western Europe.

23. The left-wing United Workers Party (Mapam), which did not belong to the coalition, took the brunt of the loss. Ben Gurion's Israel Labor Party (Mapai), the dominant

force in the government, lost only one seat. Nevertheless, the election results were correctly interpreted as a victory for the free-market forces and a defeat for those who represented anti-market doctrinaire socialism.

24. This figure refers to the entry in column 7 of table 1.4, in which unilateral payments from abroad to general government are counted as revenue on equal footing with tax revenue.

25. The U.S. Export-Import Bank, a federal agency controlled by its foreign office and operating as a commercial entity, was a case in point. The World Bank was similarly conceived as a potential source of finance for development projects.

26. This figure is an approximation of the value, in current dollar prices at the current official rate of exchange, of the fixed capital investment financed by the development budget in 1950–52. In 1951, it was about $260 million. This rough estimate was derived from data on gross capital formation and the share of general government in its finance, in Halevi-Klinov (1968), p. 232, appendix table 1, and p. 120, table 70.

27. Funds from the United Jewish Appeal, the main Diaspora fundraising organization, flowed into the coffers of the Jewish Agency for Israel, which in those years had a significant budget in terms of that of the government. These funds financed immigrant absorption, housing, and investment in agriculture. The Jewish Agency's contribution to general-government consumption expenditure was 11% of the total in 1950 and still 8% in 1954 and 1955 (Halevi-Klinov, 1968, p. 156, table 64).

28. Ten- to fifteen-year Israel Bonds issued in the early 1950s paid 3.5%–4% nominal interest (Halevi-Klinov, 1968, p. 131). Interest rates on ten- to twelve-year U.S. Government bonds were 2.5%–2.8% through 1955 and moved up to 4% in the second half of the 1950s. Since the spread did not compensate for Israel's country risk, bond sales relied on a sentimental appeal that was stirred up by the Bonds Organization in annual campaigns for Jewish communities in the United States and Canada and later, throughout Western Europe and South America. The first coast-to-coast Israel Bonds drive in the United States was launched by Ben-Gurion himself in May 1951.

29. Formally, the measure was described as an unindexed loan that would be paid back at a specified future date several years later. However, as the cost-of-living index soared by 66.5% in 1952 and as the public had noticed this development by the time the loan was implemented in the summer, the public probably considered the loan a tax.

The technical reason for the delay in implementation and of the public statement about what was still in the bag concerned the inevitable linkage of the collection of the tax on the outstanding currency balance with the replacement of the "old" banknotes, issued under the August 1948 law, with new ones. The latter would be inscribed with the name "Bank Leumi le-Israel," the new name for the Anglo-Palestine Bank, which had been inscribed on the 1948 banknote series. In February 1952, the new notes were still being printed in the United States.

30. Thus, whether the tax on M1 would have been implemented simultaneously with the official announcement and implementation of the devaluations, had this been technically feasible, is anyone's guess. Public-opinion considerations meant to obviate the shock treatment might have argued in favor of an interval between the devaluation and the tax on money.

31. Heth comments on the immediate implications on these initial "requests" by the Examiner of Banks: "Compulsory reserve ratios were [first] set in 1950 but were hardly effective since the commercial banks had sufficient liquid assets" (1994, p. 48). See also Patinkin (1956, p. 61).

32. In view of the monetization process in an economic environment of mass immigration, such as Israel's until the end of 1951, demand for cash, at least, had also been affected by this factor. Thus, demand for money in 1951–54 might have grown at a

faster rate than that estimated on the basis of the (implicit) unitary income elasticity assumption applied in this estimate. If this happened, the figure suggested in the text for the gap between money supply and demand may be somewhat excessive. See also Heth (1994), pp. 46, 50.

33. A minority of committee members, representing business and the so-called private sector, did not favor the sweeping involvement of general government in the economy and presented a minority report. This report proposed the abolition of currency control, which in practice would have required a transition to a flexible exchange-rate regime. In view of the size of the official foreign reserves at the time—about one week's worth of imports—this was the only alternative to the fixed exchange-rate regime required by the Bretton Woods rules, to which all members of the IMF adhered at that time. The alternative was obviously impractical at a time when the leading industrial countries and, effectively, most developing countries, were members of this fixed exchange-rate club and played by its rules.

Chapter 2 The Establishment of the Bank of Israel: The Legal and Institutional Framework of Israel's Central Bank

1. Kleiman (1977), pp. 239–40.

2. The details of the process and the handling of this legislation follow Bar-Joseph (1985, p. 12) and Horowitz (1975, pp. 131–33).

3. The institutional expression of this attitude and practice in the political arena at large was the eclipse of the ministries of foreign affairs in the governmental pecking order and the elevation of ministries of finance to primacy in the political arena.

4. Bank of Israel Law, 5714-1954, Section 3. This quotation from the Law and those that follow are our translations from the Hebrew original. (See Bar-Joseph, 1985, pp. 233–34.)

5. Section 49 says, "After consulting with the Committee and [obtaining] the approval of the Government, the Governor is empowered to instruct commercial banks to maintain liquid assets at a certain ratio and of a certain composition." Section 53 (III-2) empowers the Governor "to set different ceilings for different kinds of credit, investments, or other liabilities." This, too, requires prior consultation with the Advisory Committee and approval of the Government (Bar-Joseph, 1985, pp. 241–42).

6. The wording of the relevant section follows: "If the means of payment on a given day increased by 15% or more over and above their total on any day during the last 12 months, the Governor shall immediately submit a report to the Government and the Finance Committee of the Knesset, explaining the reasons for this increase . . . and suggesting to the Government the requisite measures in response to said increase" (Bar-Joseph, 1985, p. 239). The requirement to submit this statement to the Knesset Finance Committee suggests that the statement was to be published.

7. For instance, the Central Bank of Ceylon [today Sri Lanka] Law, after which the Bank of Israel Law was patterned in several respects, did not include a similar section requiring the publication of a means of payment statement (Bar-Joseph, 1985, pp. 24–26).

8. Such an accommodation—a direct central-bank credit facility to even out the government's cash flow across the well-known ebbs and flows of the fiscal year—was never available in leading industrial countries. Government in these countries tide over their finances, when necessary, by selling and repurchasing short-term securities in the money market.

9. The Banco Central de la Republica Argentina was managed by nineteen governors during the seventeen-year tenure of the first governor of the Bank of Israel, and by fifty-one governors in the sixty-six-year interval between 1935 and 2001. The Banco

Central de Brasil had twenty-six governors in the thirty-four years between 1965 and 1999.

10. The other member of the subcommittee was E. S. Hoofien. Mr. Horowitz expressed his strong preference for this kind of management structure at the central bank in the third volume of his autobiography (Horowitz, 1975, pp. 131–32). There he describes his rejection of a proposal by a member of the full committee, A. Bart, to set up a board of governors with the governor as the chair.

11. The legal powers for the supervision of commercial banking were vested in the Examiner of Banks (now known as the Supervisor of Banks), a BOI official who headed the Banking Supervision Department. As a member of the top management of the BOI, the examiner (supervisor) is appointed by the governor.

12. The Bank of England Act instructs, "In relation to monetary policy the objectives of the Bank of England shall be (*a*) to maintain price stability, and (*b*) subject to that, to support the economic policy of Her Majesty's Government, including its objectives for growth and employment" (*Banking Law Issue*, 1944).

13. The Ottoman law did not treat usury as a criminal offense. It merely prevented the legal enforcement of interest payments on debtors who refused to pay interest charges beyond the legal ceiling. Thus, even banks that overcharged overtly did not engage in criminality.

14. In a 1957 memorandum to Members of the Knesset, "Defense of a Free Interest Rate" Dr. M. A. Witkon, at that time general manager of Union Bank, presented the banking industry's case and pleaded felicitously for the abolition of the legal ceiling on interest rates. During those years, this approach and message had at best feeble support in political circles (1965, p. 22–28).

Chapter 3 Groping for and the Emergence of Monetary Policy, 1954–66

1. The value and the high variance of the series describing the high rates of monetary expansion during the first period—more than 20% annually in 1955 and 1956 for M_1—are explicable in terms of an exogenous factor: the political tension in 1955–56 that led to the Sinai Campaign of 1956 and, of course, reflected the impact of war finance.

2. The pace of monetary expansion slowed considerably in the two closing quarters of 1955 and ended the calendar year at 20.4% in annual terms—still much faster than the 15% limit (*Annual Report*, 1962, p. XIV-8, table XIV-3).

3. The report referred to the seven months terminating at the end of July 1960, during which M_1 expanded by 15%, corresponding to an annual average rate of 27%.

4. The deposits included in this calculus were current account balances and several kinds of term deposits that the central bank could redefine from time to time. Thus, lending conditions could be tightened or eased without changing the formal ratios.

5. Heth, 1994, p. 50, makes a similar statement.

6. The emergence at the turn of the 1960s, and the subsequent rapid expansion, of the volume of this de jure but not de facto "extramural" bank-credit market are discussed below.

7. *Annual Report* of the Bank of Israel. This title refers always to the Hebrew version of the report.

8. This implicit tax rate reflects the corresponding entries of index numbers for the formal and effective exchange rates in 1961 on the basis of 1954 in table 3.2. In terms of the GNP price index, the implicit tax that year was actually somewhat higher.

9. The ongoing process of this dimension of financial repression, which would generate a rapidly ever-growing accumulation of foreign-exchange deposits indexed to exchange rates or denominated in foreign exchange, obviously provided another case in point, from the monetary point of view, for making a move on the formal exchange rate sooner rather than later.

10. The Ophir-Kleiman estimate for the lagged impact of the rate of change of money on prices in the 1960–65 period is eight months for the first discrete effect and one year for the second discrete effect (Ophir and Kleiman, 1975, p. 24). The 1961 lag of prices after the 1960 acceleration of the monetary expansion is quite consistent with this estimate.

11. This market, a by-product of the Usury Law, gained momentum after inflation ticked upward in the early 1960s. The commercial banks joined the crowd by using a legal loophole that allowed them to be involved in a dominant proportion of such transactions, which were carried out on bank premises. Formally, commercial banks served only as "middlemen" between borrowers and lenders and earned commissions for this function and for lenders' guarantees, if requested. By 1961, this market already accounted for 16% of total outstanding bank credit inclusive of the "directed" credit component. The proportion would climb to 32% by 1963 and 40% by 1966 (table 3.6).

12. The impact of the credit funded by the development budget, transacted by the commercial banking system but financed by special government deposits for development credit, is shown in the grand total column (column 5) of table 3.5.

13. Long-term nominal bond yields in Germany averaged 6% in 1960–64. Since the relevant deposits in Israel paid 6% and did not involve a capital-loss risk, the Israeli interest rate was somewhat higher than that on equivalent deposits in Germany. The interest-rate figures follow Giersh, Paque, and Schmieding, 1992, p. 212, table 24.

14. This uncertainty is plainly evident in Beham's conversion data, especially figures 1 and 2, which demonstrate this change in the pattern of conversions (Beham, 1968, pp. 48–49).

15. This was largely due to the end of the ten-year inflow of German reparations and the decline and, later, the termination of the U.S. grant-in-aid in 1964.

16. The governor's letter of submission is dated November 17, 1960. The phrase "monetary discipline" appears in the means-of-payment report that was submitted in August 1961.

17. The monetary base and M_1 expanded by 38% and 28%, respectively, that year (table 3.4).

Chapter 4 Monetary Policy in a Mobilized Economy

1. The Central Bureau of Statistics index of industrial output gives clear evidence of the duration of the slowdown, from mid-1965 to mid-1967 (*Annual Report,* 1967, p. 272, table XII). Quarterly GNP data for that period are unavailable.

2. The increase in the surplus in real dollar terms, measured in terms of the U.S. GNP deflator, was 5% in 1968 and 44% in 1972, both relative to the 1964 surplus.

3. Social security contributions were increased by raising both the maximum level of contribution-liable income and the contribution rates (*Annual Report,* 1970, p. 124).

4. Table 4.4 does not convey the level of the total cash flow of general government. The cash-flow statement, which reflects general-government activities on both income and expenditure account, involving tax revenue and expenditure for goods and services, plus its operations on capital account—its own borrowing and payback, coupled with net credit transactions with businesses and households—would seem to offer much

more relevant information about the impact of general government on the monetary dimensions of the economy. However, capital-account operations involving the development-budget component of the total annual budget were always in the red, with obvious implications for the monetary dimension.

5. An alternative estimate of general-government domestic expenditures and (tax) revenues during those years was the so-called "excess demand" annual series, defined as the difference between these two flows. This measure indicates a leap of "excess demand" from 6.8% of GDP in 1966 to 18%–19% through 1970 and 14%–16% in 1971–72 (*Annual Report*, 1970 and 1974, table VII-1).

6. The potential effect of the devaluation on IL import (and export) prices is suggested by the effective exchange rate. Thus, implicit IL import prices in 1968 were 10% higher than in 1967 and 13% higher than in 1966. In terms of consumer prices, however, the price level was only 2% higher in 1968 than in 1966 and the corresponding increase in terms of GNP prices was 4.8%.

7. These, involving both GNP and the import surplus, grew at annual average rates of nearly 12% during this three-year period. The growth rate of GNP was almost 10%.

8. The price level was 3.4% higher in June 1969 than a year before and consumer prices in mid-1967 and mid-1968 were 1.7% and 1.7% higher, respectively, than a year before.

9. Up to June 1966, before the BOI moved into the market, three-month T-bills were issued at a net yield to redemption of 7.84%. After a slight dip in late November, when the BOI first became active, the yield fell to 6.50% in February 1967 and dropped in October 1967 to a 5.75% plateau that held firm until April 1969. The yield climbed to 6.50% at that time and again to 7.75% in November 1969 (*Annual Report*, 1969, p. 348).

10. M_2 and M_3 grew at even much higher annual rates, particularly from 1970 onward, reflecting the liquidity avalanche during that period.

11. The sector that our injection estimates identify as the "private sector" might better be called the "non-budget" sector. For instance, direct imports by a government ministry, such as defense imports, are included in the net injection estimate of the government sector. Imports by corporations and authorities that are partly or fully owned by general government, such as the defense industries (owned mainly by central government), the national water company (central government), the Israel Electric Corp., the Ports Authority, Israel Railways, and the Jewish Agency for Israel are counted among private-sector imports and their net injection effect on the liquidity of the system is treated as such.

12. Table 4.8 presents the inflow of reparations payments and dollar-denominated and dollar-indexed deposits in foreign and domestic currency. The formal exchange rates (table 4.2) were used to convert the inflow of reparation payments and PAZAK-TAMAM deposits into domestic currency for comparison with the IL-denominated parameters of GNP and monetary base.

13. The reversal of direction by both sectors—government moving from large injection in 1971 to small drainage of liquidity in 1972, and the private sector shifting from substantial drainage in 1971 to substantial injection in 1972—is of course not a coincidence. The 20% formal devaluation in August 1971 induced households to convert into domestic currency much more of their restitution-payment inflow and their accumulated PAZAK-TAMAM deposits. The upturn in these private conversions also traced, evidently, to the 20% devaluation (table 4.8). Similarly, the devaluation generated an increase in government receipts on foreign accounts in domestic-currency terms. This allowed government to reduce its debt to the BOI by 7.5%. The reduction led to a corresponding large negative injection (tables 4.5 and 4.7).

14. The employment series, and not just the unemployment data presented in table 4.1, suggest that the dividing line should be drawn there. According to a contemporaneous comment on the employment situation, the rate of increase of national product slowed (somewhat) in 1970 due to the attainment of full employment and the full utilization of the available reserves of factor inputs (*Annual Report*, 1970, p. 3; see also pp. 153–69).

15. We make quantitative reference to 1972 only because injection data for the three prewar quarters of 1973 are unavailable. However, the monetary-base value for that brief period suggests that the base grew at an annual rate of 19% during that time (table 4.5), slower than the average annual injection rate in 1970–72.

16. These "discounts," of course, were the BOI's contribution to the subsidized "directed-credit" component of bank credit (see *Annual Report*, 1966, p. 472).

17. The incentive to banks to promote sales and/or to purchase MAKAM on nostro account took the form of a bonus: Initially, in 1967–68, banks were entitled to acquire 9.5% MAKAM at a rate of one for every five MAKAM securities that each bank transacted. These bills carried not only a higher interest rate, on top of brokerage fees, than the longest-term MAKAM (eighteen months to maturity); they were also counted as a reserve asset in calculating the minimum liquidity ratio (*Annual Report*, 1967, p. 347). A change in the ratio of Treasury bills to the number of MAKAM sold was later used as a substitute for changes in yields offered to promote sales. Note, however, that although providing banks with high-yield reserves did boost Treasury-bill sales, this device was self-defeating because the bank reserves that it created increased the potential balance of the monetary base and, in turn, its expansionary effect on the money supply, M_1.

18. By mid-1970, when inflation, although higher than the 1969 level, was still in the 3.5%–4% range, inflation expectations might not yet have risen significantly. By the last quarter of the year, however, as inflation had crossed into a double-digit annual rate, expectations were definitely affected.

19. This is a translation of Section II-3.1 of the BOI Law. The following section, 3.2, does spell out the BOI's "second commandment": "to promote a high level of production, employment, national income, and investment."

20. The remark appeared in the Friday (October 31, 1971) weekly column of the *Economists Team,* written by members of the Hebrew University Economics Department in *Maariv,* the country's largest-circulation newspaper at the time. Patinkin's fusillade referred to the thirteenth means-of-payment report (September 12, 1971), which reported on the expansion of M_1 by 15.3% within five months (February–June 1971) and by 25% between June 1970 and June 1971.

21. Only the first of these reports appeared over the signature of David Horowitz, the first governor of the BOI, who retired in October 1971. The four subsequent reports, released after Moshe Sanbar succeeded Horowitz as governor in the last quarter of 1971, raised proposals for an across-the-board increase in interest rates, including of course those on directed credit, in a rising crescendo.

22. The significant move of the private sector from a 25% draining stance in 1971 to a similar rate of injection in 1972 also traced to an endogenous factor. The formal devaluation in August 1971 led to a major increase in conversions by recipients of German restitution payments, who had accumulated huge foreign-exchange deposits relative to the volume of M_1. The much lower draining stance of the private sector in 1971 than in 1970 also reflected, presumably, an increase in external borrowing by the private sector and, in turn, an increase in capital inflow. This foreign credit reflected a more liberal attitude on the part of the currency-control authority at the Ministry of Finance

toward applications for permits to borrow abroad, even though this undermined the BOI's attempt to impose monetary constraint. The BOI implicitly complained about the loophole (means-of-payment report, August 1972, p. 18).

23. Reported in *Maariv*, October 17, 1971.

24. The benefit of lower variance was the lowering of uncertainty and its real cost to the economy.

Part II Israel's Great Inflation, 1973–85

1. The main impact of the collapse of the Bretton Woods regime was felt only after 1973; it had little effect on the initial acceleration of inflation preceding the Yom Kippur War, which took place in the context of an overheated economy with large fiscal deficits.

2. This runs contrary to F. J. Ruge-Murcia's presentation of the Tanzi effect as an inherent feature of the inflationary process (1995).

3. Most government paper was in the form of non-negotiable bonds.

4. An important deviation from the Sargent-Wallace model is that the primary deficit was not constant but rather decreased in the inflationary period. The implications of this fact are discussed below.

5. See, for example, Barro and Gordon (1983).

6. See, for example, Woodford (2001) and Canzoneri, Cumby, and Diba (2001).

7. This is expressed in terms of the difference between the deficit on current account and the surplus on unilateral receipts account of the balance of payments.

Chapter 5 Financial Repression

1. See Fry (1988).

2. This suggests a tradeoff between inflation and growth if money is held only by households (Sussman, 1991).

3. That is, by exempting income from government bonds from taxation.

Chapter 6 War and Oil Shock, October 1973–May 1977

1. In the estimation of Meridor (1987), domestic defense consumption was 3 percentage points of GNP higher in 1973–76 than in 1967–72 (net of defense imports, which were financed by unilateral transfers).

2. The term that came into vogue was *mehdal,* signifying inaction, blunder, or even fiasco.

3. Transfer payments increased from 4.5% of GNP in 1965–69 to 6.2% in 1970–74 and from 5.7% of GNP in 1973 to 8.5% of GNP in 1974–77 (Barkai, 1998, p. 155, table A-1).

4. The directed-credit component of total outstanding commercial bank credit exceeded 60% of total credit from 1974 onward. Another highly subsidized form of credit, investment credit financed from the government's development (investment) budget, accounted for another 20% (table 4.10).

5. For a broader discussion of this phase, see Bruno and Sussman (1978).

6. This medium-term credit was managed by, but not financed from, the sources of commercial banks. The government provided the sources in the form of special deposits with the commercial banks, known by their Hebrew acronym, PAMELA (Government Deposits for Development-Budget Credit).

Chapter 7 The Liberalization Episode of 1977–79

1. See Gotlieb and Blejer (2002).

2. By the end of 1977, PATAM deposits constituted 42% of M_3, which in Israeli terms was defined as the sum of M_2 and PATAM. The ratio climbed to 76% by the end of 1980 and 85% in 1984.

3. Restrictions on bank credit were considered more effective in stemming a run on reserves than a nominal anchor such as base money or means of payment. This is because in the case of a run people usually use their money to purchase foreign exchange from the central bank, and if the latter maintains a monetary rule it will be forced to react by increasing the money supply, thus accommodating the run.

4. This makes one ask why the government introduced indexed money substitutes, which reduced the base of the inflation tax. We have already mentioned one reason: the need to divert the drift toward "green" dollars as a hedge against inflation. For a more general treatment of this problem, see appendix E.

5. See Offenbacher (1985).

Chapter 8 Early Attempts at Stabilization

1. The expectations of a construction boom proved to be exaggerated.

2. To keep real wages constant as the frequency of COLAs increases, the rate of inflation has to rise.

3. The index of import prices relative to domestic uses dipped from 108 in 1980 to 98 in 1982. The corresponding figures for exports were 105 and 95 (*Annual Report*, 1983, English version).

4. E.g., Sachs, Tornell, and Velasco. (1996).

Chapter 9 General Features of the Overall Inflationary Process

1. An analysis of the policy implications of these characteristics, drawing on Cukierman and Liviatan (1990), appears in appendix A.

2. The tendency to increase welfare-state benefits in general, and social-insurance benefits in particular, was common to many countries in the 1960–80 period. However, Israel's social-insurance benefits increased at the highest rate among industrial countries in that period. Not until the 1990s did National Insurance benefits stabilize as a percentage of GNP (Barkai 1998, tables 9 and 10). Barkai also suggests that the level of these benefits, expressed in percent of GNP after necessary adjustments for product per capita, was significantly higher in Israel than in the wealthiest countries in the world.

3. If we denote the ratios of real base money balances and real bonds to GDP by h and b, respectively, and the rate of economic growth by n, then the warranted (noninflationary) deficit is n(h+b).

4. Note that the correlation between x and y is the geometric average of the regression of x on y and of y on x.

5. See also the extensions by Liviatan (1984), Drazen (1984), and Drazen and Helpman (1990).

6. The net interest payments in line (6) of table I.2 are *real*.

7. See appendix G.

8. This argument is elaborated in Liviatan (2003).

9. Y. Djivre stressed this point.

10. See, for example Woodford (2001) and Canzoneri, Cumby, and Diba (2001).

11. Empirical studies about the demand for money that use a semi–log demand curve (Offenbacher, 1985) are inappropriate in the sense that they force on the data an elasticity of demand for money that rises commensurate with inflation.

12. One may rationalize this policy by arguing that it enhances the effectiveness of the so-called real balance effect (the "Pigou effect"), which, by definition, is absent in the case of indexed money.

13. For full discussion of this phenomenon, see Liviatan and Piterman (1986).

14. For broader discussion, see Liviatan (2002a).

15. See, for example, the 2001 Report of the Bank of Israel Comptroller.

16. The precise distinction between the Pigou effect and the inflation-tax aspect in intertemporal general-government accounts is explained in Liviatan (2003).

17. See Liviatan (2002a) for supporting evidence.

Part III The Emergence of an Independent Monetary Policy and Macroeconomic Developments after the 1985 Stabilization

1. Appendix G describes the formal connection between these rules and price stability.

2. The external debt/exports ratio moved in the same direction.

3. Inflation expectations are derived from comparison of yields of unindexed and indexed bonds of similar duration. These bonds are traded on the Tel Aviv Stock Exchange and the calculation assumes that the inflationary risk premium on unindexed bonds is small.

Chapter 10 The 1985 Stabilization Policy

1. Peres held the premiership during the first half of the government's term; in the second half, under a rotation agreement, he was succeeded by Yitzhak Shamir of the Likud.

2. This was so, even though the last-mentioned group took issue with the imposition of controls and the pegging of the exchange rate. For the detailed story of these differences, see Bruno (1993).

3. However, the formal imposition of price controls was highly relevant politically; without it, the Histadrut would not have assented to the package deal.

Chapter 11 The Consolidation of Moderate Inflation, 1985–90

1. See footnote 3, chapter 9.

2. Lavi and Sussman (2001) show that in the *long* run the real wage behaves according to the neoclassical model. See also figure II.2.

3. This follows from the model of Cukierman and Lippi (1999).

4. Although price controls were phased out over a period of two and a half years, nominal wages were much more flexible and rose more rapidly.

5. Before the 1985 stabilization policy, this was accomplished by means of credit ceilings.

6. The competition-enhancing effectiveness of this measure, introduced in 1990, was less than it might have been because the auctions entailed the intermediation of the commercial banks (Djivre and Tsiddon, 2002).

7. Djivre and Tsiddon (2002) performed a regression of these interest rates on the interest rate on the monetary loan and found that the regression coefficients converged to unity with respect to loans around 1990 and deposits around 1993, indicating increased competitiveness. (See also Geva, Samet, and Ruthenberg, 1988.)

Chapter 12 The "Russian Immigration Wave" and the New Inflation Step, 1990–94

1. At the end of the post–1985 stabilization business cycle in 1989, just before the onset of mass immigration, the unemployment rate was 8.9% of the civilian labor force.

2. This is done by Dahan and Strawczynski (2001).

3. Ibid.

Chapter 13 Monetary Developments in the Second Half of the 1990s

1. The large increase in the announced key rate in late 1991 (in response to a speculative attack on the NIS) was soon reversed (figure 13.3).

2. In these calculations, we used a crude measure of expected depreciation in quarter t (in annual terms), defined as $(E_{t+2}/E_t)^2-1$, where E_t is the average ER in quarter t. In figures 13.5 and 13.6, we used an eight-quarter moving average for all variables in order to illuminate the long-term trend.

3. The ratings of Standard and Poors and of Fitch, for example, remained at A– throughout the 1995–2001 period.

Chapter 14 The Real Economy Background

1. This is consistent with Ricardian equivalence if it reflects a temporary increase in domestic demand of general government. The increase in the deficit in 1995 qualifies as a candidate for this scenario.

Chapter 16 General Features of the Disinflation Process

1. This exceeds by far the difference between current expectations and inflation in the past twelve months (column 1).

2. This is possibly due to partial belief in the commitment to disinflation.

3. Notably, the IS curve does not capture the inflationary impact of the long-term fiscal stance.

4. In Israel, a main determinant of the BOI's estimate of future inflation is the public's inflation expectations twelve months ahead, as derived from capital-market data.

5. See for example Liviatan (1980).

6. Blanchard (2003) maintains that the above mechanism is effective only if the national debt is small.

7. See chapter 2.

8. Strictly speaking, these bonds are debentures of the government, not of the BOI. However, they were handed to the BOI for the purpose of open-market operations.

9. In regard to this kind of asymmetry in the OECD countries, see Hercowitz and Strawczynski (1998).

10. Strictly speaking, we should deduct seigniorage from the primary deficit. During the period in question, however, the value of seigniorage was very low.

11. See Bruno and Meridor (1991) for discussion of the reasons for the cycle.

12. See, for example, Lavi and Sussman (1997) and Liviatan and Sussman (2002).

13. Liviatan and Sussman (2002).

14. There was also a reduction in the size of money multipliers in the second half of the 1990s.

15. Woodford (2001); Canzoneri, Cumby, and Diba (2001).

16. For full equilibrium to exist, the *private sector* should also be in equilibrium. Full equilibrium of an economy in a simple version of the Sargent-Wallace model of

"Unpleasant Monetarist Arithmetic" is derived in Liviatan (2003). In this setting, the value of the inflation tax (im) is equal to the constant value of consumption c.

17. In regard to the Pigou effect, see Patinkin (1966). In the very short run, the shock may be absorbed by Q_0 as in the IS/LM model. After a while, however, this will be reflected in a change in the price level.

18. This means that the general-government sector is solvent if the present value of the national debt tends toward zero over time.

19. Here we use the concept of the Pigou effect in a broad sense, to reflect not only the erosion of real balances but also the erosion of real wages that were not perfectly indexed.

20. The ADF test equation was (quarterly change in inflation) = C + a(inflation in previous quarter) + b(linear trend) + e(lagged quarterly change in inflation), with C = 6.20 (9.00), a = −1.19 (−10.42), b = −0.09 (−7.29) and e = 0.08 (2.52) (t values in parentheses). The lag length was determined by automatic SIC.

21. See table I.3 in the overview to this volume.

22. It was this risk that prevented the use of this policy during the inflation era.

23. This relationship is derived formally in Liviatan (2003).

Chapter 17 The International Perspective

1. See survey in the IMF's *World Economic Report* for 1997, under the suggestive title "The Rise and Fall of Inflation."

2. See Barro and Sala-i-Martin (1995).

3. All these estimates are based on A. Heston, R. Summers, and B. Aten, "Penn World Table Version 6.1," Center for International Comparisons at the University of Pennsylvania (CICUP), October 2002. http://pwt.econ.upenn.edu/php_site/pwt_index.php.

4. Ibid.

5. See Woodford (2003) for a theoretical justification of this view.

Appendix A

1. Such a model is discussed in Yashiv (1989).

Appendix B

1. The automatic-selection method chooses the number of lags in order to minimize the Schwarz criterion, which involves a penalty term for the number of lags included.

2. The test equation was as follows. D(inflation) = C + a(lagged inflation) + b(linear trend) + four lagged D(inflation)s and their coefficients, where D denotes first difference. The numerical values (t-values in parenthesis) were C = 1.38 (0.69), a = −0.71 (−3.68), b = 0.52 (3.31), with a Durbin-Watson statistic of 1.70. We have to take into account that the distribution of the t-values is not standard. If we set the lags so as to obtain the best DW statistic (i.e., closest to 2) then the number lags is 2, the DW statistic is 1.94 and the hypothesis of a unit root is not rejected even at the 10% critical value.

3. In practice, the drift of inflation decreased after the 1985 stabilization.

Appendix D

1. This is equivalent to assuming a 100% reserve requirement where money consists only of deposits. Having a fractional reserve system does not affect the results of this

appendix if we impose a zero profit condition on the banks (see the discussion at the end).

2. This point is treated in Vegh (1989).

3. Such as that on physical capital.

4. The target h(–r) may be too ambitious for a discretionary regime.

5. Liviatan and Frish (2006) used an alternative formulation of the loss function, based on the conceptual framework of Poterba and Rotemberg (1990). The latter study introduces the ordinary tax rate (θ) as an explicit substitute for the inflation tax. In this formulation, the loss function is $L = S = (\alpha/2)\pi^2 - J(\pi - \pi^e) + (\beta/2)(m^d - m^*)^2 + (\gamma/2)\theta^2$ and the budget equation is $\psi(\theta) + \pi m^d = g$, where g denotes government expenditure. The results are similar to the present, simpler, exposition.

6. Alternatively, the fiscal cost may be offset by other advantages of increasing real balances (e.g., the utility derived from consumption) as in Correia and Teles (1999).

Appendix F

1. This section is based on Liviatan (2002a).

2. As in the model with capital controls and a fixed exchange rate. As a first approximation, we assume that λ is independent of the sterilization policy.

3. This implies that the shocks originate in the supply side of the money market, which justifies minimizing $V(\Delta MB)$, other things equal.

4. See table 9.4.

5. The results of this section are also consistent with a ΔF function of the form $\Delta F = AF - \lambda a_1 \Delta G$.

Appendix G

1. In this case, $k > 0$ if $b^* > 0$.

Appendix H

1. It may be shown that the existence of a forward solution of this model requires that $[\gamma/(1 + \gamma)]^n i_{t+n}$ tend to zero as n tends to infinity.

References

Alesina, A., and A. Drazen. "Why Are Stabilizations Delayed?" *American Economic Review* (1991).

Alesina, A., and R. Perrotti. "Fiscal Expansions and Adjustments in OECD Countries." *Economic Policy* (October 1995).

———. "Fiscal Expansions and Adjustments in OECD Countries: Composition and Macroeconomic Effects." *IMF Working Papers* (1996): 70–96.

Alesina, A., and G. Tabellini. "Rules and Discretion with Non-Coordinated Monetary and Fiscal Policies." *Economic Inquiry* 25 (1987): 619–30.

Alesina, A., and J. Tavares. "The Political Economy of Fiscal Adjustments." *Brookings Papers on Economic Activity* 1 (1998): 197–248.

Amiel, V. D. "The Effective Exchange Rate in Israel's Foreign Trade." *Bank of Israel Survey* 39 (1972): 24–46 (Hebrew).

Annual Report, Bank of Israel, various years (Hebrew).

Artstein, Y. "The Flexibility of the Israeli Labor Market." In *The Israeli Economy: 1985–1998*, edited by A. Ben-Bassat. Cambridge, MA: MIT Press, 2002.

Balassa, B. "Adjustment Policies in Developing Countries: A Reassessment." *World Development* (1984): 955–72.

Barkai, H. *The Genesis of the Israeli Economy*. Jerusalem: Bialik Institute, 1990 (Hebrew).

———. *The Lessons of Israel's Great Inflation*, Westport, CT: Praeger, 1995.

———. *The Evolution of Israel's Social Security System*. Brookfield, VT: Ashgate, 1998.

———. "A Central Bank in Chains." In *A Festschrift for M. Sanbar's 75th Anniversary*, edited by H. Barkai, 51–96. Rishon Lezion: Academic College, 2002.

Barkai, H., and M. Michaely. "The New Economic Policy after One Year." *Economic Quarterly* 37–38 (1963): 23–40 and *Economic Quarterly* 39 (1963): 2–23 (Hebrew).

Barro, R. J., and D. B. Gordon. "Rules, Discretion and Reputation in a Model of Monetary Policy." *Journal of Monetary Economics* 12 (1983): 101–21.

Barro, R. J., and X. Sala-i-Martin. *Economic Growth*. New York: McGraw-Hill, 1995.

Bar-Yoseph, I. *The Bank of Israel: Theory and Praxis.* Jerusalem: Bank of Israel, 1985 (Hebrew).

Beham, M. *Monetary Aspects of the 1962 Devaluation.* Jerusalem: Maurice Falk Institute for Economic Research in Israel, 1968 (Hebrew).

Ben-Bassat, A. "The Obstacle Course to a Market Economy in Israel." In *The Israeli Economy: 1985–1998,* edited by A. Ben-Bassat. Cambridge, MA: MIT Press, 2002.

Ben-David, D. "Israel's Long-Run Socio-Economic Trajectories." *Economic Quarterly* 50 (2003): 29–104. (Hebrew).

Ben-Schacar, H., S. Bronfeld, and A. Zukerman. *Israel Capital Market.* Jerusalem: Schocken, 1973 (Hebrew).

Berglas, E. "Defense and the Economy: The Israeli Experience." Discussion Paper 83.01. Maurice Falk Institute for Economic Research in Israel, Jerusalem, January 1983.

Blanchard, O. J. "Fiscal Dominance and Inflation Targeting, Lessons from Brazil." Working Paper No. 04-13, MIT Department of Economics, 2004.

Blanchard, O. J., and S. Fischer. *Lectures on Macroeconomics.* Cambridge, MA: MIT Press, 1989.

Blejer, M., and N. Liviatan. "Fighting Hyperinflation: Stabilization Strategies in Argentina and Israel 1985–6." *IMF Staff Papers* 34 (1987): 409–38.

Borochov, E. "Land Prices and the Inflationary Process." *Economic Quarterly* 45–46 (1965): 348–55 (Hebrew).

Brenner, M., and D. Rutenberg. "Involvement in the Capital Market in the 1978–1983 Period." *Issues in Banking* 6 (1987): 40–52 (Hebrew).

Brock, P. L. "Inflationary Finance in an Open Economy." *Journal of Monetary Economics* (1984): 37–53.

Bruno, M. *Crisis, Stabilization and Economic Reform.* Oxford: Clarendon Press, 1993.

Bruno, M., and L. Meridor. "The Costly Transition from Stabilization to Sustainable Growth: Israel's Case." In *Lessons of Economic Stabilization and Its Aftermath,* edited by M. Bruno et al. Cambridge, MA: MIT Press, 1991.

Bruno, M., and Z. Sussman. "Flexibility of Exchange Rates, Inflation and Structural Changes." *Economic Quarterly* 99 (1978).

———. "From Crawling Peg to Float." In *Michael Bruno: Growth, Inflation and Economic Stabilization,* edited by R. Melnick and Z. Shiffer. Jerusalem: Bank of Israel, 1997.

Bufman, G., and L. Leiderman, "Monetary policy and Inflation in Israel." In *Inflation and Disinflation in Israel,* edited by L. Leiderman. Jerusalem: Bank of Israel, 2001.

Burnside, C., M. Eichenbaum, and S. Rebello. "Prospective Deficits and the Asian Currency Crises." CEPR Discussion Paper 2015, 1998.

Calvo, G. A., and C. Vegh. "Exchange Rate Based Stabilization under Imperfect Credibility." In *Open Economy Macroeconomics: Proceedings of a Conference held in Vienna by the International Economic Association,* edited by H. Frisch, and A. Worgotter. New York: St. Martin's Press, 1993.

Calvo, G. A., and E. Mendoza. "Mexico's Balance of Payments Crisis: A Chronicle of Death Foretold." *Journal of International Economics* 41 (1995): 235–64.

Canzoneri, M. B. "Monetary Policy Games and the Role of Private Information." *American Economic Review* 75 (1985): 1056–70.

Canzoneri, M. B., R. E. Cumby, and B. T. Diba. "Is the Price Level Determined by the Needs of Fiscal Solvency?" *American Economic Review* (2001).

———. "Should the European Central Bank and the Federal Reserve Be Concerned about Fiscal Policy?" Mimeo, 2002.

Clarida, R., J. Gali, and M. Gertler. "The Science of Monetary Policy: A New Keynesian Perspective." *Journal of Economic Literature* 36 (1999): 1661–707.

Cohen, Y., Y. Haberfeld, G. Mundlak, and Y. Saporta. "Rate of Organized Workers and Coverage of Collective Agreements (2000)." Discussion Paper 9.01. Israel Ministry of Labor and Social Affairs, Jerusalem, 2001 (Hebrew).

Correia, I., and P. Teles. "The Optimal Inflation Tax." *Review of Economic Dynamics* 2 (1999): 325–46.

Cukierman, A., and F. Lippi. "Central Bank Independence, Centralization of Wage Bargaining, Inflation and Unemployment: Theory and Some Evidence." *European Economic Review* 43 (1999): 1395–434.

Cukierman, A., and N. Liviatan. "Rules, Discretion, Credibility and Reputation." *Economic Review* [Bank of Israel] 65 (1990): 3–25 (Hebrew).

Cukierman, A., and V. A. Muscatelli. "Do Central Banks Have Precautionary Demands for Expansion and for Price Stability? A New Keynesian Approach." Mimeo, 2003.

Cukierman, A., and M. Tomassi. "Why Does It Take a Nixon to Go to China?" Mimeo, Harvard University, 1994.

Dahan, M., and M. Strawczynski. "Fiscal Policy and Turning Points in the Inflation Environment." In *Inflation and Disinflation in Israel*, edited by L. Leiderman. Jerusalem: Bank of Israel, 2001.

Debelle, G., and S. Fischer. "How Independent Should a Central Bank Be?" In *Goals, Guidelines and Constraints Facing Monetary Policymakers* (Conference Series, no. 38), edited by Jeffrey C. Fuhrer, 195–221. Boston: Federal Reserve Bank of Boston, 1995.

Department of Treasury, *First Report on State Revenues, 1948/8–1954/5.* Jerusalem: Government Printing Office, 1956 (Hebrew).

Djivre, J., and S. Ribon. "Monetary Policy, the Output Gap and Inflation: A Closer Look at the Monetary Transmission Mechanism in Israel, 1989–1999." Discussion Paper 2000.09. Bank of Israel, Jerusalem, 2000.

Djivre, J., and D. Tsiddon. "A Monetary Labyrinth: Instruments and Conduct of Monetary Policy in Israel, 1987–1998." In *The Israeli Economy, 1985–1998*, edited by A. Ben-Bassat. Cambridge, MA: MIT Press, 2002.

Dornbusch, R. "Expectations and Exchange Rate Dynamics." *Journal of Political Economy* 84 (1976): 1161–76.

———. *Open Economy Macroeconomics.* New York: Basic Books, 1980.

Drazen, A. "Tight Money and Inflation, Further Results." *Journal of Monetary Economics* 15 (1984): 113–20.

Drazen, A., and E. Helpman. "Inflationary Consequences of Anticipated Economic Policies." *Review of Economic Studies* 57 (1990): 147–66.

Eckstein, Z. "Males in Israel Do Not Work, What Can Be Done?" *Economic Quarterly* (September 2002): 425–32 (Hebrew).

Eckstein, Z., and L. Leiderman. "Seigniorage and the Welfare Cost of Inflation." *Journal of Monetary Economics* 29 (1992): 389–410.

Elkayam, D. "Inflation Target and the Monetary Policy—A Model for Analysis and Prediction." Mimeo, Bank of Israel, Jerusalem, 2000 (Hebrew).

Feinstein, C. H. *Statistical Table of National Income and Expenditure and Output of the U.K., 1855–1965.* London: Cambridge University Press, 1976.

Fischer, S., and L. H. Summers. "Should Governments Learn to Live with Inflation?" *American Economic Review* 73 (1989): 382–87.

Flood, R., and N. Marion. "Perspectives on Recent Currency Crisis Literature." *IMF Working Papers* 98/130 (1998).

Friedman, M. *Essays in Positive Economics.* Chicago: University of Chicago Press, 1953.

———. "The Role of Monetary Policy." *American Economic Review* 58, no. 1 (1968): 1–7.

———. "The Counter-Revolution in Monetary Theory." Occasional Paper 33. Institute of Economic Affairs for the Wincott Foundation, London, 1970.

Friedman, M., and A. J. Schwartz. *Monetary History of the United States: 1867–1960.* Princeton: Princeton University Press, 1963.

Fry, M. J. *Money, Interest and Banking in Economic Development.* Baltimore: Johns Hopkins University Press, 1988.

Gaathon, A. L. "The Israeli Economy in 1950." Central Bureau of Statistics, Publication Series 100 (1951) (Hebrew); and *Government Annual* (1953): 194 (Hebrew).

———. *Capital, Employment and Product in Israel, 1950–1954.* Jerusalem: Bank of Israel, 1961 (Hebrew).

———. *Economic Productivity in Israel.* Jerusalem: Bank of Israel, 1971 (Hebrew).

Gafni, A., F. Vieder, and Z. Shiffer. "Monetary Developments and the Monetary Policy of the Bank of Israel: The Lessons of the 1970s." *Economic Quarterly* 109 (1981) (Hebrew).

Galbis, V. "Inflation and Interest Rate Policies in Latin America." *IMF Staff Papers* 26, no. 2 (1979): 334–66.

Geva, D., T. Samet, and D. Ruthenberg. "An Analysis of the Interest Rate Spread in the Sheqel Non-indexed Sector in the Banking System in Israel." *Banking Review* 77 (1988): 3–13 (Hebrew).

Giersch, H., K. H. Paque, and H. Schmieding. *The Fading Miracle.* New York: Cambridge University Press, 1992.

Giovanninni, A., and M. Demelo. "Government Revenue from Financial Repression." *American Economic Review* 83 (September 1993): 953–62.

Gotlieb, D., and M. Blejer. "Liberalization in the Capital Account of the Balance of Payments." In *The Israeli Economy, 1985–1998,* edited by A. Ben-Bassat. Cambridge, MA: MIT Press, 2002.

Gotlieb, D., and S. Ribon. "Capital Flows of the Private Sector and Monetary Policy in Israel—October 1988–March 1997." Research paper 97.09. Bank of Israel, Jerusalem, 1997.

Grinberg, L. *Split Corporatism in Israel.* Albany: State University of New York Press, 1991.

Gross, N. T., and J. Metzer. "Palestine in the Second World War: Some Economic Aspects." In *Not by Spirit Alone,* edited by N. T. Gross, 300–324. Jerusalem: Magnes Press, 1999 (Hebrew).

Guidotti, P. E., and C. A. Rodriguez. "Dollarization in Latin America: Gresham's Law in Reverse?" *IMF Staff Papers* 39 (1992): 518–44.

Halevi, N., and R. Klinov. *The Economic Development of Israel,* 1968. Jerusalem: Academon, 1972 (Hebrew).

Halperin, A. "Palestine's Balance of Payments 1932–46." Ph.D. diss., Princeton University, 1954.

Helpman, E., "Israel's Growth: An International Comparison," *Economic Quarterly,* Issue 1/99, (1999) (Hebrew).

Hercowitz, Z., and M. Strawczynski. "On the Cyclical Bias in Government Spending." Discussion paper 98.06. Bank of Israel, Jerusalem, 1998.

Heth, M. *Banking Institutes in Israel.* Jerusalem: Maurice Falk Institute for Economic Research in Israel, 1966 (Hebrew).

————. *Banking in Israel*. 2 parts. Jerusalem: Jerusalem Institute for Israel Studies, 1994 (Hebrew).

Horowitz, D. *The Development of Palestine's Economy*. Tel Aviv: Mossad Bialik, 1948 (Hebrew).

————. *The Economy of Israel*. Tel Aviv: Massada, 1954–55 (Hebrew).

————. *Life in Focus*. Ramat Gan: Massada, 1975 (Hebrew).

Howson, S. *Domestic Monetary Management in Britain, 1919–1938*. London: Cambridge University Press, 1975.

Hutchison, T. W. *Economics and Economic Policy in Britain, 1946–1966*. London: Allen and Unwin, 1968.

Israel Central Bureau of Statistics, *Statistical Abstract of Israel*. Various years.

Jeanne, O. "Are Currency Crises Self Fulfilling? A Test." *Journal of International Economics* 43 (1997): 263–86.

Kessler, A. "The Balance of Payments." In *Encyclopedia Hebraica*, 6:745–52. Tel Aviv: Massad, 1957–58 (Hebrew).

Keynes, J. M. *Indian Currency and Finance* (1913). Reprinted in *Collected Writings*, vol. 1. Cambridge: Macmillan, 1971.

————. *Collected Writings*, vol. 12. London: Macmillan, 1978.

Kiguel, M., and N. Liviatan. "Inflationary Rigidities and Orthodox Stabilization Policies." *World Bank Economic Review* 2 (1988): 273–98.

————. "The Business Cycle Associated with Exchange Rate Based Stabilization." *World Bank Economic Review* 6 (1992): 279–305.

————. "A Policy Game Approach to the High Inflation Equilibrium." *Journal of Development Economics* 45 (1994): 135–40.

Kleiman, E. "From Mandate to State." In *The Bank of a Nation in Renaissance: The History of Bank Leumi Le Israel*, by N. Gross, N. Halevi, E. Kleiman, and M. Sarnat, 3:205–96. Ramat Gan: Massada, 1977 (Hebrew).

Krugman, P. "Balance Sheets, the Transfer Problem, and Financial Crises." In *International Finance and Financial Crises*, edited by Peter Isard, Assaf Razin, and Andrew K. Rose. Boston: Kluwer Academic, 1999.

Krugman, P., and M. Obstfeld. *International Economics: Theory and Policy*. New York: HarperCollins College Publishers, 1994.

Lavi, Y., and M. Strawczynski. "The Influence of Policy Variables and Immigration on the Supply of Output in the Business Sector and its Components, Factors of Production and Productivity: Israel 1960–95." Discussion paper 98.07. Bank of Israel Research Department, Jerusalem, 1998.

Lavi, Y., and N. Sussman. "The Tradeoff between Inflation and Unemployment in Israel: A Short Run Phillips Curve Analysis." Mimeo, 1997.

————. "The Determinants of Real Wages in the Long Run and its Changes in the Short Run—Evidence from Israel: 1968–98." Discussion paper 2001.04. Bank of Israel, 2001.

Lehman, E. "Credit Policy." *Economic Quarterly* 37–38 (1963): 57–60 (Hebrew).

Leiderman, L., and H. Bar-Or. "Monetary Policy Rules and Transmission Mechanism under Inflation Targeting in Israel." Discussion paper 2001.01. Bank of Israel, Jerusalem, 2000.

Leiderman, L., and A. Marom. "New Estimates of Demand for Money in Israel." *Bank of Israel Survey* 60 (1985): 17–34.

Lindgren, C. J., T. J. T. Balino, C. Enoch, A. M. Gulde, M. Quintyn, and L. Teo. "Financial Sector Crisis and Restructuring: Lessons from Asia." *IMF Occasional Paper* 188 (1999).

Liviatan, N. "Anti–inflationary Monetary Policy and the Capital Income Tax." Manuscript. Warwick, 1980.

———. "Tight Money and Inflation." *Journal of Monetary Economics* 13 (1984): 5–15.

———. "Israel's Stabilization Program." WPS/91. World Bank, 1988.

———. "The Money-Injection Function of the Bank of Israel and the Inflation Process." Discussion paper 2002.04. Bank of Israel, Jerusalem, 2002a.

———. "The Paradox of Indexed Money Substitutes." *Economic Letters* 75 (2002b): 199–202.

———. "Fiscal Dominance and Monetary Dominance in the Israeli Monetary Experience." Discussion paper 2003.17. Bank of Israel, Jerusalem, 2003.

Liviatan, N., and R. Frish. "The Discretionary Model in a Multi-Period Framework." Discussion Paper No. 2003.07, Bank of Israel, Jerusalem, 2003.

———. "Interest on Reserves and Inflation," *Journal of Development Economics*. 80, 269–274, 2006.

Liviatan, N., and R. Melnick. Inflation and Disinflation by Steps in Israel. In *Inflation and Disinflation in Israel*, edited by L. Leiderman. Jerusalem: Bank of Israel, 2001.

Liviatan, N., and S. Piterman. "Accelerating Inflation and Balance of Payments Crises, 1973–1984." In *The Israeli Economy: Maturing through Crises*, edited by Yoram Ben-Porath, Cambridge, MA: Harvard University Press, 1986.

Liviatan, N., and N. Sussman "Disinflation in Israel in the Past Decade." In *The Israeli Economy, 1985–1998*, edited by A. Ben-Bassat. Cambridge, MA: MIT Press, 2002.

Lubel, H. *Israel's National Expenditure 1950–1954*. Jerusalem: Maurice Falk Institute for Economic Research in Israel and DBS, 1958.

Manzli, J. "The Structure and Pattern of Interest Rates in the Israeli Economy: 1955–1969." Memo, Bank of Israel, Jerusalem, 1971 (Hebrew).

———. "Measurement and Analysis of the Pattern of Interest Rates on Free Credit in the Commercial Banks, 1965–1972." *Bank of Israel Survey* 45–46: 78–112 (Hebrew), 1977.

Marom, A. "The Contribution of Inflation to the Growth of the Banking Sector in Israel." *Bank of Israel Review* 62 (1987).

McCallum, B. T. "Are Bond-Financed Deficits Inflationary? A Ricardian Analysis." *Journal of Political Economy* 92 (1984): 123–35.

McKinnon, R. *Money and Capital in Economic Development*, Washington, DC: Brookings Institution (1973).

Melnick, R. "A Peek into the Governor's Chamber: The Israeli Case." Mimeo, 2002.

Meridor, L. "The Finance of Government Expenditure, 1960–1983." *Bank of Israel Review* 62 (1987) (Hebrew).

Metzer, J. *The Divided Economy of Mandatory Palestine*. Cambridge: Cambridge University Press, 1998.

Metzer, J., and O. Kaplan. *Jewish and Arab Economies in Mandatory Palestine: Product Employment and Growth*. Jerusalem: Maurice Falk Institute for Economic Research in Israel, 1960 (Hebrew).

Michaely, M. *Israel's Foreign Trade and Capital Imports*. Tel Aviv: Am Oved, 1963 (Hebrew).

———. *Israel's Foreign Exchange Rate System*. Jerusalem: Maurice Falk Institute for Economic Research in Israel, 1971.

Morag, A. *Government Finance in Israel*. Jerusalem: Magnes Press, 1967 (Hebrew).

Mundell, R. "Growth, Stability and Inflationary Finance." *Journal of Political Economy* 73 (1965): 97–109.

Nichols, D. A. "Some Principles of Inflationary Finance." *Journal of Political Economy* 82, no. 2 (1974): 423–30.

Offenbacher, A. "Introduction: Empirical Research of Demand for Money in Israel." *Bank of Israel Survey* 60 (November 1985): 3–16 (Hebrew).

Ophir, Z., and E. Kleiman. "The Adjustment of the Quantity of Money to Changes of the Price Level in Israel, 1955–65." *Bank of Israel Survey* 39 (1972): 3–23 (Hebrew).

――― "The Effects of Changes in the Quantity of Money on the Price Level in Israel, 1955–65." *Bank of Israel Survey* 42 (1974) (Hebrew).

―――. "Inflation in Israel, 1966–65: The Wage Push on Prices." *Bank of Israel Survey* 43 (1975): 18–28 (Hebrew).

Orbach, Z. "The Financial Statements of the Bank of Israel—Principles, Developments and Economic Significance 1977 through 1988." Comptroller's Report, Bank of Israel, Jerusalem, December 1989 (Hebrew).

Orphanides, A. "Monetary Policy Rules Based on Real Time Data." *American Economic Review* 91 (2001): 964–85.

Ottensooser, R. D. *The Palestine Pound and the Israel Pound.* Geneva: Les Presses de Savoie, 1955.

Patinkin, D. "Monetary and Price Developments in Israel: 1949–1953." *Scripta Hierosolymitana* 3 (1956): 20–52. Reprinted in *Studies in Monetary Economics,* by D. Patinkin, 55–82. New York: Harper and Row, 1972.

―――. *The Israeli Economy: The First Decade, 1960.* Jerusalem: Maurice Falk Institute for Economic Research in Israel, 1967.

―――. *Money, Interest and Prices.* New York: Harper and Row, 1966.

―――. "The Increase of the Means of Payment: The Report of the Bank of Israel." *Maariv,* October 3, 1971 (Hebrew).

―――. "Israel's Stabilization Program of 1985, of Some Simple Truths of Monetary Theory," *Journal of Economic Perspectives,* 7 (1993): 103–28.

Pazos, F. *Chronic Inflation in Latin America.* New York: Praeger, 1972.

Poole, W. "Optimal Choice of Monetary Policy Instruments in a Simple Stochastic Macro Model." *Quarterly Journal of Economics* (1970).

Poterba, J., and J. Rotemberg. "Inflation and Taxation with Optimizing Governments." *Journal of Money, Credit and Banking* 22 (1990): 1–18.

Ramos, J. *Neoconservative Economics in the Southern Cone of Latin America, 1973–1983.* Baltimore: Johns Hopkins University Press, 1986.

Razin, A., and E. Sadka. *The Economy of Modern Israel: Malaise and Promise.* Chicago: University of Chicago Press, 1993.

Report of the Governor on the Increase of the Means of Payment, various issues (Hebrew). The Bank of Israel, Jerusalem.

Rodriguez, C. "A Stylized Model of the Devaluation-Inflation Spiral." *IMF Staff Papers* 25 (1978): 76–89.

Rogoff, K. "The Optimal Degree of Commitment to an Intermediate Monetary Target." *Quarterly Journal of Economics* 100 (1985): 1069–190.

Romer, D. "Openness and Inflation: Theory and Evidence." *Quarterly Journal of Economics* 108 (1993): 869–903.

Roumani, M. "Labor's Expectations and Israeli Reality: Ethnic Voting as a Means Towards Political and Social Change." In *Israel Faces the Future,* edited by Bernard Reich and Gershon R. Kieval. New York: Praeger, 1986.

Ruge-Murcia, F. J. "Credibility and Changes in Policy Regime." *Journal of Political Economy* 103 (1995): 176–208.

Sachs, J., A. Tornell, and A. Velasco. "The Mexican Crisis: Sudden Death or Death Foretold?" *Journal of International Economics* 41 (1996): 265–83.

Sanbar, M., and S. Bronfeld. "Conceptual Framework and Developments in the Monetary Sector, 1948–1972." *Quarterly Economic Review* 77 (1973): 3–46 and *Quarterly Economic Review* 78–79: 217–236 (Hebrew).

Sargent, T., and N. Wallace. "Some Unpleasant Monetarist Arithmetic." *Federal Reserve Bank of Minneapolis Quarterly Review* (1981): 1–17.

Shaw, E. S. *Financial Deepening in Economic Development.* New York: Oxford University Press, 1973.

Shiffer, Z. "Indexation, Apartment Prices and the Inflation Process." In *Inflation and Disinflation in Israel,* edited by L. Leiderman. Jerusalem: Bank of Israel, 2001.

Sokoler, M., and A. Cukierman. "Monetary Policy in Israel and Its Institutional Arrangements: Past, Present, and Future." *Economic Quarterly* 139 (1987) (Hebrew).

Stammerman, K. A. "Economic Adjustment and the Politics of Stabilization Policy in Israel." In *Israel Faces the Future,* edited by Bernard Reich and Gershon R. Kieval. New York: Praeger, 1986.

Strawczynski, M., and J. Zeira. "Reduction in the Relative Size of Government in Israel after 1985." In *The Israeli Economy: 1985–1998,* edited by A. Ben-Bassat. Cambridge, MA: MIT Press, 2002.

Sussman, N. "Monetary Policy in Israel 1986–2000: Estimating the Central Bank's Reaction Function." In *The Bank of Israel,* vol. 2, *A Monetary History,* edited by N. Liviatan and H. Barkai. New York: Oxford University Press, 2007.

Sussman, O. "Macroeconomic Effects of a Tax on Bond Interest Rates." *Journal of Money, Credit and Banking* 23 (1991): 352–66.

Sussman, Z. "From Crisis (1973) to Stabilization (1985): The Israeli Economy at the Mercy of External Shocks." *Economic Quarterly* (1995) (Hebrew).

Svensson, L. E. O. "Inflation Forecast Targeting: Implementing and Monitoring Inflation Targets." *European Economic Review* 41 (1997): 1111–46.

Szereszewski, R. *Essays on the Structure of the Jewish Economy in Palestine and Israel.* Jerusalem: Maurice Falk Institute for Economic Research in Israel, 1968 (Hebrew).

Tanner, E., and A. M. Ramos. "Fiscal Sustainability and Monetary versus Fiscal Dominance: Evidence from Brazil, 1991–2000." *IMF Working Papers* 02/5 (2002).

Taylor, J. B. "Discretion Versus Policy Rules in Practice." *Carnegie-Rochester Conference on Public Policy* 39 (1993): 105–214.

U.S. Government. *Economic Report of the President, 1975.* Washington, D.C.: U.S. Government Printing Office, 1976.

Vegh, C. A. "Government Spending and Inflationary Finance: A Public Finance Approach," *IMF Staff Papers* 36 (1989): 657–77.

Witkon, M. E. "A Defense of Free Interest Rates." In *Banking Problems in Israel,* by M. E. Witkon. Tel Aviv: Union Bank, 1965 (Hebrew).

Woodford, M. "Fiscal Requirements for Price Stability." *Journal of Money, Credit and Banking* 33 (2001): 669–727.

———. *Interest and Prices.* Princeton University Press, 2003.

World Economic Outlook, 2001. IMF.

Yashiv, E. "Inflation and the Role of Money under Discretion and Rules: A New Interpretation." PSIE, MIT Working Paper (1989): 8–89.

Index

A page number followed by the letter t or f indicates a table or figure, respectively, on that page.